Hegemony Constrained

THE SECURITY CONTINUUM:
GLOBAL POLITICS IN THE MODERN AGE

Series Editors: William W. Keller and Simon Reich

A series published in association with the
Matthew B. Ridgway Center for International
Security Studies and the Ford Institute for
Human Security

HEGEMONY CONSTRAINED

Evasion, Modification,
and Resistance to
American Foreign Policy

Edited by DAVIS B. BOBROW

UNIVERSITY OF PITTSBURGH PRESS

Published by the University of Pittsburgh Press, Pittsburgh, Pa., 15260
Copyright © 2008, University of Pittsburgh Press
All rights reserved
Manufactured in the United States of America
Printed on acid-free paper
10 9 8 7 6 5 4 3 2 1

Library of Congress Cataloging-in-Publication Data

Hegemony constrained : evasion, modification, and resistance to American foreign policy /
edited by Davis B. Bobrow.
      p.   cm.
  Includes bibliographical references and index.
  ISBN-13: 978-0-8229-4342-6 (cloth : alk. paper)
  ISBN-10: 0-8229-4342-5 (cloth : alk. paper)
  ISBN-13: 978-0-8229-5982-3 (pbk. : alk. paper)
  ISBN-10: 0-8229-5982-8 (pbk. : alk. paper)
  1. United States—Foreign relations—2001–   2. Hegemony—United States.   I. Bobrow,
Davis B.
  JZ1480.H43 2008
  327.73—dc22   2008003268

CONTENTS

TABLES AND FIGURES

Tables

Figures

Hegemony Constrained

1

STRATEGIES BEYOND FOLLOWERSHIP

DAVIS B. BOBROW

This book examines how those involved in international affairs attempt to evade, modify, and even resist U.S. government policy preferences. It explores the strategies and tactics they may use to prevent official Washington from getting what it wants in terms of quantity, quality, timeliness, or cost. The chapters focus on the options these players have used and may use in the future, their rationales, and the circumstances affecting their choices. These international factors also have strong links to domestic politics. All politics is not "local," but politicians maintain or lose their power according to how they manage homeland politics. Our observations and conclusions suggest that how Washington goes about international affairs and domestic politics has more or less helpful implications for how the United States is perceived internationally. For example, certain actions might suggest to others that the United States seeks to dominate or withdraw from the world stage, and other actions might be seen as righteous or hypocritical, competent or incompetent, benign or malignant, indifferent or exploitative.

It is hardly news that some in the world dislike and even defy the policies of the United States or indeed of any superpower. America's debacles in Iraq and Vietnam, like those of the Soviets in Afghanistan and the French in Algeria, illustrate how violence using asymmetric means can favor those far weaker in terms of the classical measures of power preferred in conventional U.S. political-military assessments. And international affairs realists have long discussed counter-balancing, in which another state, or a coalition of them, tries to enhance or pool its power to counter unipolar dominance, whether present or expected, global or regional.

This volume goes beyond those widely recognized possibilities to explore a more complex and nuanced set of options, related goals, and their implications for the United States. Many of the additional options are more available, more frequently used, and less risky than attempts to inflict a direct, militarized defeat on some American policy venture or to sharply reduce the absolute and relative international power and presence of the United States. In part, that is because the practices of interest are not limited to those centered on military ends and means but include "actions" on the whole range of international issues on which the American government might try to exert influence and apply power or to avoid involvement altogether. The goals of some challenges are to increase America's international commitments, presence, and activism beyond what Washington has preferred, in contrast to those associated with militarized resistance and hard power counter-balancing. The changes others may seek are not limited to pushing the United States out, back, or down. Further, efforts to modify, evade, or resist what official Washington wants do not necessarily run counter to American national interests, whatever U.S. policy makers may claim. Not all U.S. government policy preferences really advance American interests even if intended to do so.

As will be seen, pigeonholing others into one or two broad "grand strategy" categories (e.g., "moderate" or "extremist," "pro-" or "anti-"American) or doing so for issues on which they interact with the United States (e.g., "high" or "low" politics, economic or ecological matters) has quite limited usefulness. Different foreign actors bring different "histories in use" and domestic and regional circumstances to issues. The factors most important to particular actors vary from issue to issue, place to place, and time to time. Those specifics may be far different than the themes of any "Washington consensus" or convenient Washington dichotomy for policy debates and spin contests. They may lead foreigners to challenge U.S. policy by suggesting linkages between issues that U.S. policies treat as unrelated or by separating issues that U.S. policy glues together. Of course, the great geographic and functional breadth of official U.S. policy concerns and goals often presents others with opportunities to invoke and exploit issue linkages.

To make matters still more realistic, albeit less parsimonious, unitary actor formulations can obscure and distort the particulars of challenge strategies and tactics and predicted U.S. responses. What options would-be challengers choose depends on their internal distributions of influence, and an apparent choice may be a commitment, a probing bluff, or even an unauthorized action.

A challenger trying to forecast or interpret a U.S. response may well consider relations between key elements in a current presidential administration and between themselves and other participants (bureaucratic, political, and special interest) in American politics. Both Americans and international actors assess who on the opposing side has policy clout and look for converging interests between particular participants in American and challenger policy processes. International challengers may view some U.S. officials, bureaus, and third-sector organizations as potential de facto partners. Domestic challengers to U.S. international policies can try to gain leverage by enlisting foreign support and even strengthening foreign supporters.

Starting Points

This volume was conceived during widespread discussions of U.S. world primacy and international affairs practices early in President George W. Bush's first term, but the aspects of international affairs central to his administration did not begin and will not end with his presidency. Two premises that have ongoing importance for challengers and challenges underlie our work. First, leaders in much of the world believe that they cannot avoid being affected by U.S. acts of commission and omission. That belief plays a significant role in, for example, how nations protect their material assets and the intangible values of society as a whole (Wolfers 1952). More in line with prospect theory, a nation that strives to achieve its preferred vision for the future (perhaps restoring past values) will keep one eye focused on the United States (Levy 1997). Others will then be attentive to U.S. policies and policy-making processes and search for ways to affect them so as to advance their own priorities.

Second, the view that "the strong do what they can and the weak do what they must" fails to capture much of the reality of international affairs (Barnett and Duvall 2005). The "strong," such as the United States, often do not do everything they can because of the press of competing priorities, domestically prevailing norms of legitimate action, and the pressures posed by domestic political and policy competitors (George 1980). The strong are not always indifferent to the current and prospective costs their actions may involve. As for the weak, treating them as "clay" to be molded at will by the strong ignores the full range of actions the weak may have available to achieve their goals both now and in the future. Those who are generally considered to be the weak, or the weaker, may not actually be weak in specific situations or on specific issues that are more important to them than to the strong. Even if they are "weak," their cost tolerance may be greater. And the political elites of the weak are not any less concerned with domestic politics than their superpower or great power counterparts.

Much American thinking slights the options available to others in the world to affect what the U.S. government can achieve. In spite of alternative voices (see, e.g., Walt 2005; Pape 2005), that unwarranted underemphasis is especially pronounced when U.S. policy elites claim moral superiority. Those claims are frequently voiced by President Bush, with the consequences Hans Morgenthau warned about: "the light hearted assumption that what one's own nation aims at and does is morally good and that those who oppose that nation's policies are evil is morally indefensible and intellectually untenable and leads in practice to that distortion of judgment, born of the blindness of crusading frenzy, which has been the curse of nations from the beginning of time" (1952, 984).

Unwisely, top U.S. officials often seem to expect almost complete, unquestioning compliance from nations with fewer material power assets or to believe it desirable and feasible to deal with the noncompliant mostly through policies of domination or conversion (Ikenberry 1998–99, 54). Both Bill Clinton's and George W. Bush's national strategy statements contain a substantial pledge to engage in "world-shaping" on both realistic and idealistic grounds, albeit with differences on the effectiveness and efficiency of various means to do so (Brown et al. 2000, 351–411; Bush 2002). Both have encouraged the use of American power through some combination of direct rule imposed by force, controlled international institutions, structural leverage based on asymmetric dependence, and export of belief, governance, and economic systems. At root, there has been an implicit assumption that what is held to be good for America is good for all informed and respectable others. There are substantial indications of a resurrection of American exceptionalism and "manifest destiny" accompanied by assumptions that the United States holds an unrivaled and thus decisive share of military, commercial, and soft power assets.

Dominance advocates call for the United States to shape the world in a geographically and functionally comprehensive way based on its superior might and superior values: "American power advantages are multidimensional, unprecedented, and unlikely to disappear any time" (Ikenberry 2003). Putting those advantages to work can ensure inherently justified American national interests against numerous threats. U.S. government policy preferences are then attainable and legitimate. Evidence to the contrary (for example, the course of events in Iraq) does not point to dubious assumptions but only to poor management of details. Serving U.S. interests allegedly will advance collective global interests in world progress and peace through the stabilizing structure of a unipolar international system centered on and designed by the United States (Bobrow 2001; 2002). If necessary, dominance or conversion can feasibly be supplemented with "internal reconstruction," in which the United States directly "intervenes in the secondary state and transforms its domestic political institutions" (Ikenberry and Kupchan 1990, 292).[1]

As a practical matter, a U.S. policy portfolio whose major elements are domination, conversion, and replacing the political infrastructure of others should call for the most serious attention to what those others will attempt by way of strategies of modification, evasion, and resistance. Ironically, the conceptions underlying such an American portfolio make that studious attention seem unimportant or even unnecessary. In essence, the United States is asserted to be the international rule maker, one that can (as a practical matter) and should (as a normative matter) determine or at least exert enormous influence on the content and processes of international cooperation and confrontation. The American "superiority triad" of values, military power, and economic resources does and will allow the United States to play the rule-maker role at what for it are tolerable or even modest costs (Wohlforth 1999).

Relevant and indeed central policy contests within the United States should then primarily have two foci. One is on the policy *actions* that will be emphasized in general vis-à-vis particular foreign players and situations. There are issues about resource allocation and preferred instruments of a broad nature, most obviously military versus nonmilitary, and of relative priority within each broad category (e.g., for military defense versus force projection, or for economic liberal openness versus neomercantilist nationalism).

The second focus is on the *arenas* in which Washington will exercise its leading role: unilateral assertion; forging and commanding problem-specific "coalitions of the willing" (Haass 1997; 2002); or designing, managing, and leading broad, formally organized, ongoing multilateral institutions. The United States should not shrink from the first arena, although the second is preferable. Dominating recalcitrant foreigners and imposing regime change merits a prominent place in America's policy portfolio. The third arena, multilateral institutions, should not be allowed to hamper the United States' ability or will to pursue the others (Gaddis 2002). Institutionalized multilateralism does not have merit in its own right but only as a case-specific instrument to be used as it facilitates U.S. pursuit of domination, conversion, or regime change.

Whatever their disagreements about policy actions and arenas, those committed to the dominant superpower view tend to agree that others have only a very limited set of choices about the role they will play vis-à-vis American scripted international security scenarios. Their options, as in the run-up to invading Iraq, ostensibly are limited to ultimately self-defeating irrational and evil opposition (e.g., Saddam Hussein's Iraq), marginalization while the world passes them by (e.g., Gerhard Schroeder's Germany, Jacques Chirac's France), or compliant following (e.g., Tony Blair's United Kingdom).

Many proponents of American dominance contend that most other states and nonstate groups faced with that menu will accept followership as their only viable alternative. Their decision makers will sign on to the international security ends and means the United States prefers, thinking that doing so will at least minimize costs while acting otherwise will trigger U.S. punishments and reduce any consideration Washington gives to another's views and interests. Also, given the allegedly intrinsic appeal of the "American model," foreign elites will find compliance the course of least resistance because mass sentiments in their populations resonate with U.S. values and practices. Clarity and commitment in American policy will then produce assent. Assent to any particular American policy will create precedents and momentum for followership on other issues. Foreigners who opt for strategies of modification, evasion, or resistance are doomed to isolation and rejection internationally and domestically. As they demonstrably fail, such strategies will seem increasingly less attractive.

Compared to adherents of the "dominance school" described above, the "loyal opposition" view certainly favors much more apparent consideration for the views of others (e.g., consultations and dialogues) with less unilateral assertion and more development and use of multilateral institutions. Those are the preferred arenas favored by coalitions of the willing. With such a "velvet glove" approach, an America that acts with "tact" will get its way more often and at lower cost than one whose behavior seems like that of "a sullen, pouting, oblivious, and over-muscled teenager" (Gaddis 2002, 56). Others treated with a show of respect are more likely to comply with U.S. policy positions that are tolerable in terms of both their national pride and domestic politics and to take on some of the burdens of policy implementation.

Yet the "velvet glove" school shares a fundamental premise of indispensability with the dominance advocates regarding the extent to which the United States should, can, and must play the critical role in the evolution of international affairs. In Joseph Nye's words, "If the largest beneficiary of a public good (such as international order) does not take the lead toward its maintenance, nobody else will" (2001, 102). Most international others supposedly do and will recognize that situation and want America to act accordingly. Most others supposedly do and will view America as being the positive exemplar of secular trends (modernity and globalization) and the definitive exemplar of best practices in the political (democracy) and military (the revolution in military affairs or RMA) realms. Accordingly, for instrumental reasons, the "velvet glove" perspective differs from the dominance view in calling for America to make greater use of "strategies of restraint" and "reassurance" (as in Ikenberry 2001; 2003). These supporting assumptions are empirically dubious (Bobrow and Boyer 2005), as are those of the explicit dominance school. In any event, the two perspectives agree on the feasibility and desirability of an end result that amounts to "legitimate domination" by the United States (Ikenberry and Kupchan 1990).

These widespread views about what the United States can and should do in the early twenty-first century seem to slight what post–World War II history tells us about the options actually available to others and their likely consequences for U.S. foreign policy ventures. Much of the language in contemporary American policy circles echoes that of the Vietnam War years. Consider the November 1964 assertion by Walt Rostow that "our assets . . . are sufficient . . . if we enter the exercise with adequate determination to succeed. . . . [A]t this stage of history we are the greatest power in the world—if we behave like it" (quoted in Rosi 1973, 16). Noncompliance by and criticism from others allegedly made pursuing U.S. policy preferences even more imperative rather than indicating a need for rethinking their merits. Credibility required staying the course in the face of mounting costs lest others doubt America's "power, resolve, and competence" to discharge its morally obligatory mission (Assistant Secretary of Defense John McNaughton in 1965, quoted in Rosi 1973, 16). The Vietnam War policies of the United States turned out to have grossly underestimated the costs that counter-strategies to Washington's preferences would impose, and those policies were eventually abandoned.

In fact, the last half of the twentieth century and the years since have been rich in examples where others evaded, modified, or resisted official U.S. preferences even though the United States had a massive share of global hard and soft power assets. Such policy lines were pursued with some success even by states identified as America's closest "kin" in the international system and as members of a putative security community with the United States at its core, as well as by avowed enemies and neutrals.

In the early Cold War years, "[t]he Europeans themselves were crucial in recasting the terms of liberal multilateralism—if only in resisting, modifying, and circumventing American proposals" (Ikenberry 1989, 398). Subsequent Cold War decades saw numerous European attempts to evade and modify U.S. military deployment and doctrinal preferences. Japan evaded and modified U.S. official preferences that it assume extended military obligations or comply with the political economy of the Structural Impediments Initiative, and it secured the reversion of Okinawa. The 1970s oil shocks saw the United States having to modify its initial preferences for dealing with the

Organization of the Petroleum Exporting Countries (OPEC). Lack of simple compliance marked the behavior even of others who at the same time saw the United States as the best (or even the only) available guarantor against a common source of threats, or as a hard (or even impossible) to replace provider of economic benefits.

History suggests that there can be policy traps inherent in both the harder, more militaristic and unilateral stance ("hegemony with 'imperial characteristics'") and the softer, less militaristic and more multilateral stance ("hegemony with 'liberal characteristics'").[2] Unduly rosy anticipations of foreign compliance can lead to unrealistic estimates of a specific policy's benefits (too high) and costs (too low). Policy commitments based on such enticing estimates can entangle the United States in unproductive situations for which policy modifications are delayed because of their perceived credibility costs. In other words, U.S. policies considered attractive (primarily because policy makers underestimated evasion, modification, and resistance efforts by others) are still pursued even when there is ample evidence of noncompliance. The regret in the phrase "if we knew then what we know now" does not translate into decisive action to reverse policy (e.g., the absence of imminent WMD capability in Iraq coupled with mounting expenses and casualties). Internationally, others may well see encouraging precedents in instances of relatively successful attempts to evade, modify, and resist U.S. preferences. Eventual U.S. policy reappraisals (withdrawals and various forms of "backing down" or even tardy increases in commitments) can make such options more attractive to others. Actual or perceived foreign attempts at evasion, modification, and resistance also can foster in America a domestic climate of aversion to international commitments and responsibilities given what seems to be the unreasonable behavior of others.

Several self-inflicted circumstances are policy traps for the United States. In one, American policy elites have propagated such exaggerated images of U.S. power that the threshold for promising options that challenge U.S. policy preferences is set very low. David need not actually succeed in slaying Goliath to seem successful; it is sufficient to entice Goliath into self-exhausting and vulnerability-increasing behaviors. Success in baiting such traps would increase the chances of achieving a draw, securing substantial concessions, or even wounding Goliath enough to make him a shadow of his former self. In another self-inflicted circumstance, American officials focus almost exclusively on the possibility that "great powers" or "major states" will attempt evasion, modification, and resistance, ignoring the "little guys" with very small material power assets relative to the United States and thus getting caught unprepared. In a third circumstance, American officials believe that others are not in a general search-and-learning mode about nonfollowership strategies, that only a few are interested in them and then for only a few specific issues.[3] Finally, American policy elites may be prone to ignore potential coalitions established to evade, modify, or resist what an incumbent administration prefers. Such coalitions could be established between foreign parties and organized participants in U.S. politics (e.g., opposition politicians, dissenting bureaucrats, issue-interested business sectors, and nongovernmental organizations [NGOs]). Coalitions of that sort can make it more difficult and resource intensive to secure and sustain a domestic mandate for the major international commitments that vigorous imperial or liberal domination requires. Prudent American statecraft would take considerable pains to avoid such traps and the conditions that lead to them. That calls for a fuller understanding of the strategies of evasion, modification, and resistance available to others and their calculus for choosing to pursue one or more of them. With perceptiveness on those counts, the United States will, if anything, be more able to convince others that strategies other than followership are inferior to compliance. It would at least be more able to persuade others to adopt options that are easier for the United States to counter.

Anticipating What Others Might Conclude and Do

Developing an appropriate degree of perceptiveness about others' strategies of evasion, modification, and resistance starts by placing those others at the center of attention. This strategy follows the rules of good policy analysis put forward by Albert Wohlstetter and Richard Elmore. In analyses of "conflict systems" and "opposed systems design," Wohlstetter (1964; 1968) recommended giving others in such systems as much attention as we give ourselves; allowing them to follow their own accepted rules of the game to act rationally and intelligently to advance their interests; and conducting end-to-end analysis of the paths from an American policy choice to its impacts on a target situation and realization of initial U.S. policy objectives.

Elmore (1985) did not limit his counsel to policy systems already opposed or in conflict but instead to any system in which no single organization has sole and complete control of policy adoption, implementation, and impact. For this larger set, he in effect accepts the Wohlstetter maxims and argues for working through a "reversible logic" of "forward and backward mapping." Doing so generates a realistic understanding of the determinants of policy outcomes, the actors involved, and their options and likely choices. What difference does emphasis on the forward or the backward approach make?

From the forward mapping perspective, the problem is finding a collection of implements likely to produce the effect that policy makers want. From the backward mapping perspective, the problem is finding a set of decisions that policy can influence and specifying how policy can tip those decisions in the desired direction. Forward mapping stresses what policy makers control; backward mapping stresses the marginal influence that policy exercises over decisions by individuals and organizations. If we were to look at policy decisions only from the forward mapping perspective, we would consistently overestimate the degree of control policy makers exercise. Policy makers tend to see the world through the lens of the implements they control. . . . But the success of policy depends . . . as well on conditions outside the control of policy makers and on decisions over which policy exercises only a marginal influence . . . to be good strategists, policy makers have to calculate the consequences of their actions from the point of view of the decisions they are trying to influence. (Elmore 1985, 68–69)

The backward mapping perspective suggests that sound policy design by U.S. officials would seek to answer two questions about others providing elements that are critical or at least conducive to realizing American policy preferences: To what extent will those elements suit the self-perceived needs and values of the other actors? If providing those elements is clearly not in their interests, what could the other actor do to avoid providing them in an effective and timely manner? If there is a gap between, on the one hand, others' perceived interests and values and, on the other, their view of the implications of official U.S. policy preferences, answers to the second question amount to options for evasion, modification, and resistance.

The stimulus to challenge the United States rather than comply with it stems from judgments by foreign elites that U.S. policy preferences will impede realization of their own domestic and international goals. Judgments about domestic consequences often will get more weight, and these are shaped by evolving constituency interests, prejudices, historical experiences, ideology, identity, values, and national and group institutional patterns.[4] Those factors may well have momentum, motivational intensity, salience, and potential repercussions of far greater magnitude and predictability than the carrots and sticks the U.S. government might try to use. When foreign judgments emphasize long-term national and group futures, immediate net gains from followership may carry less weight than long-term gains from evasion, modification, and resistance.

Compliance with U.S. policy preferences is hardly a foregone conclusion. First, for many others in international affairs, there is a persistent contradiction between what they consider to be legitimate and what they consider to be domination by the United States (or even by a coalition of the willing). Consider, for example, the oft-quoted statement of Joschka Fischer, who as Germany's foreign minister contended that "alliances between free democracies should not be reduced to following. Alliance partners are not satellites" (quoted in Erlanger 2002). Refusing compliance seems especially unsurprising when displayed by others who view their historical experiences with Washington as worthy of a "justice" claim for compensation for historical damage or neglect or evidence that "legitimate domination" amounts to their elimination.[5]

Second, standards set by others for determining the magnitude, credibility, and irreversibility of American "strategies of restraint" or "reassurance" may be more demanding than what American officials and publics regard as conclusive evidence. Those external actors are especially likely to be leery of the United States asserting its "right" to curtail commitments, for example, by not ratifying or by unilaterally withdrawing from international agreements it has signed. Indeed, American persuasiveness about its own military prowess, economic wealth, technological superiority, and cultural reach may raise the bar for U.S. credibility. An America ostensibly able to do whatever it wants has fewer excuses for failure or for claiming a waiver on grounds of expense or difficulty. If America has so great an advantage over others, then U.S. rejection of a proposed reduction in its margin of superiority can seem unjustified. After all, the United States will have an abundance of private goods in any event.

Third, socialization into or conversion to exported "American ideas" may raise the threshold for American legitimacy and lower the threshold for sensing a U.S. goal of domination: "when the hegemon finds it necessary to pursue policies that are at odds with the norms it initially articulated . . . elites in secondary states may question the sincerity and credibility of the hegemon's normative program" (Ikenberry and Kupchan 1990, 294). Also, others may use these exported ideas as a lever to mobilize American public opinion and thus pressure the government to change official policy, by charging that the policy violates basic U.S. values.

Fourth, many others monitor American domestic politics and social currents, including policy ideas that have gained popular support. Their appraisals may contain grave doubts about the extent to which U.S. policy elites can sustain their commitments to "self-binding" restrictions on autonomous action, costly or risky actions, or side-payments (i.e., convenient concessions) to members of ad hoc coalitions. Some claim that the "open" nature of U.S. policy formation processes will assuage such doubts because of the opportunities it affords foreigners to influence outcomes (see, e.g., Ikenberry 1998–1999). Foreigners accepting that argument might arrive at conclusions less supportive of compliance. With regard to evasion, modification, and resistance, that openness could lead others to conclude that they have important allies in the

U.S. polity with whom they can coalesce to bargain successfully for a better deal. Alternatively, that openness might be exploited by other foreigners who have different agendas and who are better positioned to wield influence in Washington. Of course, American claims to openness might be a device to trick foreigners or embroil them in domestically oriented struggles among U.S. actors with their own parochial agendas.

While it is premature to claim to have developed a high-quality typology of nonfollowership options (a set of categories mutually distinct and comprehensive), we can begin to discern some categories with distinctly different cores, and these cores have plenty of conceptual or experiential illustrations (if only fuzzy boundaries).[6] The authors of the chapters that follow have started from a framework in which nonfollowership options always have two sorts of content: *actions* and the *arenas* in which and through which they are taken. Besides using some current action capabilities and existing arenas, others may try to build for the future more and different action capabilities and create new or enhanced arena arrangements. Actions may be taken in more than one of the arenas but not necessarily in all of them; each arena may accommodate more than one of the actions but not necessarily all of them. Those who do not simply follow the United States on some particular issue may well have the opportunity and the capacity to pursue several combinations of actions and arenas simultaneously or sequentially. If issues persist for a lengthy period, the options considered and used may change in view of others' experience with them, their domestic context, third-party behavior, and U.S. responses.

Table 1.1 sets out the cells of an exploratory matrix of options to evade, modify, or resist U.S. official preferences, with types of actions in rows and types of arenas in columns. Many of the possibilities may be used to seek expanded, not just curtailed, U.S. involvement. As suggested earlier, it is reasonable to assume that an attentive international audience seeks to learn from the success and failure of attempts to challenge the United States in any of the ways shown.

Actions

The category of "'craziness' and martyrdom" demonstrates "readiness to sacrifice self-existence" by taking steps that run counter to widely held norms of state behavior and mainstream utilitarian calculation.[7] Such actions thus seem crazy and senseless but may in fact be strategically rational (Kahn 1960; Schelling 1960). The actions are often shocking to American sensibilities and seem very difficult to prevent by normal government action. Their most extreme forms directly impose pain and suffering in dramatic ways: "genocide, . . . mass assassination of leaders, food poisoning, systematic sabotage of civilian

Table 1.1. An initial framework

Actions	Unilateral	Arenas			
		Broad agenda institutions with U.S. excluded	Coalitions of the unwilling	Clubs and caucuses in U.S. member IGOs, INGOs	Collective action networks with American participants
"Craziness," martyrdom					
Melting					
Counter-balancing					
Fait accompli					
Bloc creation					
Rule-based retaliation					
Rule expansion					
Consent and exploit					
Consent and deceive					
Promise, protest, retraction					
Conditional support commitments					
Schedule delays					
Linkage to large side-payments					
Standing aside					
Credible helplessness					

peaceful facilities, counter value terror against schools, hospitals, recreation areas, civil transportation." Such actions challenge compliance with U.S. preferences in ways beyond killing those who collaborate with Washington. They may persuade Americans to doubt the benefits of maintaining international commitments in the face of such extreme hostility. They may lead foreign elites and populations to conclude that the United States will not dominate the "crazy" challenger or will do so in illegitimate ways that impose substantial costs on bystanders. An American administration faced with such developments may change the policies that craziness and martyrdom challenge.

While craziness and martyrdom inflict pain on the United States, its foreign associates, and even innocent bystanders, "melting" evades U.S. attempts to eliminate a foe by simply disappearing, as the Taliban did for a while, to await an opportunity for later reconstitution. Then the United States must choose between abandoning its elimination preference (at least implicitly) and undertaking a longer and more resource-demanding suppression campaign than officials had anticipated (and may have promised to American and foreign audiences). After 9/11, subsequent developments in Iraq and Afghanistan, and transit bombings in Madrid and London, craziness and martyrdom as well as melting actions are by now all too familiar. Given the space constraints of this volume, the following chapters concentrate on other ways that actors may evade, modify, and resist U.S. policies.

"Counter-balancing" refers to more varied actions than the classic political-military alliance of weaker or equally matched states or the bipolarity sought by a single "peer competitor." Those sorts of structural "hard counter-balancing" actions involve a general, ongoing, and explicit rejection of U.S. primacy and its perceived status as the sole rule maker. They are, however, harder and more time consuming (and thus rarer) than smaller efforts to deprive the United States of its preferred course of action. Such situational or issue-specific counter-balancing actions are used more frequently, as they are easier and quicker to mount (and abandon). They often involve actions designed less to alter the status quo than to render too costly the American attempts to gain an advantage. This type of challenge is less direct than a potentially countervailing one. For example, a state may move to develop an international organization excluding the United States in order to counter-balance new U.S. military bases near its borders. Consider China's leadership of the Shanghai Cooperation Organization (SCO) in the context of U.S. military basing in Central Asia or the European Union and Mercosur agreements that provide some counter-balancing to a U.S.-sought free trade area of the Americas. On occasion, others in the world may seem to be tolerating or even encouraging U.S. policies, when in actuality they anticipate that that those policies can easily be blunted through soft counter-balancing.

The next action type, "fait accompli," challenges the United States by making moves that create a changed situation, as with Israeli settlement policy or North Korean nuclear testing. By presenting the United States with a new set of international facts, challengers try to make obsolete the assumptions made by American policy planners and decision makers. The feasibility of the United States achieving its policy preference at all, let alone at the initially estimated cost and schedule, can be rendered increasingly doubtful.

"Bloc creation," with the United States left on the outside of the bloc, may present considerably more opportunities for future nonfollowership coalitions. It can involve forming a new international governmental organization (IGO), adding a major mission to the scope of an existing institution, or forming a new interest group caucus within an IGO to which the United States does belong. Examples include steps toward the regional economic arrangement of the Asia-10 (the Association of Southeast Asian Nations +3), the EU pursuit of a European defense identity other than NATO, and the developing country G-20+ grouping in the Millennium Round World Trade Organization (WTO) negotiations.

"Rule-based retaliation" uses codes of behavior previously accepted by the United States to pose substantial costs for the policy preferences the federal government currently pursues or is considering for future adoption. It hinders U.S. defection from previously agreed-upon restraints on autonomous action, or at least raises the price of defection or failure to implement. Numerous cases brought against the United States in the WTO are illustrative.

"Rule expansion" proposes initiatives that, if accepted by the United States, would impose new restraints and, if rejected, would generate criticism among politically significant Americans who advocate the rules in question. The Kyoto Protocol, the Anti-Land Mine Convention, and initiatives to make inexpensive pharmaceuticals more readily available in poor countries are illustrative.

Actions of evasion, modification, and resistance do not need to be framed as opposition but can be wrapped in a cloak of consent. "Consent and exploit" actions declare and may even undertake cooperation with a general U.S. policy line while using it to justify specific practices that U.S. policy elites view with disfavor. Examples include the most expansionist versions of the Israeli wall for the West Bank and Russian actions in Chechnya. "Consent and deceive" actions amount to overt, declaratory support while acting in direct contradiction to it. Consider Egypt with regard to the promotion of democracy.

"Promise-protest-retraction" actions provide consent but later explicitly withdraw it. The consenting foreign leaders claim to find themselves overruled by protests or institutional responses from within their domestic polity. Those protests, which often are actually not surprising to the foreign leader who had issued a promise, are followed by a "reluctant" withdrawal of consent. Leaders of Japan's conservative ruling party for almost fifty years used this type of action to fend off U.S. pressures for a less restrained military posture. In such circumstances U.S. officials find themselves pressed to modify their policy preferences or risk weakening an ostensibly compliant, pro-American foreign leader or regime.

A cloak of consent may also be wrapped around "conditional support commitments." Prospects of compliance are explicitly contingent on meeting some conditions considered highly unlikely to develop or be met. The up-front conditions usually are considered legitimate by important elements of challenger, third-party, and U.S. selectorates. Consider how the French and others made their support for the U.S. invasion of Iraq conditional upon UN

Security Council approval and how Israel announced it would commit to U.S.-supported plans for resolving the Palestinian conflict only if the Palestinian Authority suppresses attacks from its territory.

Less forthrightly, "schedule delays" may be used after consent and co-operation pledges. Promises are one thing, while implementing actions are another, as with pledges of development assistance, humanitarian relief, or peacekeeping military forces that never or only fractionally ever reach their destination—as the Hamid Karzai government in Afghanistan can attest about pledges from American allies in Europe and Asia. Delaying efforts may last long enough for U.S. policy elites to adjust their priorities and lose the will to make up for shortfalls in pledged foreign contributions or to pressure dilatory foreigners to honor their pledges.

Consent, even if not denied outright, may not amount to followership if it is linked to Washington repeatedly earning it in ways that sacrifice some important U.S. priorities. Such "linkage to large side-payments" can substantially reduce, or eventually outweigh, any American policy gains from whatever cooperation foreigners have been induced to provide. Consider, for example, how Chinese officials have managed to cooperate on North Korean nuclear matters in return for official U.S. restraint from pressure for currency reevaluation, human rights improvements, or Taiwan's formal independence.

Strategies of evasion and modification can also take the form of "standing aside." Staying out of a situation altogether challenges American policy preferences under either or both of two conditions. In one circumstance U.S. policy planning assumes the availability of assets that a foreign party controls, such as military resources, intelligence assets, or financial and trade regulatory authorities.[8] The United States can find itself in a dependency trap that foreign parties can trigger (whether or not they intentionally created the trap). The second condition is that significant elements of the U.S. political scene trust particular foreign parties to certify the correctness of Washington's policy preferences. Their standing aside calls into question the judgments underlying the relevant U.S. policy preferences.

The actions discussed to this point largely involve what foreign parties may persuade Washington that they have the capacity to do. The final type of action, "credible helplessness," invokes a lack of capacity. The more Washington comes to recognize that others have large capacity deficits, the less promise U.S. officials will see in pressing followership on them. Incapacity may be a deliberate achievement, as with Japan's decades of inaction in developing the military capabilities the United States wanted it to have. In other instances, the lack of capacity may be unintended but, once credible, is useful in inducing Washington to tolerate a retreat from compliance. For example, heavily indebted middle-income countries in Latin America have used an inability to meet debt and debt service obligations to extract relief that the United States would have preferred not to provide.

Arenas

Whatever actions foreigners consider, they also have to make choices about the arenas in which to pursue them. Some major possibilities appear in the column headings in table 1.1. In the "unilateral" variant, a particular state or nonstate actor engages in evasion, modification, or resistance on its own. All the other possibilities involve joint action with one or more other states or nonstate actors. Whether intended to do so or not, unilateral efforts may encourage emulation by others if they seem effective. Such effectiveness can also trigger American responses that make nonfollowership more attractive to third parties. While unilateral actions can be taken in any of the other arenas (e.g., a single member veto in the UN Security Council), our interest lies primarily in their use outside of multi-member settings.

"Broad agenda institutions with the United States excluded" are composed of states or NGOs but do not include American organizations as more than observers. Their members provide or seek to provide them with rules of appropriate behavior, some established commitment to collective action by their members, and accepted processes to undertake it. Those commitments and processes can operate independent of U.S. approval. Such institutions need not engage in a blanket rejection of U.S. policy preferences and may on occasion even support them. They do, however, rest on the mutually recognized interests of their members in pursuing certain objectives over time, whatever the nature of U.S. policy preferences, and pooling their assets for doing so. Exclusion of American organizations may be based on regional identity (e.g., the EU and ASEAN) or economic characteristics (e.g., OPEC and other commodity cartels), or it may result from U.S. rejection or nonratification of particular international agreements (e.g., the International Criminal Court and the Kyoto Protocol).

By way of contrast, state and nonstate "coalitions of the unwilling" have a more ad hoc, issue-specific character. They lack established processes for arriving at collective decisions about anything, including challenges to official U.S. preferences, and their continued existence is highly uncertain. The French-German-Russian endeavor to hold back the U.S. invasion of Iraq in 2003 is illustrative.

A fourth type of arena for mounting challenges is that of "clubs and caucuses in U.S. member IGOs and INGOs." Resources are pooled to strengthen support for agreed-to caucus positions and to hold out prospects of bloc voting. The possibility of harmonization between club and caucus preferences and those of the United States may not be denied and may even be sought after. An underlying premise of challengers choosing this type of arena is that some part of the U.S. government or some American interest group has a stake in the future of the relevant international governmental or nongovernmental organization and in having it handle a variety of issues. Pulling an issue into such an arena where a substantial non-U.S. club or caucus exists may induce desired American policy changes, delay unwanted U.S. policy actions, and reduce the chances of substantial U.S. retaliation for nonfollowership. U.S. officials may be denied a domestically persuasive mandate justifying their initial policy preferences and may be provided with a justification for modifying them.[9] The United States may then face a more demanding carrot-and-stick problem, especially when the club or caucus is empowered by the institution's rules and norms to forestall mandates the United States seeks (as with the ASEAN caucus in the Asia-Pacific Economic Cooperation [APEC], the Islamic caucus in the UN, and the G-20+ in the WTO).

The last type of arena, "collective action networks with American participants," can resemble other arenas discussed above in terms of some ongoing commitment to collective action, established processes for decision making, and a shared sense of objectives among members. As the term "network" in this last category suggests, it need not have those characteristics any more than do coalitions of the unwilling. What makes this arena reasonably distinct is the mix of network participants: nonstate actors both foreign and American, foreign governments, and, formally or informally, some elements from American central or subnational bureaucracies and politics. Many such networks are created and sustained with one major purpose: shaping official U.S. policies in directions they might not otherwise take.[10] As a generic type, such networks may pursue almost any of the types of actions discussed previously and support use of the other types of arenas.

Our Explorations

The chapters that follow probe actors, policy issues, actions, and arenas likely to be of continuing importance in international affairs. Although they do not cover a representative sample of all nonfollowership practices, they do suggest alternatives to compliance with U.S. policies not limited to the particular time periods and situations examined.

Some chapters focus on country-specific foreign actors. Others center on strategies and behavior in multilateral groupings and organizations. Particular attention is paid to political-military issues in chapters on Iraq, Germany, Turkey, the G-7, and the Missile Technology Control Regime (MTCR). Other chapters are more concerned with nonmilitary issues: global warming, trade and trade-related issues, financial regulation, and public health with respect to dangerous substances. Of course, the same foreign actors may or may not practice nonfollowership on both military and nonmilitary issues. Differences and similarities in resorting to nonfollowership are covered in chapters on China, Turkey, and the G-7. A chapter on international public opinion addresses domestic political conditions in various countries and the incentives for their political elites to constrain American hegemony. The final chapter draws some conclusions about and implications for the perspective and framework introduced in the previous pages. It thus addresses possible future challenges to American policies as well as the development of more realistic and anticipatory U.S. statecraft.

MODES OF IRAQI RESPONSE TO AMERICAN OCCUPATION

JEREMY PRESSMAN

The United States invaded Iraq in March 2003 with a clear vision for Iraq's future. In moving to topple Saddam Hussein, Washington foresaw the development of a stable, democratic, friendly, and nonthreatening Iraq. Resistance to U.S. preferences, however, developed from day one, and over time the United States was forced to modify its policies and lower its expectations. Political and military (i.e., violent) opposition to the invasion revealed the problematic assumptions of the United States as it went into the war and led to repeated changes in U.S. policy. In addition to the direct human, financial, and political costs, the long-term implications of Iraqi resistance are significant.

This account focuses on resistance within Iraq to the U.S. occupation that followed the invasion in March 2003. While I am particularly interested in the Coalition Provisional Authority (CPA) and the Iraqi Governing Council (IGC), which ran Iraq from soon after the invasion until the handover of limited sovereignty to an interim Iraqi government on June 28, 2004, I also look at two issues that have developed since that time: the growth of militias and the 2005 national elections. The resistance largely came from domestic Iraqi actors but also included foreign fighters and jihadists who came to Iraq to violently resist the U.S. occupation. I give special attention to political methods of challenging CPA policy as seen through the actions of Ayatollah Ali al-

Sistani, a Shiite leader, and Kurdish officials, although the significance of violent resistance through "craziness" and martyrdom as well as melting actions are also considered. In terms of the options presented in Davis Bobrow's introductory chapter, actions are emphasized since the focus is on substate (domestic Iraqi) and nonstate actors.

U.S. Preferences in the Middle East and Iraq

During much of the Cold War, U.S. policy in the Middle East focused on preventing Soviet penetration of the region, maintaining the free flow of oil at a reasonable price, and ensuring Israel's survival.[1] With the collapse of the Soviet Union in December 1991, the issue of Soviet meddling became moot, and the other U.S. objectives became easier to achieve. On September 11, 2001, after a decade-long respite, a third element was added back into the U.S. policy equation: stopping the Middle East from serving as a base for violent, anti-American Islamists. To different degrees, oil, Israel, and Islamist terrorism created the fundamental base upon which the Bush administration built its case for war against Iraq in 2003.

The United States has long played in Persian Gulf politics to secure some of the largest petroleum reserves in the world. In 1953, the United States helped restore the Shah of Iran to power and toppled a nationalist Iranian leader who sought to nationalize the Iranian oil industry. By the 1970s, the United States was relying on twin pillars in the region, Iran and Saudi Arabia; the approach relied on local proxies to protect U.S. interests. The anti-U.S. Iranian revolution in 1979 ended this approach, and President Jimmy Carter then established the precursor to the U.S. Central Command, the unified U.S. forces responsible for the Horn of Africa, the Middle East, and Central Asia.[2] In the 1980s, the United States played both direct and indirect roles in Gulf politics: providing material support to Iraq in the Iran-Iraq war; reflagging Kuwaiti oil tankers to bring them under U.S. naval protection; seeking a secret deal with Iran in what came to be known as the Iran/Contra scandal; and continuing to develop U.S. relations with Saudi Arabia and the five other members of the Gulf Cooperation Council (Bahrain, Kuwait, Oman, Qatar, and the United Arab Emirates).[3]

The U.S. reaction to Iraq's invasion of Kuwait in 1990 exemplified an even stronger and more direct U.S. policy to maintain a stable and friendly Gulf region. When more than a half million U.S. forces expelled the Iraqi army from Kuwait, the United States operated out of Saudi Arabia, Turkey, and other states. Most of the financial cost of the U.S. effort was borne by Iraq's neighbors, especially Kuwait and Saudi Arabia. Throughout the 1990s, U.S.-

led forces policed northern and southern no-fly zones over Iraq, supported weapons inspections in and economic sanctions against Iraq, and continued to develop U.S. military ties with the Gulf monarchies (although relations with Iran remained cold). The proxies were thus largely serving as bases for U.S. forces and equipment rather than as U.S.-trained or armed intermediaries responsible for defending U.S. interests in the region.

Since the early 1960s, and especially after the 1967 Arab-Israeli war, the United States also has been deeply enmeshed in ensuring Israel's survival. This has meant U.S. arms sales and economic aid to Israel, diplomatic support for Israel at the United Nations and elsewhere, serving as Israel's patron vis-à-vis its Arab enemies and the Soviet Union, and facilitating Arab-Israeli political negotiations in an effort to lessen or end the conflict. Guaranteeing Israel's survival has been, at times, difficult to square with the U.S. commitment to the free flow of oil because so many of Israel's adversaries are major oil-producing states.

Islamist terrorism is the third and newest element in the U.S. stance toward the region. Although al-Qaeda was based in Afghanistan, many of its members came from and went back to the Middle East; it received financial backing and political sympathy from people located all over the region. If the United States was going to crush anti-U.S. terrorists with a global reach, as President George W. Bush pledged in the days just after 9/11, it was going to need to act in the Middle East to achieve that objective.

The premise of the U.S. invasion of Iraq was the need to get rid of Iraq's president, Saddam Hussein, but it also drew on these long-running U.S. objectives in the region. By getting rid of Saddam Hussein, the United States planned to transform Iraq from a hostile, dangerous dictatorship to a pliant democracy. More importantly, a pro-U.S. Iraq would give the United States a new anchor for U.S. security policy in the Gulf region and thereby help the United States protect its oil interests and fight Islamist terrorism.

Toppling Saddam ostensibly would open the door to three beneficial changes from the U.S. perspective. First, regime change would eliminate the threat to the United States from Iraq, its weapons of mass destruction, and Iraqi links to global terrorism.[4] The implicit U.S. argument was that these security challenges were a manifestation of the particular Iraqi regime (Saddam) rather than of the national interests of any Iraqi leader. Second, by managing Saddam's replacement, the United States could ensure that post-Saddam Iraq was a pro-American ally.[5] Third, the United States wanted to democratize Iraq. A democratic Iraq would not only improve the lot of the Iraqi people but could also serve as an example for other authoritarian states in the Middle

East. Some U.S. officials thought in terms of a demonstration or contagion effect: Iraqi democracy would serve as a role model and infect other states with the democratic bug. They hoped Saddam would be the first of many regional autocrats to fall (Bush 2003).

These specific U.S. objectives for Iraq varied greatly in terms of the amount of Iraqi cooperation and capabilities needed to achieve them. The scope of the objectives helped shape the possibilities for challenges. The U.S. military toppled Saddam's regime in a matter of weeks. The initial invasion and occupation of Iraq also limited threats from nonconventional weapons (had such weapons existed). In contrast, ensuring a pro-U.S. regime has been more difficult unless Washington plans to occupy the country indefinitely.[6] A democratic government cannot be established by American fiat; Iraqis must be willing and able to support this objective. The latter objectives have required a longer U.S. commitment and higher U.S. costs, which created more openings for challenges. If the United States had only objectives that it could achieve in a matter of weeks, post-Saddam political and military challenges would have had little significance. That Washington had aims that needed years to come to fruition set a dramatically different time frame and one that Iraqi actors could exploit much more easily.

As it turned out, many Iraqis were pleased with the initial U.S. goal of getting rid of Saddam but broke ranks with the United States on its other preferences. In October 2003, 17 percent of Iraqis wanted U.S. soldiers to leave Iraq and 43 percent saw the United States as an occupier rather than a liberator. By April 2004, the numbers had risen to 57 and 88 percent, respectively (Rubin 2004).

The U.S. preferences in Iraq were based on three interrelated assumptions about postwar Iraq that all proved to be incorrect. Washington assumed Iraqis would welcome U.S. soldiers as liberators indefinitely. Vice President Dick Cheney explained: "As for the reaction of the Arab 'street,' the Middle East expert Professor Fouad Ajami predicts that after liberation, the streets in Basra and Baghdad are 'sure to erupt in joy in the same way the throngs in Kabul greeted the Americans'" (Cheney 2002). In reality, the United States was quickly seen as an occupying force that was suppressing and harming Iraqis. This Iraqi perception was reinforced in May 2004 and afterward by the news of the torture of Iraqi prisoners at Abu Ghraib. The United States also assumed that its military forces would be able to maintain a secure environment. Lastly, U.S. officials argued that economic improvements would be rapid and follow a one-way trend (always getting better).

Violent Resistance

From the beginning of the occupation of Iraq, U.S. military forces and the CPA faced violent resistance from multiple actors, including Saddam loyalists and Sunni nationalists jockeying for power in the post-Saddam era, Muqtada al-Sadr's Mahdi army, and a small group of foreign fighters seeking to extend their global anti-American jihad into Iraq. Iraqi nationalism and opposition to foreign occupation played a role for almost all the Iraqi fighters. Though all these groups used violent tactics, they did not share the same goals. The insurgency succeeded in undermining the American ability to achieve its objectives in Iraq and increased the leverage of Iraq's political actors by creating time pressures on U.S. officials. In the face of the violence, the CPA needed signs of political progress, not stalemate.

Much of the violent resistance was designed to stoke fears of participating in a U.S.-favored new order and to promote silence if not build active support for opposition to it. The cumulative impact of many attacks on Iraqi police stations and assassinations of political officials such as the president of the Iraqi Governing Council, Ezzedine Salim, in May 2004 was probably to dampen public involvement. Since the end of the CPA, violence has only worsened, though attacks on the U.S. military became secondary to sectarian bloodletting. By 2006, Iraq was in the middle of a civil war (Fearon 2006). Whereas before the fall of Saddam Hussein there was no meaningful relationship between Iraq and al-Qaeda, as the insurgency developed al-Qaeda clearly saw Iraq as a new front in the war against the United States.[7]

Ayatollah Sistani

The most prominent political resistance to U.S. policy was from the widely respected Shiite cleric Ayatollah Ali al-Sistani. As one U.S. advisor noted, "No Iraqi commands a wider following of respect and consideration, and has more capacity to steer political developments away from violence and extremism, than Sistani" (Diamond 2004, 8).[8] Another U.S. advisor described him as "a figure whom no one could afford to ignore." He was "the democratic (or at least the majoritarian) conscience of the occupation" (Feldman 2004, 36, 67). His "religious authority was unparalleled" (Chandrasekaran 2006, 164). Sistani repeatedly pressured the CPA on the importance of early elections. Although the CPA resisted him for months, the two sides eventually agreed to hold elections earlier than the CPA wanted but later than Sistani had suggested.

What is much less clear is whether Sistani and other Shiite leaders primarily disagreed with U.S. timing and tactics or also had different objectives. Sistani is not a liberal, but he accepted a democratic system as a way to institutionalize Shiite power based on Iraq's Shiite majority. Would he support or oppose a pro-American Iraq five years down the road? What was the Shiite vision for Iraq's national security? These questions remained unanswered during the CPA period, a period that did not ask players to make final choices about Iraq's future.

On June 28, 2003, Sistani issued a two-page *fatwa* calling for the constitution to be written by elected representatives. The approved English translation rejected the appointment of members to draft a constitution. Instead, it called for a "general election" to choose representatives to a "foundational Constitution preparation assembly." Later, the constitution would be put to a referendum.[9]

L. Paul Bremer, the U.S. head of the CPA, mistakenly thought he could overcome Sistani's opposition by getting backing from other Shiite clerics for the CPA's plan or by changing Sistani's mind. As one of Bremer's "senior aides" later explained, "The view was 'We'll just get someone to write another fatwa.'" Iraqi Shiite members of the IGC fed this belief (Chandrasekaran 2006, 80, 187). The CPA tried to "work around" Sistani's objections (Bremer 2006, 189–90, 213). Yet neither circumventing Sistani nor changing his mind was likely to work given Sistani's revered status and the hierarchical nature of Shiite jurisprudence. More junior Shiite clerics did not have the authority to overrule Sistani. Moreover, his opinion was only likely to shift on the basis of new information, not political pressure.[10]

Why did the United States oppose national elections? According to one CPA advisor, "CPA thinking was dominated by the view that elections ought to be delayed as long as possible" (Feldman 2004, 114). The CPA frequently highlighted the potential logistical problems, including the absence of reliable voter rolls, suggesting that the U.S. opposition to immediate elections was based on technical issues. A second possible explanation is that U.S. officials were familiar with other post-conflict transitions in which premature elections undermined the movement toward stability and recovery. Thus, the initial U.S. position on national elections was based on the fear that such elections would be divisive and destabilizing. A third U.S. concern was about who would win the elections and how that outcome would affect future Iraqi-U.S. relations. The elections might favor those already organized, the Islamist and Ba'athist parties. In other words, the election could bring to power Iraqi forces that were anti-democratic and hostile toward Washington (Bremer 2006, 226).

Whatever the primary factor, throughout 2003 the CPA favored other mechanisms for selecting the drafters of the new constitution. Instead of elections, the United States initially thought that U.S. and Iraqi officials would jointly appoint the drafters. When the IGC was formed in July 2003, the CPA

and the new IGC members agreed the IGC would appoint a commission to set-
tle on a mechanism. In the summer of 2003, the United States pursued a second idea: partial elections, in which "the occupation authority would organize
caucuses in each governorate, or province, that would be limited to political,
religious, tribal, academic and trade union leaders as well as other influential
local figures approved by the Americans. The caucus would select the drafters
of the constitution."[11]

The IGC appointed a commission to consider the issue, but even under
U.S. pressure the commission did not endorse a mechanism favored by the
United States. In early September 2003, the commission voted unanimously
to support general elections, in part because of Sistani's position. According to
a CPA advisor, the committee "found itself completely constrained by the existence of Sistani's [June 28, 2003] fatwa" (quoted in Feldman 2004, 40; Chandrasekaran 2006, 187). The United States expressed its displeasure. Yet even in
its final report on September 30, the commission declined to endorse any of
the three options: appointment, partial elections, or direct elections. During
the fall of 2003, the United States and its allies were unable to change Sistani's
position. In addition, in the late summer and fall of 2003, some Shiite members of the IGC supported Sistani's position that national elections were the
best mechanism.

Meanwhile, the growing number of U.S. casualties in Iraq put pressure
on the United States to resolve the impasse. Whereas forty-four U.S. soldiers
died in all of October 2003, thirty-two were killed in the first week of November. (Even as of early 2005, November 2003 remained one of the worst months
for casualties for U.S. and allied forces: eighty-two U.S. dead and twenty-eight
international allies killed.)[12]

In mid-November 2003 Bremer unexpectedly came back to Washington
for consultations with President Bush and other top officials. At these meetings, the United States decided to try to overcome Sistani's objections by
deferring the writing of the constitution. It did not drop its opposition to national elections for selecting the drafters. The new plan still included partial
elections (caucuses), which were previously unacceptable to Sistani. The new
plan did call for the United States to transfer sovereignty to the Iraqis before
the permanent constitution was written, a reversal of earlier U.S. sequencing
that planned for the transfer of sovereignty after the writing of the permanent
constitution. This revised approach would give Washington more time to gain
support for a mechanism for selecting drafters other than through national
elections. The revised plan was approved by the CPA and IGC on November
15, 2003.

Sistani stated his objection to the proposed selection of an interim Iraqi government by caucuses. On November 29, 2003, responding to questions submitted by *Washington Post* reporters, Sistani codified his stance: "The mechanism in place to choose members of the transitional legislative assembly does not guarantee the establishment of an assembly that truly represents the Iraqi people." He explained what was acceptable: "This mechanism must be replaced with one that guarantees . . . elections, so the assembly will emanate from the desire of the Iraqi people and will represent them fairly without its legitimacy being tarnished in any way" (Shadid and Chandrasekaran 2003; Chandrasekaran 2006, 205).[13]

Tensions rose in January 2004, culminating in a massive Shiite protest calling for direct elections. On January 11, Sistani again called for national elections and emphasized that the lack of national elections could lead to violence. The next day, Bremer reiterated in the press his commitment to the caucus approach, and the January draft of what became the transitional administrative law or TAL included the caucus mechanism.[14] On January 19, a Shiite-led demonstration brought tens of thousands of Iraqis into the streets of Baghdad to call for direct, national elections (Shadid 2004b).

By mid-February, most IGC members opposed the caucus plan, and the United States had accepted a UN team, led by Lakhdar Brahimi, to study the feasibility of conducting national elections (Chandrasekaran 2004b). The United States and/or Sistani may have decided to rely on Brahimi to provide a face-saving way out of the stalemate over the mechanism for choosing the drafters of the constitution and for scheduling the national elections. One U.S. advisor saw the UN role as proof of Sistani's impact: "Ayatollah Sistani had done what Tony Blair could not: he had brought the United States to the United Nations, hat in hand, seeking its involvement in nation building in Iraq" (quoted in Feldman 2004, 41). His report, according to one CPA official, was a "critical" factor in determining the new framework.[15] Furthermore, the United Nations had significant experience in handling elections in post-conflict societies. Given that experience, some U.S. officials may have believed that if the UN team thought elections could be held in Iraq despite the logistical challenges, the United States was willing to go along. Even before the Brahimi report was officially released, the United States finally conceded that the caucus approach was dead.

The report from Brahimi's fact-finding mission was issued by UN Secretary-General Kofi Annan on February 23, 2004. Brahimi rejected both the caucus approach and holding national elections by June 30, 2004.[16] The report argued for decoupling the handover of sovereignty from national elections. The elections could be delayed even if the transfer of sovereignty still took place by June 30, 2004. That meant that the report had to come up with a new mechanism for choosing the post–June 30 transitional Iraqi government; the report offered some suggestions but did not advocate any single option. The report also suggested that elections for a legislative and constitutional assembly be held by the end of 2004 or shortly thereafter. (In the November 15, 2003, agreement, the United States had concurred with the plan to hold elections for a constitutional assembly by March 15, 2005.)

On February 26, 2004, Sistani responded to the UN report by accepting a six-month delay in holding the elections as long as there were "clear guarantees," such as a UN Security Council resolution (Shadid 2004a). Sistani had met with Brahimi on February 12, and the meeting apparently helped to convince Sistani of the logistical difficulties of having elections by June 30, 2004. The deal was enshrined in the TAL and UNSC Resolution 1546 on June 8, 2004. Ultimately, Brahimi chose the interim government. He allowed Sistani to assess Brahimi's list of four potential prime ministers. While Sistani did not pick one favorite, he did veto one possible candidate (Chandrasekaran 2006, 244–45).

In opposing U.S. policy, Sistani relied on a core American norm: one person, one vote. Given the Shiite Arab demographic advantage in Iraq (probably 60 to 65 percent of the population), Sistani could pay lip service to this central principle of democracy without necessarily being committed to democracy. Following the American norm would guarantee Shia political power. Implicitly, Sistani consented to the U.S. rule and then exploited it for Shiite gain. Bremer paraphrased his spokesperson: "[W]e'd have a real image problem if it looked as if America were against elections" (2006, 279).

Who prevailed? Neither the CPA nor the Sistani faction got exactly what it wanted, but the end result was more favorable to Sistani. The original U.S. plan "had been done in by a half-page fatwa written by an old man in Najaf" (Chandrasekaran 2006, 289). The U.S. effort to move forward through the appointment and then partial election (caucuses) of drafters of the constitution was stymied by Sistani, as Bremer himself conceded (2006, 167, 224, 243). The elections schedule, however, did not follow Sistani's initial preferences, although this was due to the logistical difficulties described by Brahimi and the UN mission rather than to the persuasive power of the United States. The constitution writers would be selected by Sistani's method, but the transitional government of Iraq—what became the government of Prime Minister Iyad Allawi—would not.

Why did the United States have to take heed of Sistani's opposition? As noted already, the insurgency put time pressure on U.S. officials. Sistani's religious power translated into significant political power; even many Iraqis working with the United States respected Sistani's viewpoint. If the United

States was not already aware of Sistani's strength, his popular support was made clear by the January 2004 rally. Sistani's call for national elections also raised the issue of U.S. legitimacy in Iraq. How could the United States promote anti-democratic means to force a democratic process when the democratizing aspect was being used as a central justification for American policy in Iraq? The old notion of a proconsul does not work well when the occupying power is seeking to democratize the occupied people in short order. Finally, the United States may have wanted to favor Sistani as a Shiite leader who could deliver in the face of a rising challenge from al-Sadr (Cole 2003a).

Even after the elections issue was settled, Sistani still influenced the political process. On March 5, 2004, five Shiite members of the IGC refused to sign the TAL at what was supposed to be the official signing ceremony.[17] Although the document was signed a few days later, the brief disagreement may have delayed an inevitable clash over the Kurdish desire for autonomy and legal protections from the central government. The five Shiites echoed Sistani's opposition to article 61(c), the clause giving any three provinces the ability to scuttle the permanent constitution. After meeting directly with Sistani on March 7, the five holdouts signed the TAL the next day without any changes to the draft. A few months later, Sistani successfully pushed the United States to exclude a reference to this interim document in UNSC Resolution 1546 on June 8, 2004. In a letter to the president of the Security Council, Sistani warned that any direct reference to the TAL in the proposed resolution would have "serious consequences" (Feldman 2004, 147).

Kurds

Although Kurdish leaders had worked with the United States for several years, after the fall of Saddam the two sides clashed over militias, checkpoints, and political issues. The main objective of Kurdish leaders was a conservative one: to protect their past gains. Since 1991, northern Iraq functioned as an autonomous zone outside of Saddam's control. It was under the partial protection of the United States and Britain and was dominated politically by the two main political and military Kurdish entities, the Kurdistan Democratic Party (KDP) and the Patriotic Union of Kurdistan (PUK). In 1992, Kurds held elections for a regional parliament, the national assembly. A council of ministers, including a prime minister, was first formed in September 1996. They formed the Kurdistan Regional Government (KRG), based in Irbil.

To protect their autonomy, Kurds seemingly supported the same type of Iraq that Washington wanted. Kurdish officials had already worked with the United States in the 1990s and called for "a free, federal, pluralistic and democratic Iraq" (Barzani 2005).[18] The leaders of three Kurdish political groups served as members of the Iraqi Governing Council: Massoud Barzani (KDP), Jalal Talabani (PUK), and Salaheddine Bahaaeddin of the Kurdistan Islamic Union. The Kurds accepted U.S. objectives for Iraq but added some of their own, which led to some important policy differences. One U.S. official involved in drafting the TAL later called the Kurdish issues "the most contentious, explosive, and difficult to resolve" (Diamond 2006, 161).

After Saddam's fall, Kurdish leaders, as they had throughout the 1990s, emphasized a federal solution and did not push for Kurdish independence. Much more powerful external actors objected to Iraqi Kurdish independence; they included Turkey, the United States, and the rest of Iraq. Turkey threatened to intervene if Kurdish leaders expanded the size of the autonomous region, let alone declared independence. Moreover, the practicality of independence for a land-locked country surrounded by four larger neighbors—Iran, Iraq, Syria, and Turkey—was questionable. With independence, unresolved issues such as the status of Mosul and Kirkuk and the division of Iraq's oil revenues might not be decided in the Kurds' favor. In short, the calculation seems to have been that it was better to protect what Iraqi Kurds had achieved than to risk it all by seeking independence (and thereby risking a return to domination by others, or destruction, or death).

The Kurds resisted some initial CPA policies, and the CPA backed down. The CPA initially called for the Kurds (and others) to disband militias and take down checkpoints. The Kurds resisted both policies and clearly stated that they never intended to disband their militias, the *peshmerga*. The checkpoints came down. However, they quickly went back up after a few bombings in Kurdish-controlled areas. The militia issue was not resolved until the TAL came into force and U.S. and Kurdish leaders signed a private memorandum, as noted below.

The United States opposed interim legal recognition of and sanction for Kurdish autonomy, while Kurdish leaders raised a number of issues to protect Kurdish power and, in the case of Kirkuk, improve on the status quo. In early January 2004 Bremer twice met with Kurdish leaders "to urge them to back down from their demands to retain autonomy" (Wright and Sipress 2004). U.S.-Kurdish meetings continued over the next two months. Drafts of the TAL from January 2004 did not contain a mechanism to ensure Kurdish ability to block an unfavorable version of the permanent constitution, something that was included in the final TAL (article 61[c]).

The Kurdish leaders pressed for concessions on a range of issues, including the peshmerga, protection from national legislation, the judiciary, ratification of the permanent constitution, the status of Kirkuk, and the disbursement of oil revenue. When the TAL was signed, it recognized the special status of

Kurdistan and put in place a number of constitutional protections. On the militias, protection from national legislation, and constitutional ratification, the Kurdish position prevailed. Kurdish was also an official language of Iraq, and the structure of the presidency council was a "huge victory" for Kurdish leaders (Diamond 2006, 169–71). The only area where Kurdish leaders conceded much ground was the new judicial structure. The status of Kirkuk and the oil question were in essence deferred.

Many of these concerns were contained in a Kurdish proposal for a chapter in the TAL devoted solely to Kurdistan. Although the final version of the TAL did not contain a separate chapter on Kurdistani issues, officials incorporated several of the ideas into the TAL. The Kurdish proposal was originally given to CPA officials, probably in early February, and then the Kurdish government posted the document on its Web site on February 20, 2004.[19] The proposed chapter included four relevant articles. Article 1, "Continuity of the Kurdistan Region," protected the legal, territorial, and governmental aspects of Iraqi Kurdistan and the KRG. Article 2, "The Iraqi Kurdistan National Guard: Security of the Kurdistan Region," called for the maintenance of separate Kurdish militias (security forces). Article 3, "Natural Resources in the Kurdistan Region," called for Kurdish control of land, water, and oil (including the sale of oil). Article 5, "Kurdistan Region Ratification of Successor Laws to the Transitional Law," required Kurdish popular approval of any permanent constitution. In general, the continuity of the Kurdistan region and the ratification issue were dealt with in the TAL along the lines proposed in this document, the security forces were dealt with in a separate memorandum, and the oil issue was deferred.

On disbanding Kurdish militias, the TAL is ambiguous, but the two parties signed a private memorandum of understanding that largely endorsed the Kurdish position. In January 2004, the United States had asked Kurds for the full demobilization of the peshmerga (Diamond 2006, 162). According to TAL article 27(b), all militias must be under the central government's "command structure." Article 54(a), however, allows the KRG to "retain regional control over police forces and internal security." The memorandum of understanding goes even further and directly addresses Kurdish concerns raised in article 2 of the proposed separate chapter on Kurdistan for the TAL. A small number of Kurdish forces would become part of the Iraqi National Guard under the control of the central Iraqi government. The remaining peshmerga would be known as a KRG internal security force and include rapid reaction forces, anti-terror forces, and mountain rangers. These internal security forces would report to the KRG, not to the central government.[20] After the memorandum was signed, a U.S. official asked Barzani how to translate "mountain rangers" into Kurdish. Barzani's answer was telling: "We will call them 'peshmerga'" (quoted in Chandrasekaran 2006, 257).

The TAL also provides the Kurds protection from many national laws involving Islam. In terms of federal laws, "the Kurdistan National Assembly shall be permitted to amend the application of any such law within the Kurdistan region" with the exception of foreign policy, national security, fiscal policy, natural resources, telecommunications, and a few other matters (article 54[b] with reference to 25 and 43[d]). This clause would provide the Kurds with protection against the intrusion of (Shiite) Islamic observance into daily life and governmental practice. If, for example, the federal government passed a law mandating that women must be covered when in public, the Kurdish assembly could legally block the application of the law in Kurdistan. The TAL itself contained compromise language on the relationship between the law and Islam (article 7). During the negotiations, Bremer "indicated that he will veto any interim constitution that makes Islam the sole source of legislation" (Chandrasekaran 2004a).

The definition of the judiciary in the TAL gave the Kurds some protection, but they conceded that federal courts would be above Kurdish ones. Iraq's new supreme court would operate in a framework designed to bring together, though not fully integrate, the two existing legal systems, one in Kurdistan and one in the rest of Iraq. The federal supreme court was given "[o]riginal and exclusive jurisdiction in legal proceedings between the Iraqi Transitional Government and the regional governments, governorate and municipal administrations, and local administrations" (article 44[b][1]). Local court decisions, "including the courts of the Kurdistan region," would be subject to review by federal courts (article 46[b]). While most decisions would be by a simple majority, cases between the central government and the regional governments must be decided by a two-thirds majority of the nine justices (article 44[d]). This was the result of Kurdish pressure (Diamond 2006, 150).

For ratification of the permanent constitution, the Kurds also protected themselves. The interim Iraqi constitution contained this clause: "The general referendum [to be held no later than October 15, 2005] will be successful and the draft [permanent] constitution ratified if a majority of the voters in Iraq approve and if two-thirds of the voters in three or more governorates do not reject it" (article 61[c]). This veto provided for in the article is not restricted to Kurds, but Kurds are the majority in three provinces and could have balked at provisions imposed by the Shiite majority.[21] By the time the actual vote took place in 2005, the fear was actually that three Sunni Arab majority provinces might block ratification (they did not).

One unresolved issue is the geographic definition of the Kurdish area.

Kurdish leaders would like to expand Kurdistan to include Kirkuk and Mosul, as it was defined in the 1990s. Turkey has threatened that it will not allow Kirkuk to formally fall under Kurdish political control. This issue was not resolved during the CPA period, though Kurdish leaders tried to get U.S. support during the TAL negotiations in the first months of 2004 (Williams 2004; Diamond 2006, 164–65, 167). In the TAL, article 53(a) endorsed the territorial status quo in northern Iraq without resolving the question.[22] In a separate article (58), the TAL endorsed a process to remedy the ethnic cleansing of Kurds (and others) under Saddam Hussein. The articles made specific reference to Kirkuk. Later, after the CPA's dissolution, Iraqi Kurds who had returned to Kirkuk since the fall of Saddam were allowed to vote in the national elections in January 2005. That they were allowed to vote was seen as a victory for the Kurdish political leadership (Smyth and Guha 2005). On the ground, Kurdish leaders sought to bolster constitutional battles with a favorable demographic balance. Faits accomplis—moving more Kurds into contested cities—could reshape the theoretical debates.

Lastly, the Kurds tried to ensure a more favorable distribution of Iraq's oil revenue, but the language of the TAL is ambiguous. The initial U.S. position was that Iraq's central government would have "exclusive authority" over natural resources (Diamond 2006, 162, 169). In the TAL, the federal government has the responsibility for managing Iraq's natural resources. The language on sharing the wealth takes into account many considerations: "distributing the revenues resulting from their sale through the national budget in an equitable manner proportional to the distribution of population throughout the country, and with due regard for areas that were unjustly deprived of these revenues by the previous regime, for dealing with their situations in a positive way, for their needs, and for the degree of development of the different areas of the country" (article 25[b]). Given the multitude of factors mentioned, one can imagine this playing out in several different ways, only some of which would be to the liking of the KRG.

Overall then, the Kurdish leaders cemented their autonomous status, conceded few rights (the judiciary being the exception), and kept open some issues on which they hope to expand Kurdish powers. Given the initial U.S. opposition to legal protections for Kurdish autonomy, the United States (and non-Kurdish Iraqis) conceded several important points. In short, the TAL and the memorandum of understanding respected the Kurdish red lines. The Kurds "had emerged as the most successful players in the [TAL] negotiations." Given that the United States had opposed most Kurdish provisions, "it was a remarkable political victory" for the Kurds (Diamond 2006, 171, 174).[23]

Why did the Kurds get much of what they wanted? One plausible explanation is the time pressure on the United States due to the insurgency and the need to avoid the appearance of a political stalemate in Iraq. If the CPA refused to concede the major Kurdish red lines, the Kurds could have held up the TAL negotiations and undermined yet another aspect of the November 15, 2003, agreement: the signing of a transitional constitution by February 28, 2004. If the CPA could not negotiate the TAL in a timely fashion, the United States could not move toward transferring sovereignty to Iraqis and holding elections. The sovereignty and elections issues, along with a general sense of forward momentum, helped the Bush administration on two interrelated points. First, those issues helped Bush in the 2004 presidential election; he could tell voters he had a plan that was working. Second, they helped the American people believe that U.S. troops would not be in Iraq forever. Stalemated political talks in Iraq would send the opposite message and support for the war might drop quickly. This was especially important at a time when some Americans were just starting to recognize that Bush's Iraq war would be much more costly in human and financial terms than the administration had previously admitted.

Iraq since the End of the CPA

Since the end of the CPA, the United States has continued to try to influence Iraqi politics and governance. But just as during the CPA period, local actors have frustrated U.S. designs that emphasized a national rather than regional and sectarian post-Saddam Iraq. From the perspective of U.S. desires, local actors often were in fact engaging in consent and exploit or even consent and deceive actions. The efforts by militias to capture national police and military forces and the electoral results are illustrative.

Militias

The United States has sought to create national security forces in the sense that the Iraqi police and military forces would be multi-ethnic and give primary allegiance to the Iraqi state. At the same time, local actors have worked to capture national forces for sectarian advantage. As the Iraqi civil war has intensified over time and sectarian killings have increased, many local military players have little incentive to prioritize national over sectarian needs.

One valuable prize, then, for sectarian leaders was the Ministry of the Interior because it oversees a number of Iraqi police and security forces. The Supreme Council for the Islamic Revolution in Iraq (SCIRI), one of the leading Shiite movements, got control of the ministry after the January 2005 elections; Bayan Jabr was named minister.[24]

Despite U.S. rhetoric and TAL provisions to the contrary, SCIRI's actual control of the ministry gave it the power to influence personnel selection as Iraq reconstituted its police and security forces. The Badr corps, SCIRI's militia, used the ministry as a way to get Badr members into local police slots. They also pushed Badr members into a well-armed national police force—the police commando units. At the same time, Jabr led a purge of Sunni officials in the ministry. Since the ministry was charged with the day-to-day effort of building security forces, control of the ministry meant the ability to circumvent American preferences.

The packing of "national" security forces with militia members was more than an unfair division of the spoils. These same police were often implicated in sectarian killings; some were Shia death squads masquerading as a police force.[25] Ministry of the Interior personnel also were blamed for the "vast majority" of abuses against those in Iraqi custody.[26]

Jabr's sectarian tendencies actually became clear even before he was minister of interior. Under the CPA, Jabr was minister of housing and construction. That ministry was in charge of the Facilities Protection Service, a force that Jabr also packed with Shiite recruits. U.S. officials who complained to their superiors about Jabr were brushed aside (Silverstein 2006).

Elections and Governments

Although the United States did not openly endorse particular parties during the Iraqi elections, the United States hoped the elections would be part of a process that would bring Iraq closer to both national unity and democracy. Iraqis, Bush said, had "chosen a future of freedom and peace."[27] Instead, the results produced the opposite: sectarian parties. Moreover, many members of the party that got the most votes in both elections, the United Iraqi Alliance, were sympathetic to Islamist ideologies at odds with a liberal worldview. The Alliance included the three most powerful Shia movements: SCIRI, Dawa, and the Sadrists aligned with Muqtada al-Sadr (and his Mahdi army).

In the elections on January 30, 2005, almost three-quarters of all votes went to this Shia list, the United Iraqi Alliance (48.2 percent of the vote and 140 of 275 seats), and a Kurdish list, the Democratic Patriotic Alliance of Kurdistan (25.7 percent of the vote and 75 seats). The closest approximation of a nonsectarian or more secular list, Iyad Allawi's Iraqi List, finished a distant third (13.8 percent and 40 seats). Many Sunni Arabs boycotted the election.

The impact was also felt at the local level. In Basra, Iraq's second largest city, the local government is controlled by Islamist parties, and this has deeply affected daily life in the city (Dreazen 2005). Basra elections, held the same day in January as the national elections, were dominated by two parties: Islamic Basra (twenty of forty-one seats) and the Al-Fadhila Islamic party (twelve).

In the second national elections of 2005, on December 15, ethnic parties again dominated. Since many Sunni Arabs participated, votes were now split among Shia, Sunni, and Kurdish parties. The United Iraqi Alliance (41.2 percent and 128 seats) and the Democratic Patriotic Alliance of Kurdistan (21.7 percent and 53 seats) were joined by two Sunni Arab parties: the Iraqi Accord Front and the Iraqi National Dialogue Front (for a joint total of 19.2 percent and 55 seats). Only one party with nonsectarian aspirations, the Iraqi National List, which included Allawi's Iraqi List and other parties, received more than a handful of votes (8 percent and 25 seats).[28]

Not surprisingly then, the allocation of ministries in Iraqi governments after the elections was largely along sectarian lines. Given that the parties were largely sectarian, so were their demands.

The results in terms of militias, elections, and governments were not totally at odds with U.S. preferences, but this was only because U.S. policy contained a fundamental contradiction. Washington sought to preserve Iraq's national unity and avoid sectarian bloodshed, but it also used ethnic leaders and promoted a division of political leadership along ethnic lines similar to Lebanon's system of government. Perhaps the United States thought it could use existing ethnic power bases to push the country away from ethnic divisions, but in fact the effort only strengthened sectarian lines and sectarian decision making. Power for one's own ethnic group might simply have been a tactic in the eyes of the United States, but it became an end in itself among Iraqi political and militia leaders.

Lessons from Iraq on the Variety of Challenges

Iraqi resistance to U.S. policy preferences typifies a number of ways in which weaker actors may resist dominant powers. The Iraqi case includes examples of many of Bobrow's action categories: "craziness" and martyrdom, rule-based retaliation and expansion, fait accompli, consent and exploit, consent and deceive, and schedule delays. The Iraqi case also suggests how the interaction between violence and political challenges may increase the likelihood that the great power is stymied. First, violent resistance creates time pressure that affects the time frame for political actors as well. Second, political actors may be forced to (or feel compelled to) react to events taking place in the violent realm. Differences of opinion among rival political actors may emerge that are based solely on how to deal with the violent resistance. In terms of Bobrow's arenas, this means that challengers need not be working together formally as part of a front or network in order to benefit from their respective anti-U.S. tactics. Finally, the case addresses how challengers may exploit a great power that seeks to achieve many goals simultaneously.

Some Iraqi insurgents used extreme violence, attacks on civilians, and self-sacrifice to affect policy in Iraq, the United States, and elsewhere. Suicide bombings, beheadings, and attacks on Iraqi police and governmental personnel sent a message. They might cause Iraqis who were considering working with the CPA and IGC to stay on the sidelines. By 2006, Iraqis were afraid to help a wounded Iraqi or approach a dead body in the street for fear of being seen as partisan and thus a potential target (*Los Angeles Times*, Sept. 20, 2006; McDonnell 2006). They might influence the U.S. public to back away from Iraq given the high and ghastly costs. In the international arena, this type of violence could lead other states and international actors to question whether the United States could succeed. This in turn would affect the willingness of others to get involved; why board a sinking ship? The Sadrists' battles with U.S. and Iraqi forces could have had a similar impact on Iraqis, the U.S. public, and the international community. However, the message sent may well have been a different one—that of nationalist determination, not craziness. It says, "We are here, this is our land, and we will use force to defend it"; this is meant to be a rational argument for the high costs the United States and others will pay if they continue to occupy Iraq.

Actors may use "codes of behavior previously accepted" by the United States to undermine U.S. policy. Once Washington sets the rules of the game, actors may resist by using the accepted rules against the rule maker. While the most obvious applications of rule-based retaliation and expansion may be in the international economic realm, Sistani's reliance on democratic norms is a more subtle illustration. Sistani took the general U.S. commitment to democracy and elections and insisted that the United States also uphold that commitment in the Iraqi context. He must have known that such an appeal for democratic elections would have deep resonance with Bush's constituents back in the United States. The two parliamentary elections in 2005 then led to the "problem" with elections from a loyalty perspective: the United States did not get to choose the winners. This also has resonance for Bobrow's consent and exploit action category; Shiite politicians could agree to democracy in a broad sense, only to use it as a way to build an Iraqi nationalist coalition.

The time frame for the United States and Iraqi actors was not the same, and this meant that Iraqi negotiators could threaten to wait out political disagreements with the United States and other Iraqi actors. While Washington wanted continual signs of progress in order to satisfy domestic and international observers, Shiite and Kurdish leaders could better afford to bide their time. The possibility of political deadlock, delays, and missed deadlines was alarming to the United States and gave greater leverage to the Iraqi representatives. (This may also be linked to another action type, conditional support commitments, in which "[p]rospects of compliance are held out as being explicitly contingent on some [unlikely] conditions being met.") As time passed, the Kurds were also not standing still. By working to change the demographic balance in their favor in contested cities such as Kirkuk and Mosul, they sought to use faits accompis to prod U.S. policy.

One interesting aspect of the resistance to U.S. preferences in Iraq was the interplay between the violent insurgency and political interactions between the CPA and other Iraqi actors. Unlike some cases where the militant and political actors may be linked (e.g., the Irish Republican Army and Sinn Fein), most of the insurgents were wholly distinct from many of the most powerful Iraqi political players. Neither Sistani nor the Kurds were in any way cooperating with the insurgents. Al-Sadr was not a puppet of Sistani, and the Kurds strongly opposed the insurgency. As time passed, however, and some Shiite militias and their political leaders—though not Sistani—controlled the Ministry of the Interior and other branches of the government, the political-military connections did grow stronger.

The insurgency affected CPA-Iraqi interactions in two ways. First, it created controversial decision points to which political actors had to react. For instance, in the spring of 2004, Ghazi al-Yawir, a Sunni member of the IGC and later the transitional president, said he would resign if the Fallujah standoff was not resolved diplomatically. Shia member Abd-al Karim al-Mahmadawi expressed similar concerns after coalition attacks on al-Sadr's forces.[29] In short, the counter-insurgency campaign led to splits among some Iraqi politicians and the CPA/U.S. military.

Second, the insurgency created a sense of urgency among U.S. officials that probably gave Sistani and the Kurds greater leverage in disagreements with the United States. The Bush administration needed good news to sustain domestic political support for the Iraqi adventure, especially given that President Bush was up for reelection in November 2004. The combination of insurgency and failed political negotiations would not have boded well for the Bush administration. U.S. officials could not end the insurgency by modifying American policy short of leaving Iraq, but they could accommodate political opposition through reasonable concessions. Moreover, the United States was the external actor far from home whereas Iraqis were home and fighting, whether politically or militarily, for control of that home. The Iraqis had nowhere else to go.

Iraqi resistance is also suggestive about the interplay between different U.S. objectives in a given setting. First, challengers may be selective about which U.S. objectives they can best take on. For Iraqis willing to use military means, it may have made more sense to wait until the United States had toppled Saddam's regime and then launch an insurgency rather than try to stave off the U.S. invasion in March and April 2003. The American military advantage was greatest during the initial invasion, while the battlefield became more competitive during the insurgency.

Second, challengers may embrace some U.S. goals but not others. When the United States has many broad goals, as it did in Iraq, the challengers may quickly understand the potential conflict between various U.S. objectives and then seek to exploit the areas of goal incompatibility. Sistani may have seen that he could support the democratic path even if that meant the United States might have to sacrifice its desire for a pro-American Iraqi regime. More speculatively, perhaps Kurdish leaders were willing to protect Kurdish autonomy even if that was at the expense of the territorial integrity of Iraq, an important baseline for Iraq's future from the U.S. perspective. One could also see this dynamic with the militia and elections issues after the CPA ended.

What have shifts in U.S. policy in Iraq cost the United States? While these costs are not solely the result of opposition to U.S. preferences in Iraq, the magnitude of each is greater as a result of successful challenges to American policy.

As in any war, the United States has expended blood and treasure. Up to the transfer of sovereignty, more than 850 U.S. soldiers had been killed in Iraq and the financial bill was into the hundreds of billions of dollars. By late 2006, the U.S. casualty figures exceeded twenty-three thousand dead and wounded soldiers. More broadly, Iraq failed to demonstrate the ease and replicable nature of nation-building or democratization and has instead made nation-building look very difficult, costly, and time consuming. The U.S. effort has struggled to build a secure environment, a better economy, and a legitimate government and political system. The Iraqi debacle could easily inspire future leaders to say what then-candidate Governor George W. Bush said on October 11, 2000, in his second debate with then–Vice President Al Gore: "I don't think our troops ought to be used for what's called nation-building."[30]

The same is probably true for democratization. While Iraq could yet emerge as a democratic country, the U.S. role in Iraq is unlikely to inspire democrats and liberal reformers in the near term. In addition to altering procedures on numerous occasions, the United States compromised democratic and liberal values on major symbolic and substantive issues such as the Abu Ghraib scandal and other torture allegations, the concessions in Fallujah, and the partial reversal of de-Ba'athification. In the absence of Iraqi WMD and al-Qaeda–Iraq terror links, democracy and human rights became the major ex-post Bush administration justifications for the war, but they lose some impact in the face of anti-democratic and anti-liberal behavior.

Lastly, the U.S. performance in Iraq and the Iraqi insurgency help al-Qaeda by playing on both American power and weakness. The invasion and reconstruction of Iraq serve as a motivating tool for recruitment and fundraising. The evil giant, America, invaded and occupied another Muslim land. At the same time, the insurgents' success in inflicting casualties and creating a climate of fear and disorder demonstrates that U.S. forces are vulnerable. It gives encouragement, and possibly tactical models, to others elsewhere who hope to confront the United States. Iraq became a training area for jihadists and other U.S. opponents.[31] In short, American military and economic dominance does not mean that the United States can dictate its desired outcome in every political or military arena.

The United States did make some adjustments, but they came too late. Bremer twice overhauled the CPA's political program, including the agreement of November 2003 and the acceptance of the Brahimi plan. The CPA handed over sovereignty before a final constitution was in place. Yet more generally, from 2003 to 2006, the United States was never able to overcome its initial errors, including ignorance about the likely depth and ferocity of both political and violent opposition to the U.S. occupation.

The United States could learn from the political resistance in Iraq, but the true test will not come until the next time Washington seeks to remake another government and society. Local players are not omnipotent, but they hold home-court advantage. With nowhere else to go, time is often on their side when faced by a distant superpower. Bearing this in mind, the United States should focus more clearly on the potential leverage of local actors. U.S. officials had a hard time imagining being stymied by other negotiating parties. More broadly, one can hope for greater American humility and caution when the United States considers such foreign policy ventures in the future.

THE RELUCTANT ALLY
German Domestic Politics and the War against Saddam Hussein

SIEGMAR SCHMIDT

On September 11, 2001, Chancellor Gerhard Schroeder of Germany promised the United States "unlimited solidarity" in the fight against terrorism. Only one year later a severe crisis in both American-European and American-German relations broke out. Germany not only refused to support a U.S. invasion of Iraq as part of its war on terror but also declared that it would not support even UN military action against Iraq. Germany's ostensibly strict opposition to U.S. policy toward Iraq differed strongly from the country's active role in the war against the Taliban in Afghanistan, where, for the first time in postwar German history, the German government deployed a few hundred elite ground troops to take part in combat. The conflict between the United States and the German and other European governments over Iraq reached unprecedented levels both in substance and in style. The conflict over confronting Saddam Hussein and the subsequent occupation of Iraq caused a major shift in international public perceptions of the United States. The share of Germans saying that the United States is Germany's "closest friend" dropped dramatically, from 50 percent in 1995 to only 11 percent in March 2003.

This chapter examines three main motives and reasons behind Germany's opposition to the United States, actions and arenas used in challenging the United States, U.S. reactions to those challenges, the success of Schroeder's strategy domestically and internationally, and the evolution of German-U.S. relations after the beginning of the Iraq war and the 2005 German elections.

Special attention is given to possible contradictions in German policy, contradictions such that Germany neither resisted U.S. Iraq policy in a sustained and comprehensive way nor simply followed it.

Much of relevance has already been written since the pre-invasion dispute. For example, Philip Gordon and Jeremy Shapiro (2004) cover the relationship between the United States and Europe as a whole, while Steven Szabo (2004a; 2004b) focuses exclusively on German-American relations. With the notable exceptions of Dalgaard-Nielsen 2003 and Karp 2005, most of the articles are policy oriented, with the authors usually adding to their analyses some recommendations for a rapprochement across the Atlantic, or, while comprehensive, are journalistic or descriptive (Winkler 2004). There is a broad consensus among German and American scholars and journalists that Chancellor Schroeder's domestic considerations played an important role in Germany's categorical "nein." From this perspective, Schroeder successfully instrumentalized the Iraq war for his party's victory at the polls. Yet his view does not easily accommodate the facts of simultaneous and subsequent direct German support for the American-led war on terror, including but not limited to Afghanistan, and less direct cooperation with the U.S. military engagement in Iraq. The complexities of German motivations and politics need more explication because they can help us understand what Germany has and has not done with regard to the challenge action and arena categories sketched in chapter 1. As two-level game formulations suggest (Putnam 1988), Germany pursues and rejects, sustains and terminates challenge options in light of the international and domestic contexts experienced and perceived by Germans. Those contexts include U.S. reactions to nonfollowership—reactions that can intensify rather than ease challenges.

German-U.S. Relations in Historical Perspective

It is difficult, if not impossible, to understand Germany's foreign and security policies without taking into account Germany's historical development and resulting foreign policy identity. The total military and moral defeat in 1945, the devastation, the partition of the country, and millions of refugees are deeply ingrained in the country's collective memory. The Holocaust and the war crimes committed by the German military, particularly in Eastern Europe, are part of the country's consciousness. Germans still feel responsible for the past, and this memory is kept alive. "Never again Auschwitz" ("Nie wieder Auschwitz") became a leitmotif of the raison d'état of the Federal Republic. Further, Germany has been an occupied and later a semi-sovereign state and, during the Cold War, a frontline state that imported security from the United States primarily through NATO.

The postwar limits on the political leverage of Germany, and collective experiences and memories shared by elites from all political camps and the majority of the population, created a type of foreign policy aptly described as "civilian power."[1] According to Hanns Maull (1990–1991; 2007) Germany, as a civilian power, has a foreign policy that features a strong preference for principled multilateralism instead of unilateralism; support for international organizations and regimes, in particular those favoring human rights and trade; a foreign policy culture of restraint that avoids the image of leadership in favor of consensus-oriented, often "quiet" diplomacy; a focus on economic and trade interests; a preference for economic and diplomatic instruments such as sanctions and conference diplomacy instead of military force; and an emphasis on democratic values and human rights.

These principles explain to a considerable degree the course of German foreign policy. Germany acted as a loyal partner within the NATO and EU frameworks. Between the 1970s and the mid-1990s Germany was one of the driving forces of European integration. Due to its economic power and diplomatic weight, it was able to hammer out political compromises for further deepening (the Maastricht Treaty, 1992) and widening of the EU (eastern enlargement). Although Germany did benefit from the common market finalized in 1991, commentators criticized its role as the paymaster of European integration. In the transatlantic relationship between Europe and the United States, Germany defined its role as a broker or mediator between France and the United States. During the Cold War, Germany shifted from an uncompromising policy toward Eastern Europe to a special form of détente, the Ostpolitik. It not only developed into a major supporter of the Commission on Security and Cooperation in Europe (CSCE) process, but the Ostpolitik of the Social Democratic Party (SPD)/Free Democratic Party (FDP) government (1969–1983) went far beyond détente by establishing a close-knit fabric of economic, cultural, and political relations between Germany and its eastern neighbors. Besides being a useful arena for increasing its international reputation, the UN was, in Germany's view, the most important institution for securing international peace and development. Germany became the third largest contributor to the UN and funded UN peacekeeping operations. In addition, Germany supported the development of international law and heavily supported the International Criminal Court (ICC). These aims were overwhelmingly shared by all political camps, which made German foreign policy highly predictable. One of the cornerstones of the consensus was that the missions of the German army—the Bundeswehr established in 1955 after heated debates and strong opposition—were solely to protect the country or to defend NATO territory.

From the establishment of the Bundeswehr to 1990 there was a broad consensus that no German troops should be deployed overseas for other than humanitarian reasons, for example, in the wake of natural disasters. After the sea change in international relations caused by the fall of the Soviet empire, a controversial discussion started in Germany in 1990 when a U.S.-led coalition invaded Kuwait to end the Iraqi occupation (Operation Desert Storm). Mass demonstrations, many involving young students, took place under the slogan "no blood for oil" and curtailed the government's political latitude for responding to Iraq's invasion. Despite criticism from its allies, Germany was unable and unwilling to participate in Desert Storm even though it was legitimized by a UN Security Council resolution. Instead, Germany contributed to a large extent by bearing the adjunct costs of war (similar to "checkbook diplomacy"). The controversial and emotional debate about the use of the Bundeswehr for peacekeeping missions ended in July 1994, when the Constitutional Court ruled that the Bundeswehr could participate in missions outside the NATO area, in so-called out-of-area operations.[2] The Balkan wars brought about a fundamental change in thinking about the role of the military. The atrocities, especially in Bosnia, left Germany (and other European nations) helpless since neither diplomatic initiatives nor economic sanctions could stop the massacres. When in 1995 the Serbs overran the UN "safe haven" zone around the town of Srebrenica, even the pacifist left had to consider that the "civilian" policy approach had failed.[3]

From the mid-1990s on, Germany deployed several thousand soldiers in the international peacekeeping force in Bosnia and additional troops in Kosovo and Macedonia. The newly elected SPD/Green Party government in September 1998 not only continued but extended these peacekeeping engagements (Wagener 2004). This was surprising since the SPD and the Green Party in particular traditionally harbored the "generation of 1968" (the student revolt in Germany) and its pacifism. The air strikes carried out by the German air force against Serbia during the Kosovo conflict could be regarded as the end of the historical taboo against using military force as a foreign policy instrument. This sea change in German foreign and security policy was only possible as a project of the political left, the generation of '68. Their anti-militaristic, pacifist record gave them the moral credibility that made the use of the military also acceptable to the center. In 2002, up to ten thousand German soldiers were on duty in peacekeeping and post-conflict peace-building missions. Compared to the decades after 1949, Germany transformed itself in a relatively short time span from a country that had (due to historical experiences) a pacifist orientation to a country that forms one of the pillars of international peacekeeping. It did so even though large portions of the German populace still have reservations about the active foreign involvement of German soldiers and military solutions in general. Germany became the driving force behind a large-scale, complex plan to stabilize and link the Balkan states more closely to the EU. The plan reflected a carrot-and-stick strategy. The main elements were civilian in nature, featuring conditional economic aid as well as a stabilization force to prevent renewed fighting between the different political and ethnic groups. This specific mix of military and civilian instruments developed into the main characteristics of EU post-conflict management aimed at reconstructing war-ravaged countries, as affirmed in EU security strategy in 2003 by its High Representative for Foreign Policy, Javier Solana.

Although there was considerable sympathy for the United States from all political parties after the shock of 9/11, whether or not Germany should assist in the military campaign against the Taliban in Afghanistan developed into a clash between the pacifist left and the SPD/Green leadership. Vociferous resistance also came from the Party of Democratic Socialism (PDS) and civil society "remnants of the German peace movement" (Dalgaard-Nielsen 2003, 108), who were influential during the 1980s. It became clear that although the governing SPD/Green coalition had a clear majority in the Bundestag, the necessary absolute majority of votes was not ensured. Twenty-eight coalition party MPs declared against military participation. The chancellor then decided to link the question of Germany's contribution to Operation Enduring Freedom to a vote of confidence, the ultimate instrument to induce coalition party discipline. Although Schroeder received the necessary majority in a vote held in November 2001, his "coercion" stimulated frustration and anger among the SPD and the Greens. The vote in the Bundestag did lead to massive support from Germany for Operation Enduring Freedom: the country pledged thirty-nine hundred troops, mostly for logistics and medical units and a one-hundred-member elite combat unit (Dalgaard-Nielsen 2003, 107–109). In addition, eighteen hundred military personnel were deployed on ships off the Horn of Africa to prevent the Taliban from entering Somalia. A small contingent of German soldiers was also deployed with the U.S.-led Immediate Response Force in Kuwait and had special capabilities for detecting weapons of mass destruction (WMD).

After the Taliban leadership was overthrown, Germany played a major role in military, development aid, and civilian conflict management efforts to reconstruct Afghanistan.[4] In addition to its major involvement in reconstruction, Germany took the political lead by organizing a donor conference in Petersberg, near Bonn, to coordinate the reconstruction of the devastated country. Again, the German contributions to the reconstruction of Afghanistan, like those to the Balkans, were largely but not exclusively civilian in nature. The military component was systematically downplayed by the government. The focus on civilian means and additional UN mandates increased domestic acceptance, since many Germans were still reluctant about or even opposed to military means in general and the use of force in particular.

The German Position on Iraq

In general, Germany had been supporting U.S.-led actions against terrorism. A broad majority in most political parties—except the PDS, some of the Greens, and left-wing Social Democrats—backed logistical support and even military engagement in Afghanistan. That was the context in which U.S. statements about Iraq raised fears of militarization and unilateralism. Especially disturbing were President Bush's State of the Union address of January 29, 2002, with its emotionalizing reference to an "axis of evil" and, a few weeks later at a security conference in Munich, Deputy Secretary of Defense Paul Wolfowitz's mention of a "pre-emptive strike."

The German government's position during the pre-invasion period ultimately had four major elements. First, actions against Iraq would require a UN Security Council resolution, a position of strict multilateralism. Second, only convincing evidence of Saddam's possession of WMD and Iraqi links to international terrorism, especially to al-Qaeda, would justify a military intervention. Although Saddam as dictator was a massive human rights violator, invasion to overthrow his regime would violate international law. Third, military intervention was a potentially dangerous "adventure," because it might destabilize the region and hamper a necessary Israeli-Palestinian peace agreement.[5] Fourth, given the European experience in the Balkans, the decision to overlook the lack of a postwar strategy was very unwise.

More parochial and defensive arguments by the government pointed to the €2 billion already being paid annually by Germany for international peacekeeping and to a military overstretched because of a lack of well-trained and specialized troops.[6] The government remained undecided on the acceptability of preemptive strikes. Politicians from various political parties criticized the new U.S. doctrine of preventive intervention for violating international law. Yet Foreign Minister Joschka Fischer declared on August 15, 2002, that if connections to al-Qaeda could be proved, the situation would be totally different and Germany would support a military action even without a UN resolution.

In contrast to the government, parts of the German public were opposed to the use of force in principle, not only against Iraq. The dominant view on Iraq was "without us." A minority regarded the coming war against Iraq as unjustified, aggressive U.S. imperialism. Ignoring the realities of international terrorism, some in left-wing circles had the idea that the United States had to "pay the price" for its one-sided support for Israel.

Explanations for Germany's Challenge

Three different, if not inherently exclusive, explanations for Germany's lack of compliance with U.S. Iraq policy merit attention: general and profound differences in European and American world views, German movement toward a new foreign policy identity, and domestic electoral calculations by Chancellor Schroeder.

Living in Different Worlds?

The first explanation suggests that the crisis over Iraq was the consequence of increasing long-term alienation between the United States and Europe. There have emerged different, even incompatible, strategic security cultures associated with an enormous gap in military capabilities—the omnipotent United States and a weak Europe—and equally great differences in preferred foreign policy arenas (unilateral versus multilateral) and instruments of foreign policy (military versus diplomatic). According to Robert Kagan, "Europeans oppose unilateralism in part because they have no capacity for unilateralism" (2002b, 5). For Kagan, history, especially European history, accounts for the differences in strategic culture. The traumatic experience of two world wars in the last century, and successful European integration, which solved the "German question" of how to restrain a state with hegemonic aspirations, led to an idealistic Europe rejecting *Machtpolitik.* For Kagan, the United States lives in a Hobbesian world of war and conflict and Europeans, in a peaceful, Kantian world of universal norms and the rule of (international) law.[7]

The transatlantic rift looming during the second Clinton administration burst into full bloom with the election of George W. Bush. Transatlantic tensions and antagonisms were already being fueled by American plans for national missile defense, withdrawal from the Anti-Ballistic Missile (ABM) Treaty, rejection of the Kyoto Protocol, and ongoing opposition to and sabotage of the ICC. Unlike earlier well-known disputes between Americans and Europeans about security and economic issues, those over Kyoto and the ICC discredited the idea of a transatlantic value community and undermined the basic consensus among its members.

The new American security doctrine of September 2002, presented in Bush's State of the Union address in 2003, estranged Europeans and Americans even more. Its advocacy of preventive military intervention was and is unacceptable to Europeans and in particular to Germans. More broadly, Germans came to view the United States as a major obstacle to global governance (Hippler 2003). The Iraq crisis was a catalyst that brought to the fore long-standing differences based on historical experiences and conflicting perceptions of security threats. The dispute over Iraq thus marked the beginning of a parting of ways between long-term allies. That split would not negatively affect the United States since, as Kagan concludes with barely concealed arrogance, "the United States can shoulder the burden of maintaining global security without much help from Europe" (2002, 13).[8]

There are a least two prima facie arguments against Kagan's idea of the historical emergence of an inherently antagonistic strategic culture between the United States and Europe. First, his argument is much too general in nature as the splits in the European Union over Iraq demonstrate. Second, his analysis cannot explain Germany's high profile in Afghanistan and Kosovo. From Kagan's perspective, Germany and other European nations would have shunned military involvement in the former because of their pacifist orientation. That obviously was and is not the case. The Afghanistan intervention was highly compatible with the German role as a civilian power. In a highly controversial essay, Gunther Hellmann (2004) explains that this compatibility existed because the goals of the Afghanistan mission were to overcome the Taliban's fanatic, fundamentalist, and cruel version of Islamic rule; to rebuild the country; and to secure human rights. Further, the use of force was legitimized by the collective security system (the UN and NATO). The Afghan case therefore corresponds perfectly with Germany's foreign policy identity as a civilian power—an identity distinct from generalized pacifism. Kosovo is similarly compatible with a civilian power identity since it combined a humanitarian emergency with a collective security institution mandate. Contra the view of Regina Karp (2005–2006, 74), the Afghan and Kosovo cases fit well with Germany's civilian power orientation rather than being "exceptions" to it.

A Changed Foreign Policy Identity?

Both German and American authors tend to neglect recent developments in the post–Cold War debate in Germany about the country's future role in world affairs. The disappearance of the parameters of Germany's foreign policy of the last four decades, exemplified by the unified sovereignty recognized in the Treaty on the Final Settlement with Respect to Germany (1990), raised basic questions about the future direction of German foreign policy. As Hellmann observed, the need to rethink the future course of Germany's foreign policy was for some time hidden by political rhetoric emphasizing continuity (2002, 1). Eventually, academic and public debate was sparked by Chancellor Schroeder. Unlike his predecessor Helmut Kohl, of the Christian Democratic

Union (CDU), Schroeder changed the style of foreign policy. The new look presented a reorientation of German foreign policy under the core terms "normalization" and the "German way" ("*Deutscher Weg*"), which characterized a more self-confident, sometimes even aggressive style.[9] These and similar statements by other leading politicians marked a striking departure from the past, when even the term "national interests" had a negative connotation for the majority of intellectuals and foreign policy makers. The more recent discourse is much less about a remilitarization (equated with normalization especially by the left) than was the debate in the early and mid-1990s.

Debate among policy intellectuals intensified with the transatlantic rift over Iraq, since there apparently was a major change in German foreign policy. In addition, the continuing troubles of the Schroeder/Fischer government after the loss of important regional elections were accompanied by arguments about the achievements and weaknesses of its foreign policy. Many criticized the nation's foreign policy as shapeless and without ideas or vision (Maull 2004a; Hellmann 2004). Many agreed with Josef Janning's assessment that one of the most important weaknesses of German foreign policy was its inability to build strategic coalitions based on a defined policy agenda (Janning 2002, 15). To support this line of argument, critics cited the lack of any major German initiatives in the EU framework, a deteriorating relationship with France, and the friction-laden policy agenda for China and for Russia under President Vladimir Putin. Lacking a strategic vision, Germany was an inherently difficult partner.

The lack of strategy was not yet recognized by the public. One reason for this oversight was the prevailing preoccupation with domestic issues, such as unemployment and cutbacks in social services. Another reason might have been the communication skills of Chancellor Schroeder and especially Foreign Minister Fischer. Schroeder's metaphors (Germany has "grown up" and "learned its historical lessons") have been supported by a stable majority. In addition, his announcement during the 2002 campaign that the previous "checkbook diplomacy would be replaced by real policy" was widely accepted.[10] His foreign policy was popular, and the majority of Germans praised the chancellor for his "without us" policy that kept Germany out of the Iraq quagmire.

Viewed from the perspective of a basic shift in Germany's foreign policy identity, the specifics of the Bush administration's practices and the passing circumstances of a particular German election seem to be only epiphenomena (Harnisch 2004). The simultaneity of the crisis and the German elections was only coincidental in helping Schroeder to victory. Germany would sooner or later have pursued a challenge strategy aimed at a new, more European security arrangement with a diminished role for the United States. This interpretation does have serious consequences for future American and German security and the prospects of the transatlantic security architecture, but the implications and their drivers are different than in the "Venus and Mars" view of clashing strategic cultures.[11]

Election Campaign Opportunism?

Many German (e.g., Winkler 2004) and American (e.g., Gordon and Shapiro 2004) analysts who do not deny the relevance of gradual estrangement view the German federal election campaign as the main reason for Germany's uncooperative behavior regarding Iraq.[12] In the spring of 2002, opinion polls signaled a defeat of the coalition government in the upcoming September elections. The main reason for the declining popularity of the Schroeder and Fischer government was its failure to overcome the deep structural economic and social crises (Tenscher 2005). Rising unemployment and an overall gloomy mood increased dissatisfaction with the government. The opposition parties, although lacking a convincing reform program, benefited from the political climate. The CDU and Christian Social Union (CSU) had reason to expect to become the strongest party in the elections and head a coalition with the FDP or the Greens.

A catastrophic flood in the eastern part of Germany in July 2002 and the threat of war in Iraq gave Schroeder opportunities to show determination and energy in dealing with pressing problems, opportunities he quickly took advantage of. The Oder River flood gave him the chance to present himself as a hands-on leader when TV cameras showed pictures of Schroeder—equipped with rubber boots—helping the German army build dams against the rising water. Roughly 70 percent of the respondents to an opinion poll conducted in August 2002 believed the Schroeder government did a "good job" (Niedermayer 2003, 47).

Yet for Schroeder's campaign managers, the flood peak was over at the end of July and other issues had to be found. The Iraq crisis provided the SPD/Greens campaign with an excellent opportunity for Schroeder to play the role of the peace-loving statesman (Tenscher 2005, 19). In this role he could not only keep Germany out of war but also fight for German interests by challenging the sole superpower. Immediately after the situation in the regions hard hit by the flood had begun to improve, Schroeder declared on television that Germany would not participate in a possible "adventure" in Iraq, even with a UN Security Council mandate. The SPD leadership formally decided on August 5 to include the Iraq issue in the campaign (Harnisch 2004, 182).

The Iraq issue became a multi-purpose tool for Schroeder. First, it could help achieve a precondition for victory at the polls: the unity of the party and stability of the coalition. Support for Schroeder in his own SPD and for the coalition partner (the Greens) was in doubt. The Afghanistan debate in the German parliament had revealed considerable opposition in both parties. Only by connecting the vote in the Bundestag with the vote of confidence did the chancellor receive the necessary absolute majority in November 2001. The out-of-area debate and Germany's expanding military engagement in the former Yugoslavia had already triggered a crisis in the Green Party.[13] In a context of increasingly aggressive U.S. rhetoric against "rogue states" and an "axis of evil," the left wing of the SPD and the Greens had had enough. They had agreed to the Kosovo and Afghanistan operations only because of massive political pressure. It thus seemed very likely that support for the U.S. policy toward Iraq, including the deployment of soldiers, would split Schroeder's coalition. Tough opposition to the U.S. policy offered a chance to bring moderates and radicals together and improve the stability of the coalition just in time for the election. A campaign focusing on the question of "war and peace" also might mobilize voters and counter widespread apathy, especially in the SPD camp.

In addition to Schroeder's strategic considerations with respect to his own party, the Iraq question also provided an opportunity to weaken the PDS, the successor to the former East German ruling party. In regional elections the PDS had been very successful in the East and was the strongest party in several regional coalition governments. In the previous federal elections, the party had passed the 5 percent threshold for representation in the Bundestag. One reason for the popularity of the PDS had been the party's pacifist and anti-war positions. The PDS was the only party that consistently opposed the use of force by Germany and voted against the participation of the Bundeswehr in all peacekeeping and peace enforcement actions. The PDS enjoyed high credibility among left-wing voters, especially in the East, where anti-Americanism was, for historic reasons, widespread. One of Schroeder's aims was to convince voters to shift from the PDS and to vote for the SPD as the genuinely pro-peace and anti-militarism party.

Schroeder's strategy was successful as the SPD and Greens' coalition won the September elections with a marginal plurality of only 600,000 votes, the closest race in the history of the Federal Republic of Germany. Observers agree that the Iraq crisis played a considerable role in the election outcome (Winkler 2004; Harnisch 2004; Tenscher 2005, 9; Niedermayer 2003, 57). Opinion polls revealed that Iraq and terrorism issues received more and more attention by the electorate as election day approached. Many polls revealed growing support for the SPD/Green coalition as the war of words with the United States escalated. Media coverage of the dispute with the United States helped Schroeder win the German debate over Iraq and thus the election.[14]

Although some U.S. government officials, such as Ambassador Daniel

Coats, realized that the upcoming election put the Schroeder government under extreme pressure, they were unable or unwilling to moderate Washington's rhetoric. In retrospect, the speech Vice President Dick Cheney delivered in Nashville on August 27, 2002, was crucial. To the surprise of the German government, Cheney declared that the overthrow of Saddam's regime was the aim of the United States, whether or not Iraq accepted UN weapons inspectors (Winkler 2004, 21). German officials, especially Defense Minister Peter Struck, who had taken office in July, regarded Cheney's remarks as a "mistake." Such U.S. rhetoric only fueled opposition from German politicians. The United States seemed not to be paying attention to the politics of one of its major allies. If the U.S. government was at all interested in the views of its Germany ally, it did not understand the complexity of German politics during the pre-election period and the deep roots of pacifism resulting from German history. The confrontational style of U.S. officials, especially Secretary of Defense Donald Rumsfeld, made it easy for Schroeder to play the anti-American card: reference to "the arrogant and aggressive superpower." Challenging the United States was widely viewed as legitimate and, from a moral standpoint, even necessary to prevent the "evil of war."

The SPD/Green coalition also benefited from the campaign emphases of the opposition (the conservative parties and the FDP) on issues such as unemployment and economic reforms. Those topics could not have the emotional impact of a war-and-peace question. The CDU/CSU, historically the political home of "Atlanticism" and champions of transatlantic partnership, were unable to sell their much more differentiated argument about Iraq during the election campaign.[15] The CDU/CSU leadership warned of international isolation of Germany and favored a common European policy (which proved to be unrealistic). The harsh American rhetoric made it more and more difficult even to have a balanced discussion since the political climate became overtly anti-American. For a long time, the CDU/CSU shied away from a clear position because it was unprepared for debate about and internally divided on the Iraq question. The rank-and-file party members and, according to opinion polls, their other (potential) voters, criticized the conservative parties' leadership for being too soft on the Bush administration.

Challenge "Strategies" to Prevent the Iraq War

German resistance to U.S. policy on Iraq arose from differences in threat perceptions, an emerging foreign policy identity, and short-term electoral considerations. Those factors motivated the German government, supported by a clear majority of the populace, to try actively to induce the United States not to invade and occupy Iraq. Attempts to do that used several distinguishable combinations of the actions and arenas introduced in chapter 1.

Standing Aside (Somewhat)

The SPD/Green campaign position on Iraq can be viewed as a pledge to stand aside militarily and unilaterally, if necessary, from a U.S. invasion—a categorical "nein." Yet, although it pledged to refrain from sending combat troops, the SPD/Green coalition supported the United States in a variety of military and eventually nonmilitary ways. That was true beginning shortly after the German elections with respect to deployments previously made to Kuwait, the use of military bases in Germany, and over-flight rights.

For Operation Enduring Freedom, Germany had deployed to Kuwait tanks equipped to detect chemical, biological, or nuclear weapons. In November 2002, nearly two months after the elections, the German Bundestag extended the tank deployment. There was, however, strong opposition from the Green Party. The announcement by Defense Minister Struck in January 2003 that the tanks would stay in Kuwait to protect American forces even in case of a war not supported by Germany was decried by members of the Green parliamentary faction. The issue of base use and over-flights by the U.S. military for an Iraq war also muddied the political waters. After an intense debate, the Bundestag reaffirmed those rights in November 2002, but again the Green Party declared readiness to oppose what amounted to continuity in relations with the United States (Harnisch 2004, 187). Since the government had only a small majority, the Greens could have brought the newly elected government down by insisting in the Bundestag that Germany stand aside completely from military cooperation with a U.S. war in Iraq. They did not.

It is not clear whether the German government threatened or even seriously considered withdrawing the tanks or denying use of bases or over-flight permission. On the one hand, Schroeder reportedly said in confidence that if the tanks were withdrawn, "it would be impossible for a German chancellor to fly to Washington for the next 50 years" (Harnisch 2004, 180). On the other, prohibiting use of military infrastructure and over-flights was never clearly ruled out and was even raised in a legal report the German governments announced in September 2002. It is clear that beginning shortly after its election renewal, the SPD/Green coalition did not follow through with its promises to withhold military cooperation from a U.S. war on Iraq, even if it did refrain from dispatching additional military units to participate in that war.

In the evolving context of the U.S. invasion and occupation, the German government expanded the scope of its administrative cooperation. Germany supported NATO's program to train Iraqi military officers in the United Arab Emirates. Military equipment (trucks) and spare parts were handed over to the Iraqi forces (*Sueddeutsche Zeitung*, Dec. 11, 2004). The German government actually increased its engagement in Afghanistan rather than threatening to end it as a way of challenging U.S. Iraq policy. In December 2005, the German government decided to cancel the equivalent of $5.6 billion of Iraqi debt, amounting to 80 percent of Germany's claims against Iraq. This decision, taken under considerable U.S pressure, served to signal other major creditors, especially France and Russia, that they should take similar steps.[16]

Germany, France, and Russia or a Coalition of the Unwilling

Unlike France, which declared in August 2002 that a military operation required a UN mandate, Germany rejected military intervention even if authorized by a UN resolution. Consequently, Germany found itself politically isolated, even in the camp of the anti-war states. Realizing that, the chancellor first tried to expand German political leverage by adopting a more conciliatory policy toward the United States, which took the form of continuing military cooperation. He underestimated, however, the domestic climate and the strong pacifist tendency he had so successfully activated during the electoral campaign. Accordingly, the German government then attempted to modify U.S. policy by using multilateral arenas. Perhaps most importantly, the German government started searching for diplomatic support from EU members. The search started too late, and many European governments were unresponsive to the invitation to challenge the United States. Therefore, Germany started to intensify its long-standing contacts with France. The fortieth anniversary of the German-French Elysée Treaty in January 2003 was used to demonstrate agreement on Iraq. The two governments called for authorization of a military intervention by the UN and more time for the weapons inspectors in Iraq. Each proposal would delay the U.S. timetable for invasion, thus postponing or even decreasing the likelihood of war. The United States reacted with outrage: Rumsfeld termed both countries part of the "old Europe." A few days later he compared Germany with Libya and Cuba: "There are three or four countries that have said they won't do anything; I believe Libya, Cuba and Germany are the ones that have indicated they won't help in any respect" (quoted in Gordon and Shapiro 2004, 28).

The confrontation between Germany and the United States then reached its peak four months *after* the elections. The Iraq debate and the American reactions led to a stronger and more general public aversion to the United States. A poll conducted in spring 2003 asked, "Should Germany and Europe support or halt U.S. hegemony with respect to establishing a new world order?" Nearly half of the respondents opted for halting or "containing" the United States, only 14 percent favored support, and 33 percent abstained.

The harsh U.S. reaction and Germany's isolation brought Germany into the arms of France, a matter of potential "bloc revival" if not "bloc creation" in the EU, that is, in a broad-agenda international institution that excludes the United States. Germany became the junior partner in French diplomatic efforts that started to challenge the United States more and more openly. The common stance against U.S. policy was also perceived by senior French and German politicians as a chance to reanimate the Franco-German axis in the context of the European Security and Defense Policy (ESDP) (Gordon and Shapiro 2004, 11). Franco-German cooperation had worked earlier as a "motor" of European integration but had not run smoothly during the previous two years. One grave unintended consequence of the German-French cooperation was to bring long-standing divisions within the EU to the surface. On January 30, 2003, eight European leaders expressed their solidarity with the United States in an open letter, although public opinion in most of their countries was against U.S. policy. Europe was deeply divided and the EU was therefore unable to act collectively to either oppose or support U.S. policy toward Iraq.

An attempt at a larger and perhaps potentially more potent coalition of the unwilling became evident when Germany, France, and Russia agreed on a memorandum that opposed U.S. policy preferences regarding Iraq.[17] All three countries regarded the UN Security Council as the core institution for handling the Iraq situation. For the signatories, a war against Iraq was not justified because of the lack of evidence that Iraq possessed WMD. They opted for a more robust UN inspection regime, hoping that improved inspections, more time, and tighter controls would increase pressure on the Iraqi government when combined with credible military threats. The informal coalition between Russia, France, and Germany continued even after the war began. A second meeting was held in April 2003, on the same day Baghdad was occupied, and at the end of August 2004 the French and Russian heads of state and the chancellor met again to define a common stance. They reaffirmed their commitment to a leading role for the UN in postwar Iraq.

The possible coalition of the unwilling signaled by the meetings between Russia, Germany, and France amounted to soft counter-balancing relying exclusively on political and diplomatic measures and strategies. They demonstrated that the governing coalition in Berlin had an active foreign policy and underlined that Germany was an important and equal partner of powerful states. More concretely, common projects or actions directed against the United States—a kind of hard-balancing—were never part of the meetings' agendas.

Opposition within the UN

Calls by a coalition of the unwilling to place a situation in the hands of an ongoing international institution can, as they did for Germany, complement challenges to U.S. policies mounted within IGOs. Challenges to American policies also can be multi-faceted, as Germany's were, if they are pursued in the arena of an IGO that has the United States as a member (e.g., the UN) or an IGO that does not (e.g., the EU).

In the Security Council the United States faced fierce opposition from France and, with a more moderate tone, from Germany, which became a temporary member of the Security Council and president of it on February 1, 2003. After intense negotiations, UN Resolution 1441 was accepted in November 2002 by a 15-to-0 vote in the Security Council. The resolution was a political compromise stating vaguely that Saddam would face serious consequences if he did not cooperate with the UN weapons inspectors. It can be regarded as a success of mainly French diplomacy since it avoided a commitment to the automatic use of force if Saddam failed to comply with UN conditions (Joffe 2003, 159; Gordon and Shapiro 2004, 112). At that time the French strategy to "entangle Gulliver" (Joffe 2003, 159), assisted by Russia and China, seemed to work. More realistically, the unity the transatlantic allies reached with Resolution 1441 was an illusion, since the United States was dissatisfied with the weapons inspectors' report from Iraq.

U.S. diplomats started to lobby for a second UN resolution, one that would legitimize military action. The "caucus" of the nay-saying states—France, Russia, China, and Germany—opposed the American attempt (Gordon and Shapiro 2004, 149). During the crucial months of February and March, their UN ambassadors met several times to coordinate their position. In February, the U.S.-British alliance and the anti-war coalition lobbied six nonpermanent UN Security Council members (Angola, Cameroon, Chile, Guinea, Mexico, and Pakistan). Germany acted as France's junior partner; the real opposition came from France. The American efforts for another UN resolution failed when President Jacques Chirac declared that France would block a new UN resolution "whatever the circumstance" (Gordon and Shapiro 2004, 152). German opposition gained strength from President Bush's disregard for the UN since the president made it clear that the United States intended to act even without a mandating resolution. That is, America was disposed to violate norms or rules central to Germany's civilian power conception about the conditions under which the use of force would be legitimate. Although Germany, as a temporary member rather than a permanent member of the Security Council, was not one of the main players challenging the United States, it was from the American perspective a challenger rather than a loyal ally. From the perspective of the Bush administration, Germany was trying to expand rules of international conduct that would infringe on the prerogatives the United States claimed as its right.

Opposition in NATO

NATO, the guarantor of security during the Cold War, had its post–Cold War legitimacy crisis worsen shortly after 9/11. The United States did not accept NATO General Secretary George Robertson's offer, an offer strongly supported by Germany, to play a substantive role in the war against terror, even with the unprecedented activation of article 5 of the NATO Treaty. The United States never intended to start its war in Iraq under NATO's auspices. From a European and German perspective, Secretary of Defense Rumsfeld's statement that the "mission defines the coalition" violated NATO's raison d'être (Gordon and Shapiro 2004, 61) and implied the possibility of NATO's demise (Joffe 2003, 157). The U.S. administration did insist that, under article 4, Turkey receive NATO support for defense against possible Iraqi retaliation. Germany, France, and Belgium opposed this plan and thus delayed its implementation. They argued that assistance to Turkey would signal the inevitability of war against Iraq. Massive pressure from the United States combined with diplomatic tricks—the United States moved the issue to NATO's Defense Planning Committee (DPC), which did not include France—eventually brought Germany and Belgium to accept a compromise in which assistance to Turkey was mainly from national governments rather than NATO. Yet Germany's policy on defense aid to Turkey resembled its policy on militarily standing aside, as discussed previously. This policy was at best ambivalent and perhaps contradictory. Although a compromise within NATO was reached and Turkey received, among other things, Airborne Warning and Control System (AWACS) coverage, Berlin insisted that German personnel would have to be withdrawn if Turkey entered the Iraq war (Overhaus 2006, 71).

On Iraq, Germany arguably prevented NATO from taking the role of a compliant alliance partner and doing what the United States wanted. Indeed, both the chancellor and defense minister rejected NATO General Secretary Robertson's offer to mediate between Berlin and Washington (*Der Spiegel* 2002, 112). At least with regard to NATO, Germany's challenges were made easier at home by the strong criticism of U.S. slights to NATO from the more conservative parties that historically provided the stronger support for it (Schwarz 2004).

Interpretation and Implications

The challenges Germany posed to the Bush administration's Iraq policy followed from the joint effects of the three types of motives that have been discussed: more structural estrangement, more situational elections, and an already emerging vision for the future of the country's foreign policy. The two policy systems differed because they addressed different sets of issues. Whereas the United States perceived or at least pretended to perceive that the overthrow of Saddam was part of the war against terror, Germany viewed those two situations as independent of each other. For Berlin, both Operation Enduring Freedom and the fight against the Taliban were "a legitimate form of self-defense" (Rudolf 2006, 143). Militarily forced regime change was not a legitimate means of self-defense and was therefore strongly rejected. The instrumentalization of the Iraq war for the elections in September 2002 cannot explain the increasing declaratory resistance after the victory of the SPD/Green coalition. The short-term electoral calculations did feed into and draw on a continuing process of estrangement between Germany (and parts of Europe) and the United States caused by different perceptions of risk and international relations in general (Karp 2005–2006, 68–69), differences deeply ingrained in their respective foreign policy self-conceptions (Szabo 2006, 12).

Those sources of challenges were stimulated and indeed bolstered by some particular process characteristics involving the role of the media and the style of prominent persons. On both sides of the Atlantic the style of communication was marked by unprecedentedly heated and aggressive public rhetoric from high officials. Donald Rumsfeld's infamous response to reporters' questions about the old and the new Europe fueled the conflict and increased German public sentiment against the United States. In Germany, members of parliament and the government adopted hostile rhetoric that further escalated the crisis. The "diplomatic" style of the Bush administration made it easy for Schroeder to translate deeply rooted anti-U.S. sentiment into votes securing the plurality for his party. Each side used public media to trumpet their policies and views of the other in an apparently uncompromising and somewhat disrespectful way. As some scholars noted, "Neither the Americans nor their European critics seemed to take into account the potential impact of their policies on the Atlantic alliance; some even seemed to want to undermine it" (Gordon and Shapiro 2004, 156).

Further, miscalculations and misunderstandings caused by biased interpretations of alliance history prevailed on both sides of the Atlantic. Too many American policy participants believed that Europeans would cooperate sooner or later and underestimated their willingness to challenge the United States, especially in the case of Germany, which always had been a reliable ally, "bandwagoning to the U.S. policy in the past." The American leadership, believing in its military superiority, thought that victory in Iraq was preordained and so believed that before long "the Europeans will jump on the bandwagon" (Gordon and Shapiro 2004, 65). Although much of the experience of forty years of transatlantic cooperation should have suggested otherwise, the Europeans believed that they could induce U.S. policy makers to fundamentally change their responses to an enemy that Washington viewed as evil, politically useful, and easily crushed and transformed.

The Schroeder/Fischer government used a variety of "strategies" or, more accurately, actions and arenas to challenge U.S. Iraq policy.[18] Besides the relatively prominent behaviors discussed earlier, there were rather ad hoc or at least only sporadic attempts to use pleas of credible helplessness (e.g., limited Bundeswehr capabilities, fragility of the ruling coalition), to mobilize a collective action network with American policy intellectuals opposed to war on Iraq, and to offer conditional support commitments. The last suggested that Germany would change its position with clear evidence of an imminent WMD threat from Iraq or of substantial connections between Saddam and al-Qaeda.

Several types of actions took place in the unilateral arena, but the main sites for challenges intended to prevent the United States from starting the war were international organizations with and without U.S. membership. In NATO and the UN, Germany, together with other states, tried to use established procedural rules and norms to delay mandates and drag out or halt preparations altogether. Germany used its relatively strong position in NATO and its status as a nonpermanent member of the UNSC (beginning in January 2003) to organize challenges, although France was the driving force behind the anti-U.S. coalition in the UN. Emphasis on the IGO arena for attempts to evade, modify, or resist U.S. policy reflects Germany's traditional emphasis on multilateral policy pursued through international organizations.

The German government failed to prevent the United States from attacking Iraq through its unilateral actions and attempts at collective action to influence the Bush administration. At and shortly after the time of the German challenges, the United States rejected them as based only on naïveté, resurgent German nationalism and parochial ambitions, and diffuse anti-Americanism. Germany, together with France and some other states, only succeeded in delaying the war to buy time for a diplomatic, UN-based initiative.

By blocking a UN resolution authorizing a U.S. attack, Germany and others helped delegitimize the war (Dalgaard-Nielsen 2003, 99). That, however, had the negative, unintended effect of making the UN marginal to developments in Iraq. Further, the United States managed to secure military support from several non-European states and some members of the EU. The split in the EU had the residual effect of a major setback for its Common Foreign and Security Policy (CFSP) and European Security and Defense Policy (ESDP). Another weakened IGO was NATO, an institution strongly supported by Germany. It was paralyzed by the different, uncompromising views of the allies during the conflict.

From one angle, the intensity of the disagreement in both substance and style marked the emancipation of German foreign policy from the United States and Germany's return to the stage of international politics as a more independent actor. "Germany is no longer a country which automatically says 'yes'" (Karsten Voigt quoted in *Frankfurter Allgemeine Zeitung,* Feb. 6, 2005). Thus, it would be naïve to conclude that a return to pre-crisis business as usual is likely. German and American authors (Müller 2004; Szabo 2004b) argue that the relationship has fundamentally changed and harmony is very unlikely to recur (compare Dembinski 2003). Currently, there are no clear signs that the alliance partners will develop a common security agenda, in part because of the remarkably different views of a more conciliatory American public (see chapter 12 in this volume) and a largely uncompromising Republican leadership in the United States.

From a more multi-faceted point of view, the conflict over Iraq has led to a new phase in U.S.-German relations, not necessarily to a complete parting of the ways (Szabo 2004a; 2004b). Part of the remaining alienation of the German public is shown in polling: Germans viewing U.S. leadership as desirable declined from 68 percent in 2002 to 43 percent in 2006, the sharpest decline among European countries polled.[19] Disapproval of President Bush is also extremely strong (see chapter 12). From a German viewpoint, in July 2005 Washington appeared to impose punishment for challenges to U.S. Iraq policy. Whatever its reasons, the United States denied support for Germany's much desired goal of a permanent seat on the UN Security Council.

Those developments and the more fundamental matters discussed earlier do not provide sufficient evidence that there has been or will soon be a basic and irreversible divorce between the two countries. Recall that Germany has refrained from ending or sharply reducing long-established forms of security cooperation with the United States, enhanced cooperation in the U.S. war on terror, and substantially engaged in Afghanistan. Some of those developments, as well as cooperation on curbing Iran's WMD-related programs, amount to offering energetic cooperation on some policy aspects to make up for any ill will resulting from challenges on others.

A combined emphasis on both a more independent foreign policy identity and basically cooperative relations with the United States may have become easier in November 2005. At that time Angela Merkel, leader of the conservative Christian Democratic Union, became chancellor, presiding over a "grand coalition" between the CDU and the SPD.[20] The new government could take advantage of steps already taken on both sides of the Atlantic to soothe relationship frictions. In formal terms, the conflict between the United States and Germany ended during a personal meeting between Bush and Schroeder in September 2003 (Szabo 2004a, 41). As for atmospherics, Schroeder congratulated President Bush on the successful elections in Iraq in January 2005, and several visits by high-ranking U.S. officials, such as Secretary of State Condoleezza Rice, showed a new respect. Chancellor Merkel had announced during her campaign that she would try to reinvigorate relations with the United States. Once in office, the style of the grand coalition and in particular of the foreign minister, Frank-Walter Steinmeier (SPD), proved to be less populist and confrontational (Karp 2005–2006, 75).

Expectations in the United States that Merkel would introduce a 180-degree shift in German foreign policy and offer troops or otherwise substantially "bandwagon" on the Bush administration's Iraq policies have been shown to be unrealistic. Regina Karp's observation holds true: "German governments distinguish themselves by style, not by substance" (2005–2006, 75). The chancellor would immediately risk the breakup of the coalition if she were to defy the overwhelming German foreign policy consensus by offering to send troops to Iraq. Continuing and possibly increasing support for reconstruction efforts in Iraq and the Karzai regime in Afghanistan are a different matter. Support for counter-terrorism cooperation with the United States will surely continue while Merkel and other leading German politicians openly criticize America's detention camp in Guantánamo and secret CIA rendition flights and prison facilities. The new government is less likely to even appear to be considering challenges to the United States through cooperation with China, Putin's Russia, or a France that tries to actively counter U.S. dominance. Instead, Germany may return to mediating between France and the United States.

In sum, Germany remains an ally of the United States, but a more critical and selective one. Fundamental, broad, and sustained resistance to U.S. leadership from Germany seems unlikely if U.S. policies become even somewhat more partnership oriented and if Germany follows Foreign Minister Steinmeier's formula of self-confident modesty (selbstbewußte Bescheidenheit).

4

SOFT DETERRENCE, PASSIVE RESISTANCE

American Lenses, Chinese Lessons

STEVE CHAN

The classic Chinese strategic text *The Art of War* by Sun Tzu is particularly illustrative of the imperative of developing sound knowledge about oneself and about one's counterpart(s) as a prerequisite for successful military campaigns and diplomacy. For example,

> Attaining one hundred victories in one hundred battles is not the highest achievement; subjugating the enemy without having to fight is the true pinnacle of excellence.
>
> The highest realization of warfare is to attack the enemy's plans, the next is to attack its alliances, the next is to attack its army, and the lowest is to attack its fortifications.
>
> Those who excel in warfare compel others to respond to them and are not compelled to respond to others.
>
> If the enemy must prepare to defend many positions, then its forces facing us will be few.
>
> Do not count on the enemy not attacking, but depend on one's own efforts to develop an unassailable defense.

Today, the themes of many Chinese strategists' writings resonate with the injunctions of hard-core realists (Johnston 1995). They also, however, express some ideas that tend to be, if not entirely unique or distinct, underrepresented in standard discourse among U.S. international relations scholars. These ideas offer suggestive contrasts to several themes in how Americans typically think about managing challenges to a hegemon.

One such theme features an acceleration model of power, which assumes that, if unrestrained, the strong will become stronger as gains on successive encounters create winning momentum. This expectation of cumulative advantage emphasizes positive serial dependency—success in power expansion begets further success. This view is accompanied by corollary beliefs about waves of democratization, falling dominoes of rogue states, and bandwagoning to join a hegemon. Its flip side warns against appeasement because current concessions can engender future demands for further concessions. The shadow of the future thus increases the salience of any current dispute and calls attention to the potential harm to one's reputation caused by appeasement or even inaction. This acceleration model of power highlights the accumulation over time of the material and psychological wherewithal of a hegemonic state.

Less attention has been given to a self-limiting or even a self-exhausting model of power, according to which a hegemon's foreign exertions will encounter inevitable limits and declining marginal utility. One can, however, find instances of this secondary theme in references to imperial overstretch, a loss-of-power gradient due to physical distance and water barriers, and a natural tendency for states to counter-balance any aspiring or extant hegemon (Layne 1993; Kennedy 1987; Mearsheimer 2001). These views point to the effects of systemic negative feedback, which tend to dash hegemonic ambitions. They reduce the urgency of active resistance and organized blocking coalitions to limit hegemonic rule by questioning its inevitability or durability.

An emphasis on curbing, checking, and restraining some deleterious impulse characterizes another significant current in the U.S. discourse on international relations. Despite their other differences, neorealists and neoliberals alike call for policies to constrain actors from defecting from cooperation, whether through threats of physical coercion, socialization of common norms, or binding commitments to collective action. These proposed policies are featured prominently in the recommended tool kit of those who want to manage a hegemon, although they are surely also available to the hegemon for managing others.

By their very nature, restraints are supposed to work against some assumed predisposition such as cheating, shirking, hiding, or, in the case of a hegemon, wanton abuse of power. Restraints therefore go "against the grain." Conversely, policies that seek to promote or exacerbate extant tendencies are less demanding and more likely to succeed. Accordingly, efforts to contain or undermine hegemony can be rewarding when they abet the hegemon's ambitions, encourage it to overcommit its resources, and foster its (false) sense of confidence. In other words, attempts to resist a hegemon and to modify its behavior can involve engagement, entanglement, and entrapment rather than overt and active confrontation. Declared support for a hegemon's cause does not necessarily rule out challenge to its rule, but it may be calculated to invite overextension by it or to advance alternative agendas that the hegemon may not want. Attempts to exploit and take advantage of a hegemon's hubris tend to be generally overlooked as part of the policy repertoire that U.S. experts associate with the less powerful.

A third main tendency in prevailing U.S. discourse codes the outcomes of interstate contests in terms of win, loss, and draw (see, e.g., Stam 1996). This scoring system does not fully capture how the outcomes have differed from the initial expectations of the hegemon and the challenger—whether the challenger was able to gain better terms than it would have in the absence of its challenge and whether the hegemon was forced to accept less favorable terms than it had originally expected (Fearon 1995). Even if the hegemon was eventually able to have its way, a challenger's resistance would have paid off if it raised the hegemon's costs, deflated its ego, and delayed the planned completion of its mission. These consequences matter to the extent that the hegemon is discouraged from initiating future encounters and that third parties are emboldened, by learning and imitation, to engage in similar actions to constrain and deter the hegemon. The success or failure of resistance efforts cannot be evaluated by just the immediate outcome of a bilateral episode but must take into account the effects of the current encounter on future decisions by the direct contestants as well as the onlookers. In this light, resistance to hegemonic bids becomes less a matter of trying to out-muscle the superpower than of using nonverbal communication intended to alter the latter's and relevant others' incentives and calculations about warranted and unwarranted costs, goals, and time horizons for achieving goals. (Presumably; Iranian and North Korean leaders would draw inferences from U.S. experiences in Iraq and Afghanistan.)

As with other actors, Chinese statecraft is multi-dimensional and involves opposing injunctions or bimodal reasoning (e.g., to be bold *and* cautious, to bluff strength *and* to feign weakness, to be patient *and* to be opportunistic). In comparison with standard U.S. strategic thinking, however, it is less prone to assume that a hegemon's or would-be hegemon's power will follow a linear progression and is more inclined to take a dialectical or cyclical view of the waning and waxing of national power. Moreover, it treats a hegemon's own internal conditions rather than external pressure as the principal source for constraining and modifying its behavior and as the main cause of its eventual decline.

Finally, challenges to hegemonic designs are viewed less as a contest of raw power and more as an attempt to influence the target's incentives and calculations. Success in those attempts results in the hegemon modifying its policies. The highest achievement in statecraft is not to prevail in a physical struggle of strength but rather to subjugate an adversary without having to resort to arms. Intangibles of strategy, morale, leadership, persistence, and timing and location can trump tangibles such as weaponry and money. These ideas contrast with the typical U.S. emphasis on internal or external "balancing"—that is, on arms buildup or alliances—as the principal means of containing or blocking a foreign rival. They point to ways of "going around" and delaying U.S. goals in a deeper sense. Moreover, and significantly, they underscore an important distinction between the current preferences of American officials and basic U.S. national interests. Current official preferences are not taken to be necessarily equivalent to enduring national interests. Two implications follow from this distinction. First, a strategy to indulge and even abet current U.S. preferences can circumvent and even defeat the realization of longer-term U.S. interests. Second, given the deep divisions in the United States as it attempts to define its national interests over time, internal divisions and contentions within the hegemon can be exploited to modify and even reverse its behavior.

Policy Cycles and the Principle of Conservation

In the past several decades, a new generation of Chinese analysts and policy commentators has emerged, and they are more familiar with the U.S. analytic lexicon and policy discourse than their predecessors were (Shambaugh 1991). Many have advanced degrees from American institutions and stay informed about the prevailing policy currents and intellectual fashions in Washington. What would China's America watchers have noticed during these decades?

They would have noticed that Asians do not have a monopoly on bimodal framing and cyclical reasoning. Although current discussions in U.S. policy circles and elite media emphasize a unipolar world, often assuming current and future American dominance as a given, it was not long ago that the talk of Washington was the inevitability of the United States' relative decline.[1] Pronouncements about the perils of imperial overextension and blowback and the flaws of a hard power conception of national influence have been followed in short order by a declared intention to expand the NATO alliance, develop missile defense, institute regime change abroad, and secure physical control of foreign energy sources. Triumphant celebration of a supposed universal acceptance of liberal secular values has coexisted with foreboding about civilizational clashes and even a siege mentality after 9/11. Theories of complex interdependence have been accompanied by unabashed assertions of unilateralism and the primacy of coercive instruments. Isolationism and interventionism have been simultaneous features of the Janus face of U.S. diplomacy.

What is a Chinese observer to make of these zigzags and seeming contradictions? Unsettled debates, contested visions, and policy cycling present themselves as plausible leading explanations. Gulliver would then be seen to have a conflicted self-image and a divided mind about proper and fruitful ways to conduct foreign relations. Recurrent mood swings characterize popular sentiments and elite outlook. Officeholders with different, even competing, agendas alternate in succession. Intellectual fads and fashions come and go. Phases of tough talk and militant action invoke a sense of déjà vu rather than panic because in the past they have been followed by retrenchment and reconciliation.

Limits on assertion and even abstention or standing aside would then have some appeal for dealing with the hegemon. Active resistance may not be useful or even necessary because of the likely prospect that the hegemon would be self-restrained rather than being constrained by others. Psychological and political forces inside the United States may well generate countervailing influences when the policy pendulum swings too far in one or the other direction. Powerful domestic groups with competing interests and visions will self-mobilize to moderate the policy agenda of incumbent officials. Institutions of shared power require tedious consensus building and entail the politics of logrolling. Electoral cycles and unstable mass preferences introduce additional checks against policy continuity, whatever its ideological orientation. Constancy, if not inaction and passivity as enjoined by the Taoist dictum, presents itself as a course of conservation. Vacillation and self-exhaustion by the hegemon promise constraint, possibly even in the absence of severe external pressure, given pressures for policy modification driven by the hegemon's internal conditions. The hallmark of strategic success vis-à-vis the United States is the ability to resist unnecessary agitation in the face of challenges and to eschew wanton behavior that dissipates energy. An impulsive and overconfident America will make those errors, and its mistakes will redound to another's advantage without requiring strenuous exertion.

The Power-Transition Prism and Playing for Time

Strategies for dealing with the hegemon should be based on understanding not only the U.S. self-image but also its image of China. During the Cold War, the United States cared about China primarily because of Beijing's strategic relationship, either friendly or hostile, with Moscow. Since the demise of the Soviet Union, however, China has been accorded intrinsic importance in U.S.

strategic thinking, assuming the role of a leading candidate to be Washington's strategic competitor. It would be difficult for any reasonably attentive America watcher in China to miss this shift.

What then are the prevailing analytic logics and categories fashionable in American policy and intellectual circles for understanding China? Again, it would be difficult for Chinese analysts attuned to U.S. discourse to overlook the fact that power-transition theory appears to be the dominant frame or prism being applied by Americans to the evolving bilateral relations. According to this theory, systemic war beckons when a rising challenger dissatisfied with the international status quo catches up with a dominant power in decline.[2] Peaceful transitions, however, are possible when they involve two democratic regimes or satisfied powers.[3] The clear implication is that unless China changes its domestic political character, its rising power is a threat to the United States.

What strategies might China, the designated challenger to U.S. dominance, employ to manage the hegemon? Beijing has everything to gain by reassuring Washington that it has limited goals and peaceful intentions. Contrary to the suggestion of power-transition theory, it is not in the interest of a latecomer to instigate a premature confrontation with the still-dominant hegemon. Instead, the latecomer has every incentive to avoid and postpone a showdown, as time will further improve its bargaining position. Concealment of one's true strength and fostering the hegemon's sense of superiority help to curtail the latter's motivation to wage a preventive war.[4] After all, a self-confident hegemon is far less likely to succumb to the preventive motivation than a desperate hegemon caught in a deep and irreversible decline. A distracted hegemon—one whose attention is drawn to Iraq, Iran, and North Korea—would divert its attention and resources from China. This distraction gains China time to become stronger. In the meantime, self-discipline to avoid being enticed or goaded into a futile competition with the hegemon—such as in an armament race, a mistake committed by the Soviet Union—is paramount. Contrary to the predominant concerns of those Americans sharing the "China threat" perspective, the last thing Beijing wants is to engage in an arms race with Washington, a competition in which the latter has a huge lead and a tremendous comparative advantage and which could only lead to China's economic exhaustion. This view of China's strategic philosophy hardly implies pacifism or disarmament, however. Rather, it emphasizes minimal deterrence so that Washington will have to face, in Beijing's estimation, unacceptable costs should there be a military showdown. In this fundamental sense, China's basic doctrine is strategic defense.

Convincing the hegemon that its dominant status is secure is only part of the reassurance game; the other part calls for a deliberate demonstration of good international citizenship. An avowed adherence to traditional principles such as state sovereignty, territorial integrity, and noninterference in others' domestic affairs offers tangible evidence of a status quo orientation and presents China as a vocal supporter of popular international rules and norms. These same principles provide a legal and normative defense against U.S. demands for concessions. Active participation and reasonable conduct in international governmental organizations contribute to a reputation for accepting multilateral diplomacy and help to refute charges of revisionist ambitions.[5]

Conversely, when the United States resorts to unilateralism and challenges international consensus, it undermines the very institutions and principles that it has worked to establish and has championed in the name of the entire international community. In this light, recent U.S. opposition to participating in various international organizations and conventions can be seen to subvert the normative order for its hegemonic rule. Examples of Washington's decision to stay outside rather than inside relevant international communities include the Anti-Ballistic Missile Treaty, the Comprehensive Test Ban Treaty, the Land Mines Convention, the Law of the Sea Convention, the International Convention on the Rights of the Child, the Kyoto Protocol, and the International Criminal Court. Significantly, in cases such as the creation of the International Criminal Court, Beijing also has serious reservations. Washington's announced rejection, however, makes it possible for Beijing to "hide," thereby sparing the latter the political costs of having to mount its own unpopular opposition. "Standing aside" and "taking a backseat" afford this advantage, among others.

The United States is less likely to strike against an upstart if it is distracted by other more pressing concerns. Iraq, Afghanistan, Serbia, and North Korea divert Washington's attention and disperse its forces. These episodes also enhance Beijing's bargaining leverage as its acquiescence and even assistance are sought. These so-called rogue nations assume a role in Washington's adversary category that China can well imagine itself occupying in their absence. The adversary category is more likely to be crowded with many nominees if the hegemon is self-confident than if it is doubtful of its own capacity to act. A self-confident America can also be expected to be impatient with the tedious efforts necessary to overcome the challenges of collective action and to overlook others' incentives to hitch a free ride. Concomitantly, its proclivity to resort to unilateral action on multiple fronts will alienate important third parties, which are now more motivated to form a countervailing coalition to check the United States.

The logic of power transition suggests that a dominant power in decline is more dangerous than one that feels secure in retaining its supremacy. A late-comer seeking to catch up will want to foster the hegemon's self-confidence and complacency rather than to abet its anxiety about losing its dominance. Differential growth rates should improve the upstart's strategic position over time, thus counseling against any rash action that would interrupt or cut short its growth spurt. That it is in the latecomer's interest to seek time and ensure stable conditions to realize its full development potential lends credibility to its signals to reassure others of its benign intentions. At the same time, others will be less prepared and inclined to interfere with China's growth trajectory if it succeeds in persuading foreign audiences that its domestic conditions are the primary driver of its economic expansion, that its expanding economy offers collateral benefits for others, and that setbacks in its development quest will have serious ripple effects abroad. Significantly, China has become increasingly important as an economic partner for traditional U.S. allies, including Japan, South Korea, Taiwan, and Thailand, and it has displaced the United States as the leading importer of goods and capital from some of them. This trend suggests that these significant others will now have a greater stake in China's continued economic well-being and will be motivated to dampen any disturbances in Sino-American relations that can affect them adversely. This does not, however, mean that there is necessarily a convergence of interests between China and its neighbors, which would clearly be untrue as a generalization. Rather, the emergent multilateral ties point to a mixed motive game in which Beijing has become more adept at avoiding isolation and being targeted for concerted blocking actions by others, as it was during the 1950s and 1960s.

Washington's traditional allies, its current adversaries, and significant third parties present an indirect avenue for influencing and managing U.S. hegemony. Beijing has increased its participation in multilateral forums and interdependent networks, such as the Association of Southeast Asian Nations and its sponsorship of the Shanghai Cooperation Organization (consisting of China, Kazakhstan, Kyrgyzstan, Tajikistan, Uzbekistan, and Russia, with Iran invited as an observer at its meeting in July 2005). The objective behind this pursuit is not necessarily to create formal alliances or even promote blocking action against U.S. policies but is rather to signal the potential for more intense and coordinated resistance if relations with the United States take a serious turn for the worse.

Beijing's strategy for managing the United States requires exactly the opposite modal behavior than that expected according to power-transition theory. The prevailing U.S. version of this theory hypothesizes a cocky and impatient challenger whose imprudence gets it into a premature and asymmetric fight that it is destined to lose. Instead, this analysis suggests that China will play for time (schedule delays), avoid an inflated profile, profess modesty in goals and capability, and seek to expand and strengthen multilateral ties and institutions (i.e., use the multilateral arenas introduced in chapter 1). The underlying strategic logic cautions against overplaying one's hand and extends to the United States ample opportunity to overplay its hand. Self-restraint rather than restraining the United States then becomes a cardinal policy tenet. At the same time, American failure to exercise proper self-discipline will cause overextension, contribute to domestic economic decline and social dissension, and arouse counter-mobilization abroad. Those developments will in turn set the United States on a course of eventual decline. Classic Chinese military treatises are well known for enjoinders to feign weakness (credible helplessness) and bide time, abet the other's arrogance and distract its attention to alternative targets, and prevail over the other without having to fight.[6] This strategic perspective implies an extended time horizon and a certain confidence in persevering through and recovering from the inevitable occasional setback that interrupts a generally favorable long-term trend.

Role Reversal and the Logic of Engagement

Classic Chinese thought enjoins the application of the other's spear against its own shield.[7] One adopts the adversary's strategic advice and tools to contain threats emanating from it. What would reasonably attentive Chinese observers conclude from the open discussions among their American counterparts about useful approaches for dealing with China? As discussed in the next section, some influential American voices advocate containment, emphasizing the use of coercive instruments and denial strategies to block China's power ascent and to check its perceived ambitions.

Chinese observers surely notice that the arguments of containment proponents have not gone unchallenged. There has been an ongoing debate in the United States pitting these advocates against others who argue in favor of engagement.[8] The so-called engagers wish to integrate China into existing international institutions and global conventions. They see widening and deepening economic interdependence as a way to restrain Beijing's bellicosity in its foreign relations and encourage its domestic political and economic liberalization. Either implicitly or explicitly, they hope to "reform" China by influencing its values and practices through regular interactions and positive exchanges that will shape its policy agenda and manipulate the influence and interests of its domestic stakeholders.

The engagers' arguments are embedded and elaborated in a large body of theoretical and empirical work falling under the rubric of democratic peace.[9] States with more democratic institutions, higher volumes of bilateral trade, and a larger number of shared memberships in intergovernmental organizations have maintained dyadic peace more than their opposites have. Political competition and accountability, foreign economic intercourse, and participation in intergovernmental organizations form the three pillars of the so-called Kantian peace.[10] They are each supposed to contribute to peace directly, and they are also expected to form a virtuous cycle whereby they reinforce each other and thus facilitate peace indirectly. For instance, democratization and increasing foreign trade encourage greater participation in intergovernmental organizations, which in turn strengthens international norms and promotes reciprocal adjustment.

There is little doubt that this is the policy recipe advocated by U.S. liberals for dealing with and indeed for transforming China. There is, however, sometimes dismay and even surprise when the Chinese apply these same methods in dealing with the United States, that is, employing collective action networks with American participants (as when the U.S.-China Business Council lobbied the Clinton administration to be more accommodating to China in negotiations on membership in the World Trade Organization). Chinese activities in the United Nations (especially in the Security Council) and regional forums such as the Association for Southeast Asian Nations +3 (China, Japan, and South Korea) are perceived to hamper the unilateral exercise of U.S. power.[11] Ongoing and expanding U.S. trade with and investment in China thus presents a double-edged sword. Deep, interlocking commercial interests create stakeholders, not only in China but also in the United States, for continuing and expanding these ties and guarding against their rupture. Increasing economic interdependence suggests that, just as China's access to the U.S. consumer market would be jeopardized by a worsening bilateral relationship, the U.S. debt market would be traumatized by a Chinese boycott. Whether one side or the other is more vulnerable to economic disruptions depends on a host of factors, including the ease of substitution and the evaluation of prospective economic loss relative to other policy goals.[12] It seems reasonable, however, to expect that as intra-Asia trade and cross-investments mount, China's dependence on the U.S. market and capital will concomitantly decline. Conversely, the United States may continue its heavy reliance on foreign capital, including Chinese capital, to sustain its fiscal deficit. Moreover, both sides can seek to use multilateral diplomacy and international organizations to constrain the other.[13]

The greater the tendency to see engagement approaches as exclusively American tools to mold China, the less prepared the United States is for Chinese attempts at role reversal. The ethnocentrism embodied in the view that engagement statecraft is only available to the United States overlooks the possibility that those seeking to evade, modify, or resist American designs may actually be favored by some structural advantages. Differences in domestic openness and diversity presumably imply differences in the ease with which China and the United States can influence the other's interest groups—differences that favor China. The numerical majority enjoyed by non-Western states in intergovernmental organizations with world or Asia-Pacific membership means that Beijing may well have a more receptive audience than Washington does. Nationalism on the part of the Chinese masses can enable Beijing to resist concessions, such as with respect to Taiwan, on the grounds of political legitimacy and popular mandate.

China's America watchers may also think that domestic opinion can pose significant disincentives for the United States and its allies' conducting large, multi-year military hostilities abroad. As shown in chapter 12 of this volume, public opinion in all the major member states of the Organization for Economic Cooperation and Development (OECD) was opposed to the U.S. invasion of Iraq in 2003, and a divided U.S. electorate has increasingly put the Bush administration on the political defensive. Many foreign governments have then had incentives not to join or to withdraw from a U.S.-sponsored coalition of the willing. China's experts are also aware that American business interests with the largest stake in economically engaging China also are important supporters of the neoconservative coalition governing the United States. This coalition is accordingly cross-pressured by its economic interests in the Chinese market and its political impulse to contain China.

"The Porcupine Magnified," or Why Size and Resolve Do Matter

Conventional U.S. conceptions of resistance and deterrence, relying on either internal armament or external alliance, present a game that China seemingly will be reluctant to play. Engaging in an arms race against the United States or in competitive acquisition of military allies would play into U.S. strength and China's weakness. The fatal error of the Soviet Union was its failure to recognize its own disadvantages.

That does not imply that military capability and the defense of the homeland are irrelevant or unimportant to the Chinese. They surely are. Yet war-winning capabilities and alliance politics need not be the only or even the main avenues for achieving national security. For China, a first line of defense is the projection of an image of being "too big to swallow." China's sheer size, territorial and demographic, provides a powerful deterrent to anyone who would contemplate repeating Japan's project of conquest prior to and during World War II—or what the United States is trying to accomplish in Iraq. An invader will surely have serious indigestion if it attempts to gain physical control over

China. China's comparative advantage lies in forcing an invader to fight on its home turf, thus ensnaring the invader in a protracted war of attrition. There are very few other countries that can feel a comparable sense of confidence in the protection afforded by their physical size and cultural resilience. However powerful the United States may be, it probably will not mistake China for Iraq or Kuwait. Therefore, neither dominance nor conversion appears to offer feasible options in dealing with China. To the extent that China is vulnerable to foreign encroachments, its weakness tends to stem from the danger of internal decay and fragmentation.

Deterrence against a militarily stronger adversary does not require symmetric retaliation—as when two boxers match blow for blow. Nor does deterrence require capabilities to ensure the complete destruction of the other side. Effective deterrence can rest on a declared posture of assured resistance rather than a demonstrable capability to inflict assured destruction. Visible physical and psychological preparations for a war of endurance and privation signal that a more powerful foe cannot hope to overawe China and expect a quick, easy victory in case of a military conflict. China will fight long and hard, and it professes to be willing to suffer greater hardship to outlast the adversary. Consequently, Beijing's strategy of deterrence seeks to project not a superior retaliatory force but rather a favorable asymmetry in resolve. The underlying rationale does not so much try to persuade the United States that it cannot score more points in the early rounds of a match but rather urges it to doubt whether it could bring a match to a successful conclusion. Beijing has tried to signal a willingness to challenge and fight a superior foe over Taiwan and has tried to reinforce the credibility of this threat by invoking memories of its intervention in the Korean War (which was unexpected by Americans at the time because of this decision's apparent "craziness").

Effective deterrence also does not require a demonstrable ability to defeat an enemy on the battlefield. All that is required is to convince potential adversaries that the expected disutility of war will outweigh its expected utility. One can be defeated on the battlefield—as in the case of the Viet Cong's Tet Offensive and Anwar Sadat's Yom Kippur War—and still score a political and psychological victory. That a militarily weaker party can accept war with a stronger adversary is explained by the fact that the former does not have to defeat the latter to gain from fighting.[14] For war between the parties to occur, all that is required is that both be convinced that they can perform better on the battlefield than the other side expects. Accordingly, each believes that it can gain a better deal by going to war than its counterpart would otherwise concede in the absence of war. The same logic would argue that effective deterrence to avoid war requires only that China demonstrate to the potential U.S.

attacker that the negative consequences of waging war will exceed Washington's threshold for acceptable costs.

Finally, deterrence efforts need not rely solely on one's own retaliatory or defensive capability, even when combined with active assistance from allies and partners. To the extent that unwanted events will have negative effects on others that the United States cares about, the latter will be self-restrained from playing its stronger hand. Washington will then be reluctant to take a more forceful stand if Sino-American tension will dampen economic growth in other northeast Asian countries. China's deterrence does not call for the active mobilization of a defensive alliance; it relies on the creation of cross-national stakeholders whose economic vitality and regime legitimacy are important to Washington and whose well-being is intertwined with the peaceful evolution of Sino-American relations. Indeed, deterrence in its broader sense can involve making oneself a critical, even indispensable, player in the hegemon's pursuit of its core agenda. Beijing's role in hosting the Six-Party Talks in negotiations over Pyongyang's nuclear and missile armaments indicates how China's cooperation in this case (and others, such as combating international terrorism and containing Iran's nuclear program) can have the effect of discouraging Washington from making other policies that infringe seriously on Beijing's core values.

From Doctrinal Admonitions to Policy Behavior

Some readers may be puzzled by the discussion on deterrence in the last section. Why should the Chinese worry about deterrence? Who in their right mind would want to attack or invade China? In response, the Chinese would point to the U.S. assaults on Serbia and Iraq, its avowed wish to institute regime change in "rogue states," the U.S. bombing of the Chinese embassy in Belgrade, the violation of Chinese airspace by U.S. surveillance aircraft, and Washington's ongoing development of a missile defense system to protect the United States from attack. They will also surely mention Taiwan in this litany. Beijing's approach to the Taiwan problem illustrates various strategic elements discussed earlier.

As a global power, the United States sees its interests engaged in many places and must therefore allocate its resources and attention to multiple concerns, including its ongoing military involvement in the Middle East. (Media coverage shows how Washington's attention can be drawn to one crisis after another in quick succession: the war in Iraq, Iran's nuclear program, North Korea's missile tests, and fighting in Lebanon between Israel and Hezbollah.) In contrast, China can focus on one overriding goal of national reunification. There is accordingly an asymmetry of attention in favor of Beijing, which also has a locational advantage that offsets Washington's overall force superiority. Thus far, Beijing has eschewed a military confrontation, preferring to count on long-term trends in political and economic transformation to improve its bargaining position. It has pursued a series of blocking actions, having generally succeeded in isolating Taiwan diplomatically in the international community and isolating the United States militarily, thus preventing it from sponsoring any prospective opposing "coalition of the willing" even though Washington has continued to provide arms to Taipei. Instead of contesting superior U.S. military forces, Beijing has sought to demonstrate that it has a higher stake in and greater resolve about Taiwan's status, a status that will continue to be the principal irritant and a dangerous flashpoint in its bilateral relations with Washington. In the meantime, the campaign to reunite Taiwan with the mainland serves useful domestic purposes by rallying nationalism and legitimating the incumbent elite. China has already displaced the United States as Taiwan's leading trade partner and investment destination, so that over time this trend of economic integration can present a countervailing force to political division.

Significantly, Taiwan's democratization has turned out to be a double-edged sword for both Taipei and Beijing. Whereas the pro-independence forces have gained a large and legitimate voice in Taiwan politics, other interest groups have emerged to advocate closer ties and less confrontation with the mainland. The latter groups include those experiencing rising cross-strait business exchanges and intermarriages, developments that have stemmed from the dismantling of political controls from the island's days as a garrison state. Recent elections indicate that the so-called pan-green and pan-blue forces (that is, those advocating greater independence from China and those advocating closer cooperation with China) have roughly comparable levels of voter support. The economic and social forces reflecting changes in Taiwan's internal conditions will, in Beijing's view, carry greater weight in determining the eventual resolution of the Taiwan issue than will developments in external relations, including possible U.S. military opposition to China's reunification goal.

Earlier sections also suggest that China will not blindly oppose the United States on all or even most issues of vital importance to Washington. One would rather expect the opposite, with Beijing declaring public support for international cooperation to combat terrorism, to prevent nuclear proliferation, and to resist commercial protectionism. On these matters, Beijing should find its interests converging with Washington's. That does, however, leave the United States to do the heavy lifting of organizing multilateral collaboration if possible and undertaking unilateral action if necessary. China can then "hitch a free ride" on U.S. efforts, benefiting from the ensuing "public goods" without having to exert itself.

One would also expect Beijing to profess a preference for multilateral forums in order to restrain unilateral impulses on the part of the United States and to avoid bilateral bargaining in which China has a disadvantage relative to the United States. Cumbersome institutional procedures also add to the transaction costs faced by Washington. Beijing will generally prefer to let others take the lead in opposing the United States. Thus, it took a backseat when France, Germany, and Russia resisted the UN mandate the United States sought for its attack on Iraq. Rarely will one find China isolated as the lone dissenter. When faced with such a prospect, it is far more likely to acquiesce quietly than to defy publicly. Thus, Beijing has exercised its veto prerogative on the Security Council very sparingly in comparison to Washington. When faced with a majority favoring an objectionable proposal, China prefers "not participating" to using its veto to block passage (Chan 2003) or seeking and receiving side-payments for its acquiescence.

China's leaders can also be expected to seek issue-linkage opportunities, which would involve redefining or reframing Washington's expressed concerns to redound to China's benefit. As a leading example of "consent and exploit," in exchange for Beijing's support in Washington's campaign against al-Qaeda, China was able to gain U.S. agreement to classify Muslim insurgents (such as the East Turkestan Islamic Movement) in Sinkiang as terrorists. In professing support in principle for efforts to build international regimes to prevent the proliferation of weapons, Beijing directs Washington's attention to its own arms sales to Taiwan. Human rights are defined to include national self-determination, racial nondiscrimination, and entitlement to economic development. China in effect tries to alter policy frames to make it difficult for Washington to choose selectively to have its way only on those issues about which it cares most deeply. In the language of chapter 1, one might say that Beijing seeks to expand or shape the interpretation of international rules to modify or delay the pursuit of U.S. preferences.

Given the preceding discussion, Beijing will tend to focus on matters that inherently give it more policy space and perhaps even greater bargaining leverage. These tend to be matters on which the U.S. elite and public are internally conflicted, torn by competing interests and avowed principles. "Free trade" offers an example of such a wedge issue. Access to the Chinese market is important to many large U.S. corporations, which historically tend to support conservative Republican candidates. To the extent that U.S. business groups are self-motivated to continue and expand commercial ties with China, they become the best advocates Beijing can hope to have for a friendly U.S. posture. Similarly, to the extent that liberal Democrats have historically favored a large role for international organizations, the norms and rules from existing regimes can be used to argue against unilateral U.S. actions whether in trade protection or armed intervention. Unwanted U.S. policies thus will tend to be forestalled by prolonged and often fruitless domestic debates and, if they should be undertaken, are likely to be less severe and lasting than one would otherwise expect (such as actual or threatened U.S. economic sanctions stemming from alleged Chinese abuses of human or intellectual property rights). U.S. concerns for how its actions may damage the very international regimes that it has played an active and leading role in constructing also will cause Washington to refrain from playing its stronger hand against Beijing. In short, the United States is likely to be self-deterred from fully exercising its hegemonic power. The prospect of such self-restraint, however, depends more on the dynamics of U.S. politics and the framing of its domestic debate than on active opposition from abroad. Oftentimes, tensions among competing U.S. goals and even outright contradictions create policy predicaments that tie Washington's hands and dampen its audacity, as illustrated in the discussion of Iraq in chapter 2 of this volume.

Proponents of the "China threat" theory emphasize Beijing's rising military stature and hegemonic ambitions. They point to the danger of an assertive China throwing its weight around and precipitating a confrontation with the United States in pursuit of its expansionist agenda (see, e.g., Bernstein and Munro 1997; Roy 1994). The analysis presented here suggests instead a cautious rather than reckless China, one that seeks accommodation but not acquiescence with U.S. hegemony. Its strategy of hampering the exercise of U.S. power and constraining its moves will reflect soft deterrence and passive resistance rather than active and militant opposition featuring an arms buildup and military alliance formation.

Key elements of China's approach to managing the United States place a premium on feigning weakness and conserving energy, eschewing competition in the other's strong suit, abetting Washington's excesses, diverting the latter's attention to alternative targets, and projecting an image of being too big to swallow and too tough to mess with. This approach accords with Sun Tzu's observation that "being unconquerable lies with yourself; being conquerable lies with the enemy. Thus, one who excels in warfare is able to make himself unconquerable but cannot necessarily cause the enemy to be conquerable" (Sawyer 1994, 183). By implication, fatal strategic setbacks are more likely to be due to one's own mistakes than the opponent's actions. Avoidance of such errors helps to put one in an unassailable position. Allowing one's opponent ample opportunity to commit these errors would conversely put it in a self-defeating position. These remarks underscore four points made in chapter 1. First, the management of a hegemon does not necessarily require the mustering of equivalent military capabilities. The emphasis of China's grand strategy is decidedly on "soft assets." Intangibles such as an asymmetry in policy attention, effort mobilization, cost tolerance, time horizon, and goal aspiration provide the wherewithal to achieve a balance against the hegemon's superior hard assets. Second, it would be misleading to dichotomize policies toward the United States simply in terms of containment versus engagement or rivalry versus submission. Management of the hegemon sometimes involves getting and keeping Washington committed when it would prefer not to be (or at least not in the manner or under the circumstances intended), rather than attempting to isolate or exclude the United States from particular arenas. Thus, for instance, Washington can help Beijing to defuse the danger of Taiwan declaring independence and of Japan pursuing its own nuclear weapons. Similarly, prolonged involvement in the Middle East will necessarily detract from the United States' profile in East Asia. Third, the policies of George W. Bush's administration may or may not correspond to long-term U.S. national interests. Thus, declared support for "official" Washington does not necessarily indicate agreement with or sympathy for American national interests. By the same token, efforts to modify, evade, and resist current U.S. goals also do not amount to challenging American national interests. That Americans disagree among themselves about the wisdom of administration policies suggests domestic dynamics are likely the leading source of policy change. Fourth, as this chapter has strongly implied, China is not now and in the next several decades is not likely to be strong enough to challenge and displace U.S. hegemony. At best, China is only a regional power with a role largely limited to its immediate neighborhood. Thus, concerns about whether China may eventually supplant the United States as the global hegemon are telling not so much about China's capabilities currently or in the near future. They speak more to American ambitions and insecurities.

Although this chapter dwells on Chinese strategic reasoning and conduct, it would be a mistake to infer that the characterization and interpretation given are uniquely or distinctly Chinese. Despite the predictions of neorealists, balancing against a rising or extant hegemon has not been the dominant behavior in history. When faced with hegemonic threat, states have instead tended to appease, bandwagon, pass the buck, "hide," and "transcend" by offering institutional arrangements that go beyond resolving an immediate dispute.[15] Napoleonic France was defeated only because it insisted on attacking its allies and neutrals, thus thwarting their attempts to appease and bandwagon.

By repeatedly lashing out against its neighbors, France finally produced, by its own aggressive actions, a coalition of opposing states that Britain's diplomacy had sought but failed to bring about (Schroeder 1994a; 1994b). In the same vein, A. J. P. Taylor remarked that Nazi Germany brought about its own downfall by not only fighting Britain and France but also by declaring war on the Soviet Union and the United States—the two world powers that only wanted to be left alone (Taylor 1961, 278). A would-be hegemon's recklessness and arrogance turned potential allies and neutrals into enemies. The impetus that fostered a coalition against those states came from their own aggressive actions rather than a natural instinct on the part of the weaker states to balance against them.

The logic of hegemonic (read U.S.) decline given by Chinese strategists also corresponds with another well-known process described by historians. A tendency to "overreach"—to take on extensive foreign commitments beyond the domestic economy's capacity to sustain them—has been an important part of the familiar story of imperial decline (Kennedy 1987), with the Soviet Union being just the latest empire to suffer from severe economic decay and political disintegration due to a crushing security burden (see, e.g., Wohlforth 2003). At some point military expenditures are likely to impose severe opportunity costs in forgone domestic spending, whether in public or private consumption or investment (including investment in human capital) (Russett 1970; Chan and Mintz 1992). Chinese views are hardly exceptional in attributing a tendency for a hegemon's excessive ambitions to eventually deplete its available resources and cause a domestic crisis of confidence.

In terms of the actions and arenas presented in chapter 1, the Chinese strategic conception clearly favors some elements while de-emphasizing others. There is a strong legacy behind Beijing's moves to form whatever "united front" seems useful for containing its main antagonist of the moment. Favored arenas include participation in both formal institutions excluding U.S. membership and informal caucuses inside institutions with U.S. representation. Interlocking ties with interest groups and regimes that are important to Washington make it difficult to single out China for retribution without hurting or taking on important domestic groups and third countries. Thus, China also makes use of coalitions of the unwilling and collective action networks with U.S. participants. Dense commercial networks provide an informal arena for transactions among private actors rather than formal intergovernmental institutions, but they can work equally effectively in restraining unwanted actions by the hegemon due to its concerns for causing serious collateral damage to influential private interests and their political allies and sponsors. Unilateralism is possible but not likely except in unusually favorable or dire circumstances involving core values of the regime. With respect to the action categories, Beijing tends to be eclectic. Its inventory includes signaling potential bloc creation, rule expansion, consent and exploit, schedule delays, conditional support, linkage to side-payments, and standing aside. A resort to "craziness" and martyrdom and to conjuring up system-destabilizing vulnerability (if not "helplessness") is also possible.[16] One may recall that projecting an image of "too-tough-to-be-messed-with" is based precisely on a supposed willingness to take on powerful adversaries and to endure extraordinary privation. China's revolutionary folklore, including episodes in the Korean War, celebrates extreme personal sacrifice and collective hardship in protracted struggles against long material odds. Concomitantly, one encounters occasional references to China's regime fragility and economic instability, with the insinuation that in the absence of foreign understanding or toleration of Beijing's helplessness, such vulnerabilities can well trigger severe repercussions regionally and even globally. In this sense, China's size serves not just a defensive purpose in the sense of protecting it from foreign domination. It also confers a certain external importance in the recognition that what happens inside China, for better or for worse, can cause nontrivial ripple effects for others. As the Chinese economy becomes a bigger part of the regional and global economy, this importance is only likely to grow.

THE UNITED STATES AND TURKEY
Limiting Unilateralism

ILTER TURAN

States and other actors have historically tried to modify the behavior of others, irrespective of whether the world system in which the phenomenon occurs is characterized as hegemonic, duopolistic, or a balance-of-power system.[1] In case of divergence between their policy choices, the more powerful actors work to implement their own choices while the weaker try to resist and modify the preferences of the former, irrespective of whether their relationship is characterized as friendly or adversarial. The nature of the world system in this context may only limit and constrain the means that are available to the sides and are considered permissible by them. Naturally, those that are in possession of more means through which they can induce compliance are more likely to achieve success. Yet those with lesser means also have access to resources, strategies, and actions. They may be able to deny the more powerful complete achievement of their goals and even induce their reconsideration.

The United States and Turkey developed close relations after World War II within the context of the Western defense system. The development of the relationship had been sought by both parties. Turkey had feared that it constituted a target for the ideological and geographical expansion of the Soviet Union, while the United States, in assuming the defense of Western Europe, had come to believe that an effective defense system would have to include Turkey on the southern flank of NATO.[2] This convergence of interests has constituted the underpinning of a partnership that has continued to this day.

Nevertheless, even when the severity of the Soviet threat facilitated the perception that the two nations' interests were highly convergent, thus encouraging compliance with American foreign policy preferences, there were instances in which policy preferences diverged sharply. More recently, a continuing sharp divergence of preferences has occurred with regard to the American invasion and occupation of Iraq.

This chapter examines four cases (which occurred under different systemic conditions) in which Turkey tried to evade, limit, modify, resist, control, undermine, and render ineffective the policy preferences of the United States. For each case there is a historical outline followed by a discussion of the actions Turkey employed and the arenas in which those actions were taken. The chapter concludes with suggestions of the possible implications of this analysis vis-à-vis relations between materially stronger and weaker political entities.

The Cyprus Crisis of 1964

The Republic of Cyprus was established in 1960 by trilateral agreements between Great Britain, Greece, and Turkey after a long struggle against British colonial authority initiated by the Greeks, who constituted three-fourths of the population. Turkey had become a party to the dispute to ensure that the rights of the Turkish population on the island would be protected in the event Britain gave independence to its colony. The terroristic Greek nationalist movement had also turned against the Turks once it had become apparent that they were not to be satisfied with minority status in what otherwise would be a Greek state. With the efforts of the Turkish, Greek, and British governments, a solution was eventually arrived at, creating a system of checks and balances that ensured the security and the protection of the rights of the Turkish community. The three countries would jointly and/or individually ensure the protection of the constitutional order. Each retained the right to intervene on the island if the constitutional order were violated.[3]

Soon after independence, Archbishop Makarios, the new president of Cyprus, began to argue that the constitution was unworkable and some of its fundamental provisions ought to be changed. These changes would fully undermine the system of checks and balances and make the island fully dominated by Greeks. Both Turkey and the Turkish Cypriots objected strenuously, and tensions began to rise. On December 23, 1963, Greek gangs began to attack Turkish Cypriots. Turkey began to entertain the idea of staging a military intervention on the island.

From the beginning, the United States had avoided becoming embroiled in the Cyprus problem. The problem concerned three NATO allies, and they were working for a solution. Furthermore, Britain had special interests on the island, including two military bases, and America was reluctant to get involved in what it considered the domain of its closest ally. Prime Minister Ismet İnönü, on the other hand, had judged from the beginning that Britain could not be impartial with its bases on the island and that only U.S. involvement would make it possible to protect the Turkish minority. İnönü's initial efforts to get American support had been turned down by Secretary of State Dean Rusk, who said that the United States was not a party to the conflict. To point to the urgency of the matter, Turkey then flew jets over the island, prompting all parties to agree on the establishment of a peacekeeping force. The effort failed and Greek actions against the Turks continued. İnönü told the U.S. ambassador on January 8, 1964, that unless the rights of the Turkish Cypriots were ensured, Turkey would have to intervene.[4]

The Turkish threat led to an Anglo-American plan for the deployment of a ten-thousand-member NATO force, which Makarios rejected. Sensing that a NATO force would work to sustain the existing arrangement, he said that he would accept a UN peacekeeping force. The UN Security Council decided on March 4 to send such a force to the island, and the decision was quickly implemented. This deployment, however, neither stopped the violence directed against the Turkish Cypriot community nor deterred the Greek side from efforts to change the constitutional order. Shortly afterward, Makarios unilaterally abrogated the treaty of alliance between Britain, Greece, and Turkey and announced that a new Cypriot army would be formed.[5]

The intransigence of the Greek Cypriot regime and the intensification of the attacks on the Turkish community led Turkey once again to consider a military intervention. The United States was still not interested in getting involved and encouraged the parties to work together. On June 2, however, the Turkish prime minister informed the U.S. ambassador that troops were to leave for Cyprus the next day. The latter asked that the operation be delayed twenty-four hours so that he could consult his government. Within that short period, the Turkish government received an unusually undiplomatically worded note from President Lyndon Johnson asking Turkey not to intervene militarily. Prime Minister İnönü was invited to Washington, as was the Greek prime minister. A return to diplomacy appeared to have been achieved.[6]

As the leader of the alliance, the United States had tried to stay away from the quarrelling among some members. Yet by considering unilateral military action and advising its major ally of its intentions, Turkey succeeded in bringing in the United States as an arbiter. The initial plan for a NATO force on the island and the later decision to send a UN peacekeeping force would not have been possible without American support.

The prevention of a Turkish military intervention in Cyprus, on the face of it, looks like a powerful ally preventing a weaker ally from doing what it wanted to do. Yet some later analyses have suggested that it was Turkey that actually achieved its political goal. The argument is that the Turkish prime minister was far from sure that a military intervention would succeed. Turkey did not have sufficient landing craft, its troops were not trained for landing operations, and it might not have been able to provide sufficient air and logistical support to its troops. Domestically, there were strong pressures to stage an intervention in the face of constant acts of brutality against the Turks. Only a strong American warning could justify the reconsideration of the military option. When he informed U.S. Ambassador Raymond Hare, İnönü was certain that he would be asked to withhold the action and he was only too glad to give him the twenty-four hours he wanted. The result was the Johnson letter that spared Turkey from an intervention whose outcome was uncertain. The United States got the blame.[7]

President Johnson's reference to the uncertainty of NATO protection in case of Turkish action against Cyprus led İnönü to reply that if any exceptions were made, the credibility of the alliance would be destroyed. That the point was never raised again even at the time of Turkey's actual intervention on the island (the third case to be examined) suggests that Washington understood the dangers of the statement made in a hastily drafted letter. An alliance relationship also appears to place constraints on the powerful members in terms of the options open to them when a weaker member challenges their preferences.[8]

The United States succeeded in stopping the Turkish intervention. It could not, however, prevent the Greek Cypriot regime from destroying the constitutional order that was created in 1960. It lost the moral ground on which it could offer advice to Turkey to maintain alliance harmony. Turkey began to pay closer attention to its relations with the Soviet Union and with its neighbors in the Middle East. It also began developing additional military capabilities with its own resources (i.e., without a U.S. contribution) in order to be able to intervene on the island when needed. When Turkey staged an intervention on the island in 1974, it could remind its American ally that its advice had failed to produce results and Turkey would not make the same mistake again.

The Opium Problem

Richard Nixon, as a presidential candidate in 1968, identified the use of narcotics as a major problem for American youth and a major source of crime in the country.[9] Agreeing with earlier allegations that Turkey was one of the major sources of opium and derivatives that were reaching the U.S. market, he suggested that Turkey should ban opium poppy cultivation. Turkey responded that it was already cooperating at the international level to keep cultivation under control and was ready to do more but that a total ban would inflict unacceptable hardships on a significant number of farmers whose livelihood depended on opium poppy cultivation. To demonstrate its commitment to combating illicit production and trade, Turkey had already proceeded to limit the areas where cultivation would be allowed (Erhan 1996, 86) and signed the Single Convention on Narcotics by the end of 1966 (Harris 1972, 92). For its part, the United States made only a small loan to Turkey for research on the cultivation of alternative products and to improve law enforcement (Harris 1972, 193). In any event, mutual dissatisfaction and irritation had become constant.

After Nixon's election, the U.S. administration became increasingly committed to Turkey's terminating opium cultivation, arguing that it was the major source of drugs that reached the American market. Although Turkey's entire production was insufficient to meet even one month's worth of American consumption, the idea still found adherents in many quarters of American society. The White House pursued a carrot-and-stick policy, promising on the one hand to help Turkey compensate for the losses to be incurred by opium farmers and the costs of shifting to new crops and threatening economic and military sanctions on the other (Erhan 1996, 107). Turkey reacted with indignation to American allegations but, at the same time, tried to improve its monitoring of poppy cultivation and intensified cooperation with the UN to develop additional international means to combat the drug trade. Such efforts proved insufficient to satisfy American policy makers, who appeared to have discovered a topic that could be exploited for domestic political ends.[10] In 1971, tensions generated by Turkey's opium production appeared to be spiraling to ever higher levels, with no basis of agreement in sight.

What made a change possible was an indirect intervention by the Turkish military, which called for a halt to partisan politics and the establishment of a national unity government that would enact a number of constitutional changes the military commanders advocated. The "above politics" government formed under the watchful eyes of the military was, by its nature, weak both domestically and internationally. The United States, however, was increasing pressure on Turkey to terminate poppy cultivation. The American ambassador was called back to Washington for consultations, while the Turkish ambassador was told that eradicating narcotics was the American administration's highest priority. Lacking domestic support, the Turkish government began negotiations with the United States. It accepted totally banning opium poppy cultivation in return for compensation far less than the amounts it had initially sought. While the U.S. government expressed satisfaction, there were protests in the Turkish parliament. A motion to remove the ban was introduced but defeated.

After two years of political instability under indirect military rule, the country moved in 1973 toward national elections. Parties were unanimous in their condemnation of the ban. They complained that it had been forced on Turkey by the United States without credible justification and that it imposed unacceptable hardships on Turkish farmers. Meanwhile, production soared in other parts of the world since the United States had failed to bring about a more effective international ban. In October 1973 the Republican People's Party (RPP), which prided itself on pursuing "anti-imperialist" stands, led the vote totals in the elections. Forming a coalition with the religiously oriented National Salvation Party, which also had an anti-American stance, the RPP devoted substantial attention to lifting the ban on opium cultivation. It was pointed out that the ban was not serving its purpose—America's drug problems continued unabated and there was no shortage of opium-derived drugs in the U.S. market (Erhan 1996, 153).

Nevertheless, the U.S. administration continued to insist that Turkey retain the ban. Its ambassador in Ankara pursued this line actively while some members of Congress introduced measures to terminate economic and military assistance to Turkey. Secretary of State Henry Kissinger reiterated the American position to the Turkish prime minister when they met in New York in April 1974, to no avail (Erhan 1996, 137). A concurrent congressional resolution calling for the American administration to convey that economic aid would be withheld unless the Turkish government retained the ban also failed (Sönmezoğlu 1995, 65–66). The Turkish government repealed the ban on July 1, 1974. Cultivation would be allowed in limited areas under government control, the slicing of poppies would be banned, and the government would continue to support international cooperation to fight against the illicit use of opium.

The United States reacted immediately. Its ambassador was called home for consultations; both houses of Congress passed resolutions urging that the United States withhold economic and military assistance. The debate was still in full swing when Turkey intervened on Cyprus to protect the Turkish Cypriots in the face of a Greek-instigated coup, after which the United States imposed an arms embargo on Turkey. Relations between the two countries were rapidly deteriorating, an outcome that the U.S. government wanted to avoid. In the meantime, it had become apparent that Turkey had taken serious measures to prevent illicit trade in Turkish-grown opium. Congressional testimony to that effect by Undersecretary of State Joseph Sisco and the U.S. ambassador took the poppy cultivation issue off the agenda (Erhan 1996, 150–51). Apparently, imposing a policy on a government with low levels of domestic support and low esteem in the international arena provides only a weak basis for continuing the imposition after the restoration of popularly backed, elected governments. All Turkish governments, it should be added, acknowledged the legitimacy of American demands and displayed a cooperative disposition for finding solutions.

The Cyprus Intervention and the U.S. Arms Embargo

The essential elements of the Cyprus conflict have already been discussed with regard to the crisis of 1964 and the Johnson letter. The introduction of a UN peacekeeping force (UNFICYP) had brought an uneasy and unstable peace to the island without substantially altering Greek and Greek Cypriot commitments to *enosis,* or eventual union with Greece.[11] The military regime that came to power in Greece in 1967 was dedicated to *enosis.* As their domestic popularity waned, the colonels came to think that it could be revived if they could achieve a union of the island with Greece. They moved to implement their plans by initiating a coup on July 15, 1974, against the elected Cypriot government of Archbishop Makarios, who had distanced himself from the junta. The timing appeared to be good since Turkish-American relations were tense as a result of Turkey's repeal of the poppy cultivation ban. The colonels expected that Turkey would protest but would be restrained by the United States and others from a military intervention on the island (Uslu 2000, 243–53).

After reviewing the new situation on Cyprus, the Turkish government, headed by Bulent Ecevit, concluded that, unless reversed by a military operation, the coup would mark the beginning of a process leading to *enosis.* Ecevit himself went to London and invited the British to carry out a military intervention together with Turkey to force the Cypriot government to comply with the Treaty of Guarantee it signed when it became independent. The British wanted to explore peaceful means. The United States had dispatched Undersecretary of State Sisco to join the Turco-British talks, but Ecevit objected that the United States was not a signatory to the Treaty of Guarantee. He did, however, meet with Sisco later.[12] The undersecretary tried to dissuade Ecevit from intervening and offered rewards and issued threats. The shipments of military hardware that had been delayed because of the poppy crisis would be expedited. Intervention, on the other hand, would mean an end to U.S. assistance and a general worsening of Turkish-American relations. Rather than yielding, Ecevit proposed that Turkey send a sizable military contingent to the island to match the Greek forces that had come there in violation of international agreements and that negotiations for a federal system commence immediately. Since the Greek leadership rejected both proposals, Sisco's efforts, it seemed, had not produced any positive results (Bölükbaşi 1988, 193–95). Secretary of

State Kissinger had telephone conversations with Ecevit during which the secretary was told that applying pressure comparable to that in 1964 might lead to a permanent rupture of Turkey's relations with the Western Alliance.[13]

Turkey intervened on the island on July 20, 1974, and, after fierce fighting, secured a beachhead and announced its willingness to engage in negotiations. During this period, the United States abstained from threats to stop Turkey, although military shipments did in fact slow down. On July 23, the Greek junta resigned and a civilian government under Konstantinos Karamanlis was established (Uslu 1999, 281). In Cyprus, Nikos Sampson, who had led the coup, was replaced by Glafkos Klerides, the head of the Cypriot senate. Negotiations started on July 25 but did not progress well. Both Greek and Turkish forces on the island were trying to expand their area of control as they were negotiating (Bölükbaşı 1993, 200–201). Turkish and Greek goals in the negotiations could not have been more divergent. Turkey wanted to create a new political arrangement to ensure the survival and security of the Turkish community and was amenable to proposals that would serve that purpose.[14] Greeks wanted a return to the pre-coup situation and turned down U.S. and British proposals for compromise. Seeing no way out of the deadlock, Turkey decided to return to military action and expanded its control to 36 percent of the island (Uslu 1999, 301).

Turkey's hope that the Greeks would return to the conference table did not materialize. Strong disagreements emerged within the Turkish governing coalition on what should be offered to the Greek side, resulting in the breakdown of the coalition. The void was filled by caretaker governments that were not in a position to negotiate by making commitments or concessions (Sönmezoğlu 1995, 99–102). The U.S. executive branch, for its part, became paralyzed by the Watergate crisis (Bölükbaşı 1993, 212). As a result, the U.S. Congress began to assume a more active role in foreign policy, opening the way for ethnic lobbies to have a greater influence on policy making. Several members of Congress asked Kissinger to terminate military assistance to Turkey. Later, two bills to the same effect were vetoed by President Gerald Ford. In the end, however, the president concluded that a compromise had to be reached with the Congress. Two bills were passed in late 1974, one terminating military assistance to Turkey and the other imposing an arms embargo. The American executive branch did not view the embargo as an effective instrument. It worked to convince the members of Congress that the Western defense system was being undermined, and in late 1975 it managed to get approval for a one-time only commercial sale of military equipment that had already been paid for (Bölükbaşı 1993, 96–97; Uslu 1999, 318).

Turkey's responses to the embargo included symbolic measures, such as indicating that bilateral defense talks had become meaningless and canceling a meeting between the Turkish ambassador and Kissinger. Turkey also canceled its participation in the military exercises planned for the winter of 1975 and announced that U.S. bases and installations would have to be closed if the embargo was not repealed. It partly implemented the closure in the summer of 1975 by suspending military activity at those sites and placing them under Turkish command. American personnel were nevertheless allowed to stay in order to prevent a total rupture since the U.S. administration was working hard to have the embargo lifted.[15] Turkey even signed a Defense and Cooperation Agreement in March 1976 with the U.S. government though it was clear that it could not become operational until the embargo was ended (Sönmezoğlu 1995, 109). Finally, a Federated Turkish Republic of Northern Cyprus was declared. Turkey also initiated other foreign policy actions. It turned its attention to improving relations with the Soviet Union and the countries of the Middle East (Firat 1997, 203–207). As the embargo continued, Turkey began talking about leaving NATO, arguing that it was not certain that the alliance would be able to continue to provide for Turkey's security (Sönmezoğlu 1995, 112). Only after the election of Jimmy Carter to the presidency was it possible to reverse the deterioration in Turkish-American relations. Although Carter had been unsympathetic to Turkish positions and concerns earlier, upon assuming office he became convinced that problematic relations with Turkey were harmful to Western security interests (Henze 1987, 78). After persistent efforts he managed to get the embargo lifted (Uslu 2000, 321–23; Sönmezoğlu 1995, 113–15).

The Cyprus intervention and the ensuing arms embargo brought two allies into conflict. The United States wanted to prevent two allies from engaging in armed conflict, but it failed to prevent the Greek side from initiating a coup on the island, thereby weakening its ability to restrain the Turkish side from intervening to redress the balance. Turkey felt that its vital interests might be permanently damaged and so staged an intervention. The United States judged that some accommodation would be preferable to a more permanent rupture in the relationship.[16]

The Iraq Crisis

After the stormy years surrounding the Cyprus crisis, Turkish-American relations displayed a comparatively smooth pattern after the repeal of the arms embargo in 1977. The United States used Incirlik Air Base for logistical purposes as well as raids into northern Iraq during the Gulf War and later for the implementation of Operation Provide Comfort.[17] The United States promoted the idea of developing Turkey into an energy corridor for oil and gas from the Caucasus and Central Asia and lent support to the construction of the Baku-

Tbilisi-Ceyhan pipeline. The United States, Israel, and Turkey developed a close working relationship in the field of security. It was assumed that U.S. and Turkish interests were highly convergent and the relationship could be characterized as a strategic partnership. Two thorns in the relationship, however, were allegations by some Turks that the United States was providing northern Iraq–based elements of the Kurdish terrorist organization PKK with supplies and the lack of compensation for substantial losses incurred when Turkey stopped trade with Iraq in order to support Operation Provide Comfort.

When the administration of President George W. Bush began to develop plans for invading Iraq, for allegedly harboring weapons of mass destruction, it assumed that Turkey's cooperation would be forthcoming. The idea of an intervention in Iraq was not new in Ankara. The possibility had already been raised by William Cohen, President Bill Clinton's defense secretary, on a trip to Ankara in November 1998, who was told that this would be difficult. Prime Minister Mesut Yılmaz made a more explicit statement to Secretary of State Madeleine Albright during her visit in 1999. He indicated that Turkey would be concerned with four outcomes of a military intervention in Iraq: an influx of refugees to southeastern Turkey, the founding of a Kurdish state in northern Iraq, the incurring of major economic costs, and Turkey's being a target if Iraq did indeed possess WMD.[18] A U.S. invasion of Iraq continued to occupy a critical place on the U.S.-Turkish agenda under George W. Bush. In March 2002 Vice President Dick Cheney visited Ankara and reiterated American determination to bring Saddam down, even without the support of others, but then asked for assurances of Turkish support. In September, the Turkish General Staff got a message from the U.S. Department of Defense specifying what was expected of Turkey. American ground, sea, and air units would be deployed to various facilities in Turkey, including air and naval bases, airports, and harbors. Although the message was addressed to the General Staff, compliance with many of the requests would in fact require parliamentary approval. The United States continued to communicate its expectations through visits of Undersecretary of Defense Paul Wolfowitz and Deputy Undersecretary of State Marc Grossman.

The Turkish public was generally not favorably disposed toward a military intervention in Iraq and was concerned about the evolution of an independent Kurdish entity. The coalition government, in disarray after its small partner had called for early elections, had responded favorably to a Russian offer to work together to avert the need for a military operation in Iraq that would, in all likelihood, lead to the breakup of that country. Lack of enthusiasm on Turkey's part did not deter the United States from trying to enlist Turkey's cooperation on Iraq. While visiting Washington in late August, the Turkish undersecretary for foreign affairs was told that the United States was planning to send between seventy-five thousand and eighty thousand troops through Turkey and that repair and expansion of existing facilities were needed. He responded that approval would have to come from parliament, which could meet only after elections in early November 2002. American attempts to work through the General Staff failed because the military referred the matter to other parts of the Turkish government. After the U.S. Congress authorized President Bush to declare war on Iraq without waiting for a UN mandate, American requests were repeated once again through military channels, but the response was the same. Only the parliament could give such permission and, as a practical matter, that was impossible two weeks before the elections.

The elections brought the newly formed Justice and Development Party (AKP) to power. The party was young, and many of its deputies and ministers had not had national political experience. Before they had a chance to get acclimated to their jobs, the government received a message that Wolfowitz and Grossman wanted to come to Ankara to discuss the use of military facilities in Turkey as a primary base for supplies and as a secondary base for operations associated with invading Iraq. Prime Minister Abdullah Gül, after reminding the visitors that the AKP had been in office only for a week, said that deputies would have to be persuaded to grant Turkey's American ally its wishes. After some discussion, Gül agreed that site inspection (the first stage of a three-stage operation comprised of inspection, preparation, and utilization) could be done without parliamentary approval if performed by personnel already deployed at Incirlik Air Base and accompanied by Turkish officers. He added that this step should not be construed as a commitment to go on with the other two stages. The American team was not ready to provide specific answers about how costs Turkey incurred would be met and the role Turkey might assume in Iraq's reconstruction. The Turkish side got the impression that the U.S. team was so committed to its own plans that it failed to grasp that Turkey had not made clear-cut commitments. The United States continued its efforts to get a solid commitment from Turkey without success. The head of the AKP, who was soon expected to win a by-election and become prime minister, was invited to Washington and to the White House, where he indicated that he did not want his country to be the only Muslim state to cooperate with the U.S. invasion of Iraq.

Even the earlier verbal commitment to site inspections of military facilities was not being implemented promptly, a situation Turkish authorities attributed to bureaucratic formalities. Only after another lengthy note from Wolfowitz did on-site inspections finally begin. In the interim, the Americans had begun to move military supplies into and near Turkey. The newspapers were full of stories about materiel being unloaded from ships and allegedly being sent to the Iraqi border.

The government was unsure how to proceed. It definitely did not want to be the only country in the region extending support to the invasion. The prime minister decided to go to Syria, Egypt, Jordan, Saudi Arabia, and Iran in early January 2003 for consultations. U.S. patience was beginning to wear thin because equipment was waiting to be unloaded at the port of Iskenderun and troops in the United States were ready to travel to Turkey. While the members of the cabinet agreed that the United States should be accommodated somehow, the prime minister admitted that it would be most difficult for him to persuade his party's deputies to accede to American requests. Subsequent meetings of various government agencies were equally inconclusive. Turkey did propose to the United States that separate military, political, and economic negotiations should be conducted by different committees, each producing a memorandum of understanding. That was accepted and negotiations finally started. The political negotiations in particular were rife with conflict and almost broke down several times on issues ranging from whether American soldiers should pay value added tax on their shopping in Turkey to the rules of engagement for Turkish soldiers encountering PKK terrorist gangs.

The prime minister's trips to other countries of the region had not produced tangible results. While all agreed that Iraq should cooperate with UN arms inspectors, they were sure that Saddam Hussein would not be accommodating. Gül may have hoped that these trips might facilitate passage of a UN resolution making it easier for Turkey to take part in the Iraqi operation, but that did not seem to be happening. Meanwhile, the United States kept pressing for a positive decision from Turkey.

The Turkish General Staff reported to the parliament that the United States was now determined to go into Iraq irrespective of how Saddam behaved. Plans were made to meet the influx of refugees from Iraq. Turkish concerns about a Kurdish state in northern Iraq as well as the status of Mosul and Kirkuk had been related to the Americans. The General Staff concluded that it was absolutely necessary to reach some decision about the U.S. requests. On January 16, a month after the original consent, permission was given to start site inspections.

Although the Turkish government tried reluctantly to accommodate American requests, it was well aware that there was significant opposition to them in the parliament. The opposition was fully against them, while many deputies belonging to the ruling party also raised serious objections, which the government tried to defuse. Several attempts were made without success to get the United States to be more supportive of Turkish positions on Cyprus. It tried to get Arab leaders to persuade Iraq to cooperate with the UN, also without success. It hoped that the UN might adopt a position closer to that of the United States, but that seemed unlikely to materialize. It tried to get specific commitments from the American government regarding northern Iraq, but they were not forthcoming. It invited high representatives from Iraq to visit Turkey in the hope of persuading Saddam Hussein to be more cooperative. The representatives came, but Iraq's behavior did not change. Under pressure to produce a decision, the government decided to ask the parliament to approve the next stage of site preparation, insisting that approval would not imply a commitment to the following stage of site utilization, which was still being negotiated. Fifty-three ruling party deputies went their own way and voted against the bill.

Negotiations on the economic and political fronts were not going well. The compensation the United States offered for economic losses was much below Turkish expectations. The Turkish government, unsure of the reliability of U.S. commitments, wanted congressional approval of the memorandum of understanding, but Bush administration officials said that was not their practice. The Iraqi Kurds were threatening to resist Turkish troops if they came in, while the Turkish military opposed the distribution of certain weapons to local elements in northern Iraq. The Turkish president and the speaker of the parliament insisted that a UN resolution was necessary before Turkey could cooperate. The government hoped that the military, through a meeting of the National Security Council on February 28, would recommend that the site utilization request be granted, but the military leadership avoided taking a position.

The government, under pressure to produce a decision, presented a resolution to the parliament. On March 1, as the parliament was getting ready to debate the proposal, students were demonstrating against the United States a mile away. Islamic intellectuals were lobbying AKP deputies to vote no. During the debate, an opposition member of parliament struck a chord among AKP deputies when he said, "Fear not America, fear God!" An announcement that the memorandum of understanding had been completed did not produce any effect—the resolution failed. There were more affirmative votes than "nays," but the resolution fell three votes short since abstentions were counted as negative votes according to the Standing Orders of the Grand National Assembly. One hundred ruling party deputies voted with the opposition.

After the initial shock, the United States tried to see if the vote could be reconsidered, but the timing seemed inappropriate. Recep Tayyip Erdoğan, the head of AKP, was running in a by-election a week later to become a member of parliament so as to take the place of Abdullah Gül as prime minister.

Rather than spending even more time trying for a new resolution, the United States sought permission from the Turkish government to use its airspace. The request was immediately granted. Although there was little public support for the American requests and much opposition from a variety of sources, the failure to accede to all of the requests seems to have been less because of deliberate policies and more because of the government's incorrectly estimating that it had the votes needed to pass the resolution and did not need to mobilize additional support.

Choosing Arenas and Actions

We have looked at four cases in which Turkey and the United States had differing interests and pursued different courses of policy. In each case, Turkey tried to avoid compliance with official U.S. policy preferences and indeed tried to change them. What were the arenas and actions Turkey used from among the types outlined in chapter 1?

An actor may turn to several arenas and resort to several courses of action at the same time or shift from one arena to another and from one action to another as a highly interactive process unfolds. In the events leading to the Johnson letter of 1964, Turkey initially presented the United States with a fait accompli and engaged in some counter-balancing rhetoric after receiving the letter. On Iraq, Turkey was using the unilateral arena but also considered holding out for a UN Security Council resolution, though it ultimately did not pursue that course. If it had, the arena would have been that of "clubs and caucuses in U.S. member IGOs." Of course, not all types of arenas and courses of action may be available to an actor in its efforts to evade, modify, or resist American policy preferences. During the arms embargo after the Cyprus intervention, to cite an example, the arena of "coalitions of the unwilling" seemed not to be an option Turkey could pursue. That was not only because the United States and Turkey had a close and multi-faceted alliance relationship but also because there were no other "unwillings" with which to form a coalition. Standing aside was not an action option in the opium poppy ban because Turkey was the target of the American demands.

The choice of arenas and actions may be constrained by the nature of the issues at hand. By way of illustration, the Turkish desire to involve the United States in the Cyprus conflict by its nature made the unilateral arena the necessary choice since Turkey did not want to involve countries other than the United States or international organizations in the affair. In choosing arenas and actions, one must always consider the effects of choices on third parties. Prior to the U.S. invasion of Iraq, the Turkish government displayed sensitivity about how its behavior would be viewed both by EU members and countries in the Middle East. Such sensitivity constrained the choices Turkey could make. Finally, the policy-making agencies in a country do not necessarily offer unanimous support for a particular policy. This is especially so in the United States, where the political system is characterized by a separation of powers and is rich in checks and balances. Therefore, foreigners working to evade, modify, or resist U.S. policy preferences need to be careful not to weaken (and ideally should try to strengthen) the position of those elements in the policy process that are favorably disposed toward them. For example, the arms embargo the United States imposed on Turkey after the Cyprus intervention was demanded by Congress but not supported by the executive branch. In its actions, Turkey had to take into consideration that the U.S. government (including the Departments of State and Defense) was not the source of the embargo and was open to a cooperative approach for coping with it. Thus, Turkey and the United States signed a Defense and Cooperation Agreement while the arms embargo was still in effect. "Collective action networks with American participants" can involve elements of the U.S. executive branch as well as of other branches and nongovernmental organizations.

Table 5.1 shows the arenas and actions employed by the Turkish government in the four cases. The table shows that the most frequently used arena was the unilateral one, followed by clubs and caucuses in U.S. member IGOs. As mentioned above, dealing with the arms embargo did involve a particular sort of collective action network with American participants. Other arenas were not used. This is not surprising. Turkey has not belonged to many broad agenda institutions that exclude the United States. Therefore, if Turkey turns to IGOs to influence U.S. policy choices, those are generally IGOs in which the United States is also a member. Those to which Turkey belongs but the United States does not were not relevant for the four cases examined. The Council of Europe, for example, was not an appropriate organization in terms of functions and agenda that would make it a helpful resource for dealing with the pertinent U.S. policies. The Islamic Conference Organization (ICO), which Turkey eventually joined, was not seen by Turkey as an effective organization in international politics. Furthermore, it has not been one that Turkey would particularly want to turn to for dealings with the United States. After all, the only topic on which the ICO could achieve a somewhat clear, if symbolic, consensus has been a pro-Palestinian stance that the United States has not appreciated.

Turning to NGOs and INGOs, several observations may be made. First, the growing role of NGOs and INGOs as important actors in international relations is relatively recent. In general, the use of this arena in international affairs was more limited in the past. Second, while ethnic lobbies in the United

Table 5.1. Turkish choices

Actions	Unilateral	Broad agenda institutions with U.S. excluded	Coalitions of the unwilling	Clubs and caucuses in U.S. member IGOs, INGOs	Collective action net-works with American participants
			Arenas		
"Craziness," martyrdom					
Melting					
Counter-balancing	JL			JL, OP, CYP	
Fait accompli	JL, CYP				
Bloc creation	IRQ			CYP	
Rule-based retaliation					
Rule expansion					
Consent and exploit	CYP				
Consent and deceive					
Promise, protest, retraction	OP, IRQ				
Conditional support commitments	OP, CYP				CYP
Schedule delays	JL, OP, IRQ				
Linkage to large side-payments	OP, IRQ				
Standing aside					
Credible helplessness					

Key: JL = Johnson letter; OP = opium ban; CYP = Cyprus/military sales embargo; IRQ = Iraq

States have a long history, Turkey has not had an ethnic lobby of its own since the number of Turks that have settled in America has been relatively small. Turkey has, with exceptions, enjoyed the support of the Jewish lobby as a result of its close relations with Israel. In the four cases considered, however, that lobby was not especially active on Turkey's behalf. Third, so-called civil society organizations have only recently been growing in Turkey, in some ways in parallel with increasing economic prosperity and intensifying urbanization. Turkish democracy has also only recently been expanding such that governments have begun to see NGOs and INGOs as both legitimate and indispensible parts of the political scene. Taken together, the absence of a propensity to turn to NGOs and INGOs seems amply explained.

In examining the actions Turkey took to evade, modify, or resist U.S. policy preferences, it seems useful to consider the cases separately, leaving comparisons for later. In the string of developments that culminated in the infamous Johnson letter, Turkey made a fait accompli, which included Turkish planes flying over the island, but then scheduled a delay to allow the U.S. government to respond. After a possible Turkish intervention had been averted, Turkey worked with the United States in NATO and later the United Nations to have a peacekeeping force on Cyprus. Turkey also tried to counterbalance the U.S. threat that NATO protection might not apply in the face of a Turkish intervention in Cyprus by raising the specter of the dissolution of NATO and the reorganization of the global security system.[19]

The ban on opium poppy cultivation and its repeal presents a longer, multi-stage process. Turkey had been cooperating with the UN Narcotics Commission and had limited cultivation to four provinces. It had also made conditional commitments to support U.S. policy by saying that it would welcome American assistance in processing the drug and improving controls at both the production and marketing stages. As the American administration pressured Turkey to ban the cultivation of opium poppies, Turkey delayed action and hoped that it would be able to persuade U.S. policy elites that it was not the source of the problem. The military-backed government that came to power in 1971 agreed to negotiate about a ban, and negotiations moved to the question of compensation and other side-payments. The ban that the government introduced was opposed by all parties and was lifted after the elections of 1973 marked a restoration of civilian political control. A military-backed Turkish government had made a promise to ban cultivation while all political parties had protested, and finally the ban was retracted by the elected government.

When a mainland-directed coup toppled the Greek government of Cyprus, Turkey responded by taking steps toward a military intervention to redress the balance. The United States was against a Turkish military intervention. The Turkish government announced that it would support negotiations on the condition that Turkey increase its military presence on the island and that the principle of a federal system be accepted. When the Turkish government quickly judged that the *status quo ante* could be restored only by a military intervention, the United States was faced with a fait accompli. Although Turkey had consented in the past to accept U.S. weapons for NATO purposes, it exploited them for a purpose for which they were not intended. While Turkey also consented to negotiations after its initial intervention, it exploited the interim to consolidate its military presence and created a second fait accompli by expanding the military operation to take control of 36 percent of the island. Upon the imposition of an arms embargo, Turkey tried to counterbalance it by canceling NATO exercises, threatening to close NATO bases, and developing better relations with the Soviet Union and Middle Eastern countries. A final fait accompli came in the form of the declaration of an independent Turkish republic in the northern portion of Cyprus. Although calling this move "bloc creation" would be an exaggeration, Turkey received spare parts and military supplies during the arms embargo from some NATO member countries, such as Germany and Italy, which helped Turkey maintain its military readiness for NATO purposes.

Finally, when the U.S. government made plans to invade Iraq, Turkey insisted that the basics of the American request required parliamentary approval. By finding legitimate reasons, including elections and change of prime minister, the government kept delaying compliance with U.S. demands in the hope that Washington would give up its attack plans. The measures included consultations with a group of regional countries that might constitute some kind of a bloc that would persuade Iraq to honor American demands and avoid the invasion. Turkey also tried to put forth conditions for its approval of U.S. demands. These included extending support for the Turkish position on Cyprus, making sure that Turkey was not the only country with a majority Muslim population that would support America's planned invasion of Iraq, and insisting that a pertinent memorandum of understanding be approved by the U.S. Congress. Given convictions that support extended to the U.S. operations would inflict high costs on Turkey, side-payments were negotiated. While the Turkish government promised to accede to American demands, many organized groups in society, the opposition party, and many of the ruling party deputies in parliament protested to a point where the government proposals failed to win approval.[20]

In relations between two states, the weaker uses various arenas and actions to prevent the stronger from imposing its policy preferences. In this context, describing a stronger country as a hegemon simply implies that it has strength or power that the weaker may find difficult to resist. It does not mean that the weaker simply engages in automatic and complete compliance. The preceding discussion looked at four cases of policy divergence between the United States and Turkey. Three were during the bipolar world; the fourth, when the world system was characterized as unipolar, featured the United States as the hegemon. The arenas and actions Turkey employed in the four cases were sufficiently similar to suggest that they did not change when the prevailing characterization of the international system did.

Although a hegemon may have many resources at its disposal, the case studies confirm that weaker states can have means at their disposal to deny it the full realization of its policy preferences. These means may vary according to the issue at hand and the nature of the relationship between the hegemon and the weaker state. Several may be employed at the same time or they may be employed in sequence as needed. The four cases studied contain examples of the use of arena-action combinations simultaneously and in sequence. They show how Turkey tried to evade, modify, or resist the policy preferences of the United States and achieved some degree of success in each instance.

What can we learn from Turkey's experience with the United States regarding challenges to the policies of a hegemon? First, in a multi-faceted, complex relationship, the hegemon, and not just the weaker state, is constrained in its choice of arenas and actions to produce compliance with its demands. That condition can work in favor of the weaker party. Even in the case of Iraq, when the United States could not get its way, it produced a restrained response against Turkey both in order to minimize collateral damage to other matters where the two countries had mutual interests and ongoing cooperation and to maintain a reserve of goodwill that could be drawn on in the future. Second, since the United States government is not a monolith, there are often differences of opinion between (and within) branches of government. At times of confrontation, the weaker country tries to enlist the support of elements having a friendlier disposition toward it in order to temper the influence of those that would exert harsher pressures on it. For example, note the reluctance of the U.S. executive branch to terminate arms shipments to Turkey during the opium ban and later after the Turkish intervention in Cyprus. Third, as a world power, the hegemon has a busy and constantly changing agenda. If a weaker state can resist a demand by the hegemon long enough, it is entirely possible that other developments and concerns will demand the hegemon's attention. That will relieve the hegemon's pressure on the weaker state. In the Iraq case, Turkey's refusal of the American demand to use Turkish territory for troop and equipment transit was overtaken by events. As the United States invaded Iraq, it began to consider how Turkey could contribute in other ways to the invasion and then to Iraqi reconstruction. Finally, the hegemon may feel that it is at least substantially responsible for ensuring stable, if not warmly harmonious relationships among its weaker friends. This provides an opportunity for the weaker to bring in the United States as an arbiter, peacemaker, or police officer in their antagonistic relationships with other associates of the hegemon. The success Turkey had in getting the United States involved in the Cyprus conflict is a good example of this phenomenon.

Looking ahead to future research, it may be possible to change and enrich the list of arenas and actions, though caution in generating too many categories is advised, to preserve elegance. To illustrate, a country may try to preempt a demand from a hegemon by taking measures in advance. This, in a sense, was the case with Turkey's cooperation with international agencies in the fight against the illicit trading of drugs in advance of the U.S. demand to terminate opium poppy cultivation. A country may also offer other compensation for failing to accede to a specific demand of the hegemon, as distinct from seeking compensation. This is what Turkey seems to have done when, after not accepting the U.S. request to send troops through Turkey to Iraq, it later offered to send Turkish soldiers for patrol duties that would facilitate the job of the Americans. We must also remember that, especially among countries with friendly relations, persuasion may be the first step employed in the face of a policy divergence, with other actions deferred until persuasion attempts seem ineffective.

Understanding how weak states resist stronger states, including a hegemonic one, may be considerably enhanced by expanding the analysis to include the arenas and actions the stronger employ and by placing any specific instance of policy divergence in the context of the more comprehensive and multilateral relationships between a weak and a strong state. The analysis may be strengthened further by examining how relations with third parties may strengthen or weaken the ability of the weaker polity to evade, modify, or resist the preferences of the strong.

RESISTANCE TO HEGEMONY WITHIN THE CORE

Domestic Politics, Terrorism, and
Policy Divergence in the G-7

THOMAS J. VOLGY, KRISTIN KANTHAK,
DERRICK FRAZIER, AND
ROBERT STEWART-INGERSOLL

Our approach to the topic of challenges to American hegemony places
these challenges in a context focused on changes in hegemonic
strength. We expect the nature, location, and salience of challenges to vary
with the strength of the United States. Declining U.S. structural strength will
affect both American strategies of maintaining the world order it desires and
the nature of challenges from major allies and the institutions within which
they work to maintain the status quo. We focus not on those in international
politics who are dissatisfied with the status quo but on essentially status quo
states in the hegemonic core. We do so since we believe that as U.S. hegemonic
strength declines, America is likely to come to depend more on institutions
and groups of states sharing its perspective and commitment to the status
quo.[1] When those relationships weaken, U.S. control over global affairs becomes more tenuous.

Perhaps more controversially, we focus less on strategies to resist U.S.
leadership and more on variation in policy cohesion between America and
its key allies, that is, on policy divergence. It is almost a trivial and obvious
but often ignored point that policy divergence is a critical condition for challenging hegemony.[2] That is almost by definition true for dissatisfied states.
For pro–status quo coalition partners, however, it is not at all obvious that
such policy dissension is or will be substantial. Further, there is often much
less than full understanding of the roots of such policy dissension among the

101

"satisfied" states. While policy dissension can be overcome and challenges to hegemonic U.S. control minimized (even in the core), costs are much higher than when there is policy congruence. The possibility of major challenges to U.S. leadership in the core creates fundamental problems, especially when U.S. leadership requires core support to supplement its capabilities. For these reasons our chapter focuses not on menus of challenge actions and arenas but on the critical condition (policy dissension) that gives rise to their use by others in the hegemonic core.[3]

Finally, we focus not on individual states or regions of evasion, modification, and resistance but specifically on the G-7 as a group and particularly on variation in the G-7's aggregated level of policy cohesion. We do so because the G-7 was established and institutionalized to supplement declining U.S. hegemonic capabilities and, as a group, has overwhelming economic, political, and military capabilities in the international system. For more than a quarter century, spanning both the Cold War and post–Cold War eras, the G-7 has played an important role in maintaining the U.S.-centered international order (Volgy and Bailin 2003). Whether it continues to do so may in no small measure depend on the extent to which its members maintain a substantial degree of policy cohesion regarding critical international problems and the strategies for dealing with them.

The results of our analyses highlight the difficulties G-7 states face in creating a common perspective on new systemic disturbances, such as international terrorism. We suggest that international terrorism is likely to increase both policy disagreements and G-6 challenges to U.S. hegemonic initiatives.[4]

Hegemonic Strength

Hegemony (or global leadership) requires much from a leading state, including preponderant strength along with the motivation, desire, and competence to use it in developing rules and norms for the international system.[5] Strength alone is clearly not enough, nor is it necessarily accompanied by motivation or competence. Nevertheless, global leadership becomes a dangerous illusion in the minds of foreign policy makers if there is not sufficient strength to impose a roadmap on global events and to enforce the rules and norms required for implementing it.[6]

Much of the neorealist literature assumes that sufficient strength will exist among the great powers in the system to allow them to fashion a global architecture. According to these assumptions, changes in the distribution of strength among great powers determine changes in the shape of the system (e.g., unipolar/hegemonic, bipolar, multi-polar) (e.g., Waltz 1979; 1993). For us, it is an empirical question as to whether or not sufficient strength exists to fashion global architecture and to enforce the norms accompanying it, especially with respect to hegemony or global leadership.

What type of strength is needed? Susan Strange (1989) argued forcefully that global leadership requires two types of strength: relational and structural. Relational strength refers to the capabilities of a hegemon or a global leader vis-à-vis other actors in the system and its ability to get some groupings of others, by persuasion or coercion, to do what they would not otherwise do (Strange 1996, 165). Structural strength reflects a different dimension of capabilities, referring to the capacity of a hegemon to create essential rules, norms, and modes of operation for various aspects of the international system. A global leader/hegemon enjoys "structural power through the capacity to determine the terms on which those needs are satisfied and to whom they are made available" (ibid.). Hegemony then creates and/or sustains critical regimes that extend patterns of cooperation and reduce uncertainty as states pursue their objectives.[7]

Strange left operationalizing these two approaches to hegemonic strength to others, a challenge we have pursued previously.[8] The results provide a longitudinal perspective on U.S. strength, covering both the Cold War and the post–Cold War eras. They show important differences between relational and structural strength and suggest important implications for challenges to U.S. hegemony in general, and for the salience of policy congruence within the G-7.

Recall that relational strength involves the types of capabilities needed when responding to dissatisfied states that challenge global rules and norms. In this sense, relational strength is relative to the strength of potential chal-

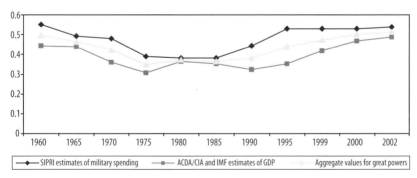

Figure 6.1. Estimates of the U.S. share of great power military and economic capabilities, 1960–2002

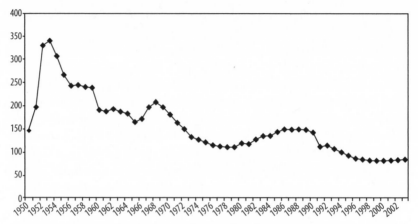

Figure 6.2. Estimate of U.S. structural strength index, 1950–2003

lengers of the status quo.[9] From that perspective, post–Cold War international politics seem unipolar, as the United States seems to exhibit preponderant capabilities, compared to other "great powers."

Figure 6.1 summarizes U.S. relational capabilities, as shares of great-power economic and military capabilities. U.S. relational strength among the great powers is overwhelming, whether in the aggregate or in disaggregated forms. For our most recent data point, U.S. relational capabilities are in excess of 50 percent of all great-power strength.

A very different picture emerges when we view strength from a structural perspective, as seen in figure 6.2. Here, the focus is on the amount of resources made available to foreign activity as modified by both domestic constraints and international system complexities (for example, the growth in system membership and the extent of state autonomy as measured by its international trade dependence as a percentage of GDP).[10] The picture conveyed by the U.S. structural strength index is one of dramatic decline and is nearly monotonic over time. Rather than a picture of stable unipolarity, we have one in which resources for foreign policy activities by the United States have not kept up with changing global circumstances, including the growth and complexity of the international system and the increased loss of autonomy created by growing dependence on international trade. If the measure is a valid one of the strength used to fashion global architecture and help create new rules and norms for the system, then its low levels since the 1970s, and especially since the end of the Cold War, suggest insufficient structural strength for the United States to act hegemonically unless it successfully integrates its resources with those of like-minded core allies.

Policy Dissension within the G-7

The G-7 was created during the mid-1970s to respond to potential systemic disturbances, not coincidentally at a time when both U.S. structural and relational strengths were in decline. The willingness of the G-6 to enter into this institutional arrangement was no doubt facilitated by the reality that the other members of the group were also experiencing declining capabilities vis-à-vis the rest of the world (Volgy and Bailin 2003). Created as a partnership between states in the economic realm (where the United States was the strongest but less than predominant), the G-7's scope has gradually expanded into the political/ military realm (where the United States is much stronger than the other actors). The norms of partnership from the economic realm have been carried over to a variety of noneconomic matters.[11]

When acting together, the G-7 controls a predominant share of military and economic capabilities in the international system. Its control is sufficient to shape the contours of international politics in a manner that the United States simply may not be able to accomplish with its own structural strength.[12] That is why, elsewhere, we have referred to the period between 1975 and 1997 as a period of "group hegemony" in which the G-7 acted as an important institutional mechanism for system maintenance purposes and for designing a new global architecture, albeit incrementally (Volgy and Bailin 2003).

Accordingly, we view the G-7 as a critical mechanism to supplement missing U.S. structural hegemonic strength. That supplement may not be forthcoming unless there is substantial policy congruence among G-7 members. Although the G-7 is now deeply institutionalized, challenges within it to U.S. leadership are likely if and when policy cohesion is substantially diminished.

As Davis Bobrow highlights in chapter 1, there has been a history of disagreement with U.S. strategies and policy preferences, even among states identified as "America's closest 'kin,'" a label clearly represented by the members of the G-7. More recently, the events leading up to the invasion of Iraq underscored substantial divisions between the United States and its G-7 partners. While Britain remained a staunch ally of the United States and eventually Japan and Italy chose to support (albeit nominally) the war option, Germany, France, and Canada challenged American initiatives toward a war-based approach to regime change in Iraq. With the exception of Tony Blair's enthusiastic support, the "coalition of the willing" has been cobbled together overwhelmingly from outside the G-7.

The policy dissension over Iraq is not without precedent. Since the end of the Cold War, French policy makers have consistently questioned American leadership, challenging what they perceived as American hegemony.[13] French,

German, and (even) British policy makers agreed—after the dominant role of the United States in the Bosnian conflict—to create an "independent" military capability for the European Union separate from NATO (and U.S. and Turkish) control (Ginsberg 2001). American withdrawal from the Kyoto Protocol has been denounced by most G-7 states. Japan has at times challenged American leadership in the global political economy, for example, by at one time seeking (in cooperation with China) an alternative financial structure to the International Monetary Fund (IMF) in Asia (Bergsten 2000).

Policy disagreements between the United States and its G-7 colleagues also pre-date the end of the Cold War. French initiatives for an independent foreign policy were featured in its relations with the United States as early as the 1960s and as late as 1986, when France denied "overflight" privileges to U.S. warplanes attacking Libya. German chancellor Willy Brandt's policy initiatives toward the Soviet Union and Eastern Europe pre-dated moves toward détente between the Soviet Union and the United States. For the Italian government, American involvement in Beirut in the early 1980s stimulated major policy differences over the Middle East and Israel.[14] Descriptions of such disagreements fill the pages of analyses of transatlantic relationships (e.g., Hodge 2004; Lindstrom 2003).

Nevertheless, we should be mindful of the larger dynamic uniting G-7 states: policy disagreements have coexisted within a substantially broad range of policy congruence among these status quo powers. For the most part, G-7 states have been satisfied with the direction of affairs in international politics. Policy agreements are crucial for the G-7 to act in concert. The fact that it has often done so indicates that policy disagreements have not been sufficiently disruptive to destroy the ability of the G-7 to act collectively.

Yet troubling questions persist. How much policy cohesion remains in the G-7 when one of the pillars of cohesion—the Cold War—has disappeared? How can we account for the diminution of policy cohesion when any pillar is removed? To answer the first question, we look at two types of data that provide a longitudinal perspective on policy cohesion between G-7 states: alliance portfolios and voting patterns in the General Assembly of the United Nations.

Alliance portfolios have been used previously to indicate similarities in policies and orientations to international relations.[15] Annual observations are available for most states, and there is a substantial history of data validity and reliability. A major disadvantage, however, is that a state's alliance portfolio is not sensitive to rapid fluctuations in the international environment. Even with that caveat, analysis of the alliance portfolios of G-7 states clearly demonstrates a substantially similar policy orientation, showing disruptions only in response to major fluctuations in the international environment (e.g., the end of the Cold War).[16] The absence of policy dissension—except in response to major turbulence—suggests that this measure of policy congruence is insufficiently sensitive to the range of policy disagreements within the G-7. Accordingly, we turn to a second measure, one more controversial but also potentially more sensitive to fluctuations in policy disagreements: commonality in voting on resolutions in the UN General Assembly (UNGA).

While not an ideal way to measure policy cohesion between states, votes cast on UNGA resolutions by powerful states—which are generally satisfied with the status quo—usually reflect little more than their policy preferences on issues. The UNGA may be a quasi-legislative arena for some UN members, but that is not the case for the strongest of states.[17] Few (if any) incentives exist for strong states to deviate from their policy preferences when voting in the UNGA.[18] Also, we find no other available measures or data sets that provide consistent observations of the G-7's policy preferences over its lifetime and over a broad range of issues.

Essentially, there are two methods for assessing the cohesiveness of policy preferences through voting in the UNGA. One uses factor analysis; the other develops a group defection ratio. Factor analysis allows for an empirical, inductive clustering of votes on a variety of dimensions that show the relative cohesiveness of a group of states on those dimensions. Unfortunately, factor analysis limits our observations in two crucial ways. First, given the type of data we have on UNGA voting, factor analysis can at best provide snapshots aggregated to several years rather than annual observations. Second, the method itself generates data that discount a large percentage of contested votes, often dismissing as much as 50 percent of the "explained variance" in voting. Its strength, on the other hand, lies in identifying dimensions of voting over time and the extent to which policy congruence changes on the most salient ones.

Figures 6.3 and 6.4 illustrate both the strengths and weaknesses of the factor analysis method.[19] The two primary dimensions of voting in the UNGA in both the 1990–1992 and 1997–1999 periods consisted of a north-south and a Middle East dimension. Figures 6.3 and 6.4 illustrate very strong policy congruence between all G-7 states on the first dimension and substantial variation between the United States and the G-6 (and within the G-6) on the second dimension in both time periods.

We also examine cohesion by creating a group value for each year's votes and then estimating defections from the group's voting norms. Previous re-

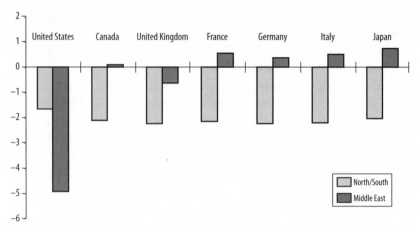

Figure 6.3. Factor values for G-7 states for sessions 45–47 (1990–1992)

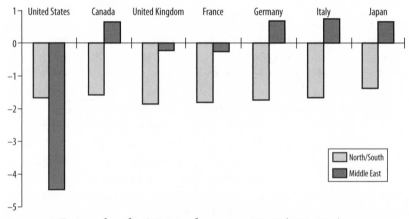

Figure 6.4. Factor values for G-7 states for sessions 52–54 (1997–1999)

search examining the cohesion of third world states in the UNGA used the same defection ratio measure to estimate the deviation of individual members from a common group position.[20]

Figure 6.5 displays the annual defection ratio for the G-7 from its inception through 2003. We include in the figure the defection ratio for the UNGA as a whole to allow for a comparison between the relative cohesiveness of the G-7 and a General Assembly that is meant to be relatively cohesive.[21] We also display "individual" state defections in figure 6.6.

Figures 6.5 and 6.6 reveal considerably more variation in policy congruence than indicated by alliance portfolio data, although there is some corre-

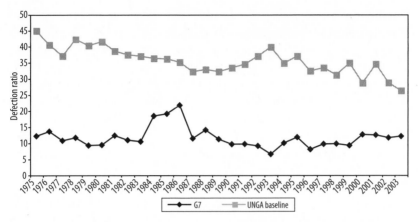

Figure 6.5. Defection scores for the UN General Assembly as a whole and for G-7 states, 1975–2003

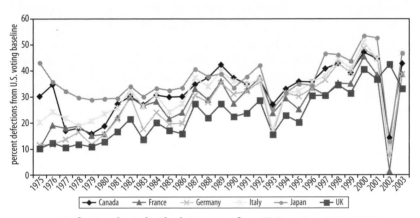

Figure 6.6. Defections by individual G-7 states from U.S. voting, 1975–2003

spondence (and therefore a bit more validation for the voting measure) between the two. For example, the alliance portfolios indicate that Japan is most remote and the UK is most proximate to the United States. The voting data average scores on individual state defections reflect these relationships.[22] In a similar vein, as the congruence of alliance portfolios declines after the end of the Cold War, so does voting congruence with the United States after 1989 for all the G-6 states.[23]

Two trends merit further note. First, while policy disagreements with the George W. Bush administration are clearly noticeable in the data (showing post–Cold War level highs in defections among G-7 states), they appear to indicate a broader pattern of growing policy disagreements with post–Cold War American administrations. Although the Iraq war and the policy disagreements over American use of coercion to achieve regime change received the most public debate, a substantial amount of policy disagreement already existed, as it did prior to 9/11. Second, the pattern of defections continues to underscore substantial underlying policy agreements between the G-7 states compared to the level of policy agreements within the global community as a whole (see figure 6.5).[24] This is consistent with the notion that the G-7 includes primarily very powerful states that benefit from the global status quo.

Accounting for Policy Dissension in the G-7

The evidence presented, including both the factor analysis and defection ratio results, offers a twofold image regarding policy cohesiveness within the G-7 and consequently for concurrence with U.S. hegemonic leadership. On the one hand, there has been—and continues to be—a substantial amount of policy cohesion within the group. On the other hand, there is significant variation in cohesiveness, both before and after the Cold War. While there is a notable decline in policy support of hegemonic preferences after 1989—with the collapse of the Cold War pillar of the status quo—the post-1989 period has not been the only period of significant policy dissent. Although there has been more individual country deviation from U.S. preferences since 1989, the substantial variation in policy congruence before the end of the Cold War is consistent with Bobrow's injunction in chapter 1 that challenges to U.S. global leadership are a phenomenon not unique to present circumstances.

Our primary task then becomes discerning reasons for variation in G-7 policy cohesiveness across both the Cold War and post–Cold War periods. Recall that the G-7 was created in the belief that institutionalization of the group, in the context of common policy preferences toward the status quo and within a framework of overwhelming strength, would facilitate collective responses to systemic disturbances and challenges to the international status quo. The G-7 was also intended to help create the new norms and rules that would be needed. The G-7 envisioned three types of systemic disturbances: interstate wars, crises, and turbulence within the global economy. These are "typical" disturbances in the sense that much of international politics has been historically focused on them. Much of the cohesion the G-7 has historically demonstrated was due to the similarity in policy preferences of states relatively satisfied with the status quo in response to traditional systemic disturbances. Thus, we do not expect interstate wars, interstate crises, and global economic threats to have a negative impact on G-7 cohesiveness.[25]

Instead, the cohesiveness of G-7 policy preferences is more likely to be tested by relatively new types of systemic disturbances affecting the status quo. Two such types are international terrorism and intrastate conflicts. Both are relatively "new" in international politics, at least in their scope and the growth of their impact on relations between states.

While terrorists have acted throughout the history of international politics, the sheer magnitude of recent international terrorist activity since 1968 presents disturbances relatively new to the international system.[26] As the events of September 11, 2001, demonstrated, international terrorism has come to rival—if not surpass—interstate wars in its potential to disrupt international politics.

International terrorism has clearly left its mark on the last third of the twentieth century. An average of more than four hundred international terrorist acts annually has been recorded by the U.S. State Department since 1968.[27] The United States, the one G-7 state relatively immune to international terrorism on its own soil, experienced the shock of the destruction of the World Trade Center towers. Even before 9/11, while the frequency of terrorism declined in the 1990s compared to earlier periods, the level of violence per attack increased significantly (Müller 2003, 24).

Growth in the volume of intrastate war qualifies it as another new type of systemic disturbance that has become a numerically far larger threat to the status quo than interstate wars. In the nineteenth century, roughly 60 percent of all wars were international (interstate) in character. By the last third of the twentieth century intrastate wars constituted 70 percent of all conflicts (Sarkees, Wayman, and Singer 2003). Over the last quarter of the twentieth century, nearly three such conflicts occurred per year, at a total loss of nearly 9 million lives, compared to fewer than 1.3 million lives lost in interstate wars (Sarkees, Wayman, and Singer 2003, 65). Furthermore, intrastate violence contributes substantially to turbulence internationally because it often results in large migration flows that create additional ethnic conflicts, militarized interstate disputes, and occasionally interstate wars.[28]

Both "new" types of disturbances pose substantial challenges to the international status quo and to the G-7's leadership and maintenance of global relations. As relatively new phenomena, they challenge existing G-7 institutional mechanisms. Involving essentially nonstate actors, they threaten historically embedded norms and rules regarding the primacy of interstate relations. What then explains variation in the cohesiveness of the G-7 under these conditions?

Domestic Politics and Foreign Policy Congruence

We primarily approach policy makers' responses to new systemic disturbances from the perspective of domestic politics.[29] Key foreign policy makers are domestic political actors. While they may pursue critical foreign policy objectives, they are at least as motivated by domestic political considerations—and view new systemic disturbances through domestic political lenses—as they are by foreign policy considerations.[30]

From a domestic political perspective, all new systemic disturbances are not alike. There are at least three types: disturbances with minimal immediate and/or long-term domestic political consequences in any of the G-7 states; disturbances with similar, substantial short- and long-term domestic political consequences in all of the G-7 states; and disturbances with varying, substantial domestic political consequences for G-7 members. Fashioning policy congruence among the G-7 nations on systemic disturbances that have minimal domestic political costs or have similar domestic political costs should not pose great difficulties. Systemic disturbances laden with different but large domestic political costs for G-7 members are the ones most likely to create policy dissension and defections from U.S. policy preferences.

We think this has been happening when G-7 members entertain a collective response to international terrorism, an issue that carries with it at least two types of nonuniform domestic political consequences for G-7 members: selectorate turmoil and domestic security risks. Terrorism carries the potential of selectorate turmoil by creating or increasing conflicts within the selectorates and winning coalitions that determine the political fortunes of G-7 governments (Bueno de Mesquita et al. 2000). G-7 states vary greatly in the nature and composition of their selectorates—for example, in the size of their Arab and Muslim populations. In France, for example, nearly 10 percent of its population consists of Arabs and Muslims, while Japan's Muslim population is negligible. Subgroups may withhold support from their governments in solidarity with groups being targeted as terrorists from the Middle East. Just as difficult from a political perspective, such electoral groups may clash with others within the domestic political system over Middle East issues. We do not expect a uniform impact on the G-7 through such selectorate turmoil, but that is precisely the point: different domestic electoral situations will lead to different foreign policy positions on international terrorism.

A second domestic political consideration regarding terrorism involves varied perceptions and experiences of domestic security risks. If G-7 members articulate strong common policy responses to terrorism, they run the risk of increasing terrorist violence affecting all members of the group. Foreign policy makers experiencing little or no terrorist activity at home risk becoming terrorist targets, and—through their foreign policy decisions—of alienating their selectorate for having increased national insecurity. Even for those G-7 members with extensive previous experience with terrorism, there is considerable variability in success in dealing with it and in the willingness to risk more incidents by partaking in a common, U.S.-favored counter-terrorism policy.[31]

We do not expect such domestic political considerations to have a uniform impact on all G-7 states. Britain, for instance, with a long history of terrorism experience, is likely to respond differently than Japan. American policy makers post-9/11 are likely to see terrorism in a different light than the French, who survived the terrorist attacks of the 1980s and 1990s and may be less likely to take the risk of another round on French soil. Domestic political considerations regarding security may drive an American president and a French president to far different policy perspectives in the aftermath of tragedies from international terrorist attacks.[32]

Since international terrorism is laden with varying domestic political costs for G-7 members, we expect that increasing levels of international terrorist activity pose conditions conducive to G-6 challenges to U.S. leadership in counter-terrorism, that is, less policy cohesion in the G-7.[33] Our expectations about how the G-7 addresses intrastate conflicts are very different because their impact on the domestic politics of G-7 members differs in kind from that of international terrorism. Most intrastate conflicts will either not translate directly into the domestic politics of G-7 states (e.g., the Sudanese civil war), or, if they do, they will likely have a uniform domestic political impact on most G-7 states (for instance, a civil war in Saudi Arabia). While some intrastate conflicts may have differing domestic political impacts on G-7 members (e.g., the conflicts in Bosnia and Kosovo), those are likely to be relatively rare compared to the variation in the domestic consequences of international terrorism. Accordingly, our domestic politics approach should be of significant help in accounting for G-7 responses to international terrorism but not for G-7 policy congruence in dealing with intrastate conflicts.

Alternative Perspectives

Due to their prominence in international relations theorizing, two alternatives that may help account for fluctuations in G-7 policy cohesiveness deserve our attention. A realist/neorealist explanation emphasizes the relative strength of the dominant actor (the United States) in a group (the G-7); a liberal/institutionalist explanation emphasizes patterns of institutionalized cooperation within the group in response to potential threats to the status quo. These alternatives challenge the value of the domestic politics explanation and may shed more light on G-7 responses to intrastate conflicts.

While realist/neorealist accounts of conflict and cooperation (where cohesion is one aspect of cooperation) come in many forms (see, e.g., Schweller and Priess 1997), they share a primary focus on the relative power capabilities of major actors in international affairs while disagreeing on how power and relative strength matter. Hegemons, or states with asymmetrically strong capabilities, may deter conflict with potential competitors and foster cooperation through leadership (Mastanduno 1997). Alternatively, sustained periods of predominance can foster coalitions against a dominant nation (Modelski 1987; Rasler and Thompson 1994). Relative parity between states may foster much greater competition—all things being equal—among states than asymmetrical power relationships (Lemke and Werner 1996). Additionally, power transitions between states may be symptomatic of ongoing challenges to the lead nation and the global status quo, or the dynamics of such transitions may motivate (dissatisfied) states to reconsider their roles and opportunities, leading to greater conflict between states (see, e.g., Doran 1989; Tammen et al. 2000).

Although competing concepts and operational measures are involved and sometimes yield contradictory results (see, e.g., DeSoysa, Oneal, and Park 1997; Mansfield 1993), the idea that power and relative strength matter in shaping patterns of conflict and cooperation between major states continues to enjoy currency. At first glance the idea appears to be relevant for an analysis of G-7 cohesiveness. Since the United States is the strongest of the G-7 actors, variation in its strength relative to the group should influence the group's cohesiveness. As American strength increases, the United States' ability to influence how G-7 actors view and respond to global circumstances should be enhanced. The more other G-7 states reach parity with the United States, the more they may question American policy positions. The G-7's policy cohesiveness when faced with either intrastate conflicts or international terrorist threats will covary with relative American strength.

The liberal/institutionalist tradition offers yet another perspective. Most relevant here is John Ikenberry's theorizing about the dynamics driving the creation and maintenance of global order mechanisms.[34] International governance institutions are possible because members benefit more from cooperation relative to the cost of participation and the surrendering of some autonomy, and they gain when the major power in the system (such as the United States) surrenders some sovereignty through its willingness to abide by institutional rules (rules that are consistent with its own interest). Thus, irrespective of power differences, members cooperate through major institutional arrangements and do so to help perpetuate their interests. For the G-7, that interest is warding off threats to the status quo.

Given a successful, institutionalized history of cooperation between G-7 members and all else being equal, the members will continue to use existing institutional mechanisms and respond similarly to systemic disturbances and threats to the international status quo. The G-7's cohesion would increase when such threats occur. Intrastate conflicts will increase G-7 cohesion, since such conflicts have substantial consequences for immigration flows, other intrastate and interstate ethnic conflicts, militarized interstate disputes, and even interstate wars—all of which can have substantially negative consequences for the status quo.

For assessing these claims, the UNGA voting measure of defections (designated in the test that follows as "defect"), reported in figure 6.5, serves as the dependent variable. We use four independent variables to predict changing levels of G-7 cohesion. The first is simply the defection ratio lagged (the variable "LDR"). We use it to assess the extent to which the previous level of cohesion may have an impact on the present level.[35] A second independent variable assesses the relative strength of the United States vis-à-vis the rest of the G-7 using an aggregate measure that averages U.S. military spending and GDP, divides that average by the index for the group (the variable "LUSRS"), and lags it one year behind the other variables.[36] The third independent variable deals with the frequency of intrastate conflicts annually in the international system (labeled "DMCON").[37] The fourth independent variable is based on annual frequencies of international terrorist acts (labeled as "TERROR").[38] Overall, we use the following model to predict defections:

Defect = LDR – LUSRS – DMCON + TERROR.

Besides the base model, we applied regression analysis to three others, as shown in table 6.1. The external disturbance model is meant to capture a range of interstate challenges to the status quo. The "factored-in" model represents the cumulative effects of interstate wars and crises on levels of defection. The mixed disturbance model focuses on both domestic and external disturbances. We test these alternative models for two reasons. First, crises and interstate wars may already be "factored" into the policy cohesiveness of the group and thus be unlikely to predict variation in G-7 defection scores.[39] This argument finds support in equation 2a (see table 6.1). Second, these disturbances may amount to exogenous considerations that alter policy commonalities between G-7 members. That is, they may nullify the predicted relationship between policy cohesion, intrastate conflicts, and terrorism by giving priority to more established concerns about crises and wars. If, however, the relationships predicted by our base model are robust, then we should be able to find them even in models that include disturbances such as crises and interstate wars (equations 2 and 3; see table 6.1).

Table 6.1 shows that, consistent with our predictions, the models yield no significant relationship between varying levels of U.S. relational strength and variation in G-7 defection scores. Relational strength seems to contribute little

Table 6.1. OLS regression equations for G-7 defection ratios with selected independent variables

	Equation 1 (predicted model)	Equation 2 (external disturbance model)	Equation 2a (factored-in model)	Equation 3 (internal/external disturbance model)
LDR	.022 (.107)			
TERROR	.021*** (.006)	.022*** (.007)		.021*** (.006)
LUSRS	−5.542 (24.975)	.601 (30.586)		−9.739 (28.5)
DMCON	−.238* (.116)			−.237* (.115)
CRISES		−.04 (.206)	.201 (.185)	−.068 (.187)
WARS		−.447 (.651)	−.087 (.755)	
Constant	5.046 (12.107)	2.023 (15.044)	10.45*** (1.456)	7.396 (14.048)
R^2	.49	.40	.05	.49
Adjusted R^2	.39	.28	.03	.39
Probability > F	.007	.029	ns	.007
N	25	25	26	25

* $p = .06$
** $p \leq .01$
*** $p \leq .001$ (standard errors in parentheses)

to policy cohesion in the G-7.[40] In addition, the results for the predicted model indicate that lagging the defection ratio adds little to the amount of variation explained. Unsurprisingly, the group's prior level of defection does not predict its present level of defection. This should come as no surprise: UNGA resolutions change substantially from year to year, and G-7 responses to these resolutions are primarily a function of policy preferences rather than legislative dynamics that may endure across sessions of the UN.

Variation in the frequency of intrastate conflicts does have a modest impact on the group's defection ratio. The relationship between this variable and the defection ratio is negative, as expected for the predicted model and the internal/external disturbance model, suggesting that increased levels of intrastate conflict are associated with modest decreases in the group's defection ratio.

On the matter central to the previous domestic politics reasoning, however, there is a very strong negative relationship between the frequency of terrorist activity and G-7 cohesiveness, as demonstrated by its significance level and positive relationship with the defection ratio. The relationship is dramatically evident for the predicted external disturbance and the internal/external disturbance models. We reasoned earlier that there are substantial differences among G-7 members in the anticipated domestic political costs for a unified approach to international terrorism. We expected to find substantial policy differences in response to increased international terrorist activity, and that is precisely what table 6.1 shows.[41]

Finally, as suggested by the results for the factored-in model, the typical systemic disturbances of interstate wars and crises appear to have no significant impact on the G-7's defection ratio. As noted earlier, those types of events have long been of concern to the G-7 and appear to act more as constants than variables in accounting for G-7 policy cohesion. Results for the external disturbance and the internal/external disturbance models suggest that variation in crises or in interstate wars does not reduce the impacts of intrastate conflicts and terrorist activity on the G-7's defection ratio.

The Future of G-7 Policy Congruence and Challenges to the United States

Our findings suggest a number of conclusions regarding the likelihood that even within the G-7 we will find increased challenges of evasion, modification, and even resistance to U.S. leadership in the future.

The typical "old" systemic challenges to the status quo are likely to be met with a relatively unified policy response in the near future, as they have been in the past.[42] G-7 states will likely exhibit similar policy preferences when major interstate conflicts erupt, interstate crises threaten established norms of international affairs, or international economic turbulence threatens the well-being of G-7 states. These types of issues will continue to generate relative consensus and little resistance to American leadership if the United States employs the G-7's institutions and pursues its own policies in consultation with its G-7 partners (unlike U.S. Iraq policy).

The greater dangers for policy defection and G-6 challenges to U.S. leadership revolve around issues that are relatively new (and for which there are no well-developed, relatively successful, institutionalized group responses) and that pose differential and significant domestic political consequences for the member governments.

International terrorism is one such divisive issue. While there has been substantial collaboration between G-7 members in certain areas (e.g., hindering terrorist economic networks and sharing intelligence), more visible tactics in the hunt for terrorist organizations and states that may harbor them are likely to continue to create major rifts.

Although clearly not the identical issue, nor one that is particularly new, the Middle East conflict, and especially the relationship between Israel and Palestine, and their surrounding neighbors, is fraught with consequences similar to the issue of international terrorism. Throughout the Cold War and its aftermath, U.S. leadership on this issue has been aggressively challenged by some of the G-7 members and, as shown in figures 6.3 and 6.4, has substantially split the group. We suspect that a significant reason again involves the domestic political consequences associated with an international issue. Those differences have not yet split the G-7 on a permanent basis. The current intersection between this issue, the ongoing conflict in Iraq, and differences over how to combat international terrorism makes it more problematic than before for G-7 partners. Even as staunch an ally as Tony Blair demanded that the United States create a new peace process in the Middle East in exchange for continued British support in Iraq. Joint German, French, and British efforts under a common EU umbrella to negotiate Iran's nuclear capabilities—coupled with a skeptical response by the United States—underscore further the divisive nature of the Middle East for G-7 partners.[43]

It is likely as well that U.S. leadership also will be challenged in other issue areas, particularly when domestic political consequences divide the G-7. Global ecological issues, as illustrated by conflicts over the Kyoto Protocol (discussed in chapter 8 of this volume), constitute a relatively new issue area for the G-7 and have substantial domestic political consequences for member states with large "green" groupings within their selectorates. Even for U.S. policy makers, political support within the prevailing coalition appears critically dependent on domestic actors unwilling to risk the economic impact of timely achievement of the goals of the protocol.

Changes to the membership of the G-7 constitute another potential problem for continued policy cohesion. With the exception of Japan, the other members of the group as of 2007 carry very similar alliance portfolios, reflecting similar orientations to international affairs. All of the G-7 states are democracies, with widely varying selectorates but similarly democratic processes determining the fortunes of political leaders. That is not the case with Russia, the next state likely to become a full member of the group. Russian domestic politics play out with dramatically different rules than those of the G-7 states, and Russian policy makers are likely to respond with different domestic imperatives in mind.[44] This divergence is likely to be magnified by a generic Russian orientation to international politics substantially different from that of the original G-7 members.[45]

The addition of China to the G-7 would amplify these differences even further. China would bring a new group of policy makers to the G-7 table, and they would be responsive to a pattern of domestic politics with an even narrower selectorate than that of Russia and even less exposed to democratic processes. Further, its foreign policy preferences have been demonstrably different from not only the G-7 but also Russia (Volgy et al. 2003). It is not likely that an institution historically based on the relative homogeneity of its members—both in terms of preference for the international status quo and the democratic nature of their polities—would be able to survive such a challenge to its cohesiveness.

Finally, there is much that remains unexplained by the previous analysis. Statistically speaking, our best model does account for nearly half of the variation—an outcome that is substantial given no more than four variables per equation—but nearly half of the variation in G-7 cohesion remains unexplained. The power of that model, based on the domestic politics approach, may well be substantially increased by inserting one of the missing elements often used in domestic politics explanations of foreign policies: the foreign policy orientations that new political elites bring to office (Bueno de Mesquita 2003). Newly elected, appointed, and promoted foreign policy makers are more than just domestic political actors and may well have foreign policy orientations and interests that differ from one G-7 state to the next.

Who is in office is likely to matter, but primarily in the context of broader forces working in domestic and international politics. For example, the foreign policy orientations found in the Bush administration, tempered by domestic political dynamics, have been far from identical to the foreign policy orientations of Bill Clinton's presidency. If domestic political imperatives and external pressures had remained the same across the two administrations, fundamental differences in policy orientations might have been more muted and difficult to detect. As contexts and pressures changed, as they obviously did after 9/11, foreign policy orientations favoring more unilateral action and regime change came to the fore under George W. Bush in a manner quite different from what would have likely played out under Bill Clinton or Al Gore with their different initial policy preferences. Obviously, building in policy makers' beginning preferences could improve our model's capacity to predict G-7 policy cohesion.

To conclude, arguments and evidence have been presented that underscore the importance of varying domestic political conditions for policy congruence with and divergence from the United States in the G-7. While much remains to be done, it seems clear that domestic factors play a central role in determining on what issues what governments will mount challenges to U.S. policy preferences from within the core of the American-centered part of the international system.

7

THWARTING U.S. MISSILE DEFENSE FROM WITHIN THE MISSILE TECHNOLOGY CONTROL REGIME

DENNIS M. GORMLEY

America's accretion of military, economic, and "soft" power since the end of World War II has led most scholars and security practitioners to assume an incontrovertible U.S. dominance of the international security system. Yet there are subtle actions that states might wish to take to increase the costs or call into question the effectiveness of U.S. dominance. This case study examines how states may thwart America's presumed dominance in military power—specifically the perceived effectiveness of its global missile defenses—through actions taken from within the thirty-four-nation Missile Technology Control Regime (MTCR). The MTCR is the only existing multilateral mechanism governing the transfer of missiles and related technologies relevant to the delivery of weapons of mass destruction (WMD).[1] In terms of the framework in chapter 1, the MTCR case illustrates the actions of fait accompli, consent and exploit, and consent and deceive. The pertinent arenas are the unilateral and coalition of the unwilling types and especially IGOs to which the United States belongs.

Global missile defenses consist of regional missile defenses protecting U.S. forward-based forces and America's friends and allies and national missile defenses protecting the American homeland against rogue-state or non-state actor missile attacks. U.S. national security strategy no longer depends as heavily as it once did on nuclear deterrence. Instead, American defense policy formulations reflect a transition to a denial strategy, one that depends critically on the broadly perceived effectiveness of denying one's adversaries the achievement of their military objectives. Although global missile defenses are by no means the only component of America's emerging denial strategy, they are expected to play a central role. Missile defense effectiveness will hinge chiefly on meeting important technical challenges largely defined by the quality and number of offensive missiles that attempt penetration. Thus, the MTCR, which seeks member-state adherence to an agreed-upon set of export-control guidelines on missiles and technology, offers an important example of how others might thwart the effectiveness of U.S. global missile defenses and thus America's deterrence-by-denial strategy.

From Nuclear Deterrence to Deterrence by Denial

Until very recently nuclear deterrence formed the foundation of U.S. national security strategy. Nuclear weapons were expected to deter strikes not only on the American homeland but also upon allies in Europe and Asia. Nuclear deterrence hinged critically on the delivery of a devastating second-strike attack against the Soviet Union, although the nuclear utility theorists sought more discrete attack options than those associated with mutual assured destruction (Ikle and Wohlstetter 1988). The end of the Cold War found a growing community of nuclear abolitionists arguing that a rare historical turning point had been reached in the long-standing quest to eliminate nuclear weapons globally (Report of the Canberra Commission 1996).

Coming on the heels of the collapse of the Soviet Union and dissolution of the Warsaw Pact, the performance of precision guided conventional strike munitions (PGMs) during the first Gulf War triggered a reassessment of nuclear weapons policy within the defense community. Although virtually all the weapons used during that conflict were decades old and no new doctrinal, conceptual, or organizational innovation was displayed, signs of revolutionary progress were evident in the use of PGMs. While constituting less than 5 percent of the weapons employed, PGMs demonstrated at least an order of magnitude increase in effectiveness over unguided air-delivered bombs (Keaney and Cohen 1993, 243).

The idea that "smart" conventional weapons might represent a far more credible and usable instrument of deterrence and warfighting was expressed by many military officers. In a series of RAND Corporation–sponsored war games (1991–1993), military participants generally found nuclear weapons largely extraneous because smart conventional weapons seemed capable of destroying virtually every military target that had once been assigned to nuclear weapons (Millot 1993, 50–51).

The views of Paul H. Nitze, a principal architect of America's Soviet containment and nuclear deterrence policy, had especially great impact. Nitze argued that the time had come for the United States to reexamine its long-standing reliance on nuclear deterrence. The threat of nuclear retaliation would be unlikely to deter aggression by regional powers. Even more important, American decision makers would be unwilling to use nuclear weapons to punish such aggression. Accordingly, Nitze recommended converting the principal U.S. strategic deterrent from nuclear weapons to conventional PGMs. Such a conventional strategic force would furnish the United States with a more credible and flexible deterrent. According to Nitze, "It may well be that conventional strategic weapons will one day perform their primary mission of deterrence immeasurably better than nuclear weapons if only because we can—and will—use them" (*Washington Post,* Jan. 16, 1994).

In that context, the Bush administration in January 2002 issued its Nuclear Posture Review (NPR), required by the National Defense Authorization Act of fiscal year 2001.[2] The review was greeted largely as evidence of growing U.S. reliance on nuclear weapons (Gormley 2006b). Attention immediately was focused on the NPR's call for the potential development of new types of nuclear weapons designed to destroy deeply buried underground targets. Lost in the noise were the report's truly revolutionary features that augured transformation of strategic deterrence away from nuclear dependence and increasingly toward a combination of conventional offensive and defensive forces.

The NPR's denial strategy hinges on developing credible warfighting options to deny potential adversaries the capacity to harm America and its allies and friends—most notably by using WMD. Because post–Cold War threats are more diverse, the NPR calls for better integration of the full range of offensive and defensive weapons and doctrines. While this integration includes nuclear and conventional weapons, it is far more likely that conventional ones will become the primary means of executing America's new denial strategy. This is due not only to their potential effectiveness but also because decision makers are vastly more likely to use conventional than nuclear options.

The NPR of 2002 takes on the credibility issue in a radically new way. It joins Nitze's notion of the strategic conventional strike to a greatly reduced nuclear stockpile, active and passive missile defenses, and a revitalized nuclear infrastructure to create a "New Triad." The NPR argues that the New Triad will actually reduce U.S. dependence on nuclear weapons while improving the ability to deter attack because of increasingly robust long-range conventional strike and missile defense capabilities. With global missile defenses, the United States will be less dependent on nuclear strike systems to enforce deterrence; with global conventional strike forces, it will be less reliant on nuclear forces for offensive deterrent capability.

A Primer for Making Missile Defenses Effective

Achieving the truly revolutionary transformation of global strike and missile defense capabilities will rest as much on conceptual and organizational agility as on technological achievement. The history of purported "revolutions in military affairs" attests to the shortsightedness of focusing only on the technological challenges of military transformation (Knox and Murray 2001).

Despite persistent development problems and the elimination of any realistic, system-level flight testing, the U.S. Missile Defense Agency (MDA) pressed ahead and met President George W. Bush's directive of December 2002 to deploy initial missile defense capabilities beginning in 2004.[3] Although the Bush administration's objective is to provide a layered defense of the entire U.S. homeland, American overseas forces, friends, and allies, the first increment of global missile defenses will consist only of twenty ground-based interceptors (GBIs) employing exoatmospheric kill vehicles (EKVs), three Aegis-class cruisers/destroyers armed with Standard Missile-3 interceptors (SM-3s), and an unspecified number of Patriot PAC-3 interceptors. These interceptors are to be supported by various early warning and command, control, and communications capabilities. Secretary of Defense Donald Rumsfeld claimed that as a set they would provide a "better than nothing" shield against a limited number of enemy ballistic missiles (quoted by Bradley Graham, *Washington Post,* Jan. 22, 2004).

Missile defense proponents argue that the president's rush to deploy has been driven by strategic imperatives, not domestic political necessity. Critics see a determination to deliver on a long-standing Republican Party policy commitment that may lead to neglect of more imminent threats. Beneath the political disagreements lie substantive differences between diametrically opposed acquisition strategies. For critics who support a more traditional "fly-before-you-buy" strategy, any missile defense system should undergo enough operational testing to determine its potential effectiveness, suitability, and survivability in combat before a commitment to full-rate production or deployment. Missile defense supporters, in contrast, abjure relying on extensive intercept flight tests to determine system reliability and performance and would rely instead on flight simulation and a system architecture based on block development in which product improvements are made roughly every two years. They recognize the risks inherent in their approach but argue that it would be negligent to deny the nation at least some capability, however problematic, to meet an "urgent need" to defend against ballistic missiles. Some Pentagon officials argue that even an unproven missile defense system will provide some degree of deterrence by notifying adversaries that the United

States has fielded at least some missile defense (Bradley Graham, *Washington Post,* Feb. 2, 2004).

The presumptive threat emanates from North Korea, which first tested a three-stage Taepo-Dong-1 missile in 1998 (although only the first two stages worked). Then, after negotiations with the United States in 1999, it announced a moratorium on long-range missile testing, only to resume testing in July 2006 with multiple launches of several ballistic missiles, including the Taepo-Dong-2, which failed after forty-two seconds of flight. Resumption of testing may indicate Pyongyang's intention to pursue a two-stage or three-stage truly intercontinental missile capable of striking U.S. territory. Critically important, too, is North Korea's development of countermeasures against U.S. defense interceptors. The CIA believes that a country capable of developing long-range ballistic missiles can also produce simple but effective countermeasures that could potentially weaken or cripple a limited defensive system (Sessler et al. 2000).[4]

The most significant technical hurdle in the way of even a patchwork missile defense capability concerns the production of an operational launch booster capable of carrying the exoatmospheric kill vehicle into space. The missile defense program has also failed to deal with problems in midcourse tracking and discrimination, particularly when countermeasures are employed. These problems aside, the GBI finally had a successful missile intercept test on August 31, 2006, after a series of embarrassing test failures. The sea-based Aegis defensive system has encountered far fewer problems than the GBI midcourse segment. After seven successful intercept tests and more than ten tracking tests, in September 2006 the latest version was certified for deployment.

Notably absent from the initial defense capability plan is any capacity to intercept ballistic missiles in the boost phase of their flight—a phase lasting no longer than three to five minutes while the target missile thrusts to gain acceleration to reach the early midcourse phase outside the earth's atmosphere. Although the boost phase is short, successful interception would destroy the missile before countermeasures are deployed, regardless of the missile's range or intended aim-point. Ideally, boost-phase intercept furnishes global protection against ballistic missiles. More practically, it complements the limitations inherent in each segment of a layered missile defense system. The United States has under way two programs aimed at furnishing some boost-phase defense capability: the Airborne Laser program and a sea-based program involving high-acceleration interceptors, likely to be deployed on Aegis-class ships. More controversial space-based options, entailing strikes from low-earth-orbit satellites, may be examined in a test-bed configuration by 2010. This array of possible options attests to the importance of intercepting missiles as they are being launched.

For protecting U.S. forces, friends, and allies abroad, additional Patriot PAC-3 and Aegis-based interceptors would eventually complement the U.S. Army's Theater High Altitude Area Defense (THAAD) system, designed to intercept short- and medium-range ballistic missiles at high altitude. The Airborne Laser program would also focus on shorter-range missile threats. The decision to place the midcourse GBI system on alert at Fort Greely earlier than planned may have stemmed in part from lessons learned in March 2003. That was when Patriot PAC-3 hit-to-kill interceptors were rushed into service prior to the U.S.-led invasion of Iraq despite repeated problems experienced during PAC-3's operational testing (author interview of defense industry official, Sept. 15, 2004). Earlier Patriot models had performed poorly during the Gulf War in 1991.[5]

During the invasion of Iraq in 2003, Patriot missile batteries performed admirably against Iraq's short-range ballistic missiles (all nine of their threatening missile launches were intercepted and destroyed) but failed to detect or intercept five low-flying, antiquated Iraqi cruise missiles. Also, two Iraqi ultralight aircraft (very light piloted airplanes) that U.S. intelligence officials feared might carry chemical or biological agents were belatedly detected (but not engaged). They were spotted only after flying over a U.S. Army division's troops, equipment, and command facilities prior to the unit's advance on Baghdad. Iraq's use of low-flying cruise missiles and slow-flying ultralights also contributed to the Patriot's unfortunate series of friendly-fire incidents, two of which led to the loss of two aircraft and the deaths of three crew members (Gormley 2003).

These events are sad reminders of the weak state of cruise-missile defenses, which, by comparison with the high priority given to ballistic missile defense, have always been treated as an afterthought. In fiscal year 2005, for example, the Pentagon requested $9.2 billion for ballistic missile defense and a paltry $239 million for cruise missile defense (Rumsfeld 2004). This situation may be desperate, but it is not hopeless. Solutions have less to do with seemingly insurmountable technological challenges than with new conceptual and organizational thinking and determined leadership.

Perhaps the most egregious weakness impairing cruise missile defenses is inadequate connectivity among each military service's air defense systems because of unique military service data links using different techniques for target tracking. Improving the capacity to distinguish friendly aircraft from enemy cruise missiles will require merging various service and MDA battle management command, control, and communications programs to achieve connectivity. The quest for a joint approach, now known as the Single Integrated Air Picture (SIAP), was initiated as far back as 1969 to improve tactical air control but has yet to be realized. However much improved tracking through SIAP interoperability makes sense, its effectiveness depends ultimately on improved airborne sensors for detecting low- and slow-flying cruise missiles and unmanned air vehicles (UAVs).[6] Given that each Patriot PAC-3 interceptor costs between $2 million and $5 million, about 60 percent of which is attributable to the missile seeker (Gormley 2001), cheaper seekers will become essential for dealing with saturation attacks from much cheaper cruise missiles.

If regional cruise missile defenses are a difficult challenge, protecting the homeland against both offshore and domestic cruise missile threats is even more daunting—and perhaps more expensive. Cruise missiles or UAVs might be launched from concealed locations at modest distances from their targets or brought within range and launched from freighters or container ships—in effect, a "two-stage" form of delivery (Central Intelligence Agency 2002). Progress in national cruise missile defense will not be made without corresponding improvements to respective service programs and actually implementing the SIAP program. Affordability looms large also, since even a limited defense against offshore cruise missiles would cost $30 billion to $40 billion.

As for dealing with unmanned threats launched from domestic points of origin, America's capacity remains virtually nonexistent. A U.S. House of Representatives hearing on July 8, 2004, drew grim attention to the lax state of America's defenses against low-flying airplanes by examining the near-catastrophic circumstances surrounding the funeral for President Ronald Reagan. On that occasion, June 9, 2004, the governor of Kentucky's official airplane was mistakenly identified as a possible terrorist threat.[7] The nation will remain ill prepared to cope with such threats for the foreseeable future. The best defense one might hope for is a preferential form that protects the nation's capital, other major urban areas, and critical infrastructure targets.

Perceiving and Reacting to Missile Defense Effectiveness

Missile defenses help deny adversaries the achievement of their military objectives. The perceived effectiveness of missile defenses, whether seen from an adversary's or a U.S. perspective, is a product of more than just how well active missile defenses on their own are seen or expected to perform. To contend with ballistic and cruise missile attacks, the Joint Chiefs of Staff embrace a multi-faceted doctrine comprising attack operations (or counterforce), active defenses (Patriot, GBI, etc.), and passive defenses (e.g., vaccines for biological attack). Although the lion's share of funding goes to active missile defenses, military planners recognize that counterforce strikes offer "the greatest lever-age at [the] lowest cost," as one U.S. Air Force briefing put it, because they find and attack missiles, launchers, warheads, and supporting infrastructure, preferably before they are used (Gormley 1999). Leverage derives from destroy-ing the warhead on enemy rather than friendly territory and eliminating the missile defense challenge of coping with countermeasures in the subsequent midcourse phase. The military services have achieved notable progress in counterforce capabilities since their abysmal performance in finding and at-tacking Iraqi Scuds during the Gulf War in 1991 (Gormley 2006b).

Yet no matter how much active missile defenses may continue to suffer from adverse perceptions due to repeated test failures, the existence of an os-tensibly robust missile defense program appears to be accepted by the Ameri-can public. Although missile defense critics frequently comment and write about missile defense flaws, a poll shortly after 9/11 found only 31 percent of those surveyed correctly responding that the United States does *not* currently possess a national missile defense system against long-range ballistic missiles (Herron et al. 2000, 2006).

How do and will current and possible future adversaries of the United States perceive the effectiveness of active U.S. missile defenses (separately or in combination with counterforce and passive defense measures)? There is lit-tle evidence that foreign audiences share the harshest critics' belief that avail-able or even conceivable missile defense technologies will never perform as claimed. Indeed, even critics realize that many of the reasons for poor missile defense performance to date have less to do with the mission's impossibility than with intense pressures to maintain politically mandated schedules, which have virtually eliminated risk reduction and sensible developmental testing. This so-called "rush to failure" was self-evident even to supporters of missile defenses late in the Clinton administration; President Bush's directive in 2002 to deploy an initial if limited system only exacerbated it (Government Ac-countability Office 2003).

Even if the hurried and incautious rush to deployment were brought un-der control, the harshest critics of missile defense are unlikely to abandon their firm belief in the impossibility of a credible and cost-effective system. Many other critics remain gravely concerned that, given the amount of resources be-ing devoted to missile defense, American technological ingenuity may well succeed in making global missile defenses work in a decade or so—at least well enough in the eyes of both U.S decision makers and America's chief ad-versaries (Sauer 2003). Given the Bush administration's intentionally opaque deployment strategy emphasizing block development, with no overarching architecture specified, these critics worry that Moscow and Beijing will grow increasingly concerned about the survivability of their strategic nuclear arsenals.

Russian and Chinese reasons for concern about where America's missile defenses are headed differ slightly. What animates Russian officials most is that with the eventual U.S. deployment of highly powerful ground-based X-band radars and spaced-based infrared sensors (known as Spaced-Based Infrared System or SBIRS-Low), America will have a "break-out" potential in place for a thick, global system of missile defense (Mendelsohn 2000). More ominously, once deployed globally, not only will midcourse GBI interceptors be able to take advantage of their improved resolution but so too will a growing network of sea-based interceptors on Aegis cruisers/destroyers and land-based upper-tier THAAD, the size of which is no longer subject to ABM treaty restrictions. Of course, X-band and especially SBIRS-Low may not be as effective as promised, but that does not lessen the desire of arms control experts and Russian defense planners alike to see the uncontrolled expansion of American global missile defenses avoided through numerical caps on defense interceptors. China, for its part, appears to be sufficiently concerned about the consequences of American missile defense expandability, particularly in space, that it has stalled further negotiations on a fissile material cut-off treaty in the Conference on Disarmament in Geneva contingent upon the start of negotiations within that forum on banning space-based weapons.

Not unexpectedly, Bush administration officials view such arms control restraints on expanding missile defense as unnecessary in today's changing strategic environment and antithetical to their emerging strategy of military denial. Although the adverse impact of missile defenses on strategic stability seems to have largely disappeared from today's strategic discourse, few strategic analysts doubt that it will reappear as layered defenses begin to demonstrate more effectiveness than their currently feeble performance shows. Tied to an ever-increasing gap between American military capability and any conceivable competitor's, especially in prompt, global conventional strikes, and a national security strategy explicitly emphasizing preemption, effective global missile defenses are sure to resurrect concerns about strategic stability.

Absent confidence in American restraint, it would not be surprising for Moscow and Beijing, either unilaterally or as a coalition of the unwilling, to mount challenges from within the MTCR to thwart the perceived effectiveness of U.S. missile defenses or at least raise their already high costs. Since missile defenses are only one component of a multi-dimensional mix of offensive and defensive forces that constitute a denial strategy, it will remain difficult to establish useful metrics for calibrating the perceived effectiveness of missile defenses. Nevertheless, the ever-increasing costs and prospective adverse international repercussions of expanded missile defenses could stand as the most compelling motivations for Moscow and Beijing to resist American pretensions from within the MTCR.

Why Export Controls Matter

A major reason for instituting effective nonproliferation mechanisms is to control the quantitative and qualitative evolution of threats. Few avid supporters of missile defenses are willing to admit that the diffusion of technology can be effectively controlled. Arguably, however, the MTCR has achieved notable success in bringing a significant degree of order and predictability to containing the spread of ballistic missiles. Most missile programs that raise concerns today have their design origin in the widely proliferated Scud missile, essentially a 1950s Soviet improvement on the Nazi V-2 missile. The poor accuracy, clumsy logistics, limited payload, and other weaknesses of the Scud and its many derivatives inhibit their users' capacity to create flexible and confident attack options that go beyond crude delivery of WMD.[8] Their poor performance also makes them easier to defend against than ballistic missiles that impose much more severe burdens on missile defenses. The latter have logistical demand-easing solid-rocket motors and sophisticated guidance, navigation, and control technologies that permit not only great accuracy but also maneuverable reentry vehicles.

Certainly the MTCR's most notable success thus far was the forced dismantling of the Condor missile program sought by Argentina, Iraq, and Egypt during the 1980s—a missile that included sophisticated Pershing II–level technology. Yet just as important has been the blocking, through effective export controls, of hundreds of components, technologies, and production capabilities—the necessary ingredients for developing complete ballistic and cruise missile systems (Speier 2000).

A few brief examples illustrate why even imperfect export controls can have an important constraining effect on missile proliferation. It has increasingly become the general presumption that almost any person or small group with modest engineering knowledge and skills could build a simple, autonomous self-guided UAV or small cruise missile at minimal expense and based entirely on off-the-shelf component technologies.[9] Too much should not be made of do-it-yourself cruise missiles. Just because Radio Shack offers all the component parts does not imply that they can be readily integrated to produce a reliable system. System integration skills, particularly those needed to integrate actuators and servo controls that are crucial for moving the UAV's control surfaces based on commands from the flight management computer, represent the most significant integration challenge. The mere diffusion of technology, as reflected in tangible components and engineering drawings, is necessary but not sufficient to enable the widespread proliferation of missile systems (MacKenzie and Spinardi 1995).

Integrating new guidance technology or an alternative propulsion system into a proven design has typically proven far more difficult and time consuming than predicted. It took the United States nearly a decade to succeed in integrating global positioning system technology into the family of general-purpose dumb (inaccurate) bombs to create the highly accurate Joint Direct Attack Munition. Both long-range ballistic missile development and converting anti-ship cruise missiles into land-attack systems have proven more daunting than many originally foresaw. The Commission to Assess the Ballistic Missile Threat to the United States (1998, known as the Rumsfeld Commission, after its chairman Donald Rumsfeld) concluded that countries like North Korea and Iran could compress the development of a long-range ballistic missile into a much shorter time than it took either the United States or Soviet Union. Yet North Korea and Iran have notably struggled over the last five years—ironically, the time the Rumsfeld Commission argued it would take to move from primitive Scud technology to an intercontinental range ballistic missile capable of striking U.S. territory. Even though notable experts had predicted that countries such as Iraq and Iran could convert their aging Seersucker anti-ship cruise missiles into land-attack models in about one year, Iraq was found to have struggled for over a year just to integrate an alternative propulsion system into the existing airframe (Kay 2003).

Given the complexity of such seemingly easy development programs, even imperfect export controls can impose severe time delays or dissuade developing countries from pursuing such efforts altogether.

Circumventing the Intent of the MTCR

The MTCR seeks to delay if not altogether block unwanted acquisition and development of missile delivery systems or at least make it so expensive that interested states and nonstate actors are dissuaded from acquiring missiles for WMD delivery. These goals are sought by bringing together thirty-four states that say they agree on a general set of guidelines governing exports of missiles and the equipment and technology used in their production.

Yet, unlike the nuclear, chemical, and biological nonproliferation regimes, the MTCR has no legal treaty provisions or international organization to ensure compliance. Instead, a common set of guidelines backed up individually by national export control legislation within each participating state governs the MTCR's administration. Given the voluntary nature of the regime, it is not surprising that most member states seek to maintain some flexibility in their export rights. Generally speaking, international norms against the acquisition of nuclear, biological, and chemical weapons are fairly robust, while consensus on the need to control delivery systems can be shaky at times. This is especially the case for cruise missiles and UAVs, which have only recently begun to spread as widely as ballistic missiles (McMahon and Gormley 1994; Gormley 2006a).

The Black Shaheen Sale

The MTCR's most restrictive "presumption of denial" guidance to its member states applies to Category I systems: complete missiles or UAVs capable of carrying five-hundred-kilogram payloads to a range of at least three hundred kilometers, as well as certain major subsystems for them. The Black Shaheen cruise missile and its various French and British derivatives feature a highly stealthy aerodynamic shape, low-observable materials, low infrared (IR) signature, and a combination of guidance and navigation schemes designed to achieve a high probability of survival and high terminal accuracy—in short, a weapon of grave proliferation concern (Gormley 2001). Even though the Anglo-French Black Shaheen cruise missile appeared to be a Category I system, Paris and London decided to sell the missile to the United Arab Emirates (UAE) in 1998. The decision by this coalition of the unwilling came notwithstanding strong protests from Washington about the adverse consequences of such a transfer. Paris and London both argued that the Black Shaheen sale presented no proliferation danger, an argument that narrowly had some merit.[10] The MTCR's guidelines do stipulate that on the rare occasion when a Category I item is exported, governments must obtain binding end-use assurances from the recipient that the missile will be used only as a conventional weapon and will not be reexported to another state.

The export market for land-attack cruise missiles (LACMs) is expected to grow dramatically in the next decade. To compete with the United States, European manufacturers of LACMs have leapt to the top rung of world producers, led by the Anglo-French firm Matra Bae Dynamics (MBD). As of 2001, MBD was believed to have at least $2.1 billion worth of development and early-production contracts and orders for more than two thousand of its LACMs. These orders largely will satisfy internal French and British requirements, but it remains obvious that for every export of this family of LACMs, unit costs for French and UK missiles will decline. The fact that the Black Shaheen sale occurred in the midst of intense negotiations for sixty advanced fighters helps to explain why France was persuaded to defy MTCR guidelines. Whatever the explanation for the Franco-UK decision to export the Black Shaheen, the fear among security analysts is that the decision will negatively affect export control by states with far more worrisome export records than either France or Britain. Those most notably include Russia and China.

Russia and the Past as Prologue

Russia joined the MTCR as a full member in 1995 after a bitter controversy with the United States over Russia's agreement in 1991 to provide cryogenic rocket engines and related missile technology to India (Pikayev et al. 1997). During the controversy, Russia's MTCR status was that of an informal "adherent"—a category designed to encourage the observance of international norms on missiles and related technology transfers. Even as Russia became a full-fledged member, controversy continued over reports not only of Russian exports supporting India's missile program but also of exports by Russian state entities for Iran's ballistic missile program (Speier 2000).

Russian entities involved in missile proliferation have diverse pedigrees. While North Korea has supplanted the former Soviet Union as the principal exporter of ballistic missiles globally, it appears that Pyongyang's missile programs may have benefited significantly from assistance by former Russian missile designers and engineers.[11] North Korean and Russian activities appear to come together in Iran's emerging long-range missile programs. According to Israeli sources, Iran's Shihab series of ballistic missiles depend critically on North Korea's No-Dong missile and various Russian missile designs, including the SS-4 and SS-9. The exact nature of Russian assistance to Iran remains ambiguous, but if Russian state officials accelerate the quality of engineering assistance together with the provision of more sophisticated missile subsystems (most notably, advanced propulsion technology), it would put Iran on a clear path toward an intercontinental-range ballistic missile system.

Intentionally sanctioned activities of Russian entities, or simply unwillingness to implement effective monitoring of entity activities, are not the only transfer pathways Russia might employ to thwart American missile defenses. Direct transfers of complete missile systems, the MTCR notwithstanding, are also conceivable. A spate of news reports from Israel and Russia in early 2005 pointed to a possible missile deal between Russia and Syria involving the transfer of the Iskander-E medium-range ballistic missile, which appears to be a Category I missile. The Iskander possesses the two most worrisome features of the Black Shaheen LACM: precision guidance and difficulty of defense. The missile has a reported accuracy of twenty meters and a terminal maneuvering scheme, which, according to the Russians, renders the Iskander impossible to intercept.[12] In spite of strong defense industry pressure to approve Iskander export to Syria, the adverse foreign policy consequences for

Russia in early 2005 made it highly unlikely that any formal transaction was likely to occur.

Even though the MTCR membership tightened its guidelines for cruise missile exports after the Franco-British Black Shaheen sale to the UAE, Russia could still use the sale as a pretext for transgressions with regard to its own cruise missile exports. Russian arms manufacturers began marketing LACMs in earnest during the premiere Moscow Air Show in 1992, when a shorter-range version of the three-thousand-kilometer-range Kh-55 air-launched cruise missile was offered for sale (Gormley 2001). The offerings demonstrate not only the inherent modularity of cruise missiles but also a clumsy attempt by the Russian manufacturer Reduga to keep the offerings below the MTCR's range and payload thresholds.

Russia has also exploited the modularity of its sea-launched 3M-55 Yakhont cruise missile to produce the 3M-54E1, or Club, for the export market. This missile is believed to have both anti-ship and land-attack options built in. According to a Russian Internet news service, India and China have already received Club exports and the UAE is a prospective recipient (Moscow Agentstvo Voyennykh Novostey, Aug. 24, 2006, http://www.militarynews.ru). Equally controversial because of its impact on the MTCR's effectiveness is the co-development by India and Russia of Brahmos dual-mode (anti-ship and land-attack) supersonic cruise missiles, which both nations wish to market internationally. While the Brahmos and Club cruise missile exports do not appear to fall under the MTCR's Category I provisions, India and China clearly possess WMD and the missile can readily fly to a range of three hundred kilometers, which compels Moscow to secure end-use assurances that the missile will not be used to deliver WMD. Practicing a strategy of consent and exploit, Russia could cooperate with the general guidelines of the MTCR while at the same time acting counter to the regime's intent as well as U.S. policy preferences. In sum, Russia clearly possesses ample financial and strategic incentives to exploit its strong position as a cruise missile manufacturer should U.S.-Russian relations deteriorate further.

China's Dubious Compliance

China's relationship with the MTCR has been problematic from the start. In becoming an "adherent" in October 1994, China took the unusual step of formulating its own version of what adherence meant. China agreed to "not export ground-to-ground missiles featuring the primary parameters of the MTCR"—which suggests that its adherence applies only to complete Category I systems and not to air-to-ground cruise missiles (Gormley 2001). Prior to China's adherence to the MTCR's guidelines in 1994, Beijing had pledged in 1991 not to sell complete Category I missiles. Despite its pledge, and consistent with a consent and deceive strategy, China transferred at least thirty-four M-11 ballistic missiles to Pakistan. When confronted by the United States, China denied the transfer and Washington imposed economic sanctions it lifted, in late 1992, after yet another pledge by Beijing to adhere to the MTCR's guidelines and parameters. Early in the Clinton administration, Washington implemented sanctions again after learning that China had engaged in missile trade with Pakistan. Even though the U.S. intelligence community reported in February 2000 that "some [Chinese] ballistic missile assistance [to Pakistan] continues," Washington and Beijing struck another deal in November 2000 to waive sanctions then in place for missile-related exports to Pakistan and Iran in exchange for China's publication of a specific export control list pertaining to missiles (U.S. CIA 2000). Discussions even began to occur informally within the MTCR to admit China as a full member state. Yet intelligence reports continued to implicate China in an ongoing flow of component missile technologies to Pakistan and other states.[13] Unsurprisingly, Beijing's bid for MTCR membership during the MTCR plenary meeting in Seoul in 2004 did not succeed, largely due to Washington's insistence.

Strategic, commercial, and foreign policy reasons underlie China's willingness to defy Washington's wishes to see Beijing curtail its missile sales. In regard to Pakistan, China maintains a strong strategic relationship and partnership that entails a full range of major weapon system transfers and other forms of defense cooperation. Countering India and Soviet designs originally informed this strategic partnership, but post–Cold War needs, including using Pakistan as a balance against India, remain critically important to China. From the beginning of China's opening up in the early 1980s, Chinese defense industries were expected to exploit commercially the increasingly lucrative international market for arms. Pakistan's need to compensate for Indian conventional superiority with advanced ballistic missile systems fit well with China's aggressive export needs. Finally, and most important for this study, Beijing understood well Washington's sensitivity to uncontrolled missile proliferation and has masterfully exploited it to provide leverage with Washington on missile defense deployments in East Asia and arms sales to Taiwan.

The potential convergence of Russian and Chinese interests—the former operating from within formal MTCR deliberations, the latter on its edges—to make America's emerging missile defenses more costly and suspect in the eyes of their prospective recipients could play out in a number of plausible ways. There are signs of growing common interests between Moscow and Beijing. Shortly after Russia suffered the apparent loss of its traditionally close relationship with Ukraine (in that nation's election of December 2004), Moscow announced two accords with Beijing signaling a closer long-term relationship. One involves a new degree of economic cooperation in exploiting Russia's vast energy resources; the other, a historic first—large-scale joint military exercises on Chinese territory. According to Charles Krauthammer, these developments signify the formation of a new "anti-hegemonic" bloc consisting of Russia, China, and its covert relationships with such rogue states as North Korea, Iran, and Syria, among others (*Washington Post,* Jan. 21, 2005).

Regional Settings

Mutual Russian and Chinese interests in complicating America's pursuit of effective missile defenses have compelling plausibility because missile proliferation has already begun to show a new toxic character: a volatile mix of increases in medium- and intermediate-range ballistic missiles together with the acquisition of land-attack cruise missiles. States considering acquiring a delivery system for WMD are now likely to acquire both ballistic and cruise missiles, especially if they face an adversary having ballistic missile defenses. They are motivated in part by lessons from the American invasion of Iraq in 2003 (viz., that defending against both cruise and ballistic missiles severely complicates and increases the costs of effective missile defenses). Most missile defense interceptors in regional settings will be asked to defend against both ballistic and cruise missiles. States wishing to deter U.S. or regional military interventions were unlikely to invest heavily in cruise missiles until American missile defenses performed decisively better than they had during the Gulf War in 1991. Patriot's success against Iraq's ballistic missiles in 2003 coupled with the problems Patriot faced in detecting and intercepting cruise missiles increases incentives to acquire cruise missiles (Gormley 2003).

Increased Russian assistance to China could adversely affect performance and increase the cost of American and allied missile defenses in a future military conflict between China and Taiwan. Recent developments in the missile competition between China and Taiwan illustrate how the addition of cruise missiles—particularly increasingly advanced designs provided with the aid of Russian engineering—can greatly exacerbate tension in the region.

China has been deploying its M-series ballistic missiles in provinces within reach of Taiwan at the alarming rate of fifty to seventy-five a year for several years. Estimates suggest they have eight hundred deployed as of the end of 2006. These missiles are thought to possess sufficient accuracy to make conventional payloads effective against Taiwan's ace in the hole vis-à-vis a cross-strait invasion—its large air force, reputed to be significantly more potent than China's and capable of defeating any cross-strait invasion. Taiwan, however, can deploy its highly effective air force at only a handful of airfields.

By themselves, ballistic missiles armed with conventional munitions are not capable of closing Taiwan's airfields. They could temporarily delay the take-off of Taiwan's superior air force in the critical first hours of any cross-straits military campaign. They could thus enable China's inferior air force to more effectively attack Taiwan's pinned-down planes and to penetrate Taiwan's air space due to Taipei's aircraft being delayed from meeting China's in air-to-air engagements (Gormley 2000; U.S. Department of Defense 2004).

In response to China's ballistic missile buildup, Taiwan has purchased missile defenses, including U.S. Patriot PAC-2 interceptors, and scheduled acquisition of the latest hit-to-kill PAC-3 interceptors. Patriot batteries alone, however, have difficulty defending against both ballistic and cruise missiles. *Space Daily* (Sept. 19, 2004) reported that China had tested a new LACM (the Dong Hai-10) with a range of fifteen hundred kilometers and accuracy of ten meters and had already deployed a shorter-range LACM (the Ying Ji-63) with a range of four hundred to five hundred kilometers, as well as Harpy UAVs furnished by Israel. This news sparked an open debate among Taiwan's legislators about the feasibility of relying solely on costly missile defenses to counter these developments. One Taiwanese government official stated, "Relying on purely defensive systems to protect ourselves from China means we will have to outspend them 10 to one; we have to buy anti-missile missiles plus more early-warning and other detection equipment. That is impossible in the long run" (quoted by Kathrin Hille, *Financial Times* [Asian ed.], Sept. 25, 2004). As an antidote, Taiwan is pursuing an LACM program of its own, believed to be within four years of completion (Gormley 2006a).

Besides making U.S. missile defense effectiveness more uncertain and costly, Russian-Chinese collaboration could foster a missile arms race in northeastern Asia and elsewhere. Unlike the Cold War doctrine of mutual assured destruction, which involved the threat of nuclear retaliation, the classic missile arms race developing along the Taiwan straits involves, initially at least, conventionally armed missiles, suggesting a lower threshold for a decision to commence hostilities. Even worse, Taiwanese military analysts have discussed instituting a "preventive self-defense" strike option entailing early use of cruise missiles to confound China's strike plans (Gormley 2006a). As the brief analysis of Taiwan's air force and early-warning vulnerabilities shows, there is a compelling urge to usurp control at the outset of conflict and a perceived benefit in doing so.

Japan also is not immune from considering the merits of cheaper offensive solutions to the growing missile threat it faces. In 2004, an advisory panel to the prime minister concluded that Japan might require a preemptive strike capability to launch against foreign threats such as ballistic missile launch installations (*Japan Times,* Oct. 2, 2004). Although Japan's prime minister, Juni-chiro Koizumi, rejected such a notion as inconsistent with Japan's "defense only" policy, the high cost of missile defenses and growing recognition that these defenses might be overwhelmed by a combination of ballistic and cruise missiles may explain why Japan continues to analyze the need to develop its own offensive missile capability—at first thought to be a ballistic missile but later confirmed to be an LACM (Gormley 2006a). Prominent news accounts of the costs of missile defense illustrate Japan's dilemma (Shigeru Handa, *Toyko Shimbun,* Dec. 24, 2004). Because each Patriot PAC-3 missile costs an esti-mated $4.75 million, Japan's budget allocation for missile defenses will buy no more than thirteen interceptors. Even worse, the Aegis-based SM-3 interceptor missile costs four times as much as Patriot, meaning that fewer than ten can be purchased each year. With North Korea's arsenal of No-Dong ballistic missiles numbering more than two hundred, the arithmetic is stark. If China lends as-sistance to North Korea's nascent cruise missile development program, Japan may be unable to afford a sufficient number of missile defense interceptors to protect major population centers and critical military and industrial facilities. Under such circumstances, much cheaper offensive strike options could be-come an acceptable alternative.

Mixing cruise missiles with already growing arsenals of ballistic missiles in the Middle East could offer yet another Russo-Chinese pressure point af-fecting the performance and cost of American and Israeli missile defenses. Until recently, Israel had dominated development and acquisition of cruise missiles and UAVs. Besides being a major developer of reconnaissance drones and the air-launched Popeye LACM, Israel has explored using armed UAVs to perform counterforce missions against enemy ballistic missile launchers. Iran's Shihab ballistic missile has motivated Israel to pursue its own missile defense system—the Arrow—with substantial financial support from the United States. As Arrow and Patriot deployments have proceeded, Iran has become noticeably interested in both LACMs and UAVs. Tehran has acquired cruise missile systems and technology from Russia and China in support of its new anti-ship cruise missile program, called Nur. And China has exported various versions of the Silkworm anti-ship cruise missile to Iran. Older ver-sions, like the HY-2 or HY-4, could be converted into LACMs with a range of at least one thousand kilometers (Gormley 2001).

Iran has responded to Israel's brisk deployment of missile defenses by converting around three hundred Chinese-furnished anti-ship cruise missiles into land-attack missiles, equipped with turbojet engines and new guidance systems. Iranian dissidents also claim that Tehran has successfully reverse-engineered Russia's Kh-55 LACM, a three-thousand-kilometer-range missile that Iran (and China) obtained illegally through Russian and Ukrainian arms dealers in 2001 (Gormley 2006a). Acquiring more cruise missiles to complement its already substantial ballistic missile arsenal would also send a strong message to Gulf Cooperation Council states, including Kuwait and Saudi Arabia, all of whom have been offered or expressed interest in American missile defense systems. Israel, too, has become alarmed about Iran's growing interest in cruise missiles and UAVs.

Russia and China could also choose to exacerbate a dangerous mix of offensive and defensive missile developments unfolding in South Asia. Not only could Russian and Chinese activities destabilize a delicate balance of power in the region but they could also make any potential U.S. intervention to stanch a potential nuclear catastrophe more problematic than it might otherwise have to be. The barely stable balance of forces between India and Pakistan could be adversely affected by the substantial addition of cruise missiles and UAVs to growing deployments of ballistic missile systems.

India is already active in developing and acquiring cruise missiles and UAVs. Its Lakshya unmanned target drone, thought to be capable of delivering a 450-kilogram payload over a range of 600 kilometers, is expected to be exported to an unknown country (probably Israel) (New Delhi All India Radio, Dec. 13, 2002). Of course, India's codevelopment with Russia of the Brahmos cruise missile, declared ready for deployment in early 2005, and the leasing of a Russian Akula II nuclear submarine equipped with nuclear-capable cruise missiles, present Pakistan with a robust offensive strike force. One sure way to aggravate regional arms racing would be for Russia to accede to nascent Indian military ambitions to rapidly incorporate advanced, longer-range versions of the Brahmos cruise missile into Indian air and land forces. With its missile partner Russia providing certain "restrictive technologies," the Indian military could integrate a turbojet engine to achieve a range of around 500 kilometers and perhaps even a more advanced turbofan engine to propel a miniaturized nuclear warhead to strategic ranges (approximately 2,000 kilometers). Indian military sources note that such an expansion of the capabilities of Brahmos is feasible. Unlike India's ballistic missile development programs, the Brahmos is "not under the global scanner" and, because Brahmos is a joint venture, India can turn to Russia for technological help (Gormley 2006a).

The development most animating Chinese action is New Delhi's pursuit of ballistic missile defenses. New Delhi has no choice but to balance comparative Pakistani advantages in offensive ballistic missiles (aided by North Korea and China) and its strategy of nuclear blackmail with a no-first-use nuclear strategy complemented by missile defenses (C. Raja Mohan, *Indian Express,* Feb. 22, 2005). India has long sought Israel's Arrow missile defense system, an acquisition that would violate MTCR restrictions because the interceptor's propulsion system exceeds the regime's range and payload thresholds. After first thwarting New Delhi's Arrow ambitions, the Bush administration reportedly relented as part of a deal in July 2005 to reengage in civil nuclear cooperation with India after more than a quarter century hiatus following India's nuclear test in 1974 (Gormley and Scheinman 2005). India has also expressed interest in the U.S. Patriot missile defense system. Within a month of Washington's nuclear deal with India, Pakistan conducted a surprise launch of its own new cruise missile, a land-attack system with a range of five hundred kilometers. Immediately after the successful launch, Pakistan's President Pervez Musharraf declared, "The biggest value of this system is [that] it is not detectable. It cannot be intercepted." Despite Islamabad's claims to the contrary, China's fingerprints are all over Pakistan's new cruise missile (Gormley 2006a).

Armed then with a substantial arsenal of ballistic missiles complemented by a growing number of LACMs, both India and Pakistan now face accelerating their already costly arms race with unpredictable implications for future regional stability. Those would inherently extend to any contingency involving U.S. military engagement.

The Homeland Defense Setting

We have seen how Russian engineering and component technology support have already and could further benefit North Korean and Iranian long-range ballistic missile programs. There are other ways to threaten the U.S. homeland that might be indirectly aided by Russia's lack of cooperation within existing missile nonproliferation regimes. Those involve low-tech aircraft converted to fly fully autonomously as UAVs. Analysts have begun to worry about such unfamiliar attack mechanisms for two principal reasons. First, they represent perhaps the most effective way to deliver biological, chemical, or certain forms of nuclear materials (powdered cesium-60). Second, these low-flying UAVs could exploit the previously discussed gap in air defense coverage of the continental United States below three thousand feet. Al-Qaeda has asserted that it is a religious duty to acquire WMD. The director general of Canada's armed forces stated publicly in early 2004 that terrorist groups have already purchased ultralight aircraft and hang gliders to work around the post-9/11 improvements against hijacking large commercial airliners (David Pugliese, *Calgary Herald*, Mar. 26, 2004).

The MTCR did take an important first step toward addressing possible terrorist use of UAVs in 2002 with a plenary meeting commitment to examine ways of limiting the risk of controlled items and their technologies falling into such hands. Nevertheless, given the MTCR's consensus nature, Russia, among several other states, could stall substantive efforts to meet the MTCR's new mandate.

The United States took the initiative in January 2003 to prevent the flow of dual-use technology that might enable a terrorist group to acquire a small UAV. Using the Wassenaar Arrangement (WA) as a starting place, the United States introduced an "anti-terrorism" proposal to the WA's thirty-three co-founding nations. It was intended to achieve transparency and greater responsibility in transfers of conventional arms and dual-use goods and technologies (including UAVs). Expressing concern about the possible terrorist use of kit airplanes and other manned civil aircraft as makeshift UAVs, the U.S. proposal sought export control reviews and international notifications for all equipment, systems, and specially designed components that would enable these airplanes to be converted into UAVs. Although the WA membership failed to reach consensus in 2003 on the U.S. proposal, it did so in late 2005. Nevertheless, a more appropriate venue for such a proposal is the MTCR because the WA does not incorporate the MTCR's strong denial rules and no-undercut provisions (if one member denies a transfer, others are obliged not to transfer as well). Yet Russia might choose to drag its feet on any U.S. initiative, if only because it may figure that such terrorist threats are far more likely to affect U.S. interests than Russia's.

Adjusting U.S. Behavior to Encourage Cooperation

Previous sections have established that others associated with the MTCR can directly and, by transfers to third parties, indirectly pose serious challenges to the effectiveness of the missile defense pillar of the U.S. strategy of denial. This section offers suggestions about what U.S. actions may make those challenges less substantial or likely.

Western arms control theory is predicated on the importance of transparency or making both sides of any competition aware—as specifically as is possible within the limits of security—of what the other side is doing. In considering how the United States might adjust its behavior to mitigate Russian and Chinese actions designed to thwart the effectiveness of U.S. global missile defenses, nothing is more important than increased American transparency about its defense programs. The Bush administration simply dismisses the necessity for such transparency. According to the Nuclear Posture Review of 2002, Russia no longer figures into American nuclear targeting plans as a primary threat. Russia and China need not fear American global missile defenses because they are aimed only at protecting American interests from comparatively small missile attacks from rogue states, not strategic attacks from Russia or China.

These assurances notwithstanding, Russia and China face a decidedly opaque U.S. missile defense program characterized by an open architecture and yearly block purchases of additional capabilities as they mature. As noted earlier, Russia is most concerned about the future deployment of ground- and space-based sensors that would provide the basis for a "break-out" scenario in which the United States could rapidly expand a "limited" system into one that threatened even Russia's offensive forces and certainly China's substantially smaller offensive arsenal.

The purest form of reassurance would resurrect formal arms control constraints, involving limits on the number of missile defense midcourse and upper-tier interceptors, or even constraints on ground- and space-based sensors.[14] China clearly has serious concerns about prospects for the United States deploying weapons in space, including space-based kill vehicles for midcourse intercept. The United States might allay international concerns, including China's, by agreeing to an international code of conduct to promote peaceful uses of outer space.

Even if it rejects an American about-face on formal arms control, the Bush administration could pursue informal outreach activities with Russian and Chinese military and diplomatic officials to inform them about the direction, scope, and pace of its offensive and defensive military programs—notably those in the Nuclear Posture Review's "New Triad." Such outreach efforts might not entirely mitigate Russian and Chinese concerns, but at least they would dissipate the veil of secrecy surrounding America's longer-term strategic direction.[15]

A more progressive approach to addressing missile proliferation concerns within the thirty-four-nation MTCR is not just the responsibility of Russia but of America as well. Were America to adjust its behavior with regard to multilateral regimes generally and the MTCR and the Hague Code of Conduct (HCOC) against the proliferation of ballistic missiles specifically, it might make less likely future Russian and Chinese actions inconsistent with the MTCR's and HCOC's intentions. For example, if the United States wishes other members of the MTCR to avoid a repeat of the Black Shaheen stealth cruise missile sale to the UAE, it would be advisable to adjust its own behavior with regard to promoting the looser MTCR rules on large UAVs and missile defense interceptors.[16] The danger of loosening controls after nearly eighteen years of experience is to foster a more pliable attitude toward other Category I controls, perhaps even on space launch vehicles, which can rapidly form the basis for an intercontinental ballistic missile program.

The same caution applies to the Bush administration's wishes to promote sales of missile defense systems by loosening controls on missile defense interceptors. For one senior administration official, the "MTCR is not, should not be, and is not intended to be a restraint on missile defense. It is intended to restrict trade in ballistic missile technology" (quoted in Amy Svitak and Gopal Ratnam, *Defense News,* July 14, 2003). In fact, however, missile defense interceptors are proscribed under Category I MTCR rules if their rocket motors can propel a five-hundred-kilogram payload to ranges over three hundred kilometers. One option under Bush administration review removes missile defense interceptors from MTCR consideration altogether. In retaliation, Russia or China could decide to present Washington with a fait accompli, consisting of transfers of uncontrolled countermeasure technologies to non-MTCR states.[17] That could worsen rather than reduce the threat American missile defenses would face.

Another example of a more enlightened U.S. approach to nonproliferation relates to improving the scanty normative guidelines that currently exist for missile restraint. One blatant shortcoming of the HCOC, implemented in November 2002, was the omission of cruise missiles and UAVs, even though that normative regime's progenitor was the MTCR, which covers both missile categories. While the HCOC was being formulated, the United States either did nothing or actually prevented cruise missiles and UAVs from being included in the code's language. Since its creation, the HCOC members have focused on expanding membership rather than deepening normative coverage by including cruise missiles and UAVs. However insubstantial the HCOC is as a normative mechanism, this shortcoming solidifies the second-class status of cruise missiles and UAVs precisely at a time when their proliferation has become inextricably linked to the spread of ballistic missiles. America would be wise to change this perception rather than fostering actions that make the effectiveness of future U.S. missile defenses more problematic.

Finally, U.S. behavior regarding formal Chinese accession to membership in the MTCR will surely affect Beijing's calculations about thwarting America's missile defense ambitions from within the MTCR. As an informal adherent to the MTCR, China has carefully crafted a self-serving interpretation of the MTCR's guidelines that affords sufficient latitude to proliferate when it suits China's security or economic interests. Thus, China has managed to evade and resist U.S. wishes by generally consenting to the regime's guidelines while exploiting its intentions through deceptive practices.[18] U.S. decision makers have denied China the membership it, and most other MTCR members, prefer. On balance, it would be better to have China operating from within the MTCR than from the convenience of "adherent" status. Formal accession to the MTCR would mark China's full involvement in a key international security institution (Zaborsky 2004). Surely in anticipation of achieving formal membership, Beijing has upgraded its national export controls dealing with MTCR systems and component technologies. Continuing to prevent China's accession to the MTCR will only increase Beijing's predilection toward icono-clastic behavior regarding missile sales. That would make it easier, not harder, for China to subvert U.S. policies from the comfort of its currently informal relationship with the MTCR.

EUROPA RIDING THE HEGEMON?

Transatlantic Climate Policy

ALEXANDER OCHS AND DETLEF F. SPRINZ

Prominent and committed supporters of mutually rewarding transatlantic relations have identified climate change as the most important global problem in this century. Counteracting major impacts of climate change requires cooperation among the major emitters of so-called greenhouse gases (GHGs) or agreement on compensation for impacts. Since 2001, the United States has abandoned the international treaty architecture of the Kyoto Protocol (KP), which is presumed to be a first step in the direction of limiting global climate change. Since much of the rest of the world has subscribed to the architecture of the Kyoto Protocol, a major rift has arisen between Europe, a fervent defender of the architecture, and the United States, which considers the protocol unworkable and against its interests. This chapter investigates the history of transatlantic climate relations, the major issues debated, and options for a rapprochement on global climate change.

Excluding the U.S. intervention in Iraq in 2003, climate policy is the most prominent example of a transatlantic rift compared to a history of mostly harmonious relations since World War II. The divide became most prominent with the decision of President George W. Bush in the spring of 2001 to abstain from the Kyoto Protocol. In the wake of this decision, widely criticized by Europeans, climate policy has been elevated to the level of "high politics," a symbol of the underlying disunity in transatlantic relations.

The United States is the largest single emitter of GHGs, that is, gases that are having an impact on the climate system. In 2000, U.S. emissions accounted for more than one-fifth (20.6 percent) of global emissions. The U.S. share is about one-third higher than that of the world's second largest emitter, the People's Republic of China (14.8 percent) and that of the third ranking, the enlarged EU 25, which has 14.0 percent (Baumert and Pershing 2004, 4).[1] Apart from its role as a major emitter, the United States is also a potential leader in developing technologies to deal with the causes and effects of climate change. These characteristics make U.S. cooperation essential for dealing with global climate change.

The importance of the United States does not diminish the relevance of the European Union. Indeed, the decision of the United States to abandon the Kyoto Protocol galvanized European efforts to unify politically around this issue. Perhaps counterintuitively, the EU is now attempting to exert leadership on global climate change. Can Europa ride the hegemon back to a safe "climate haven"?

The Transatlantic Foreign Policy Context

The current divergence between Europe and the United States on global climate policy should be judged against the broader background of transatlantic relations since World War II. Through shared goals, resource aggregation, and extensive cooperation, the United States and Western Europe were able to meet the challenges of the Cold War, advance the liberalization of international trade and finance, and promote democracy, pluralism, human rights, and other shared values. Since the events of "9/11" (2001) and "11/9" (1989, the fall of the Berlin Wall), the reshaping of the European political landscape and ensuing changes in the global agenda have severely tested the stability of the transatlantic partnership.

The United States came to the rescue of Europe in two world wars. Following the end of World War II, the United States did not abstain from influencing the political, economic, and military order of the old continent as it did after the first world war. Against the backdrop of the emerging Cold War in the late 1940s, the United States essentially united Western Europe through its first monetary union (the European Payment Union to disburse Marshall Plan funds), stabilization of investment patterns by way of the Marshall Plan itself (to the tune of about 3 percent of U.S. GDP) (Neuss 2003, 7), and continued military presence, the last making sharp deviations from Western forms of democratic political systems very unlikely. This also stabilized political expectations among Western European nations, which had to reconstitute themselves politically after a terrible war. The United States, at various stages, provided continuous support for the uniting of Europe. Conversely, the transatlantic partnership provided political support for the major interventions of the United States on the world political stage.[2]

Until about 1990, transatlantic relations were largely managed by way of multilateral institutions and occasional U.S. unilateral decisions. When some European countries went ahead on their own, for example, France and the UK (with the support of Israel) during the occupation of the Suez Canal in 1956, the United States forced them to retreat. The creation of the European Economic Community and its sister organizations in the 1950s, the creation of NATO, the use of the fixed exchange rate monetary system by way of adjustable U.S. dollar parities until the early 1970s, and the creation of institutions such as the Organization for Economic Cooperation and Development (OECD) and General Agreement on Tariffs and Trade (GATT) all reflected the benign leadership approach of the United States toward Europe. Europe, by itself, was essentially incapable of initiating and maintaining such institutions immediately after World War II. Other events, such as the Vietnam War and the Cuban missile crisis, reflected U.S. supremacy in global decision making within the Western bloc. By winning the Cold War, the United States successfully achieved its most important foreign policy goal.

American support for German reunification in 1990 was also substantial. This process, in turn, served as a catalyst for Europe's contemporary political, economic, and monetary unification. Yet outside its borders, Europe has essentially no vision for creating a world order other than to conceptually aim at multilateralism and the rule of law, predominantly by strengthening the UN system of governance. As a united actor, the EU has mainly been successful in the economic sphere of international trade where it, more precisely, the European Community as an institution, has a mandate on the world stage and is well respected by its counterparts, among them the United States. Major security initiatives, however, all relied on U.S. leadership—even in containing turmoil in Europe, as witnessed in the Balkans.

With the end of the Cold War and the continuing integration of Europe, the transatlantic security alliance lost its preeminence on both sides of the Atlantic. Faced with new, increasingly global challenges, the United States and Europe were often unable to overcome their disunity. Apart from the Iraq war and finding the best strategy to deal with global terrorism, they have taken different stances toward a vast array of topics: climate change, the UN Convention on the Law of the Sea, the landmine and anti-ballistic missile treaties, general approaches to international law, and the politics of economic globalization. In an influential article, Robert Kagan concluded, "on major strategic and international questions today, Americans are from Mars and Europeans are from Venus: they agree on little and understand one another less and less" (2002b, 3).

The Transatlantic Policy Challenge of Climate Change

The Challenge of Climate Change

Economic activities—such as the burning of fossil fuels for energy generation or the use of fertilizers and other agricultural practices—produce carbon dioxide, methane, and nitrous oxides, the three major GHGs released by human activities.[3] These anthropogenic emissions add to the preponderant natural GHG level in the atmosphere. It is feared that this anthropogenic addition of GHGs leads to an enhanced "greenhouse effect" and sufficiently disturbs the climate system to cause grave dangers.

The Intergovernmental Panel on Climate Change (IPCC) was created in 1988 by the World Meteorological Organization (WMO) and the United Nations Environment Program (UNEP) to provide scientific yet politically guided expertise. Much of its work revolves around writing comprehensive assessment reports every five years (starting with the 1990 assessment) and more specialized reports in between. The second assessment report (IPCC 1995) concluded prudently that "[t]he balance of evidence suggests a discernible human influence on global climate" (Houghton and IPCC 1996, 22). The third assessment, however, displayed more confidence that this is indeed the case and that a combination of natural and anthropogenic "forcing" of GHG emissions explains the observed temperature record of the past 150 years (Houghton and IPCC 2001, 10–12).

Having corroborated the human impact on the climate system, the IPCC also synthesized the prospects for future climate development. Different emission scenarios were explored for the twenty-first century, and some involve phasing out the fossil fuel-based energy system during this period. Even if this were accomplished, the earth seems committed to a "globally averaged surface temperature [that] is projected to increase by 1.4 to 5.8°C over the period 1990 to 2100" (Houghton and IPCC 2001, 13).

Changes in temperature are not the only impact of climate change. Three other impact domains are illustrative. First, human health may suffer from heat waves, such as that witnessed in France in the summer of 2003. Furthermore, the increase in malaria and dengue infections is a likely consequence of increasing temperatures. Second, climate change may lead to an increase in droughts and water shortages in some regions and more precipitation and flooding in others. Finally, the insurance sector is affected by major climate-related incidents, for example, when hurricanes and tornadoes more frequently hit insured property. As a consequence, insurance premiums may increase or insurance firms may avoid covering certain climate-related risks.

Climate policy and energy policy are closely intertwined because energy use generates the emissions that climate policy seeks to curb. Projections of future energy use suggest substantial increases of GHGs as the developing countries (especially China) become leaders in emissions sometime during this century. Thus, the challenge will be to curb emissions while keeping the world's economies on a prosperous trajectory.

The State of Play in Global Climate Policy

While a publication in 1896 by the Swedish chemist Svante Arrhenius is considered the first modern conjecture about the anthropogenic greenhouse effect, climate change did not become a political issue until the 1980s. Following a series of conferences held by governments, the WMO, and UNEP from the mid-1980s to 1990, substantial political attention was paid to potential dangers posed by anthropogenic climate change. That attention led to the creation of the IPCC in 1988 and of the Intergovernmental Negotiating Committee for a Framework Convention on Climate Change (INC) in late 1990.

In five sessions, the INC managed to compile a draft treaty on time for signature at the UN Conference on Environment and Development (UNCED) at Rio de Janeiro in 1992. The United Nations Framework Convention on Climate Change (UNFCCC) was signed by many countries at UNCED and thereafter; it entered into force on March 21, 1994, and had been ratified by 189 countries by October 6, 2006 (UNFCCC 2004b).

The UNFCCC is a framework convention "plus," that is, it follows the legacy of the regulations on stratospheric ozone depletion and transboundary air pollution by providing a general document that lays the foundations for future regulatory efforts. In particular, it stipulates that the "ultimate objective of this Convention and any related legal instruments that the Conference of the Parties may adopt is to achieve . . . stabilization of greenhouse gas concentrations in the atmosphere at a level that would prevent dangerous anthropogenic interference with the climate system" (United Nations 1992, art. 2).[4] In addition to that ultimate goal, the UNFCCC advised industrialized countries to bring their year 2000 emissions of GHGs back to 1990 levels (UNFCCC 1992, art. 4[2a]), but the careful wording avoids setting clear obligations that could become the object of noncompliance procedures. Many signatories failed to freeze emissions, but as a group they managed to reach this goal. Among the major emitters, the performance of the EU during 1990–2000 has been particularly encouraging.[5]

Following the principle of "common but differentiated responsibilities," the UNFCCC has set the path for industrialized countries to exercise leadership in reducing GHGs, to be followed by developing countries. While the former countries have largely created anthropogenic climate change by their economic development path, the latter wish not to preclude their opportunity to become wealthier soon. Therefore, the UNFCCC includes a range of obligations that are more demanding for industrialized as opposed to developing countries (e.g., financial assistance in favor of developing countries and a transfer of technology and knowledge). In essence, the global climate regime combines environmental with development goals—a more demanding objective than a solely environmental agreement.

While the UNFCCC set an ultimate goal and an institutional architecture, the first Conference of the Parties (COP) at Berlin in 1995 decided to begin negotiations on a protocol to the Convention that would lead to concrete and binding emission reductions in the industrialized countries (the "Berlin Mandate"). Subsequent rounds of negotiations resulted in the Kyoto Protocol (1997). In contrast to the UNFCCC, this treaty is comparatively focused. For a range of industrialized countries, it stipulates legally binding emission reduction targets for six GHGs and groups of GHGs during the period 2008–2012. These reduction targets appear in table 8.1.

The fifteen members of the European Union and some other European countries accepted an 8 percent reduction goal for their average 2008–2012 GHG emissions compared to their emissions in 1990; the United States, a 7 percent reduction; and Japan, a 6 percent reduction. The Russian Federation was allowed to keep its 1990 emissions level, while, for example, Norway and Australia were granted an increase of their emissions by 1 and 8 percent, respectively.

To achieve such emission reductions in an efficient way, countries are allowed to use specific mechanisms, including emissions trading (ET), joint implementation (JI), and the Clean Development Mechanism (CDM). In ET, a country with more emission rights than it anticipates using can sell this surplus to countries that would otherwise exceed their permitted amounts. JI and the CDM are quite similar to each other yet affect different countries. In both, an investor (country or enterprise) invests in an emission-reduction project abroad, the reductions are verified, and in exchange for the investment, the investor receives GHG credits, that is, it can now emit the total of its allowances under the Kyoto Protocol plus these credits. The difference between JI and CDM is that the host country of the emission-reduction project is an industrialized country for JI and a developing country for CDM. In CDM, a contribution is also made to an adaptation fund to help developing countries deal with climate change.

Table 8.1. Changes in GHG emissions for UNFCCC Annex I parties, 1990–2004

Total GHG emissions without LULUCF (million tons CO2 equivalent)				Changes in emissions (%)		Emission reduction target under the Kyoto Protocol[1,2]
Party	1990	2000	2004	1990–2004	2000–2004	(%)
Australia	423.1	504.2	529.2	25.1	5.0	–[3]
Austria	78.9	81.3	91.3	15.7	12.4	−8(−13)
Belarus	127.4	69.8	74.4	−41.6	6.6	no target yet
Belgium	145.8	147.4	147.9	1.4	0.3	−8(−7.5)
Bulgaria	132.3	64.3	67.5	−49.0	5.1	−8
Canada	598.9	725.0	758.1	26.6	4.6	−6
Croatia	31.1	25.3	29.4	−5.4	16.5	–[3]
Czech Republic	196.2	149.2	147.1	−25.0	−1.4	−8
Denmark	70.4	69.6	69.6	−1.1	0.1	−8(−21)
Estonia	43.5	19.7	21.3	−51.0	8.4	−8
European Community	4252.5	4129.3	4228.0	−0.6	2.4	−8
Finland	71.1	70.0	81.4	14.5	16.4	−8(0)
France	567.1	561.4	562.6	−0.8	0.2	−8(0)
Germany	1226.3	1022.8	1015.3	−17.2	−0.7	−8(−21)
Greece	108.7	131.8	137.6	26.6	4.5	−8(+25)
Hungary	123.1	81.9	83.9	−31.8	2.5	−6
Iceland	3.28	3.54	3.11	−5.0	−12.2	+10
Ireland	55.6	68.7	68.5	23.1	−0.4	−8(+13)
Italy	519.6	554.6	582.5	12.1	5.0	−8(−6.5)
Japan	1272.1	1345.5	1355.2	6.5	0.7	−6
Latvia	25.9	9.9	10.7	−58.5	8.2	−8
Liechtenstein	0.229	0.256	0.271	18.5	6.0	−8
Lithuania	50.9	20.8	20.2	−60.4	−3.1	−8
Luxembourg	12.7	9.7	12.7	0.3	31.3	−8(−28)
Monaco	0.108	0.117	0.104	−3.1	−11.0	−8
Netherlands	213.0	214.4	218.1	2.4	1.7	−8(−6)
New Zealand	61.9	70.3	75.1	21.3	6.8	0
Norway	49.8	53.5	54.9	10.3	2.7	+1
Poland	564.4	386.2	388.1	−31.2	0.5	−6
Portugal	60.0	82.2	84.5	41.0	2.9	−8(+27)
Romania	262.3	131.8	154.6	−41.0	17.3	−8
Russian Federation	2974.9	1944.8	2024.2	−32.0	4.1	0
Slovakia	73.4	49.4	51.0	−30.4	3.3	−8
Slovenia	20.2	18.8	20.1	−0.8	6.6	−8
Spain	287.2	384.2	427.9	49.0	11.4	−8(+15)

continued

Table 8.1. *continued*

Total GHG emissions without LULUCF (million tons CO2 equivalent)				Changes in emissions (%)		Emission reduction target under the Kyoto Protocol[1,2]
Sweden	72.4	68.4	69.9	−3.5	2.1	−8(+4)
Switzerland	52.8	51.7	53.0	0.4	2.6	−8
Turkey	170.2	278.9	293.8	72.6	5.3	−[3]
Ukraine	925.4	395.1	413.4	−55.3	4.6	0
United Kingdom	776.1	672.2	665.3	−14.3	−1.0	−8(−12.5)
United States	6103.3	6975.9	7067.6	15.8	1.3	−[3]
Annex I EIT parties	5551.0	3366.9	3506.0	−36.8	4.1	−
Annex I non-EIT parties	13000.5	14147.7	14425.6	11.0	2.0	−
All Annex I parties to the Convention	18551.5	17514.6	17931.6	−3.3	2.4	−
Annex I Kyoto Protocol parties	11823.8	9730.3	10011.5	−15.3	2.9	−5

Source: http://unfccc.int/files/essential_background/background_publications_htmlpdf/
application/pdf/ghg_table_06.pdf (Nov. 12, 2006).

[1]The national reduction targets as per the "burden-sharing" agreement of the European Community are shown in parentheses.

[2]The national reduction targets relate to the first commitment period under the Kyoto Protocol, which is from 2008 to 2012.

[3]A party to the Climate Change Convention but not a party to the Kyoto Protocol.

Note: LULUCF refers to land use, land use change, and forestry. EIT refers to countries in transition from planned to market economies. Base year data (under the Climate Change Convention) are used here instead of 1990 data (as per COP decisions 9/CP.2 and 11/CP.4) for Bulgaria (1988), Hungary (average of 1985–1987), Poland (1988), Romania (1989) and Slovenia (1986).

Furthermore, countries can form bubbles, that is, be considered as one emission air space and agree on common liability, so that it does not matter which actually undertakes the emission reductions as long as the aggregate emissions meet the combined obligations of the bubble's countries. The EU has formed such a bubble for its member countries.

The Kyoto Protocol was concluded in 1997, yet only in late 2001 did countries agree on how to interpret the treaty in more detail. During the interim, President George W. Bush's national security advisor, Condoleezza Rice, declared in spring 2001 that "Kyoto is dead" (quoted in Grubb 2001, 9). Against this backdrop, the Marrakech Accords of November 2001—following failed negotiations in The Hague in late 2000 and intermediate compromises at Bonn in mid-2001—were an attempt under EU leadership to salvage the Kyoto Protocol. They finalized a compliance mechanism with a facilitative and an enforcement branch, made all different types of GHG emission reduction efforts interchangeable currency, and granted generous allowances for the sequestration (binding) of carbon by forest resources and other types of so-called terrestrial sinks.

To take effect, at least fifty-five countries accounting for at least 55 percent of industrialized countries' emissions of CO2 had to ratify the Kyoto Protocol. After the United States refused to ratify the protocol, Russia (due to the size of its emissions) became the pivotal country to determine its fate. After years of ambiguity about its ultimate decision, Russia ratified the Kyoto Protocol in late 2004, which allowed the treaty to become legally binding on its parties on February 16, 2005. At that time, only four industrialized countries—Australia, Liechtenstein, Monaco, and the United States—had not yet ratified the Kyoto Protocol. Australia and the United States had stated that they did not plan to do so (UNFCCC 2004a).

Key Transatlantic Disagreements

Since climate change appeared on the international agenda, the United States and Europe have each promoted different views about several aspects of climate policy, including assessment of the state-of-the-art of science, the necessity and magnitude of binding emission reduction targets, the choice of instruments as well as their implementation, and the inclusiveness of the international regime.[6]

First, the EU takes the IPCC findings as guidelines for action in favor of mitigation whereas the Bush administration has been rather reluctant to accept the scientific mainstream. Second, the United States has opposed binding targets during negotiations, while Europe has promoted them. The United States ultimately agreed to binding emission targets in the Kyoto Protocol, only to revoke that pledge in 2001. Third, even if policy is deemed necessary, there are strong differences in the basic approach. For a long time Europeans preferred direct regulation (coded as policy and measures), which allows for the fine-tuning of government intervention in industrial activity. The United States has preferred market-driven systems such as free and unlimited emissions trading. It took the EU many years to appreciate market-oriented instruments like ET and CDM in order to reduce the burden of adjustment. Yet the EU also still believes in political and economic planning for interventions— as reflected in its past emission reductions, its plans for further cuts, and its support for the institutional structure of the Kyoto Protocol. By contrast, the United States has absolved itself from offering an alternative architecture to govern anthropogenic emissions of GHGs and relies mostly on domestic, bilateral, and multilateral research and technology programs, as well as voluntary emission cuts by U.S. companies. Fourth, the EU has supported the idea that mitigation should begin with the advanced, industrialized countries, while the United States has pushed for the inclusion of developing countries from the outset.

As climate change has advanced on the international political agenda, the debates about it in Europe and the United States have been conducted in very different ways. In the United States, there is no consensus that binding emission reductions are necessary, whereas a broad cross-party consensus exists in much of Europe. In Germany, for example, the Bundestag unanimously backed the Kyoto Protocol. Likewise, in the United Kingdom, both Labour and Conservative governments have endorsed ambitious climate change policies domestically and internationally. By contrast, the United States has yet to achieve congressional majorities favoring emissions control or an executive branch firmly committed to the Kyoto accord or any other binding global architecture to control the dangers of climate change.

The EU still believes that the top-down architecture offered by the Kyoto Protocol is "the only game in town. It is the best we have" (Jan Pronk, chair of UNFCCC COP-6, at The Hague).[7] More precisely, enthusiasm varies among EU members in support of the protocol and relevant internal policies. Yet this should not obscure the fact that, at the aggregate level, the EU remains unified in support of the KP architecture as well as serious efforts at compliance with it.

EU Climate Policy

Some key aspects of the EU's climate strategy are its burden-sharing system and current efforts at compliance, the emissions trading system, and renewable energy goals. The EU's bubble, as part of the burden-sharing system, advocates a common obligation externally while having internally differentiated obligations, resulting from negotiations among member countries. As a group, the EU agreed to a 15 percent emission reduction position before the global negotiations at Kyoto. The internal distribution formula, however, covering only 10 percent, calls into question whether the EU was ever credibly prepared to reduce emissions by 15 percent. Once the EU had agreed to an 8 percent emission reduction at Kyoto, the original agreement was quickly reopened and internal obligations adjusted downward without hesitation. In this process, it became obvious that the late developers in the EU could not retain their generous allowances in the final allocation scheme (Schröder et al. 2002, 129).

While the EU at large succeeded in honoring the nonbinding obligations of the UNFCCC to limit its 2000 emissions to those of 1990, it barely managed to reduce emissions between 1990 and 2004 (see table 8.1). Compared to a linear reduction benchmark for reducing GHG emissions between 1990 and the average Kyoto commitment year of 2010, the EU falls short of being unambiguously on track by way of internally generated emission reductions.[8] As could be expected within a heterogeneous union, compliance records actually vary substantially. Both Germany and the UK—which shoulder most of the net burden of emission reductions—as well as Sweden and France, are well on their way to complying with their EU obligations. Spain, Austria, Portugal, and Finland currently seem to be faltering with respect to achieving their European emission reduction goals. Current and planned policies for domestic emission reductions, plus planned purchases of GHG permits through the Kyoto Protocol mechanisms by Austria, Belgium, Denmark, Finland, Ireland, Italy, Luxembourg, the Netherlands, Portugal, and Spain, are projected to allow the EU 15 to achieve its 8 percent reductions goal (European Environment Agency 2006).

The EU—a latecomer to market-based regulation—passed an EU Directive in 2003 on CO_2 emissions trading among roughly twelve thousand companies. The directive covers about half of the EU's CO_2 emissions (European Commission 2004). In essence, the directive uses cost differences in CO_2 abatement among EU member countries as an efficient way to reduce the costs of compliance with the Kyoto Protocol. The 2005–2007 period serves as a time for easing the way toward achieving real accomplishments in the 2008–2012 period. It thus parallels potential global efforts at emissions trading (e.g., Japan with Russia). In the EU, long-standing member countries had until March 2004 to divide up their national allocations. Not all countries managed to submit their national allocation plans to the European Commission on time; some even had to fear infringement procedures (European Commission 2004). What at first glance looked like submitting plans for the simple implementation of a previously agreed upon EU Directive actually reflected major domestic disputes between governments and industry over who gained what, who could keep entitlements (e.g., old versus new industries), and who governed the environment (industry ministries or environment ministries). Plans in some member countries were politically astute because they used the lack of clarity over the ratification of the Kyoto Protocol by Russia as an excuse to initially over-allocate emissions nationally. Nevertheless, by 2005, the European Commission had approved all twenty-five European allocation plans.

The EU and some of its member countries have pushed renewable energy as an alternative to the carbon economy. Unlike the United States, the EU and some member countries try to set specific goals. There is a goal for making renewable energy 12 percent of overall energy consumption in the EU 15 by 2010 and 22 percent for the EU 25, but the European Commission does not expect the EU to meet these goals (European Environment Agency 2006). Moreover, the EU was unable to enter the Bonn Renewables Conference of 2004, a pet project of the then- environment minister in Germany. It followed the Johannesburg summit in 2002 and its more concrete results and had a longer-term numerical goal of its own. By 2010 the German government plans to double its share of electricity from renewable energy sources from a low level of 6.3 percent in 2000 and reach at least 20 percent by 2020.[9] In 2003 the UK released an energy white paper in which it announced that it "should put itself on a path towards a reduction in carbon dioxide emissions of some 60% from current levels by about 2050" (UK Dept. Trade and Energy 2003, 8). Renewable energy sources are destined to play an important role in this long-term scheme, with a numerical short-term goal of 10 percent of electricity by 2010 (UK Dept. Trade and Energy 2003, 12). France has a national target of 75 percent emission reductions by 2050—which would necessitate massive use of renewables.[10] Whether these goals are politically feasible remains to be seen. The EU has also set up a range of programs to assist in meeting its renewable energy goals (Gupta and Ringius 2001).

In addition to these three policy arenas sketched briefly, the EU has a monitoring system as well as other support programs for European climate policy. Whether the combination of all programs is sufficient for achieving the Kyoto goals is debatable; a report by the European Environment Agency suggests that the EU might just be able to reach its 8 percent emission reduction goals under certain circumstances (European Environment Agency 2006, 5).

U.S. Climate Policy

When George W. Bush declared shortly after his inauguration as president of the United States in 2001 that his country was no longer bound by the Kyoto Protocol, it came as a shock to most in the international community. One should note, however, that the KP never had a chance of ratification under the Clinton administration either.

Calls for the agreement to be "dead on arrival" could already be heard at Kyoto in 1997. Half a year before the negotiations, the U.S. Senate adopted in a bipartisan vote the so-called Byrd-Hagel Resolution (U.S. Congress, Senate 1997). It set the tone for (non)ratification of any future international commitment on climate change by stipulating that the United States should not sign any treaty that does not "include commitments for countries with developing economies" or would "result in serious harm to the economy of the United States."

After passage of the Byrd-Hagel Resolution, the Clinton administration essentially had to downgrade its initial reduction goals and submit a negotiation position paper that was clearly "based more on political pragmatism than environmental purity."[11] After dramatic negotiations in Kyoto, the U.S. delegation finally accepted both higher emission reduction goals and an exclusion of developing countries from binding commitments. Governmental gridlock between the U.S. executive and legislative branches became inescapable. Accordingly, when the U.S. government finally signed the Kyoto Protocol at the fourth UNFCCC Conference of the Parties (COP-4) in 1998, the accompanying Senate delegation reaffirmed at an ad hoc press conference that the Senate would not support it. Subsequently, the Clinton administration never put all its political capital behind the treaty, despite the fact that it continued to officially support it. The protocol was never forwarded to the Senate for a vote.

American domestic climate policy has gone back and forth for two decades. In both Clinton terms, the president initiated programs, but Congress more often than not blocked their implementation. In Clinton's second term, Congress even tried to weaken or abolish earlier measures, repeatedly accusing the administration of implementing Kyoto through the back door. For example, House Resolution 4194 for fiscal year 1999 explicitly prohibited any measures aimed at the Kyoto goals and even put a halt to any publicly financed information campaigns relating to climate change.

New changes arrived with the inauguration of George W. Bush. Opposing Clinton's standpoint, the new president argued that the consequences of global climate change remained uncertain. He echoed the congressional position of the late 1990s that developing countries like China ought not to be free of substantive emission reductions. The Kyoto targets were "unrealistic, . . . arbitrary and not based upon science," so the protocol was "fatally flawed in fundamental ways" (U.S. White House, Office of the Press Secretary 2001). One should note, however, that the United States under Bush has continued to support the general goals of the UNFCCC.

At the time of writing, the Bush administration has not come up with any effective alternative to the Kyoto approach or with decisive domestic measures. Some specifics are illustrative. On February 14, 2002, President Bush announced his Global Climate Change Initiative. Intended to "recognize [U.S.] international responsibilities," it is a legally nonbinding proposal to reduce the greenhouse gas intensity of the U.S. economy (i.e., emissions per unit of GDP) 18 percent by 2012. The initiative claims that "sustained economic growth is the solution, not the problem" (U.S. White House 2002). Its goal will be reached by agreements with industry on voluntary emission reductions. The National Climate Change Technology Initiative of June 11, 2001, had already put technology research and development (R&D), including CO2 sequestration, at the forefront of the administration's climate policy. Bush's approach includes tax reductions for those reducing emissions as well as government-funded subsidies for R&D (Fay 2002).

At first glance, an 18 percent energy intensity reduction goal looks ambitious. Experts point out, however, that this number is roughly in line with current trends in decarbonizing the economy, that is, the goal might be reached without any additional measures as a result of energy efficiency improvements and ongoing structural changes in the economy. In absolute terms, U.S. emissions are expected to rise by about 12 percent by 2012—resulting in levels that are more than 30 percent higher than the U.S. Kyoto Protocol commitments (Pew Center on Global Climate Change 2002). Therefore, Bush's program contradicts his announcement that the United States would play "a leadership role on the issue of climate change" (U.S. White House, Office of the Press Secretary 2001).

Most interestingly with regard to the reversal of the Clinton administration's environmental rhetoric, Congress during the Bush presidency has tried to initiate stronger climate policy measures, often thwarted by the White House. There have been an impressive number of climate policy initiatives in both houses of the U.S. Congress in recent years.[12] The most prominent and far-reaching bill was introduced in the Senate on January 8, 2003, by Joseph Lieberman and John McCain. Their Climate Stewardship bill included a national cap on U.S. greenhouse gas emissions and trading of emission rights. The bill, however, was defeated in the Senate, 43 to 55. On the positive side, this result was better than even its proponents expected. Against a strong coalition of climate skeptics in the executive and legislative branches, key elected officials such as Senate Foreign Relations Committee Chair Richard Lugar changed sides and supported the bill. In 2005, the bill was rejected again. The Senate instead adopted a nonbinding resolution by a vote of 53 to 44 calling for a "national program of mandatory market-based limits and incentives on greenhouse gases" (U.S. Congress, Senate 2005), at least putting the Senate on record for the first time with a demand for mandatory action on GHGs. McCain and Lieberman announced plans to reintroduce their bill. And the fact that other aspirants for the 2008 presidential election have introduced climate change legislation indicates increasing support in the United States for ameliorative action.

European observers tend to reduce U.S. policy to the actions of the federal government. Yet states such as California, New Jersey, and those in New England have been at the forefront of pushing for climate policy initiatives. California State Assembly Bill No. 1493 (passed on July 22, 2002) calls for substantive reduction of CO_2 emissions from vehicles. The most active states are also cooperating with nonstate actors, such as private companies and NGOs, on effective mechanisms for ameliorating climate problems (Rabe 2002). Some states have even tried to interfere with the national government's international policy. For example, California's Senate Joint Resolution 20 (September 26, 2002) stressed the need for the United States to ratify the Kyoto Protocol. In their Regional Greenhouse Gas Initiative (RGGI), northeastern states plus the eastern Canadian provinces have called for a GHG emission inventory as basis for a cap and trade scheme similar to that of the EU.[13] In August 2006 Governor Arnold Schwarzenegger of California and leaders of the Democratic-controlled state assembly announced an agreement that imposes the most sweeping controls on CO_2 in the nation. It calls for a 25 percent reduction in California's emissions by 2020 compared to business-as-usual projections (Barringer 2006).

Clearly, local and regional initiatives should be seen as valuable components but not substitutes for effective (inter)national climate policy. Altogether, the United States remained the climate policy outsider, just as it was in 1993 (Pfaff 1992). It also remains divided internally—a division that has to date resulted in the absence of significant domestic action (Riggs 2004).

Europa Riding the Hegemon?

Over the course of the climate regime negotiations, the European Union has emerged as a leading player. Yet Europe's leadership position has long been undermined by internal divergences. At the Kyoto negotiations, for example, the United States was still able to employ "salami tactics" with the EU, and EU ministers supposedly yelled at each other rather than prepare themselves better for the negotiations. Ultimately, the Kyoto wrestling match in 1997 had no clear winner. The United States managed to largely shape the protocol's instruments according to its preferences yet had to agree to emission reductions and was unable to have developing countries included in the accord. The EU—in coalition with its pro-Kyoto partners in the developed, developing, and NGO worlds—was able to modify the United States' preferred course of action.

With the near collapse of UN climate negotiations in 2000 at The Hague, it became apparent that the EU needed to establish a more outward and forward-looking strategy. Rather than mainly focusing on internal efforts, it had to invest more in global diplomacy, including stronger ties with developing countries. The EU had always been supportive of the principle of common but differentiated responsibilities, which enables developing countries to expect industrialized countries to be first movers in climate change activities.

Now, it forged a tacit coalition with developing countries to limit softening of the Kyoto obligations, conveniently lubricated by support for funds to assist them. For example, in coalition with other developed countries, the EU has offered €450 million annually for climate-related measures.

When President Bush withdrew the United States from the Kyoto Protocol, the question arose of who could and would lead global climate policy formation. A president abstaining from a treaty signed by his predecessor is unparalleled in environmental diplomacy. Equally embarrassing to Europeans was the fact that Bush presented his domestic program only weeks after Christine Whitman, then head of the U.S. Environmental Protection Agency, acting on National Security Advisor Condoleezza Rice's assurances, promised America's European allies that the president would honor his presidential campaign pledge in 2000 to set mandatory reduction targets for CO_2 emissions from power plants (Semple 2005)—which his energy intensity approach failed to do.

The EU then changed its strategy from modifying to resisting. Instead of accepting the death of Kyoto that the U.S. administration had unilaterally announced, it agreed to take the lead in continuing the UN plan. It managed to gain external capacity by not only concentrating on internal policy cohesion but also preparing for negotiating as a union (Grubb 2001). To the surprise of many, further negotiations not only survived the U.S. retreat but resulted in the Marrakech Accords, which serve as the executive rules for the Kyoto Protocol.

Many believe that the Bush administration had hoped to kill off Kyoto by opposing it (Shah 2004). Since America's withdrawal, Europe has been at the forefront of those calling on the United States to rejoin or, at the very least, not to oppose further development and entry-into-force of the Kyoto Protocol. This was clearly the message of the Gothenburg summit in 2003 and the whirlwind diplomacy the EU initiated thereafter. At least at the surface of public diplomacy, the EU has been successful with the latter. While being very clear about its reluctance to rejoin, the United States repeatedly announced that it would not try to force others to leave the protocol.

EU diplomacy followed largely what Herman Ott and Sebastian Oberthür (2001) called for in the "EU Leadership Initiative on Climate Change," namely, early ratification of the Kyoto Protocol, steps at domestic implementation, and engagement of the developing countries. On all three points, the EU scores well. It ratified early, nationally as well as at the Commission level, in 2002. Internally, the EU has taken a range of steps to reduce emissions and establish an EU-wide CO_2 trading regime. Finally, it has tried to engage developing countries diplomatically and financially, in part by member countries offering tenders for Clean Development Mechanism projects and establishing a dialogue on their engagement in a second commitment period of the Kyoto Protocol.[14] In so doing, it has also maintained considerable pressure on the United States to effectively contribute to global climate change mitigation.

Given U.S. opposition, substantial diplomatic efforts were directed at Moscow because Russia's ratification decision would decide the fate of the Kyoto Protocol. Russia was quite aware of its pivotal role and managed to derive substantial concessions from the EU on so-called sinks in the Marrakech Accords.[15] In addition to UN agencies, European sponsors supported the World Climate Change Conference (WCCC) that took place in Moscow in fall 2003. Although this summit did not result in a firm and unambiguous Russian commitment to ratify the protocol, the conference did display a strong new coalition of European and Canadian advocates supported by other lobbying groups, among them U.S. NGOs. Subsequently, the EU continued its pressure on Russia. As part of its strategy, it did not shy away from linking climate policy with other topics of great importance to Russia such as energy policy and Russia's application for WTO membership. In the end, these efforts sufficed. Together with its "climate allies," most prominently Canada, Japan, a vast majority of developing countries, relevant UN bodies, and environmental NGOs, the EU celebrated Russian ratification as an important diplomatic success and a milestone in saving the earth's climate. During this critical time period, there were constant rumors that American representatives from the private and public sectors were trying to keep Russia from ratifying. If those rumors were true, the EU won the Russian ratification tug-of-war.

At the G-8 Gleneagles summit in 2005, UK Prime Minister Tony Blair made climate change a key issue. The main outcome was an agreement by the G-8 and major developing countries with significant energy needs to launch a "Dialogue on Climate Change, Clean Energy, and Sustainable Development." Once again a European leader was able to force the U.S. president to fight for his credibility: "I've also told our friends in Europe that Kyoto would have wrecked our economy. I don't see how you can be president of the United States and agree to an agreement that would have put a lot of people out of work" (U.S. White House, Office of the Press Secretary 2005). The continuation of the G-8 dialogue will keep climate change and U.S. climate policy on the agenda (Ochs 2005).

More recently, the United States, together with Australia, China, India, Japan, and the Republic of Korea, launched the Asia-Pacific Partnership on Clean Development and Climate. According to U.S. Secretary of Energy Samuel Bodman, its aim is to "work together with the private sector . . . to take concrete action to meet energy and environment needs while securing a more prosperous future for our citizens" (Kelly 2006). While the launch of the partnership came as a surprise to the EU, the United States was quick to state that the initiative "will complement, but not replace, the Kyoto Protocol" (U.S. Department of State 2005). This itself might be an indicator of the strength that the UN process and its primary leader have gained.

Besides international alliance-building, de facto partnerships with state and nonstate actors, and direct engagement of the U.S. government, the EU has cautiously started to help increase U.S. public pressure on the government and has thus joined forces with powerful domestic actors. EU representatives often have openly applauded initiatives on the U.S. state level, which points to the policy vacuum the federal government has left. The EU has collaborated on policy, for example, with regard to the Regional Greenhouse Gas Initiative emission trading plan in the northeastern U.S. states. Still somewhat secretly, European Commission officials have discussed the possibility of linkage with the EU emissions trading system to allow emission permits to be traded across the Atlantic.[16] In 2006, Prime Minister Blair and Governor Schwarzenegger signed an agreement to do cooperative research on new clean-energy technologies. For their part, U.S. actors point to EU positions and actions in demanding a more proactive stance by the U.S. federal government.

Can EU-Europe ride the hegemon? Europa has certainly taken a ride, but any observer of rodeos knows that the rider will ultimately discontinue his or her ride more or less gracefully. If the United States proves to be a youthful bull, Europa has no chance to solve the problem on its own. In the long run the United States has to be willing to contribute to the solution. If the U.S. leadership turns out to be a wild horse ready for domestication, chances are that the EU can succeed in the long run. This seems the more probable scenario since the U.S. public—the rodeo spectators, if you will—increasingly seems to favor the rider domesticating the bull. Despite the dramatic discrepancy between actual U.S. emissions and the Kyoto target—reaching the target emission level would now indeed involve extensive adjustment of the economy—in 2005 a plurality favored rejoining the treaty.[17]

In essence, while Europe has seized the opportunity to advance global climate policy without the United States, the EU clearly prefers to have the United States included in some future policy architecture for tackling the challenge. The EU is not yet courageous enough to embark on long-term proclimate brinkmanship on its own. Its weak foreign policy performance may be improving over time, but the EU has not really mounted a fundamental challenge to its erstwhile closest partner (trade policy is a notable exception).[18] The EU, however, has successfully resisted hegemonic U.S. dominance over climate change policy, adhered to its own preferences, taken over international leadership, and, through a wide repertoire of strategies employed in different arenas, been able to modify U.S. action. A successful continuation on this path would be full implementation of the Kyoto Protocol ratifiers' commitments. For some years to come, the entry into force of the protocol appears to vindicate the EU's position, but it is unclear whether the treaty architecture in its present form will provide the backbone for a successful long-term strategy to limit the dangers posed by climate change.

Most importantly, the EU tries to build coalitions of the willing within universal membership institutions. For climate change, it has put all its eggs in one basket, the "Kyoto basket." Nevertheless, it is unlikely to be in a position to offer the U.S. a side-payment large enough to make it play along in the only game in town. Accordingly, the EU will either have to develop a set of Kyoto modifications that the United States cannot decline to accept or be constrained to wait and see if domestic political pressure in the United States will increase to the point where Washington can no longer refuse to cooperate.

Elements of a Transatlantic Rapprochement on Global Climate Change

Since Europe cannot simply dominate the United States and determine its policy, given U.S. material sources and political strength, we have to explore the chances of the EU reengaging the United States by means of more sophisticated diplomacy. What might future transatlantic relations on global climate change look like? We consider three scenarios: continued EU leadership in, and the United States refraining from participation in, global climate policy; selective linkage of decentralized policies, for example, emissions trading systems; and active transatlantic reengagement on global climate policy.

Given U.S. hostility to the Kyoto Protocol, it may abstain from any global climate policy approach in the years ahead. Reopening negotiations for a U.S. return would inevitably mean reducing the protocol's commitments. The resulting "Kyoto light" would mean a serious loss of credibility for the EU and would therefore be unacceptable. It is now commonly acknowledged that Kyoto is only a first step in preventing dangerous climate change. Thus, Europe will attempt to demonstrate that GHG emission reductions can be achieved without too much harm to economic growth and without relying on the functioning of the U.S. political process, since many participants in the Kyoto Protocol already realize that the United States is generally isolated by the fact that it has not suggested any specific long-term climate strategy. In this scenario, Europe will most likely push for U.S. participation in a post-2012 international climate agreement.

Linkage of selective domestic policies is another possible scenario. Various

U.S. states increasingly press for a more ameliorative national policy. Historically, the United States most often came up with domestic environmental legislation first and only later tried to internationalize such domestic regulation. Also, federal environmental legislation was often anticipated by regulation at the state level. Current state-level climate policy may ultimately beat the status quo by pushing the federal government to cap GHG emissions. Should a national emissions cap materialize, the United States is likely to use market-based instruments, such as a national emissions trading system, to lower the costs of compliance with domestic law (Victor 2004). Eventually, there may be opportunities to link decentralized emissions trading systems by internationally harmonizing rules of trade and verifying offsets. This would parallel the successful history of international trade in goods and services. Emissions trading—invented by Americans but first implemented in European climate policy—would then become *the* transatlantic climate mitigation tool.

A final scenario features a structured attempt at reinvigorating the transatlantic partnership by way of a joint climate policy. Three possible elements would be cooperating on technology R&D, agreeing on a long-term target, and establishing a liability fund for climate-related impacts.[19]

Achieving limits on GHG emissions at acceptable social costs will have to involve far-reaching technological change in the energy, transportation, and other sectors. This seems to be one of the few points about climate change on which the United States and Europe agree. Cooperation to promote development of climate-friendly technologies thus appears to be a promising focus for rebuilding a transatlantic dialogue on global climate change. There are, however, disagreements on the best way to promote technological change. The "technology push" view of the Bush administration puts primary emphasis on the development of low-GHG technologies, typically through publicly funded R&D programs. By contrast, the EU's "market pull" view holds that technological change originates from technology-based regulatory limits or GHG emission caps (Grubb and Stewart 2004).

Overall, choice between a target-based regime and a technology-based policy presents a false dichotomy. Investing in technology will not work efficiently enough if there is no clear target justifying those investments. Conversely, technology programs can vastly improve the acceptability and "implementability" of politically administered reduction targets (Grubb and Stewart 2004). Technology and market regulation are then two sides of the same coin. If the IPCC findings are reinforced in the coming years, and the ineffectiveness of the U.S. climate strategy broadly recognized, a more forthcoming U.S. approach to market regulation is not improbable. Likewise, the EU might face increasing pressure to assist its businesses in their development of climate-friendly technology to enable them to reach the politically mandated emission goals.

Even if we will not see such basic rapprochement anytime soon, there are alternatives for transatlantic R&D cooperation. A number of prominent voices have called for joint massive investment in the development of climate-friendly energy production and energy efficiency technologies. On the upper end, such an enterprise would be comparable to the Apollo program that successfully sent humans to the moon. On a more modest scale, investment could focus on partial solutions, such as capture and storage of GHG emissions, development of emission-free coal-fired energy production plants, and hydrogen and solar technology.

A second starting point for renewed transatlantic climate cooperation would be an intensified debate on the long-term target of climate policy. The UNFCCC should frame the debate. Article 2 of the Convention describes its ultimate objective as the avoidance of "dangerous anthropogenic interference" with the climate system. Transatlantic discussion could focus on how to operationalize that. It could even try to do so in terms of a *quantified* long-term target. Friedemann Müller and Michael Oppenheimer (2004) point out that short-term emission goals considered in isolation provide no road map for the ultimate response to climate change. Emission growth can be decreased with existing technology, but a time frame that covers several decades is needed to develop and implement new technologies that substantially reduce emissions. Short-term international emission objectives, like those embodied in the Kyoto Protocol, are determined fundamentally by political and economic feasibility. A long-term global target, to the contrary, is likely to be determined by an assessment of environmental risks. Appropriate quantification of what can be seen as a "safe" climate trajectory would enable decision makers to align short-term steps with long-term risk. Most interestingly, business on both sides of the Atlantic has called for a long-term goal (for 2050). Only that sort of time frame provides the opportunity to plan capital turnover. Its absence has led firms that are otherwise supportive to refrain from supporting the Kyoto Protocol's 2008–2012 time frame for obligations. This, in turn, has stiffened the resolve of Kyoto's political opponents.

An informal process involving policy makers, experts, NGOs, and the business community should be undertaken to stimulate governmental negotiations on a quantification of UNFCCC's article 2. Formal choice of a target would not have to be set in stone. It could be seen as a first step subject to periodic revision to accommodate current uncertainty and future learning. One reasonable approach to dealing with current scientific uncertainty would be to focus first on those outcomes for which general agreement on the importance of avoidance could be more easily achieved (like collapse of the thermohaline circulation of the Gulf stream, disintegration of the West Antarctic ice sheet, or loss of the Greenland ice sheet), and then to agree on a GHG concentration goal commensurate with avoiding such unwanted outcomes.

Even stronger mitigation measures than those applied now will be unable to fully prevent human-induced climate impacts, although the less we reduce emissions now, the higher the anticipated damages are likely to be. This raises the question of who will be held responsible for such damages and directs attention to the third possible area for transatlantic cooperation: collaboration on a global adaptation and compensation fund. Countries would be responsible in proportion to their share of global anthropogenic emissions.[20] Countries would have to pay into a liability fund over decades, and these resources would be used for adaptation and compensation. As liability would be proportional to emissions, the fund would have to indemnify itself from the proportion of impacts caused by emissions of nonmembers. The EU could create such a liability fund, and if countries wish to receive awards for compensation and adaptation, damaged parties would have to go through a court-like system establishing a causal link between the damage claimed and the emissions of GHGs. For the non-EU share of damages caused, they would have to sue other countries independently.

This liability system has three attractive features. First, it may grow as countries may wish to join a worldwide insurance system rather than being harassed in national courts and by the media, NGOs, and IGOs. Second, if future research alters the science of climate change substantially, the remaining funds could be returned to their contributors. Third, there is a clear incentive to mitigate emissions irrespective of the decisions of other countries. As the structure of emitters changes over time, so would their responsibility for liability. While the industrialized countries would initially be most liable for climate-related damages, this burden would shift proportionally to countries that are the dominant emitters of the future—thereby providing incentives for developing carbon-poor energy systems.

Ever since the United States withdrew from the Kyoto Protocol, the EU has managed to increasingly act as an international leader for dealing with the problems posed by global climate change. We have reviewed the strategies Europe has employed to, first, resist hegemonic U.S. dominance and, second, modify U.S. behavior. The EU has applied these strategies (coalition building, de facto partnerships, and issue linkage) on different levels of political organization, from the (U.S.) domestic to the global arenas. The latter has been the most important arena, with the Kyoto Protocol as of today qualifying as a "broad agenda institution with the United States excluded," in the language of chapter 1. This status quo, however, is an outcome of America's unilateral withdrawal from international climate policy and not a preferred result of EU action. To the contrary, U.S. reengagement has been and will continue to be a goal of European climate policy. On climate change, like many others issues in the post–Cold War era, the transatlantic elites hold divergent priorities and may no longer understand each other (Neuss 2004). Yet as Jessica Mathews (2002) notes, there is little that cannot be done if Americans and Europeans agree—but very little that can be done if they do not. We cannot be sure whether the suggested strategies for transatlantic rapprochement will succeed, but by not trying we could run an even graver risk: climate change as a reason for the transatlantic partners drifting farther apart.

DEVELOPMENTAL OPPOSITION IN INTERNATIONAL TRADE REGIMES

Regional Groupings and State and Civil Society Coalitions

DIANA TUSSIE

Challenges to U.S. preferences on development issues had lost all vigor in the 1990s as liberal ideas set in and wrought changes across a range of countries. As the century drew to a close the pendulum swung: many governments came to recognize that trade commitments made in times of euphoria turned out to be highly uneven, and strident discontent arose from civil society. Once again a fresh mood of querulousness and agitation set in. For many, the returns of the North American Free Trade Agreement (NAFTA) provided cold comfort. At the same time, the commitments of the World Trade Organization (WTO) led to increasing pain and disquiet as they reached their implementation deadline and began to bite. Civil society demonstrated forcefully in the "Battle of Seattle" during the WTO summit there in 1999; governments expressed their dissent from U.S. policy preferences loudly and clearly at the WTO gathering in Cancun in 2003 and then held out and finally derailed the meeting. Compounded by the new power configuration that emerged from the end of the Cold War and the ascendance of China, the international trade regime has become a wrestling camp where competing projects vie, revolt, and hold out in an attempt to shape distributive outcomes. Implicitly and explicitly, challenges to the hegemony of American interests and values lie at the core of development policy conflicts.

Regimes, including trade regimes, lay out a set of mutual expectations, rules and regulations, organizational plans, efforts, and financial commitments (Ruggie 1998, 56). Their advocates claim them to be useful tools for providing public goods or solving collective action dilemmas. Regimes and regime-forming arenas also are sites of power contests. Those contests do, of course, involve already existing power hierarchies and organized interests. What must be recognized is that regime arenas and power contests in them also involve efforts by the historically weak or underrepresented to coalesce in order to trim and reshape rules and reduce pressures to accept policies they wish to evade or delay.

Tensions have emerged in multilateral regimes where numerous coalitions of governments, and associated civil society groups, have now become active to an unprecedented extent and are in a position to place obstacles in the way of U.S. policy preferences. Examples of that form of resistance are explored for global warming in chapter 8, for tax competition in chapter 10, and for public health in chapter 11. Trade and related international economic issues, the focus of this chapter, are no less marked by such activities. Even in Western hemisphere regime building, in what is usually regarded as the United States' backyard, the crude assertion of American power has become contested. To what extent and in what ways do these patterns pose challenges to American policy preferences?

This chapter analyzes coalitions that have increased the visibility of trade by posing challenges to U.S. economic power. After a brief overview of basic features in U.S. trade policy, it focuses on the G-20 at the global level and Mercosur states at the regional level that currently constitute sustained challenges to U.S. trade proposals. Coalition building in the WTO can be categorized as manipulating value conflicts and related rules according to the framework discussed in chapter 1. Opposition to the U.S. Free Trade Area of the Americas (FTAA) project by the Mercosur members also involves other types of action introduced in chapter 1: schedule delaying and standing aside, actions couched as assertions of autonomy. The chapter concludes with an exploration of the interconnection between governments and civil society in the Americas. The simultaneity of these processes shows how the trade regime has become a complex, multi-layered arena where social forces and contending political projects compete—a far cry from being simply sites of the United States' preferred uncontested hegemonic project for market-driven integration.

The Uniqueness of Trade

The trade policy process has unique features that we must take into account when thinking about global regimes. Trade policy is inherently distributive. It has a direct impact on consumption, production, fiscal revenues, and employment. Trade policy thus produces a particular form of political conflict and requires that policy actors astutely take advantage of political cooperation opportunities.

The trade policy–making process also has tended to be quite secretive and not easily accessible to governments and societies at the receiving end. Negotiations are characterized by a great deal of bilateral bargaining over reciprocal measures on commercially sensitive issues. There is little or no emphasis on plenary-based open negotiation. Private meetings and "flexible" decision-making processes are often a euphemism for a system of governance deeply flawed by lack of transparency and accountability. Further, there are substantial requirements for legal and economic expertise, which heighten the barriers to meaningful participation by governments and social sectors less well endowed with those assets. These factors make developments in national (i.e., domestic) political arenas and their civil society complexes extremely important.

The processes and structures affecting trade-related challenges to the United States are not, of course, static. In terms of domestic opposition, the run-up to the "Battle of Seattle" marked a turning point. By then, the Global South had abandoned most traces of the import substitution policies that had allowed domestic trade politics to be heavily insulated from external pressures. Under high tariffs, business and labor had been able to fix a price structure that favored the Keynesian compact and brought together domestic producers and workers. The international distributional impact of trade was then under cover; if and when it emerged, business and labor met on the same side in favor of protection, high wages, and domestic consumption. As layer after layer of trade protection was shed, the international price structure became internalized. The international negotiations that followed had an immediate impact on prices and incomes.

The requirement for reciprocity in negotiations, whereby the gains of one sector abroad require another sector to adjust to increased import competition, intensified domestic sensitivity to adjustment processes. Trade has thus come to have unprecedented salience in domestic politics in the Global South. The emergence of articulate international coalitions and domestic pressure groups now constrains government action and requires intense efforts at interest articulation and coalition building.

For the United States, trade policy has never been just about trade. Since 1914, and especially from the 1930s onward, the United States has considered it a national duty to lead a "free trade" crusade. This mission was conducted under a variety of political imperatives, depending on the particular circumstances. The multilateral trade regime of the postwar period, centered on the General Agreement on Tariffs and Trade (GATT), was born of American dominance. As an institution, the GATT developed as an extension of American and, over time, transatlantic rules of the game. As a framework created in the image of the U.S. economy, it sought almost exclusively to deal with internal impediments—institutions and practices—to free competition. GATT assumed a U.S. model of domestic political economy. When this was not the case, the imperatives of the Cold War allowed impediments to coexist despite aspirations to multilateralism. In spite of its contribution to the creation of the international organizations and regimes of the Cold War, U.S. foreign policy never ruled out mercantilist interests and unilateral action, especially when multilateral institutions hindered U.S. goals. According to one scholar, "The United States has had a long tradition of ambivalence towards international law and institutions. This has varied across administrations but has been a constant element in U.S. policy. It has engaged both liberals and conservatives, often united in not wishing to stand in the way of the U.S. promoting both its hard interests and its great moral purposes" (Hurrell 2004).

Accordingly, trade liberalization has become mixed with other causes, including the conflation of markets and political freedoms under U.S. leadership. In essence, this was the universal projection of the American dream— a vision of economic plenty in the context of political freedom as expressed some decades later in the notion of a "free world." Often the looming presence of a menace or an enemy was necessary to garner consensus on further liberalization. These conceptions were explicitly reaffirmed in Title XXI of the U.S. Trade Act of 2002: "The expansion of international trade is vital to the national security of the United States. Trade is critical to the economic growth and strength of the United States and its leadership in the world. Stable trading relationships promote security and prosperity. Trade agreements today serve the same purposes that security pacts played during the Cold War, binding nations together through a series of mutual rights and obligations. Leadership by the United States in international trade fosters open markets, democracy and peace throughout the world" (sec. 2101[b]).

That multilateralism is an effective means for managing global economic integration is an arguable premise. The GATT was singularly unsuccessful at integrating Japan, the newly industrialized countries (NICs) of East Asia, Latin America, and now China into global trade. In its present form, multilateralism is also in tension with further globalization. Discriminatory barriers continue to proliferate, and the accomplishments of the Uruguay Round were more about imposing U.S. conceptions of trade relations on the world through anti-dumping rules, selective safeguards, investment codes, and intellectual property agreements than about genuinely global issues. As dissatisfaction grew, the United States abandoned its traditional antipathy toward bilateral treaties and gradually started to build a web of bilateral and regional agreements, both as a reassurance strategy and as a way to exert pressure on the noncompliant. The view that "if the multilateral road is obstructed, then we will just have to explore other roads" gained ascendancy.

During the Cold War years the United States was confident that multilateralism was good for its broad strategic interests, as well as the interests of American business. Since the collapse of communism, U.S. policy toward multilateral institutions has hardened. At the same time, U.S. trade policy has a heightened aspect of concern with security (Higgot 2004). America's continued rhetorical commitment to multilateralism has been replaced by a new strategy of first signing free trade agreements with regional partners and then preferential trade agreements with allies. United States Trade Representative (USTR) and later Deputy Secretary of State Robert Zoellick, of the George W. Bush administration, coined the phrase "competitive liberalization." The policies under that umbrella amount to creating a race among trade pacts for access to the U.S. market while granting favorable terms to American business interests abroad. Competitive liberalization rests on the premise that the content of each agreement becomes the negotiating floor for the next agreement. Concessions in bilateral negotiations can reinforce U.S. positions in the Western hemisphere negotiation, which in turn can increase U.S. leverage in the multilateral arena and eventually Washington's ability to shape the international trading regime. Bilateral and regional free trade agreements can be interpreted in this light as a part of a piecemeal strategy to shape the multilateral trading system. The bilateral and regional arenas are useful for placing issues on the agenda that would, without such a boost, generate strong resistance in the global multilateral bargaining arena. Different negotiating layers can contribute in this way to entrench U.S. hegemony (Phillips 2003).

The asymmetrically great power of the United States, especially when joined with the EU and Japan, need not and increasingly does not limit the options of others to mere inaction and immobilization. Quite the contrary, other governments and their citizens have formed challenging movements and coalitions to evade, modify, and resist America's hegemonic trade project in order to reduce the costs and pain they associate with it. We will now review the challenge strategies employed by state and societal actors in the context of the inherent tensions associated with different levels of development.

Manipulating Value Conflicts in the WTO

State-led trade coalitions may be classified into two types: bloc-type coalitions and issue-based alliances. They may be seen as representing the opposite ends of a spectrum. There are two key differences between bloc-type coalitions and issue-based alliances. First, the former come together against a backdrop of ideational and identity-related factors, whereas the latter are formed for utilitarian reasons. Second, bloc-type coalitions bring together like-minded states to find common ground across issue areas and over time. In contrast, issue-based coalitions are directed toward specific threats and dissipate after the particular issue has been addressed. While bloc-type coalitions dominated third world diplomacy until the early 1980s, issue-based coalitions came into vogue in the Uruguay Round (partly as a reaction to the failures of bloc-type diplomacy). The coalitions of today, having been built on the lessons of their ineffective predecessors, utilize some elements of both bloc-type coalitions and issue-based alliances.

Developing countries' dissatisfaction with multilateral negotiations has been long-standing. Prior to the Uruguay Round and during the prenegotiations of that round, developing countries had formed a broad-based coalition of "the South." The so-called Group of Ten (G-10), led by a "Big Five" comprising Argentina, Brazil, Egypt, India, and Yugoslavia, formed as soon as the United States began its push to launch a new round in the mid-1980s. The coalition successfully blocked some aspects of the U.S. initiative. Although the G-10 soon split as it tried to formulate positions as the negotiating evolved, it did highlight the potent ability of coalitions to alter the structure of bargaining in which the Quad (the United States, the EU, Canada, and Japan) enjoyed so much power.

Developing countries did not leave the Uruguay Round negotiations empty handed. The inclusion of agriculture, the commitment to phase out the restrictions on textiles, and the creation of a much stronger dispute-settlement mechanism were significant gains. Yet they were more than outweighed by concessions. The most significant concessions were a more restrictive, special, and differential treatment for developing countries; commitments made in intellectual property and services agreements; the binding of all tariffs on goods; and new disciplines on subsidies and customs valuation (Tussie 2003). Disappointment with the results of trade negotiations has come to be closely connected with the notion of participation—or more precisely the lack of participation. The decision-making process is one of the crucial dimensions of participation. Resentment was rampant when the commitments stemming from the Uruguay Round began to sting at the same time that a new round was mooted in late 2001. Developing countries again tried to avoid getting pressured into agreeing to definitions and an agenda that would exclude their interests.

Now, for the first time, there is a helpful constellation of conditions in place that will allow developing countries to challenge policy proposals. After the widespread trade liberalization of the 1990s, export lobbies in many countries have gained center stage. In addition, the accession of China into the WTO has changed the institutional balance of power. The labeling of the Doha Round as the "development round" is indicative. The features of the new coalition challenging U.S. policies also derive from the previous experience with coalitions, which suggests a process of social learning. Coalitions that negotiate instead of merely blocking policy have become more prominent.

This new (and stronger) bargaining position, under the leadership of middle-range powers such as Brazil, India, and South Africa, resulted in 2003 in the formation of the G-20+ at the Cancun ministerial meeting. The origins of this coalition can be traced to the Brasilia Declaration signed in June 2003 by India, Brazil, and South Africa—the so-called IBSA initiative. The coalition that emerged at Cancun was a response to the EU-U.S. text on agriculture, arguing correctly (and forcefully) that the offer would not have changed American and European policies very much with regard to export subsidies and trade-distorting domestic support. One of the main assets of the G-20 has been that it went beyond being a simple blocking coalition and adopted an agenda combining developing countries' proactive and defensive stances on agricultural issues.

Admittedly, the initial strength of the G-20 lay in its structure. As far as the EU and the United States were concerned, they could not easily ignore a coalition that represented more than two-thirds of the world's population and more than 60 percent of the world's farmers and was led by a powerful core of emerging powers (particularly Argentina, Brazil, China, India, and South Africa). But recall that the G-10 of the Uruguay Round had also constituted a core group of emerging powers, and it still collapsed. The reason why the G-20 has preserved its cohesion when other coalitions have failed lies in its strategies. The strength of the G-20 is that it has managed to incorporate the concerns of net food importing and food exporting countries and build linkages between them. Brazil, India, and South Africa have played a key role in unifying these traditionally oppositional groups. Even with a predominantly liberalizing thrust, the agenda has made detailed references to interests that must be protected.

By balancing interests, the G-20 stands in contrast to the Cairns Group, in which agribusiness is represented with a more avid push for full free trade. Memories of failed bloc-style diplomacy have persisted, and hence most delegates are quick to claim publicly that their coalitions are based not on identity or ideology but on shared interests in particular issues. However, closer investigation reveals that many of the recent coalitions at the global and regional levels have also reincorporated the key features of blocs. They are often limited to the developing world, outlive the issue around which they coalesced, and operate across issues. They may also be bound by a collective idea that the developing world shares several problems and needs to address them collectively. These "smart" coalitions thus combine elements of both issue-based alliances and bloc-type coalitions (Narlikar and Tussie 2004).

Akin to issue-based coalitions, "smart" coalitions stress the importance of research in facilitating negotiations in the area under discussion. Also, like their issue-based predecessors with whom they have such close affinity, they may focus on one central issue even while addressing broader issues. By incorporating elements of old bloc-style diplomacy and appealing to the shared weaknesses of developing countries (or a similar principle), they are able to acquire a longevity that the short-term, ever-shifting, ever-blocking coalitions of earlier days never enjoyed. The resulting openness to other coalitions, rather than a "United States versus them" antagonism, and logrolling that is not completely random but more focused on a smaller set of issues (partly as a result of research undertaken) make the more recent coalitions considerably more evolved than their bloc-type ancestors.[1]

The G-20 carries weight because of its sheer market power, but the development component of the final outcome of the Doha Round is of particular significance to smaller developing countries, which remain at the margin of the negotiating process. In this sense, another coalition—the G-90—plays a key role with regard to transparency and democracy in the WTO. The G-90 does this mainly by questioning participation conventions in the rule-making process, especially the negotiation practices that have emerged without consultation. On the one hand, "friends of sector meetings" have brought together countries with substantial interests in a given area; they take the lead and then share information with others. On the other hand, invitation-only gatherings of trade ministers have become the favored way of making agreements in a selective, less transparent fashion.

Most of the least developed countries (LDCs) joined other countries from Africa, the Caribbean, and the Pacific during the Cancun conference to form the G-90. These countries have interests they need to protect, and in the end game of the Doha Round they are seeking side-payments. In the Doha Round developing countries that resist pressure have a stronger veto power than they had in the Uruguay Round. That is because they now are part of the WTO and cannot be forced to accept a totally unbalanced agreement once again without substantive side-payments. The goal of the G-90 nations is not to block an agreement for its own sake but to change, to a certain extent, distributional outcomes in their favor.

A third coalition, the G-33, has also been trying to shape negotiations in agriculture. This is a grouping of more than forty developing countries with interests in protecting special products and obtaining special safeguards for them. Arguing that, in the absence of deep pockets, tariffs are the only instruments available to protect their farmers, the G-33 calls for an approach to tariff reduction that does not result in developing countries paying high prices and experiencing disruption in their rural economies. It also wants recognition of a category known as "special products" for special treatment (i.e., lower market access obligations). The United States has indicated that it was against such flexibility for the G-33; instead it proposes limiting this category of products and defining it with a very strict criterion.

In contrast, the G-20 has been building bridges, but because export interests are at stake it is concerned about a wide loophole in the special category. It would like strict limits on the number of tariff lines that can be designated as "sensitive." However, in coordinating efforts the G-33 and G-20 members have recognized the need for some special products and special safeguards as an integral element of the differential treatment to which developing countries have a right. The G-20 thus proposes that the number of sensitive products be determined after the tariff reduction formula has been developed, and it has expressed an interest in working closely with the G-33 to do so. Since agriculture cannot be self-balancing, members of the G-20 are also participating in the drafting of proposals on nonagricultural issues so that those do not become stumbling blocks in the overall process.

A trade agreement that is favorable to the Global South requires a technically driven agenda, but that alone is not sufficient to bring about the desired outcome. WTO negotiations do not generate winning coalitions like the coalitions that win elections in a political party system. Group life in GATT history has been characterized by loose, temporary, and opportunistic coalitions (Drahos 2003). The decision making by consensus that WTO requires puts extra pressure on any type of coalition because strength in voting numbers does not in itself translate into a winning coalition with market power. The rule of consensus casts serious doubts on the longer-term sustainability of trade coalitions. Nonetheless, the emergence of the new coalitions just discussed shows a process of systemic interaction giving substance to developmental values and collective policy responses by developing countries on a range of trade issues. Regional coalitions, to which we now turn, offer prima facie a more stable arrangement than global ones, given that the former are more likely to involve binding commitments.

Delaying and Standing Aside from U.S.-Sponsored Regionalism

Perhaps because the Americas were the only U.S.-influenced region largely un-contested after the Cold War (Castañeda 1993), the most comprehensive U.S. attempt to establish a model of regional economic governance was the FTAA (Phillips 2001; 2003). The FTAA's relevance here stems not only from issues of regional market access for trade and investment but also from a broader set of global power issues. As originally envisaged, the FTAA was intended to do more than just counter the regional erosion of U.S. hegemony due to greater European investment during the 1990s. It was also meant to increase U.S. le-verage in the WTO negotiations.

The initiative was warmly received by Latin American heads of govern-ment at a time when the "Washington Consensus" was the dominant frame of mind. Countries in the region were making progress on both the political and economic fronts, leaving behind the worst excesses of authoritarianism, regu-lation, and protectionism. When the heads of state of the Western hemisphere signed the Miami Declaration and Plan of Action in 1994, there was a consen-sus accepting American leadership in the post–Cold War world and favoring trade liberalization. Today the picture is one of political backlash. Disappoint-ing growth rates have led to doubts about the promise held by U.S.-initiated reform policies. The regional annual average GDP and GDP per capita growth rates during the 1990s barely hit 3.2 and 1.4 percent, respectively. These fig-ures fall far behind the growth rates experienced from the 1950s to the 1980s. Although no country in the region has reverted to protectionism, market-opening policies have come under fire and are being blamed for political, eco-nomic, and social malaise. Governments in South America are attempting an *aggiornamento* of state-led import substitution—combined with a nationalist project of regionalism and resistance to the FTAA.

State-led developmental opposition to trade rules that benefit only the United States can be clearly detected in the Mercosur trade agreement. The Mercosur grouping, shaped by Argentina, Brazil, Paraguay, and Uruguay, has often been described as a reluctant participant in the U.S. project to create the FTAA. There are several reasons why this is an apt description. In the first place, the two main partners, Argentina and Brazil, are sizeable economies with dense domestic markets; both are the least open economies of the region, having the highest average regional tariff (14.3 percent) and exports that ac-count for less than 10 percent of GDP. Business interest in the hemispheric ini-tiative has been lukewarm, and public opinion has been indifferent at best. In 2002 a referendum in Brazil, organized by more than sixty civil society orga-nizations and supported by the National Confederation of Catholic Bishops, revealed that more than 90 percent of the people who cast a vote were opposed to the FTAA and in favor of quitting negotiations altogether.

Brazil stands apart in other respects, too. Brazil's main exports to the United States include relatively high-tech goods such as aircraft, tractor parts, engines, and telecommunications equipment; low-skill-input labor-intensive goods such as footwear; and natural resource-intensive goods such as oil, steel, and paper. Each type has often been the target of a wide range of U.S. protectionist instruments (tariff peaks and anti-dumping and countervailing duties, to name a few). That has been the case, for instance, with orange juice, footwear, apparel, and sugar exports. Brazil's interest in the FTAA lies in the ability and willingness of the U.S. government to relax its trade remedy laws. Counter to this need, the U.S. Congress's passage of a protectionist farm bill in 2001 and the imposition of countervailing duties on Brazilian steel exports in March 2002 reinforced skepticism and lack of enthusiasm.

These issues have not led to a call for or against liberalization. While the technical aspects of a U.S.-led project may be desirable, they are not worth a high cost. These Latin American nations do not want to be dominated by the United States, yet they do want access to the American market to generate economic growth. Economic growth is probably possible even if only some segments of that market are opened. In order to limit American influence, these nations are also making overtures to Europe. At their core is a developmentalist reaction that seeks to redesign trade adjustment. This development-oriented stance and concern about global redistribution accepts the inevitability of Latin American liberalization while trying to manage its potentially destructive aspects by continually offering counterproposals. In this approach, disagreements with the United States on procedural and substantive issues are pursued relentlessly, a strategy that delays established schedules. Further, stand-aside strategies help deny to the United States the full achievement of its policy objectives.

As for the norms of negotiating, the United States has favored country-by-country negotiations while Mercosur has upheld not only decision making by consensus but the acceptance of subregional blocs as well. The United States promoted an "early harvest," while Mercosur has upheld the principle of a single undertaking for the entire package, in other words, that no issue be brought to a final decision until the whole set of trade-related issues is agreed upon. In regard to liberalization of services, the United States has insisted on a broad liberalization scheme, a top-down approach to services trade liberalization based on negative listing, whereby all sectors and measures are to be liberalized unless otherwise specified in annexes containing reservations or nonconforming measures. Mercosur, however, has counter-proposed a positive list approach, following the policy lines applied in its own Montevideo Protocol on Services Liberalization. The positive list approach entails a gradual step-by-step mechanism whereby countries specify the type of access or treatment offered to a particular service (or service supplier) in scheduled sectors.[2] In order to carve out and retain a slice of the government procurement market for itself, Mercosur opposes the U.S.-sought extension of open bidding to state companies and subnational entities.

At the Buenos Aires ministerial meeting in 2001, the Brazilian delegation rejected (with Chilean backing) the U.S. proposal to move up the deadline for concluding an FTAA. Finally, Mercosur expressed broad disagreement with a good part of the FTAA agenda at the ministerial meeting in Puebla in February 2004. The U.S. attempt to shift agriculture and trade relief measures to the WTO was mirrored by Mercosur, which had its own interests to defend; it suggested that such topics as government procurement, intellectual property, and services should be pursued in the WTO global talks. Mercosur's interests are biased toward the global negotiations. Use of the global arena of the WTO has the twofold advantage of requiring lower concessions than the ones demanded in the FTAA and of coalition activity with China, India, and other non-Latin American G-20 countries that can provide greater influence over the agenda.

Against this backdrop the Mercosur agreement has also pursued a hedging strategy, opening negotiations with other South American nations both to weave a fabric of agreements that allow mutual access and to increase leverage vis-à-vis the United States. The interest in extending the reach of Mercosur and obtaining a free trade area with the Andean community and Central America exemplify this vision. Throughout these negotiations Brazil's posture toward the United States has been critical, but never as confrontational as Venezuela's. The distinction is important. Economic isolation is not in the cards. The aim is to preserve the Mercosur market while at the same time gaining access for business abroad. Ultimately, the aim is to build consensus with new players capable of making that balance viable.

If the so-called South American Community of Nations, which is meant to bring together Mercosur and the Andean countries, finally achieves its objective, the union could potentially challenge U.S. hegemony in the region. The initiative faces various problems, however: huge economic constraints, lack of institutional stability, widespread corruption, and doubts engendered by past failures. Similar initiatives, such as the Latin American Free Trade Area of the 1960s and the Latin American Integration Association of the 1980s, were not able to meet their goals. Yet even the existence of Mercosur serves the purpose of challenging U.S. dominance in the hemisphere.

Regionalism as an Arena for Civil Society Contestation

The previous discussion has looked at the ways in which government-led coalitions contest U.S. policy preferences in government-led arenas. This section shifts the focus to civil society activities and stands. The heightened impact of trade negotiations in the post-import substitution era has sown the seeds of domestic discontent and contestation. The anti-globalization movement consolidated these new forms of participation and protest, forms which were subsequently fueled by fresh levels of anti-American sentiment in the context of the war on terrorism after 9/11 and a large-scale U.S.-led war in the Middle East.

Polls show that discontent and disillusion simmer. Citizens (and in particular semi-skilled and unskilled labor) are demanding a greater role for the state. A mood of disenchantment and at times resentment has swept through most of South America, leading to either a rapid erosion of presidents' popularity or, even worse, the collapse of governments amid violent riots. Since the launching of the FTAA initiative by the United States, six Latin American nations (Venezuela, Argentina, Ecuador, Peru, Paraguay, and Bolivia) have been in the throes of institutional crises, and another, Uruguay, made a left-leaning candidate its president for the first time in the history of the country.

Whether or not trade reform and the rest of the neoliberal agenda lie at the root of economic hardship, citizens associate overdependence on the United States with stagnation, unemployment, and poverty. At the same time, American pursuit of aggressive unilateralism has tapped into deeper fears about the consolidation of U.S. hegemony globally and its implications for a Latin America held to be America's inherent sphere of influence. The push the United States gave to the FTAA, perhaps controversial in any case, aroused suspicion because a U.S. presidential administration pursuing a right-wing domestic and foreign policy agenda had advocated the agreement. The way the United States has presented its war on terrorism and quest for regime change in Iraq revived anti-American sentiment. In particular, President Bush's preference for unilateral over multilateral initiatives and general unwillingness to compromise with others in pursuit of U.S. foreign policy goals has been blamed. In short, it has become easier for activists and critics of further regional trade integration to characterize FTAA plans as part of a broader political strategy for consolidating U.S. hegemony in the region.

The fear of being swamped by the massive asymmetries in political power and social, cultural, and economic resources has translated into the emergence of a heterogeneous ensemble of civil society actors active throughout the hemisphere. These increasingly mobilized actors have created transnational networks and coalitions demanding participation in regional integration processes. Moreover, some of these civil society actors have taken the next step: constructing social movements in an attempt to articulate responses to the U.S. project (Smith and Korzeniewicz 2005).

The social legitimacy of the FTAA and the influence of the United States have been called into question. A Latin American poll conducted by Zogby International in 2003 found almost universal dislike of President Bush in the region. A Latinobarómetro poll in 2003 showed that 87 percent of Latin American opinion makers rated Bush negatively. Moreover, the percentage of Latin Americans who have a negative image of the United States has more than doubled, from 14 percent in 2000 to 31 percent in 2003. Sixty percent of Latin Americans still had a positive view of the United States, but that percentage was 71 percent in 2000. In key countries, such as Mexico, the sentiment of anti-Americanism is growing faster (58 percent of those consulted had a negative image of the United States, a share that rose from a mere 22 percent in 2000). The percentage of people with a negative view of the United States reached 62 percent in Argentina, 42 percent in Brazil, and 37 percent in Chile in 2003. The implosion of the one-time "best student" of America, Argentina, has played a key role. Argentina, followed by Mexico, has been the country in which the negative view of the United States was highest.[3]

These misgivings have grown in a context in which many countries have, in recent years, elected left-leaning governments. Those governments, at least potentially, are likely to be more receptive than right-leaning ones to the concerns and claims being articulated by civil society groups and social movements. The emerging alliances forged among Luiz Inácio Lula da Silva in Brazil, Hugo Chávez in Venezuela, Juan Morales in Bolivia, Néstor Kirchner in Argentina, and the Frente Amplio in Uruguay suggest an interesting configuration in which agendas advanced by groups resisting the FTAA are accepted and to some extent articulated by governments. What this suggests, however, is less a full ideological swing to the left with associated anti-Americanism than a harmonization of agendas between governments and civil society movements, a marriage of convenience. Governments seek allies to consolidate their power and legitimate their positions with grassroots movements and labor groups. Civil society networks do not have the capacity to participate consistently and effectively in international policy-shaping debates, but there is ample evidence of the skill they have acquired in recent years in playing the politics of information, symbols, leverage, and accountability (Smith and Korzeniewicz 2005; Khagram et al. 2002). In the new political climate, weaker governments are motivated to make overtures to civil society networks for the purpose of mobilizing public support in contentious negotiations with the United States.

Specific strategic political motivations are generating an alignment of perspectives, an ideological affinity of governments with those groups more resistant to American-led patterns of regional trade integration. We have then a special political moment that provides an accommodating space enabling left-leaning governments and movements in power to advance elements of the agendas articulated by popular movements. Concessions in which some civil society actors are allowed selective participation, a common currency used by the United States in classic two-level games to increase leverage in negotiations (Putnam 1988), are being emulated by weaker Latin American governments in their strategies that challenge the United States.

Each of the Latin American government leaders mentioned above face the *realpolitik* dilemmas of avoiding open confrontation with powerful, established commercial interests while at the same time enhancing and maintaining important domestic civil society support to shore up their domestic popularity. As governments and civil society alignments converge to increase their mutual effectiveness and base of support, the FTAA (perceived as "the onslaught of empire") has become a leading case in the new generation of contested trade agreements that cannot be insulated from public concerns. What emerges from these trends is an interesting relationship between the use of mobilization and resistance. In this relationship it is not always clear how governments will balance the risk-adverse mindset of elites with popular disaffection and adapt in response to claim-making and mobilizing by civil society (Borón 2004). What is clear is that as public opinion organizes in networks and coalitions against the FTAA, governments cannot afford to treat it simply as an extension of the Washington consensus, a mere reflection of U.S.-claimed spheres of influence and policy preferences.

At both the global and regional levels, the United States has attempted to lock in its hegemony by internationalizing its domestic regulations and practices. American desires to shape the multilateral and regional trade regimes can be best understood within the tradition of exporting U.S. rules to the rest of the world in order to provide a more secure and profitable environment for its private interests. In this respect, it is worth highlighting that the United States is the only country that has developed a body of doctrine and practice favoring the extraterritorial application of its laws, a set of claimed rights initially restricted to anti-trust cases and export controls in the context of national security. For the United States, a rule-based order has increasingly come to mean the extension of American rules and procedures to the rest of the world. Of late, this has been clearly evident in the drive to extend U.S. standards of regulation and protection for the issues encompassed in the so-called new trade agenda: foreign investment, services, government procurement, and intellectual property.

As the United States attempts to extend its power and influence abroad, challenges to its doing so have multiplied and will continue to do so. This assertiveness by others is expressed through numerous efforts to build state and nonstate coalitions. What should be apparent is that as developmental values regain legitimacy, the trade arena has become a site of noncompliant challenges where the weak or underrepresented seek windows of opportunity to reshape rules and reduce pressure for policies they wish to evade or for which they want offsetting concessions. These challenges are not necessarily a general rejection of present and future cooperation with the United States at all times or on all issues. As emerging players in international affairs grow in strength and stature, they are investing in becoming technically empowered to challenge what Washington wants through evasion, modification, and resistance. They are adopting more complex ways of shaping a number of outcomes, including trade-related ones. While civil society in major developing countries may tend to demand outright resistance and confrontation, governments are more prone to accommodate by manipulating value conflicts, trimming U.S. proposals, and vying with counterproposals both through regional agreements with binding commitments and the looser coalitions in the WTO. Dealing with the United States becomes less of an exercise in helplessness. Instead, it becomes more of an exercise in negotiated accommodation in which state and nonstate actors interact and feed off each other in a process whereby values become shared, rules gradually are codified, and all actors get to reinvent themselves.

A project of semi-autarky and "nationalist regionalism" based on the scenario of an attempted "populist revival" and the aggrandizement of executive power promises no more than meager, and probably short-lived, economic compensation for the losers in processes of market integration. Delaying one's own market opening and tying it to concessions received from abroad offers opportunities for a more balanced result, one in which citizen allegiance can be attracted or at least domestic opposition can be reduced. In the different arenas in which U.S. policy is contested, civil society has become an important vehicle for attempts to shape international distribution of goods and ills. There is then a constant interweaving of negotiations to build consensus at home by co-opting some anti-globalization movements (particularly those affiliated with more combative labor organizations) and by generating technocratically empowered proposals that buy time and accommodate domestic commercial interests. State policies thus are moving from ultra resistance to crude U.S. interests to evasion and proactive modification strategies in order to achieve an inner circle of consensus with key domestic constituencies and some other selected states. Once achieved, that inner circle can be expanded to broader and broader international sets of governments and civil society networks until it is shared by enough of the world to persuade Washington that its policy aspirations are unachievable.

In the pursuit of such a "new international order," partnership and cooperation with the United States are not precluded. Imagine a triangular policy space whose points with regard to U.S. policy preferences are grudging acceptance of the inevitable, eager compliance, and blanket hostile rejection. Within that triangle lies abundant space for mixed motive games or conflict of interest situations that others in international affairs pursue by means of technically informed proposals, which pose challenges short of harsh and absolute confrontation. Although not every player in such an international order will be ready to adjust at the same time on any given issue, what happens with regard to any single issue will affect actions on others. All actors look like wrestlers nervously circling one another in a continuous process, none wanting full disruption, failure, or long-standing deadlock. That is what has happened with international trade-related issues. Trade has become a complex, multi-layered arena in which social forces and contending political projects compete—a far cry from the simple and conceptually neat hegemonic project for market-driven integration initially conceived and spearheaded by the United States.

10

U.S. DEFECTION FROM THE OECD "HARMFUL TAX COMPETITION" PROJECT
Rhetoric and Reality

ROBERT T. KUDRLE

According to *Tax Havens and Their Use by United States Taxpayers,* a report issued in 1981 by the U.S. Treasury, "The United States alone cannot deal with tax havens. The policy must be an international one by the countries that are not tax havens to isolate the abusive tax havens. The United States should take the lead in encouraging tax havens to provide information to enable other countries to enforce their laws" (Gordon Report 1981, 10).

This chapter addresses an area of European resistance to U.S. preferences that few persons—even in the attentive public—have heard much about. This little-known area, chiefly involving tax avoidance and evasion, will likely become one of the premier public policy challenges of the twenty-first century. The logic is hard to deny: globalization as economic enmeshment across political boundaries is proceeding at a rapid pace. Few signs from either private markets or public policy suggest that this trend will abate, and almost nothing points to a reversal. The increased mobility of goods, services, capital, and labor has, in turn, posed ever-increasing challenges to national tax authorities.

In the case examined in this chapter, the United States found itself in a situation in which the combined economic weight of U.S. opponents matched or exceeded its own. Economic power has been particularly important in the Organization for Economic Cooperation and Development (OECD) because that institution deals mainly with economic issues.[1] The main challenges came not in response to U.S. initiatives but to ones from the EU and Japan. An open difference emerged after the United States rejected part of an OECD plan favored by others and for which the United States had earlier provided enthusiastic support. The text of the OECD's manifesto, *Harmful Tax Competition* (1998), and initial follow-up activities generated so much hostility that the United States was provided with an unusual opportunity to claim the cause of some small developing states against rich-state presumption.

The OECD campaign against tax havens illustrates one set of dynamics drawn from the framework in chapter 1: temporize, maintain good relations based on a declared and actual willingness to engage in some compromise, and fully recognize the extent to which one's own position is shared by important segments of opinion within the hegemon. International business on both sides of the Atlantic found much fault with the *Harmful Tax Competition* (or *HTC*) project, while government fiscal professionals all over the OECD warmed to it and domestic politics ebbed and flowed—with a sharp discontinuity in the United States following the inauguration of George W. Bush as president early in 2001.

The appearance of *HTC* in 1998 seemed to signal a new determination by the high-income countries to coordinate their attack on both (illegal) evasion and (legal) avoidance of personal and corporate income taxes.[2]

HTC declared a special interest in "mobile economic activity" and was seen as only the first of a series of attempts to address tax competition issues. More than six years later, as the *HTC* project reached its final stage, few predicted any similar future initiatives. Moreover, commentators disagreed on how much the project had accomplished and what the entire episode implied for U.S.-EU relations and for the OECD. The United States had moved from a champion to a revisionist critic of the OECD efforts early in the Bush administration, and the most influential actors in the OECD and the EU were obliged to adapt as best they could. But the initiative had already shifted course, toward the U.S. position, before the open rift, and how much developments would have differed had Al Gore been president remains in doubt.

Actors and Options in International Taxation

The immediate actors in this drama of tax avoidance and evasion consist mainly of government enforcement officials on one side and corporations and high-income persons (along with their agents, interest groups, and other political supporters) on the other. The issues have seldom had much salience with the general public. The role of NGOs has been quite modest because the issues are so complicated that other policy areas look much easier to understand and to address with particular actions. When the policy discussion gets specific, defenders of avoidance and evasion tend to outgun their opponents through specialized knowledge.

The United States has always insisted that all earnings of its citizens are subject to American taxation—a "global" approach. Foreign corporate taxes are credited against U.S. tax liability (if a tax treaty is signed between the United States and the other country). Moreover, payment of corporate income tax owed can be deferred until the revenue to be taxed is repatriated to the United States. The Kennedy administration proposed eliminating this provision (Picciotto 1992, 111), and until quite recently many analysts favored this change (Bergsten et al. 1978, 196–202, 462–63). However, the growth of foreign competition from firms based in nations with more permissive regimes diminished the pressure for reform and increasingly led economists to defend deferral (Hines 1999).

Other countries, for example, Germany and France, have dealt with the double taxation problem by using a "territorial" system that draws a sharp distinction between foreign earned corporate income that is not taxed at home and domestic earned income that is (Hufbauer and Rooij 1992, 57). This method of taxation appears to give a national competitive advantage to firms with subsidiaries in low-tax jurisdictions.[3]

Taxation of loans by individuals or firms from abroad has posed another challenge. Decision makers in most states had concluded by the last quarter of the twentieth century that *any* tax on local borrowing was paid not by the lender but by the borrower.[4] Hence most modern states (those not looking for immediate revenue above all else) greatly reduced or abolished such taxation, leaving earnings to be taxed by the lending country.

Just as corporate taxation can be treated on a global or a territorial basis by the home country, so too can personal income tax liability. Although high-income countries other than the United States do not tax income from labor services performed abroad, nearly all states try to tax the earnings of their own citizens' overseas assets. But the increasing ease with which virtually anyone can place funds abroad has created a huge opportunity for tax evasion because, unlike domestic investments, foreign earnings are not accompanied by automatic or easily obtainable information for the home government.

U.S. and EU Policy Concerns

A comparison of several features of U.S. tax collection with those of many EU members might suggest that the former have been more geared to social democracy and the latter more compromised by incentives and global competition. The United States leans relatively heavily on revenue from income taxes. It collected almost half of its total revenue from personal and corporate income taxes in 1999—40.7 percent and 8.3 percent, respectively—while the EU collected only 25.6 percent from the personal income tax and just slightly more than the United States in corporate income tax: 8.7 percent (Heady 2002, 1). The United States has also been exceptionally comprehensive in taxing its citizens' overseas earnings. Further, the United States has been notably insistent on information sharing in tax treaties and has pressured states with strong bank secrecy laws and traditions to reform.

The United States has long realized that it cannot enforce its tax policy without considering what other states are doing. The same concerns about competitive disadvantage that increasingly led economists to doubt the wisdom of eliminating corporate income tax deferral bred a cautious, if not sympathetic, view of some nominally "abusive" U.S. corporate practices that served to lower effective rates on overseas earnings. Such contortions could sometimes be seen as merely putting U.S. firms on a more level playing field with their foreign rivals. This concern has grown in recent years as U.S. corporate tax rates have increasingly risen above those of competitors.[5]

While the United States takes a global approach to income taxation and most EU countries take a territorial approach, there is another arguably far more important reason why the two jurisdictions view international taxation differently. Each state in the EU—including the new low-income members—depends overwhelmingly on its own fiscal resources. Only about 2 percent of EU expenditure takes place at the Union level, and that comes from member state coffers (Demertzis 2000, 15). The transatlantic contrast is startling: American federal government tax collection is about two-thirds of the U.S. total.[6]

Recent years have seen some convergence of European VAT, personal income, and corporate tax rates, but this has come mainly from independent adjustment. Several attempts have been made to coordinate tax rates across the EU, but all (except for a minimum VAT rate) have ultimately been rejected by some members as a violation of sovereignty (Tanzi 1995, 117). Nonetheless, fears of "unfair competition" and a "race to the bottom" rivet the attention of both politicians and voters in Europe, where economic competition is generally viewed more skeptically than it is in the United States. France and Germany, the two most influential states in the EU, have long favored a floor on corporate tax rates and perhaps even harmonization (Webb 2004, 17).

Several intra-European tax issues were under close scrutiny as the OECD project began. Ireland had emerged as the fastest growing country in Europe (and, after China, the fastest growing state anywhere), in part by "ring fencing": using systematically more favorable corporate (and other) tax advantages for entering foreigners than for domestic firms (and persons). Banks in Luxembourg, Belgium, and Austria were notorious for giving other Europeans the opportunity to evade taxes on earnings from savings because accounts there were essentially as safe as domestic accounts but without automatic reporting to fiscal authorities.[7] Finally, nearly all EU states had some special advantages for non-national business investors that could be construed as violating a level playing field. In short, tax competition within Europe—and not just with the rest of the world—appeared to threaten the resource base for national budgets that were proportionately much higher than that of the United States.

The *Harmful Tax Competition* Project

A benchmark must be used to identify "harmful tax competition" in a world of independent, differing tax structures. Much previous literature, as well as *HTC,* endorses a fairly weak but easily observed standard: countries should maintain a uniform tax structure with the same rules for foreign and domestic factors.

The international consistency standard aims to control competition for real economic activity. But states may also lose tax revenue, rather than productive factors, from a kind of legal fiction: the mere appearance of activity in a place so that taxation can be avoided in other jurisdictions. This fiction is mainly of three kinds. The first is when firms utilize subsidiaries in a "harmful" jurisdiction, and these subsidiaries absorb and reinvest funds that would otherwise be taxed at higher rates in the jurisdictions where the owners reside.[8] In the second type, firms directly incorporate in another jurisdiction and avoid any residual headquarters corporate tax payments where the owners reside.[9] In the third scenario, individuals' funds are secretly routed through such jurisdictions as a means of tax evasion.[10]

The OECD decided to study various types of possibly "harmful" tax competition in 1996, an initiative ratified by the G-7's summit in Lyon in 1996.[11] The OECD's Committee on Fiscal Affairs set up a task force in 1997 that reported in 1998.

The Initial Report

Harmful Tax Competition (1998) identified two broad categories of unacceptable behavior: "harmful tax regimes" and "tax havens." The former were implicitly the province of OECD members themselves, while the latter referred generically to perhaps two score typically small polities that appear to structure their corporate and personal income taxes to attract foreign investment that is overwhelmingly financial rather than real.[12] These jurisdictions typically have stable governments (about two-thirds are members of the Commonwealth), good transportation and communications, and, of course, freely convertible currencies.[13]

According to *HTC,* tax havens are defined as having little or no tax on relevant income, and they feature one or more of the following: a lack of effective exchange of information, a lack of transparency, and "insubstantial" activity attached to the claim of haven location. The two "lacks" are linked because when no local laws compel appropriate transaction recording, there is no information for the authority to share.

Harmful tax regimes are identified further by an additional criterion that deviates from the final one for tax havens. Instead of requiring that the activity be "substantial," the standard is "ring fencing," that is, whether the jurisdiction essentially uses a different tax rate for foreign business than it does for domestic firms. The apparent rationale is that nonhavens will have a sizable taxed domestic business sector to serve as a benchmark for tax comparison, while the havens will not and instead present the threat of "sham" activity.

The original report of 1998 has been subject to great scrutiny and much criticism. It professed to target only one category of harmful tax competition: the inappropriate enticement of "mobile" financial and similar services, leaving other problems for subsequent investigations.[14]

OECD documents often begin as analysis but become increasingly murky as representatives of approving governments add their contributions. For *HTC,* an inadequately formulated problem statement contributed to a generally confusing report. The core problem is not solely, or perhaps even primarily, that financial services are "mobile." More centrally, the physical proximity of the intermediary to either lender or borrower is almost irrelevant, giving rise to tax evasion problems when foreign placement of funds lowers visibility to home authorities. In addition, the value added in service production may be locationally complex, opaque, or both, inevitably giving rise to tax-driven and challengeable claims of jurisdictional location for corporate income tax advantage.

The financial secrecy that facilitates tax evasion was the critical "service" for individual investors. Initially not given special emphasis in *HTC,* this secrecy ultimately became the focus of the entire project.[15] A jurisdiction's competitive advantage for individuals may lie entirely with that secrecy, which must be distinguished from the location of value added, which is one candidate criterion for corporate tax liability. The haven may be little more than an address when the actual depositor interface, accounting, lending, and all important decision making take place in Europe or North America. This was presumably what the "substantial activity" criterion was aiming at, but no operational measures were suggested.

HTC distinguished three different categories of "tax competition": (a) "substantial" direct investment (e.g., manufacturing), (b) "more mobile" direct investment (e.g., financial services), and (c) "passive portfolio" investment. The report declares a focus on (b), but it fails to acknowledge that the distinction between (a) and (b) is largely one of degree, with (nearly) zero value added in the claimed polity marking one end of the spectrum. Much of the really harmful tax competition, such as tax haven banking, involves a combination of (b) and (c). Another large part, such as Luxembourg's banking system, which allowed safe and effortless tax evasion by other Europeans, combined (a) and (c). HTC moved across virtually all income tax avoidance and evasion problems at one point or another without adequately relating them to each other or linking them carefully with remedies.

HTC made a series of recommendations for joint action by OECD members. These suggestions included tighter surveillance and control of the activities of tax haven subsidiaries; strengthening rules on information provision by the tax havens, including less bank secrecy; better control of internal (transfer) pricing by multi-national corporations (MNCs); more thorough exchange of information among OECD members on tax haven activity and better coordinated administration among them; new and renegotiated bilateral treaties with tax havens to embody elements of the guidelines recommended by HTC; endorsement of HTC by the OECD membership; and establishment of a new institution, the Forum, to implement the guidelines and draw up a list of offending jurisdictions. HTC also mentions a number of already familiar retaliatory measures, including restricting tax deductions made for payments to offending jurisdictions and introducing withholding taxes on earnings paid to them.

HTC's nominal logic, notably its call for self-study of "harmful" intra-OECD practices, implied that the OECD would clean up its own house but could not do so without a coordinated response to what would otherwise be opportunistic behavior by outsiders (Easson 2004, 1040). This jibes with the observation of Frances Horner, head of the OECD's tax competition unit in 1998, that "the Report added the tax haven section almost an as afterthought" (Horner 2001, 3).[16]

Early Implementation

The OECD was apparently surprised by the furor HTC produced among the havens—immediate loud protests of unfairness and neo-imperialism. It was also apparently unprepared for the eagerness of many of the havens to reach an agreement—even before a proposed "name and shame" list had been published.

The *2000 Progress Report* identified forty-seven potentially harmful tax measures in twenty-one OECD countries, as well as a list of thirty-five tax havens from an initial candidate group of well over forty. Those dropped from the list had made advance commitments to meet some specific standards identified in *HTC*. The remaining thirty-five were essentially put on notice that if they did not subscribe to *HTC* principles by July 2001 and agree to end inconsistent practices by the end of 2005, they might face a set of "defensive measures."

There was an immediate outcry from the tax havens that they could not possibly conclude one-on-one negotiations with the OECD before the deadline. In response, the OECD in November 2000 proposed a "fast track" escape from the blacklist in the form of a public declaration of adherence to a Collective Memorandum of Understanding (OECD 2000a). This commitment was both more detailed and more limited than the letters of acceptance that kept six havens from being blacklisted in the first place. It focused on transparency and the exchange of information on criminal tax matters (by December 31, 2003) and then on all tax matters (by December 31, 2005).

The tax havens' unique criterion of "substantial" activities underwent an odd metamorphosis during 2000, as represented in the May OECD Fiscal Committee report adopted by the Council of Ministers in June. The criterion of "substantial" activity that applied only to the tax havens had become "the jurisdiction facilitates the establishment of foreign owned entities without the need for a local substantive presence or prohibits these entities from having a commercial impact on the economy" (OECD 2000b, 10). A kind of ring fencing had been grafted onto insubstantiality as a source of concern.

In the Collective Memorandum of Understanding of November 2000 (OECD 2000a), the new material essentially replaced the old. The criterion labeled "not attracting business without substantial domestic activity" had a short-term (December 31, 2003) and a long-term (December 31, 2005) version. In the short term, jurisdictions could not deny firms "qualifying for preferential tax treatment" the opportunity to do business in the domestic market. The long-term requirement states, "For any preferential tax treatment accorded to other service activities, each Party will remove any restrictions that deny the benefits of that preferential tax treatment to resident taxpayers, to entities owned by resident taxpayers, or to income derived from doing the same type of business in the domestic market" (OECD 2000a, 4).

This was a bizarre and wholly inadequate operationalization of "substantial" activity. It was predicated on explicit tax preference (a jurisdiction may have no corporate income tax for anybody) and essentially treated the absence of "ring fencing" as exonerating insubstantial activity.[17] A major state will care if subsidiaries of firms incorporated in that state can avoid tax by claiming they operate in a tax haven nation although little value is added there; a major state will likely have scant interest in how legally sequestered that possibly almost nonexistent activity is from the rest of the tax haven economy.

Remarkably little commentary has focused on the "substantial" activity criterion for the tax havens, either at the time of the report or since, yet it was removed in 1999 at the explicit insistence of the United States. Two points are essential. First, the criterion was effectively neutralized before the outcome of the American presidential election of 2000. Second, if the OECD had attempted to pursue the criterion seriously, defining "substantial" operationally would have been difficult.[18] Many haven businesses could claim some degree of non-negligible value added relative to firms of similar volume in a high-income country. So guidelines would have been needed, and they might have been difficult to devise. The requirement for a very high level of value added could have counterproductively increased the migration of real activity from the OECD countries to certain havens. Moreover, the varying uses of "sham" havens for both types of activities with different effects on MNC home countries could have generated competitive concerns among the OECD states as specific cases were examined.

What would the haven itself be expected to do if the original meaning of "insubstantial" had been retained? Would it really have to require a minimum level of real activity or refuse an investment? Each rich state, after all, was legally in a position to bar its firms from using any of the havens. Moreover, the U.S. position was necessarily conditioned by its global approach to corporate taxation. Some of the flexibility the havens provided to U.S. firms put them on a more equal footing with competitors based in states with territorial systems.

The main rationale for an OECD agreement on minimal activity for jurisdictional claims would be to remove any competitive disadvantage from acting alone. Yet attempts to forge a common position would involve complex judgments and possible intra-OECD conflicts. The difficulty of the task would have forced prolonged bilateral consideration of the situations of each of the tax havens prior to any imposition of "defensive measures." In sharp contrast, a set of information-gathering requirements and a willingness to share information could be easily and generically stated for everyone. Transforming "no substantial activity" into something equally simple, if largely irrelevant, may have seemed an obvious solution. And, by establishing a standard almost identical to the one facing the OECD countries, some might have concluded that greater equity had been achieved.

The initial opposition to *HTC* by the havens and various established business voices within the OECD (International Chamber of Commerce 2000) was soon joined by a formidable new organization: the U.S.-based Center for Freedom and Prosperity (CFP), founded in October 2000. The CFP pursued two goals, one at home and the other abroad. Within the United States it aimed to persuade the Congress and the administration to oppose the OECD efforts. The CFP declared that if the United States resisted, the entire effort would fail. Internationally, it urged the tax havens to resist. In the years that followed, the CFP visited the havens to give them advice and counsel. It even participated in their delegations at meetings with the OECD (Webb 2004, 35–36; Easson 2004, 1053–54).

A U.S. Shift and Formal Project Revision

The U.S. presidential election in 2000 resulted in a Republican administration that differed substantially from its predecessor by being strongly opposed to tax increases, favoring tax cuts, and viewing the size of government in the EU as an important contributing factor to its poor economic performance. One of Bush's opponents for the Republican nomination in 2000, Steve Forbes, had made a "flat tax" the cornerstone of his campaign. The flat tax resembles the EU's value added tax in taxing only that part of income that is not saved. But American proponents often see it as a virtually complete substitute for the current personal and corporate income taxes (Cassidy 2004) rather than a complement to them, as the VAT is in Europe. If the flat tax replaced all major national taxes—including the estate tax—the tax haven problem would essentially disappear. Advocates could argue that government revenue difficulties with the tax havens are well deserved and should serve as a stimulus to rethink government revenue sources rather than to beef up enforcement efforts.

The Bush administration did not endorse the end of the personal income tax, but key officials, including Treasury Secretary Paul O'Neill, openly questioned the corporate income tax.[19] The Bush administration also differed sharply from its predecessor in being determined not to be bound by precedents for international cooperation, instead emphasizing unilateralism rather than cooperative joint policies. For the new administration the tax haven project was doubly suspect. It seemed tailored by high-tax Europeans for their own purposes, and its rhetoric about "coordinated defensive measures" involved U.S. cooperation in undefined enforcement. Nonetheless, part of the project served a long-standing bipartisan U.S. goal: thwarting evasion of U.S. taxes.

For the CFP, the *HTC* project was anti-competitive, would result in higher taxes, infringed on national sovereignty, discriminated against non-OECD countries by treating them more harshly, and threatened privacy (Easson 2004,1054). Some of these arguments clearly resonated with the new Bush administration. Treasury Secretary O'Neill failed to endorse the OECD initiative when asked about it in February 2001, and in May he expressed concern that the initiative involved interference with countries' abilities to set their own tax rates and that it constituted a step to "harmonize world tax systems" (Easson 2004, 1061).

O'Neill explained to Congress in July 2001 that the United States had been far more successful than other high-income countries in gaining information exchange agreements with other countries. He also indicated that multilateral pressure within the OECD framework could be useful in overcoming the resistance of some jurisdictions. He made clear, however, that his only objective was to shore up the enforcement of U.S. tax laws and that the OECD should not "stray" into other areas (O'Neill 2001, 2, 3). Consistent with this view, O'Neill announced that the OECD project had eliminated the "no substantial activities" criterion (even in its largely meaningless "ring-fencing" reformulation) from its criteria for haven cooperation, noting that criterion's "lack of clarity" (O'Neill 2001, 4, 6). He also expressed concern that OECD's posture was unusually "condemnatory" and "aggressive" (O'Neill 2001, 3).

In retrospect, O'Neill was largely pushing on an open door. The project had already been refocused on transparency and information exchange. Yet the Bush administration probably saw major advantages in putting a bright line around what it regarded as appropriate activity. The United States was at the time embroiled in a WTO dispute with Europe. It concerned the use of tax havens for relief from corporate taxation of U.S. firms' export sales to third countries through "foreign sales corporations." This practice could be seen as both substance-less jurisdictional manipulation and ring fencing. Also, some subnational U.S. practices, such as Delaware's treatment of foreign corporations, were questionable. No U.S. administration, let alone one committed to maximum sovereignty, wanted to become embroiled in federal-state disputes solely to meet foreign demands.[20] Partisan politics surely provided another motivation. Part of the Republican right was not getting its desired "privacy." This might be swallowed more easily with a chaser of rhetoric about the horrors of a high tax cartel and the virtues of tax competition. So, instead of glossing over differences with the EU in the interest of OECD solidarity, the Bush administration appeared anxious to exaggerate them. This triggered a barrage of criticism at home and abroad accusing the administration of being soft on tax avoidance and evasion (see, e.g., an editorial in the *New York Times,* May 26, 2001; Giridharadas 2001).[21] Nevertheless, O'Neill's congressional testimony announcing the OECD project changes began with a ringing endorsement of the essential need for increased transparency and information exchange.[22]

Cooperation on tax evasion implied a U.S. policy adjustment. The United

States had not taxed foreign-owned U.S. portfolio investments and had not collected ownership and earnings information since 1986. The Bush administration's moves to satisfy both OECD information-sharing demands and European aspirations to reduce EU tax evasion infuriated groups such as the CFP (Center for Freedom and Prosperity 2004), which insisted on a right to "financial privacy" (Hamilton 2003) that no administration had ever acknowledged.[23] Some Republicans even attempted to withdraw U.S. funding from the OECD.[24]

Reactions from Business

The OECD was attacked by its own Business and Industry Advisory Committee (BIAC) even before taking fire from the new U.S. administration (BIAC 1999). The two assaults were not independent. Some of the misgivings of U.S. and European business were given voice by the Bush administration. The OECD had not engaged in what the BIAC regarded as sufficient consultation prior to the release of *HTC*. Substantively, it was hard to find a major business on either side of the Atlantic opposed to the view that much corporate tax avoidance was legitimate "tax planning."

In an attempt to shore up business support for the OECD and acquiescence in the effectively refocused project, Jeffrey Owens, director of OECD's Center for Tax Policy and Administration, and Richard Hammer, chairman of the Committee on Taxation and Fiscal Policy of the BIAC, issued a joint statement praising tax competition and "legitimate tax planning" (Webb 2004, 34–35). Their statement was issued on March 6, 2001, about two months before O'Neill's public indication of the U.S. position. Eventually, with the project refocused on transparency and information exchange, business opposition largely ceased.[25]

The OECD's progress report of 2001 reflected U.S. pressure. It dropped "no substantial activity" as a criterion for an uncooperative jurisdiction.[26] In addition, it extended the deadline for cooperation by several months, to November 30, 2001.[27] Similarly, no "coordinated defensive measures" would be taken against the tax havens until they were taken against a similar OECD country.[28] And the OECD used the Forum—apparently originally envisioned as a site for demands to be formulated—as a place for an ongoing, collegial exchange of views among OECD members, the tax havens, and other interested states (OECD 2004b; 2004a).

The Post-9/11 World

The attacks of September 11, 2001, shifted the dynamics of tax haven discussions. Financial secrecy became linked to dangers far greater than fiscal loss.

The Financial Action Task Force on Money Laundering (FATF) had been established at the 1989 Paris G-7 summit mainly as an attack on organized crime. In 1999, as part of an explicit "name and shame" approach to enforcement, the FATF listed fifteen noncooperative territories that fell short in various areas of financial regulation, transparency, information collection and sharing, and anti-money laundering activity (Reuter and Truman 2004, 86).[29]

After 9/11, the FATF explicitly shifted its focus to emphasize terrorist funding, and its prominence began to eclipse that of the *HTC* project. This change reflected a shift in nearly every major polity toward an emphasis on security and away from whatever local privacy norms had prevailed previously. Local authorities found, however, that the information gathering and sharing requirements for tax matters and FATF initiatives were quite similar (Sharman 2004, 8).

The post-9/11 period has seen a host of new and pending measures in response to the FATF, the European Anti-Money-Laundering Directive of October 2001, and the USA PATRIOT Act of October 2001. Together they greatly increased intra- and intergovernmental cooperation by facilitating information flows, the service of documents, and the attachment of property. Some jurisdictions took a more comprehensive view of what constitutes an offense severe enough to warrant international cooperation to counter it.

Another source of concern about haven financial practices grew from the Asian financial crisis of 1997, which highlighted the unsound practices of many regional financial institutions and the need for much greater supervision. The International Monetary Fund investigated forty-four jurisdictions for the Financial Stability Forum (FSF) and found several major tax havens lacking in internal supervision and external cooperation (Reuter and Truman 2004, 87–88; Financial Stability Forum 2000, 2).

Moving to Completion

Many havens continued to declare their cooperation with the *HTC* project's demands during 2002 and 2003.[30] By the time its progress report was released the following year (OECD 2004), only five holdouts remained: Andorra, Liechtenstein, Liberia, Monaco, and the Marshall Islands. There also had been considerable change within the OECD. Of the forty-seven potentially harmful regimes noted in 2000, all but two were removed, modified, or found innocuous.

The *Harmful Tax Competition* Project in Retrospect

The *HTC* project had largely run its course by 2004, although the Forum on taxation continued, as did relevant activity in the FSF and the FATF.[31] As for the oft-touted "defensive measures," according to Jeffrey Owens, not only are "coordinated defensive measures" an option of last resort but "whether to impose defensive measures is a matter within the individual sovereignty of each country. . . . The OECD itself has not power to impose defensive measures" (quoted in Goulder 2004, 1191–92).[32]

Inadequacies of the Original Report

The original HTC report got the initiative off to a bad start. The title has been acknowledged to be a major gaffe (the project soon became "Harmful Tax Practices"), and the benefits of tax competition may have been given too little emphasis. Although "harmful tax regimes" can presumably exist anywhere, they were identified only with the OECD countries, while the "tax havens" were entirely different jurisdictions. Both "ring fencing" and "no substantial activities" should have been applied to all jurisdictions. As it turned out, "no substantial activities" for the havens was recast as the absence of "ring fencing" and essentially disappeared as a criterion long before its formal removal at U.S. insistence.

Failure to think through the practical difficulties of trying to control activity in the havens and the opposition of organized business to attempts to do so resulted in improvised revisions that damaged the project and undoubtedly the confidence of the business community in the OECD. This was matched by awkward behavior toward the tax havens, a failing that generated piecemeal corrections and long-lasting reputational damage.

The Fairness Issue

The non-OECD tax havens complained from the beginning that they were essentially treated as career criminals while OECD countries were regarded as minor offenders. Some important non-OECD financial centers with prima facie characteristics of tax havens were omitted from the original list without explanation.[33]

The midcourse corrections of 2001 redressed some of the asymmetry between the OECD countries and the havens in terms of the timetable for "coordinated defensive action," but the EU Savings Directive of 2002 added another complication. It aimed at banking secrecy that clearly abetted tax evasion in EU members Luxembourg, Belgium, Austria, and nonmember Switzerland. The compromise approved in February 2002 called for a seven-year transition period during which Austria, Belgium, and Luxembourg would gradually increase their withholding taxes from 15 to 35 percent from 2005 to 2011 while retaining 20 percent of the revenue for themselves. These EU states also insisted that Switzerland, Andorra, Liechtenstein, Monaco, and San Marino participate—thus fingering three of the noncooperating tax havens from the OECD list as well as the most important problematic tax jurisdiction within the OECD. Under the directive, banks and other financial institutions in the other states would automatically report information to fiscal authorities across the EU (Keen and Ligthart 2004, 540–41), but only on interest earnings, a restriction that many see as easy to circumvent (Wright 2005). After the transition period, the EU states with the special dispensation are expected to shift to information exchange. And the EU Commission intends to pressure Switzerland to do the same (Scott 2004, 1102).[34] The withholding compromise seemed to leave some European jurisdictions with greater bank secrecy than the havens were required to relinquish, again generating a barrage of criticism from defenders of the havens.[35]

Interpreting the Course of OECD Policy

The OECD's ultimate embrace of the tax havens as partners rather than opponents seems to have resulted from an increasing role for higher level OECD officials with greater political sensitivity. This occurred as the project emerged from the obscurity of the Committee on Fiscal Affairs. One observer close to the unfolding conflicts noted that those connected with the fiscal committee were naïve about the politics of tax reform—both vis-à-vis the tax havens and within the OECD—and that if persons with greater political acumen had been involved at the outset, the report and its implementation would have been quite different.[36] Yet in the earliest days of the HTC, relatively low-level national appointees to the OECD appeared to be giving marching orders to prime ministers in the tax havens.

Some commentators have emphasized the persuasiveness of tax haven arguments.[37] Discussions with OECD principals do suggest that their engagement with some of the havens generated sympathy. Yet the nominal parity between the havens and the OECD members ostensibly established by transmuting substantiality into the absence of "no ring fencing" hardly reflects a careful equity argument; it does reflect OECD business interests. One OECD participant said that he and his colleagues determined that the early formulation amounted to asking the havens to turn business way. But instead of developing rules about sufficient local content, a quest that presumably promised delay and intra-OECD conflict, the problem was finessed. Some of the principals may have honestly believed that was the correct solution out of sympathy for the havens—there are reports of haven ministers crying in meetings with the OECD—but the lion's share of gains from this sham activity went to jurisdictions that were not poor. The few crumbs that a permissive corporate regime offered to the poor havens hardly seem a persuasive reason for abandoning a stand on the necessity for real activity.[38]

The lack of symmetry in timetables between the OECD and the havens resulted from a political tin ear, and the problem was easily corrected. The OECD accepted the havens' demand for a "level playing field," which implied that all jurisdictions should meet any minimum standards, and accommodated the havens by engaging them as equals in a prolonged series of meetings. In doing so, the OECD gained endorsement of the basic transparency and information exchange principle that the tax havens had never accepted prior to the HTC project. Such a principle was at odds with the "financial privacy" goal of their metropolitan champion, the CFP.[39] The drive to extend the project to previously unexamined jurisdictions paralleled the EU Savings Directive's concern that money driven out of the OECD–tax haven spheres could go elsewhere. Highlighting the need for attention to such additional money centers as Singapore and Hong Kong was scarcely a concession to the havens, particularly as they did not attempt to use it as an excuse for inaction. Money is fungible, and fairness for the havens is efficacy for the OECD.

The American politics of the HTC project presents the case of a "fifth column," most visibly the CFP (whose funding is not known but is suspected of coming from wealthy Americans and foreigners who benefit from "financial privacy"). Exceeding the rhetorical power of foreign voices by orders of magnitude, the CFP spearheaded the U.S. propaganda drive, and some of its appeal to part of the Republican base was appropriated by the Bush administration.[40] Nevertheless, the CFP's core "privacy" aim, also much trumpeted by the havens at the level of principle early on, was largely ignored.

Unrealistic Expectations

HTC can be accounted at best a mixed success in its own terms, and no follow-up initiatives are likely in the near future. The important goal of abolishing nominal corporate location and the associated tax avoidance was abandoned. Tax evasion may have been somewhat more effectively addressed at the level of principle. HTC aimed to increase transparency and information sharing, and this may be happening, albeit slowly. That prospect will not be realized unless the standards are extended to a handful of financial centers not originally considered. It also was and is clear that on-demand rather than automatic information sharing can offer only limited deterrence. Increased resources for enforcement and stiffer penalties might reinforce the transparency that may be developing in the havens, but even the most determined efforts will be only a partial success. In the future the tax havens might be obliged to cooperate in providing automatic exchange of information. Only transparency may be acceptable in the post-9/11 world, and the alternative of compulsory withholding would affect only earnings tax evasion.

Implications for Future U.S.-EU relations

The *HTC* project yields lessons about U.S.-European relations and the strategies pursued by each side. The United States may dominate with both "hard" and "soft" power, but the "sticky," that is, economic, power of the EU roughly equals that of the United States by most measures. That has important implications for major international economic institutions, including the OECD, the IMF, and the World Bank.[41]

The *HTC* saga shows considerable restraint by both U.S. and European participants. Treasury Secretary O'Neill stated his opposition to both real and fancied weaknesses in the original OECD position in restrained language that included much praise for the *HTC* project. The original OECD position—apparently designed to put maximum pressure on the havens with respect to both avoidance and evasion—always enjoyed considerable bipartisan support within the United States. That, in turn, undoubtedly gave OECD staff in Paris grounds for continued optimism about transatlantic accommodation.

As argued earlier, O'Neill's public rejection served as the coup de grâce for the "no substantial activities" criterion, and the leadership of the OECD publicly treated the United States' rethinking of the entire project as a valuable contribution to the development of the project rather than as an attack on its essence.

The Bush administration's actions had both a critical and a supportive aspect. On the one hand, Secretary O'Neill made sovereigntist statements that offered reassurance to the unilateralist part of the GOP base. On the other, he embraced an attack on personal income tax evasion in much the way his predecessors had. After the official OECD revision, there is no record of further U.S. criticism. Indeed, the subsequent signing of bilateral information-sharing agreements was publicly celebrated by the Bush administration (U.S. Department of the Treasury 2003).

There also are some implied lessons for what should be done differently in the future than what was done in the *HTC* project. First, the OECD must resist tendencies to see and treat the world in "Eurocentric" terms. The United States still often dominates the OECD, but when Europe tackles an issue with a relatively high level of internal cohesion—as it clearly did in the tax project—trouble can result both with the United States and the rest of the world. The United States also needs to guard better against the snares of self-centeredness. The United States apparently paid insufficient attention to the intra-European issues that drove much of the *HTC*. A more attentive and forceful U.S. voice during Bill Clinton's administration might have increased the viability of the project in both tone and content.

Second, the OECD—both the EU and U.S. parties—should be more alert to how its policies may affect nonmembers and to their relevant responses. The ill-starred Multilateral Agreement on Investment (MAI) suggests that the *HTC* initiative was not an isolated instance of OECD failure to map likely reactions by outsiders.[42]

Third, the OECD and its dominant European members should individually and collectively prepare for intermittent "sovereignty eruptions" from the west side of the Atlantic. The EU members that share leadership with the United States in the OECD should certainly have engaged in more forward and backward mapping about relevant U.S. developments from the very beginning. The Democrats were never a sure election bet after the Monica Lewinsky scandal hit the Clinton administration, and several major elements of the tone and content of *HTC* were clearly red flags for the Republican right wing that could not have survived much serious scenario spinning. That said, even if *HTC* had been more carefully drafted, the Republicans might well have found attacking aspects of the project to be politically irresistible.

Finally, U.S. politicians, at least in the executive branch of the government, should more fully recognize that world attention to the style and substance of Washington rhetoric rivals domestic attention. This requires finding a declaratory policy line that minimizes trade-offs between what will build support at home and what will build support abroad. Treasury Secretary O'Neill's public handling of the OECD's tax competition project typified Bush administration practices. It appeared to place U.S. interests on a far higher plane than those of others, thus making a small but still damaging contribution to the collapse of European confidence in American leadership.[43]

11

SAVING THE WORLD FROM BIG TOBACCO
The Real Coalition of the Willing

JUDITH P. WILKENFELD

A group of nongovernmental organizations and states, feeling victimized by U.S. pressure, formed an unprecedented alliance and achieved an impressive goal: an international treaty. The issue that inspired the alliance was not national security, disarmament, or world peace but public health. By working together they were taking the opportunity to help forestall or mitigate the coming health pandemic of the next fifty years: diseases resulting from tobacco use. As the authors of *The Oxford Medical Companion* note, "tobacco is the only legally available consumer product which kills when used as intended" (Walton et al. 1994).

This chapter focuses first on the negotiations leading to the adoption of the first-ever public health treaty, the Framework Convention on Tobacco Control (FCTC) associated with the World Health Organization (WHO). As scholars have noted, "nongovernmental actors tend to gain more prominence in policy areas where there has been significant state failure. . . . Some are stand-ins for states; others work to influence the diplomatic agendas of states. Global diplomatic actors—whether individual scientists or activists, or vast networks of NGOs—represent a new force in the international negotiation arena. Their ability to mobilize public opinion and political action is unprecedented and closely tied to the information revolution of the late twentieth century" (Starkey et al. 1999, 61–62). Another focus is on the birth and growth of a new international, nongovernmental network of advocates.

The success of the alliance between civil society and the countries of Africa, Southeast Asia, and the island nations of the Pacific and Caribbean was brought about by persistence, patience, and stamina on the part of the various actors. Civil society brought to the alliance its technical expertise in public health, its media contacts, and its political contacts within friendly and not so friendly governments; the governments of the Global South brought their votes, their voices, and their unwillingness to be bullied.

Tobacco Marketing as the Disease Vector

Cigarettes kill half of all regular users, and of those, half will die during the productive years of middle age—thirty-five to sixty-nine. Currently the death toll is almost 5 million per year worldwide, but by 2025 the total will rise to 10 million per year and 70 percent of those deaths will be in the developing world. Tobacco exacts an enormous toll in health care costs, lost productivity, and pain and suffering inflicted upon smokers, passive smokers, and their families (World Health Organization 2004). The burden of disease is perhaps more shocking since it will overwhelm the already overtaxed and inadequate health care systems of low- and middle-income countries. A short list of the ills directly caused by or suspected of being caused by tobacco use include lung cancer; cancers of the larynx, oral cavity, esophagus, bladder, pancreas, uterus, cervix, kidney, and stomach; chronic obstructive pulmonary disease, emphysema, and chronic bronchitis; heart disease, stroke, and the progression of atherosclerosis; and spontaneous abortions, stillbirths, and sudden infant death syndrome after birth.[1]

The synergies between diseases and smoking are equally terrible (Esson 2004). Smoking most affects those who are ill and whose immune systems are weak. Smoking causes subclinical tuberculosis (TB) to advance to clinical TB and possible death; 1 billion people worldwide may have subclinical TB (Esson 2004).

The Internationalization of the Disease

Tobacco use spread from North America and Europe to the rest of the world as a result of industrialization, modern mass marketing techniques, and the increase in international commerce (Kiernan 1991). The globalization of trade in the late twentieth and early twenty-first century extended modern tobacco use to the rest of the world, to low- and middle-income countries. Multinational tobacco companies now operate in more than 180 countries (Yach et al. 2007).

The epidemic that follows tobacco use, therefore, will now move to the developing world. Death and disease from tobacco use have already begun to decline in wealthy countries due to years of aggressive tobacco control advocacy and government action. But the epidemic has yet to hit full force in low- and middle-income countries (World Bank 1999; Peto et al. 1996). Moreover, estimates of projected deaths in low- and middle-income countries are based on current male smoking rates. The emerging markets for the tobacco transnational corporations are women and children. If the companies succeed (as they did in developed countries), the death toll may be even larger than currently predicted (Yach et al. 2007).

As *Fortune* magazine reported, "An important thing to understand about Big Tobacco is that its future lies, in large part, in the developing world. 'You buy Philip Morris in the long term for their international business,' says Bonnie Herzog, an analyst at Credit Suisse First Boston in New York City. '[T]hat's their growth engine'" (Brown 2001). This movement of tobacco marketing from developed countries to developing countries has not gone unnoticed by the intended target and is often recognized as being predatory and pernicious.

The spread of tobacco use is more than just a potential public health disaster. According to the World Health Organization, "The economic costs of tobacco use are equally devastating. In addition to the high public health costs of treating tobacco-caused diseases, tobacco kills people at the height of their productivity, depriving families of breadwinners and nations of a healthy workforce. Tobacco users are also less productive while they are alive due to increased sickness. A 1994 report estimated that the use of tobacco resulted in an annual global net loss of US$200 thousand million, a third of this loss being in developing countries" (WHO 2004).[2]

The secretary-general of the United Nations, in a report to the UN Economic and Social Council in 2004, warned that tobacco production and consumption help to increase poverty and undermine sustainable development: "Tobacco and poverty create a vicious circle. . . . Tobacco increases poverty, and tobacco products tend to be more widely used among the poor. . . . The U.N.'s Millennium Development Goals (MDGs), aimed at eradicating extreme poverty and eliminating deadly diseases by 2015, are being undermined by the rise in tobacco consumption." Therefore, the report continues, tobacco control has to be "a key component of efforts to reduce poverty [and] improve development."[3]

The Role of the United States

The U.S. government played a considerable role in the development of this epidemic and impoverishment by helping U.S.-based tobacco companies expand overseas. During the 1980s, the U.S. government used the threat of retaliatory trade sanctions (section 301 of the Trade Act of 1974) to force countries in Asia to either open up their markets to imported cigarettes or face trade sanctions

(Taylor et al. 2000, 356–58). The results were catastrophic. Smoking rates in Japan, South Korea, Thailand, and Taiwan rose 10 percent higher than they otherwise would have following the massive inflow of U.S. products and sophisticated marketing techniques (Frankel 1996). In South Korea, the smoking rate among teenage boys was 18 percent in 1988. A year later, after the market was opened to U.S. imports, it rose to 30 percent, while rates for teenage girls climbed from 2 to 9 percent (Yach et al. 2007).

The Bill Clinton administration substantially changed the U.S. government's trade posture and backed away from the forceful opening of foreign markets to tobacco products. It sought to increase domestic regulation of tobacco and extend tobacco control rather than tobacco marketing to the rest of the world (Shapiro 2002). The administration's policy still recognized the importance of the tobacco trade to the United States, but it did represent a change. The policy, as enunciated in an executive order of the president, stated in part that:

> [i]t shall be the policy of the executive branch to take strong action to address the potential global epidemic of diseases caused by tobacco use. The executive branch shall undertake activities to increase its capacity to address global tobacco prevention and control issues through coordinated domestic action, limited bilateral assistance to individual nations, and support to multilateral organizations. In the implementation of international trade policy, executive departments and agencies shall not promote the sale or export of tobacco or tobacco products, or seek the reduction or removal of foreign government restrictions on the marketing and advertising of such products, provided that such restrictions are applied equally to all tobacco or tobacco products of the same type. Departments and agencies are not precluded from taking necessary actions in accordance with the requirements and remedies available under applicable United States trade laws and international agreements to ensure nondiscriminatory treatment of United States products. (U.S. White House 2001)

Recent events suggest that U.S. policy may be changing again. The actions of the George W. Bush administration during the negotiations on the FCTC may indicate a return to a more aggressive tobacco export policy.

The Proper Role for Civil Society

On May 24, 1999, the World Health Assembly (WHA) passed a resolution setting in motion a multi-year negotiation leading to the adoption of the FCTC. The World Health Organization sponsored the FCTC as the first ever public health treaty: a treaty to combat the internationalization of the death and disease caused by tobacco marketing. In 2003 Chitra Subramaniam wrote that "someday someone will write the story of the role of NGOs in leading the FCTC. . . . [T]heir role in educating the world about tobacco over the last four years has been . . . tremendously successful in sustaining the debate at the right pitch."[4]

Between 1999 and 2003, a group of public health NGOs from every region of the world had established a network of public health, human rights, consumer rights, and women's and children's rights organizations, as well as environmental activists, to lobby for a strong treaty. This network, which by mid-2004 had grown to more than two hundred organizations from almost one hundred countries, operated on a shoestring budget, with each group contributing its own expertise, materials, and hard work. Working with a coalition of willing governments, such as those of India, Thailand, Canada, New Zealand, the island nations of the Pacific and Caribbean, and the entire continent of Africa, this coalition was able to thwart the desires of the U.S. and other governments that sought a weak and nonbinding treaty. On March 1, 2003, at around 2 A.M., the negotiations ended with most countries giving speeches of congratulations; only the United States was threatening to try to derail the treaty before the WHA could adopt it and place it before the world for ratification.

Assuming that the role played by this network of NGOs assisting low- and middle-income countries was a determinant in the outcome of the negotiations, was it a proper role for NGOs to play? The United Nations recently issued a major report on the role of civil society in international negotiations and generally found it to be a positive force. As the Report of the Panel of Eminent Persons on UN–Civil Society Relationships noted, "Public opinion has become a key factor influencing intergovernmental and governmental policies and actions. The involvement of a diverse range of actors, including NGOs and private sectors, and local governments is not only essential for effective action on global priorities but is also a protection against further erosion of multilateralism." This, however, may not always be perceived as a benefit, noted the report: "Governments do not always welcome sharing what has traditionally been their preserve. Many increasingly challenge the number and motives of civil society organizations in the United Nations—questioning their representativeness, legitimacy, integrity or accountability" (UN Non-governmental Liaison Service 2004, 7–8). In the past, governments have negotiated and discussed and compromised and threatened until agreement was reached. Now, they often must deal with civil society, which wants to enter negotiations, form alliances with like-minded governments and international organizations, and attempt to be as forceful as possible in putting forth its agenda.

On the whole the report concluded that "[c]ivil society can also raise new issues, focus attention on the moral and ethical dimensions of decisions in the public sphere, expand resources and skills, challenge basic assumptions and priorities and protest unfair decisions. So enhanced engagement, carefully planned, will make the United Nations more effective in its actions and in its contributions to global governance. There is a synergy here, not a contest" (UN Non-governmental Liaison Service 2004, 28).

Nevertheless, some, particularly in the Bush administration, have questioned this role of civil society. U.S. Secretary of Labor Elaine L. Chao, speaking before the Federalist Society, stated that:

> the United States has always encouraged other nations to adopt . . . principles of free association in civil society. These ideals make possible the formation of private organizations that play a pivotal role in opening up repressive, undemocratic regimes. . . . But what is notable, and what you need to pay attention to . . . is the growing alliance of unelected NGOs and multilateral bodies, such as the United Nations, its various affiliated organizations, and the European Union, to influence the politics and laws of democratic societies. . . . In addition to the official delegation at a meeting, there often will be a long list of non-governmental organizations accredited as "observers." . . . These organizations, as you can suspect, do more than observe. . . . Their views help to shape the final outcome by lending international credibility and the mantle of grass roots support through ideas and recommendations. . . . [T]he reality is that multilateral organizations, NGOs, are becoming major, key players in global public opinion and global standard setting. Conservatives need to pay attention to these organizations and the NGOs that influence them. (Chao 2003)[5]

NGOs clearly performed all those functions that Chao decried during the FCTC negotiations. Patricia Lambert, head of the South African delegation in the FCTC negotiations, would disagree with Chao's statements of concern: "The NGO community kept pace with the negotiations all the way, did enormous amounts of research in-between sessions, were constantly keeping us up to date with things that were being hidden, things by the corporations, by other governments. So there was this percolating of information, that, speaking as an African, I can certainly say, helped us to be better informed, and therefore to take a clearer and stronger stand."[6]

One's views of the propriety of NGOs' involvement in international affairs in general and in this treaty process in particular may well depend largely on how positively one views securing a strong treaty containing a comprehensive road map for international tobacco control.

Creating a Structured Network of Non-Governmental Tobacco Control Advocates

Prior to the World Health Assembly decision to sponsor an international treaty to combat the diseases and early deaths caused by tobacco use, most tobacco control NGOs acted at the national and local level and met at the international level only infrequently. Nevertheless, those international meetings were opportunities to educate one another about advances in the science and new means of confronting the tobacco industry. As the tobacco companies looked beyond their borders for new customers, however, tobacco control activists had to try to increase their collaboration in order to find new ways to confront the industry (Yach et al. 2007).

Early collaborative efforts were the biennial and triennial world tobacco control conferences, which brought together tobacco control advocates, scientists, and policy makers from around the world. First held in 1967, these conferences have continued to serve as useful venues for the exchange of scientific and advocacy information, and more recently, online technologies have been used. One cannot overstate the importance of the Internet to help level the playing field for civil society. It provides small and geographically dispersed NGOs the ability to quickly disseminate information about the industry and its agents; answer each others' scientific, economic, and strategic questions; mobilize support and international pressure; and provide other technical assistance in a quick and efficient manner (Yach et al. 2007).

Following the resolution passed by the WHA in 1999, staff members of the Tobacco-Free Initiative (TFI) of WHO approached Action on Smoking and Health (ASH) in London with the offer of financial assistance for starting an international coalition to facilitate the involvement of NGOs in the FCTC. ASH contacted a number of prominent tobacco control groups primarily focused on domestic tobacco control issues and enlisted them in the process of developing the coalition.[7]

The primary concern initially was creating a working structure for this new alliance. A name was chosen that reflected the initial limited focus of the network: the Framework Convention Alliance (hereafter FCA or the Alliance).[8] At a minimum, the Alliance needed a closed e-mail conference and regional contact points to bring in new members and funnel information in to the Alliance and out to the membership, and it needed small working groups and individuals to take on tasks. The form that the Alliance ultimately chose turned out to be a structured network.[9]

That was appropriate because the Alliance was a geographically dispersed group with differing economic and skill levels. It covered twenty-one time zones and was made up of public health groups, environmental activists, women's and children's rights groups, consumer activists, corporate accountability groups, human rights groups, faith-based groups, and more. Some were from very wealthy Western NGOs that could afford to have two or three people work full time on international tobacco control, but most were from small under-funded organizations for which tobacco control was only one of many issues they addressed. The challenge was to have groups deal with a complex issue on a voluntary basis. Like other such networks, the Alliance had two overarching functional needs and desired outcomes. The first was to be a communication tool so that individual NGOs could learn from each other and quickly dis-seminate information to each other about the negotiations. The second was to be a vehicle for action, enabling disparate groups to take joint actions either in parallel in home countries or as a lobbying bloc when in Geneva, Switzerland, for negotiations. Coordinated lobbying was one of the main reasons for form-ing the FCA.

Groups join a coalition or network if they accept the general framework under which it operates and see that joining the network would benefit their own efforts. The Alliance initially required that new members subscribe to a set of core principles. Over time, through a process of discussions and the development of trust and friendships, the Alliance was able to establish consensus-lobbying positions on more than ten specific substantive provisions in the FCTC.[10] The Alliance expressed this consensus through joint position papers and press statements. Addressing form was only the first organizational requirement; addressing questions of representation was equally important. The UN and the Alliance realized that to be truly effective the Alliance would have to reach out and recruit more members from low- and middle-income countries.[11]

In March 2000, prior to the formation of the second FCTC working group, the FCA held its first official meeting in Geneva. Committees were formed to pursue agreed upon activities. In furtherance of the goals discussed with the WHO to bring into the movement as many NGOs from developing coun-tries as possible, one of the first committees established was the fundraising committee. This committee was tasked with finding funds to help developing country NGOs attend the negotiations. Over time, an initial grant provided to the Alliance by WHO was supplemented with funds from the member orga-nizations of the FCA, as well as grants from the Open Society Institute, the Canadian International Development Agency, Swedish International Coop-eration Agency, and other sources. As a result the Alliance was able to fund the attendance of a minimum of ten to twenty groups from developing country NGOs at the six negotiating sessions, called Intergovernmental Negotiating Bodies (INBs).

In order to ensure that the widest range of NGOs and the most diverse number of countries and regions were represented, the Alliance established eight different operational points: (1) the office of the coordinator would be located in a developing country, initially in the offices of ASH Thailand; (2) there would be no fees and no dues in order to ensure maximum participation by NGOs; (3) the broadest possible outreach would be directed at low- and middle-income country NGOs; (4) money would be sought to bring developing country NGOs to the negotiations and to support the national work of some advocates; (5) lobbying, media advocacy, and strategy planning training would be provided for the less experienced FCA members; (6) briefing papers would be developed by a policy committee and submitted to the membership for approval by consensus; (7) materials, such as how-to manuals on FCTC participation, would be produced and made available on the Web site; and (8) decisions would be taken only by consensus.

What the Alliance members got in return was the ability to speak to regional delegations in their own voice and culture; an education for Western NGOs on the needs of other countries so that Alliance positions were based on actual needs and not just on Western perceptions; an alliance with dedicated governments; and a strong and potentially effective public health treaty.

Negotiations on the Framework Convention on Tobacco Control Begin

As Allyn Taylor has succinctly pointed out, because of globalization, "governments must turn increasingly to international cooperation to attain national public health objectives and achieve some control over the transboundary forces that affect their populations" (Taylor 2002, 975). That is especially true when the transboundary health threat is to developing countries, which often have not been the prime beneficiaries of globalization and which can be negatively affected by it.

In 1996, the forty-ninth World Health Assembly adopted resolution WHA49.17, requesting that the director-general (DG) initiate the development of a WHO FCTC. It also requested that the DG "include as part of this framework convention a strategy to encourage Member States to move progressively towards the adoption of comprehensive tobacco control policies and also to deal with aspects of tobacco control that transcend national boundaries." But it required the efforts of a new WHO director-general, Dr. Gro Harlem Brundtland, to push the strategy. On May 24, 1999, the World Health Assembly paved the way for multilateral negotiations to begin on a set of rules and regulations to govern the fight against tobacco (Fidler 2003).

From the beginning, many of the developing countries' delegates to the FCTC were interested in strong tobacco control measures and saw the necessity of banding together. But not all countries endorsed the concept of a strong FCTC. There were in fact at least four categories of country actors, each with varying degrees of domestic tobacco control and different agendas in Geneva (Yach et al. 2007).

The first category consisted of high-income countries (e.g., Canada, Australia, and New Zealand) that had instituted strong tobacco control policies domestically and wanted to see such measures adopted internationally. In many cases, these countries took positions consistent with public health proposals emanating from NGOs. And a few had NGOs on their delegations. The second category was made up of low- and middle-income countries (e.g., South Africa, Thailand, Poland) that either had strong tobacco control measures in place or were considering enacting them. They believed that a strong FCTC could help them domestically and ensure international pressure for others to follow. Many of these countries spoke out in favor of strong provisions and helped form alliances within their respective regions. The third category consisted of low-income states with little or no capacity to institute effective tobacco control programs and that looked to the treaty process and other states for assistance in fending off the tobacco companies and their client countries (tobacco-producing states of Africa such as Malawi, and small Asian states, such as Cambodia). Finally, there were high-income states, home to tobacco transnational companies, that took pro-tobacco positions and tried to weaken or derail the process (e.g., the United States, Germany, and Japan).

The Alliance came to the negotiations in Geneva determined to educate delegates about the science of tobacco and tobacco control, to lobby for an effective treaty, and to work with the delegates to achieve that end. The Alliance first, however, had to educate itself before it could educate the delegates. Most NGOs and country delegates who attended were neophytes in international law and treaty making, and almost as many needed education in tobacco science and tobacco control.

When the U.S. NGOs, for example, first became involved in the process, they held a series of workshops on how to be effective in negotiations. Representatives from NGOs who had been involved in various treaty negotiations were asked to participate. They came from work on persistent organic pollutants, climate change, child rights, landmines, and the International Criminal Court, and they were asked to tell all that they knew. When the Alliance came to Geneva it applied these lessons. Accordingly, it:

- provided science-based talking papers supporting the key FCTC provisions and legal expertise in exposing weakening language in the successive treaty drafts;

- produced a daily bulletin with news and analysis; held luncheon briefings in order to educate delegates on the etiology of tobacco-caused diseases and the various elements of the FCTC;

- provided media advocacy experts to the FCA cause and gained effective media highlighting of the FCA's messages;

- brought to Geneva expert witnesses to persuade the delegates to support particular positions;

- furnished a death clock that WHO director-general Brundtland unveiled at a press conference prior to each INB to dramatize the lives at stake in producing a forceful FCTC; and

- helped mobilize flurries of international letters to key country political decision makers when requested by members in recalcitrant countries.

These activities helped educate and assist small or understaffed delegations to the negotiations and provided legal and technical support to ally governments.[12]

The actual negotiation of the terms and text of any new multilateral international agreement is a clearly political process, and that of the FCTC certainly was. Like the negotiation of other such instruments, different interests were pursued and mediated enough for an agreement to result.

The formal negotiations occurred during six Intergovernmental Negotiating Body meetings, starting in October 2000 and ending in March 2003. A large number of countries (150 to 170 on average) attended each of the six negotiating sessions, indicating a high level of interest and state participation. The first three to four INBs helped identify the important issues and schisms and key proponents of each. The last two or three sessions involved the hard bargaining. A major and primarily divisive role was played by the U.S. delegation, particularly after INB 1, when the George W. Bush administration began.

The negotiating sessions covered a plethora of issues that were contained in the draft text, for example, product regulation, education, prevention, cessation, and second-hand smoke. Two of the issues that produced the most contentious disputes and helped forge alliances between like-minded nations and NGOs were the regulation of advertising and the relationship between trade treaties and public health concerns. These two issues emerged at the first negotiating session, during which many countries urged that the FCTC include a complete ban on tobacco advertising and promotion. The Clinton administration, which could not support a total advertising ban due to constitutional concerns, instead posited a provision that would prohibit tobacco advertising that appealed directly to children.[13] The initial draft text of the treaty also contained a trade provision that would subordinate health concerns to trade concerns and was problematic for many developing country participants.

Responding to what it anticipated would be contentious issues in the negotiations, the Alliance produced briefing materials relevant to these topics, held luncheon briefings for delegates to educate them on the scientific and/ or legal basis for provisions that would advance public health objectives, and started drafting and providing alternative text language for delegates to consider. At each INB, the Alliance produced side-by-side analyses of the draft text giving the Alliance's preferred language and corresponding rationales.[14] The delegates began to become familiar with the Alliance and its work and to overcome their suspicions about civil society. Many developed relationships with individual Alliance members so that information and intelligence could be exchanged in both directions.

Before each negotiating session, WHO organized meetings of the WHO regional groupings.[15] Although countries in these groups often had differing views on what measures the FCTC should contain, having them meet in the regional groups did allow some strong countries and strong voting blocs to emerge. For example, Thailand and India emerged as strong forces in the South-East Asia Regional Office (SEARO) constituency, which would be important to the negotiations.

Perhaps the most important regional grouping was the Regional Office for Africa (AFRO) group. Patricia Lambert has provided insights into how it emerged and came to feel empowered:

> AFRO was a region, and I met with my colleagues from the other 45 African countries as part of that. . . . [W]e discovered that we were at something of a disadvantage in terms of how we didn't have international treaty making experience, and how not all of us understood tobacco, and tobacco control in the same way. So South Africa hosted a meeting in Johannesburg for four or five days to get positions together. . . . [W]hat in fact did come out of the meeting was that we discovered that we had far more in common than what divided us . . . even though we have countries that produce tobacco. . . . And so we made it, we issued a statement . . . [the Johannesburg Declaration on the FCTC, March 14, 2001] at the end of that meeting that Africa would henceforth speak with a single voice. I remember very clearly, saying . . . [at INB 2], "I'm speaking on behalf of the 46 member states of the AFRO region." And I just felt the whole room become silent. And people's heads began to turn around . . . when

I unpacked it afterwards I realized that if ever it came to a question of voting, there . . . were 191 at that stage, now there are 192 member states. So 46 of that is almost a quarter of the house. If we then could get consensus on the issues that were important to us, if ever it came to a vote, we felt that we would carry a great deal of power against other countries that perhaps were not looking for such stringent tobacco control as we were.

The countries of AFRO remained a potent voting bloc, and several countries from that region, primarily South Africa and Côte d'Ivoire, became staunch allies of the Alliance.

INB 2 was the first negotiating session attended by a delegation answerable to the Bush administration. At the first INB, the U.S. delegation under the Clinton administration had presented some pro-health positions. Under the new administration, the delegation in Geneva received instructions for a radical midcourse change. Following the directions of the new director of the U.S. Office of Global Health Affairs, the U.S. delegation repeatedly made proposals that would have weakened critical provisions of the convention and severely undermined its potential to reduce the death and disease caused by tobacco around the world. This should not have been surprising; the tobacco industry had invested many millions in campaign contributions to Republicans prior to the elections of 2000.[16]

From the point of view of the NGO community the bright spot in the negotiations was the ability of the AFRO group to continue to speak as a bloc and for the first time support a total ad ban, for which it also had SEARO's support. Thailand and India continued to be reliable voices for strong treaty language. Australia, Canada, and New Zealand also took supportive positions.

U.S. members of the Alliance decided that the U.S. delegation and its positions needed to become a major focus of their efforts. These NGOs reported on U.S. positions to the media and to friendly congressional offices. The idea was not only to put pressure on the Bush administration but also to show other delegations that U.S. actions did not represent the best public health positions. For example, following the first round of negotiations attended by Bush administration officials, Rep. Henry A. Waxman (D-CA), in the first of many broadsides against the administration's position during negotiations, accused the Bush administration of marching in lockstep with "Big Tobacco" to undermine or eliminate significant global regulations to curb tobacco use (*Los Angeles Times*, Nov. 19, 2001).

U.S. NGOs used the Waxman letter to follow up with the media and thus expose the U.S. position at the negotiations. They also sought to capitalize on the resignation of the delegation chief who had served under Clinton to highlight the change in the U.S. position. They then circulated media stories about the resignation via Globalink to NGOs in other countries for use in their efforts to diminish the effect of U.S. positions and pressure (Chelala 2001).

At INB 3, the United States used states' rights arguments as a defense against stringent requirements on most substantive issues and to argue that it could not support language requiring federal legislative action. It sought to weaken key provisions, but developing countries took strong positions and succeeded in keeping them under consideration as the negotiating process moved forward. Again, the AFRO bloc ensured that countries too often marginalized in international negotiations were represented and heard. Their representation also dispelled the tobacco industry's argument that poor countries somehow have more important things to consider than the tobacco epidemic.[17]

The debate on trade surfaced as a real threat to the forward movement of negotiations. Although a majority of countries appeared to want a provision in the treaty that would have prioritized health concerns over trade treaties when they conflict, the United States wanted to retain a provision that in effect gave preference to trade treaties. Its favored language stated that "parties agree that tobacco control measures shall be transparent, non-discriminatory, and implemented in accordance with their international obligations."[18] Although this language appears conciliatory, it ensures that international trade obligations (e.g., existing trade treaties) would continue to predominate.

Because of the importance of the trade language, the Alliance, in addition to producing a wealth of written materials, believed that it needed to bring an expert to Geneva to speak to this issue. As a result, it asked Ambassador Ira Shapiro to attend the negotiations. He had served as general counsel and chief negotiator with Japan and Canada in the Office of the United States Trade Representative under President Clinton. At the FCTC negotiations, he conducted luncheon briefings, one-on-one discussions with delegations, and even addressed the negotiating body itself. Ambassador Shapiro's powerful presentations helped force the removal of the provision that the United States favored and the inclusion in the preamble of health primacy language.

AFRO continued to be a major force for a strong and effective treaty. Its ability to maintain loyalty and cohesiveness among its members made it a target for countries favoring a nonbinding and weak treaty. The AFRO meeting following INB 3 was held in Côte d'Ivoire, and AFRO held firm to its strong positions and continued the practice of having francophone and anglophone Africans meet together in spite of efforts to divide them.

As with any negotiations, the toughest part began during the last two or three sessions. These presented the NGOs and allied governments with a problem. The new chair elected to guide the negotiations advocated and adhered to a policy that no provisions would be accepted for the draft text without the consensus of all those attending. This gave a small number of dissenting countries, such as the United States, an extraordinary amount of power to disrupt the negotiations.

At INB 5, the United States, Germany, Japan, and Turkey became quite vocal in their opposition to language that would unequivocally place health concerns over trade policies. Perhaps to placate those countries, WHO weighed in with an opinion that article XXb of the GATT (language similar to that proposed by the United States) was sufficient to protect health. However, the SEARO region and Pacific island countries continued to push for an explicit health-over-trade provision.

On advertising, the chair's text, instead of recognizing the overwhelming support for a total ad ban that emerged in INB 4, used weak language to promote the protection of "vulnerable groups" from advertising. The U.S. delegation maintained that a total advertising ban was a "red line they would not cross" and would not sign or accept any treaty with an ad ban provision, even if there were exemptions for countries with constitutional constraints. Ireland spoke for twenty-four countries and supported an ad ban on all direct and indirect advertising, which left Germany isolated in the European Union while AFRO, SEARO, and Pacific island countries held firm to a total ban. The World Bank also intervened in the negotiations, saying a total ban was an essential component in reducing the harm of tobacco.

NGO access to the negotiations was severely curtailed, as deliberations moved from open, "general" sessions to closed, "informal" sessions. NGOs began to rely heavily on allied delegations for information about the content of closed meetings, getting copies of text proposals from these delegates and asking them to act as "conduits" who would take text and analyses to the negotiations. They had a war room and roving lobbyists using walkie-talkies to respond rapidly to problematic text proposals and arguments. They also used advocates and experts like Ira Shapiro to meet with individual delegations, and they created on-the-spot analyses of each new text proposal and provided new text language. Dr. Caleb Otto of Palau affirmed the role that NGOs played:

> The United States was, . . . whether they intentionally tried to intimidate [us], or were just intimidating by who they were, and who they brought with them, you know like lawyers, very good eloquent speakers, people who knew about the law, international law. . . . It was hard for us to always know whether or not we were being derailed by laws, or whether there was some truth that we needed to understand. This is where I think the NGOs . . . help[ed] us know what the law was about, or where . . . there was truth or untruth in what the

U.S. was saying. . . . For instance, . . . one of the . . . tactics that the United States delegation used was to say our constitution cannot allow us to do this. . . . And so this is where the NGOs were able to help us and say it is not entirely correct that the constitution does not allow [it]. And [the NGOs] would give us examples on . . . the constitution, or . . . federalism. . . . And we had some assistance from the NGOs to say there are instances where the federal government . . . was able to get the states to behave by saying we can give you certain money if you . . . [do] . . . this."[19]

The last negotiating session, INB 6, was held February 17 to March 1, 2003. It began with a new and final chair's text. That text outraged NGOs, as well as AFRO, SEARO, and Pacific island countries by omitting reference to widespread support for a total ad ban. Instead, the draft reflected the much weaker positions taken by the United States and favored by the tobacco industry. At the insistence of the United States and China, NGOs were shut out from all substantive negotiating sessions. NGOs received information from the friendly delegations in AFRO, SEARO, and Pacific island countries. NGOs took to picketing and street theater outside negotiating rooms, while maintaining good contacts with friendly delegations and providing language and rationales to prop up delegations involved in negotiations that took on the aspect of trench warfare.

This last negotiation session was contentious, reflecting the deep divisions between voting blocs. After three years of negotiations, the treaty was in danger of ending up as a weak and preemptive document that would discourage countries from going beyond what was contained in the text. Much of this was a result of the U.S. government's increasingly heavy-handed efforts to weaken the treaty.

In frustration, the U.S. NGOs called a late-night meeting to debate future actions. Early the next morning, they held a press conference calling on the United States to stop supporting the interests of Philip Morris over public health. U.S. NGOs called on the U.S. government to withdraw from FCTC negotiations rather than continue to undermine the efforts of the rest of the world to adopt a strong treaty. The American Cancer Society, the American Heart Association, the American Lung Association, and the Campaign for Tobacco-Free Kids made the demand, citing heightened U.S. efforts to water down nearly every provision of the treaty. For example, John Seffrin, chief executive officer of the American Cancer Society, asserted that "at this crucial juncture, the United States government is working methodically to weaken virtually every aspect of this treaty. This is unconscionable. We call on the U.S. government to observe the first rule of the Hippocratic Oath: do no harm. The time has come for the U.S. to stand aside and allow the rest of the world to complete a treaty strong enough to change the course of the tobacco epidemic."[20]

Taking advantage of relationships built over the years of negotiations, the NGOs asked a delegate to the negotiations to speak at a press conference and provide evidence of the U.S. government's bad behavior. Hatai Chitanondh of the Thai delegation told reporters about U.S. threats in which delegations were told to accept weakened positions or risk losing U.S. aid. The story caught the media's attention and was picked up by outlets all over the world. Counting on the reputation that NGOs had achieved with delegates, the Alliance gave copies of the press statement to all the delegations so they would understand that the U.S. negotiators did not represent the views of the U.S. public health community. Bolstered by this support, the countries finished negotiations and finalized a strong and comprehensive treaty, including the comprehensive ad ban that the United States had strongly opposed.

The United States, however, was not yet defeated. Speaking angrily at the final negotiating session, the U.S. officials vowed to get the treaty changed before it could be finally adopted. Its objections were legion. The required minimum health warning size was unacceptable. The United States could not accept a prohibition on sales to or by minors, citing federalism concerns. The language referring to "indigenous individuals and communities" was an unrecognized formulation in international law. Citing constitutional concerns, they complained that advertising, sponsorship, and promotion definitions were too broad. Perhaps most importantly and generally, the United States was unwilling to sign a treaty that would not allow it to "take reservations," that is, opt out of any treaty provision it found unacceptable.

Early in the morning on March 1, 2003, the negotiating countries, fed up with U.S. intransigence, finally agreed to a strong and comprehensive treaty. Yet the United States still had two months in which to weaken the treaty before final adoption by the World Health Assembly. Three weeks before the countries were to meet in Geneva to finalize the treaty, the United States began to carry out its threats. Derek Yach, of the World Health Organization, alerted U.S. NGOs that the U.S. government was sending a communiqué to every government involved in the negotiations and demanding changes that would significantly weaken the treaty, including the insistence that reservations be permitted. The communiqué contained an implicit threat that the United States might withhold its continued support for funding a variety of international tobacco-related activities if changes were not made.

After the NGOs got a copy of the communiqué, they provided it as an exclusive to the *Washington Post,* probably the daily newspaper most read by U.S.

"inside the Beltway" national political circles. The resulting story, headlined "U.S. seeks to alter anti-tobacco treaty: Reservations clause sought as way out of some provisions," merits quotation:

> The Bush administration says it needs the "reservations" clause to ensure that the U.S. could disregard treaty requirements it considered constitutionally questionable. But anti-tobacco activists and foreign diplomats say the demand is an attempt to water down the treaty to benefit tobacco companies or to unravel the agreement entirely.
>
> "I think it is impossible to reach a consensus, and this could easily be the end of the entire tobacco convention," said Belgian negotiator Luk Joossens. "If you open one article, it will encourage other nations to open articles they don't like. And if the reservations are included, then crucial aspects of the entire effort will be weakened. There is a lot of anger in so many countries about this American action."
>
> The treaty also includes tobacco-control programs that require considerable funding. The U.S. has been the largest donor to that effort, and some delegates said they believed that the U.S. was using the threat of cutting off its funding to persuade [delegates] to vote for its positions. . . . William Pierce, spokesman for HHS, said the "primary concern of U.S. negotiators is that parts of the treaty could prove to be unconstitutional by interfering, for instance, with tobacco companies' free speech rights. . . . Senate Democratic leader Thomas A. Daschle and House Democratic leader Nancy Pelosi said in a letter to the Administration, "In contrast to these public statements, your Administration went to great lengths to weaken many important provisions of the treaty. . . . In addition to advancing weak language, the U.S. delegation also inappropriately pressured other nations to adopt U.S. positions." (Kaufman 2003)

The story got attention from print media and networks across the United States, just as the NGOs wanted. Illustratively, Ellen Goodman, syndicated columnist for the *Boston Globe,* wrote, "But couldn't we make common cause with the rest of the world in pursuit of an international killer, a globally certified bad guy? Like say the Marlboro Man?" (Goodman 2003).

The U.S. NGOs immediately circulated the stories to Alliance members around the world and encouraged them to communicate directly with their governments to urge them to reject U.S. demands. The media attention was so intense that the press secretary for President Bush had to answer questions at a White House press briefing about the position the United States had taken on the treaty. The U.S. media attention prompted governments around the world to speak out in support of a strong treaty. The publicity made it impossible for the United States to pressure individual governments behind closed doors. When the U.S. efforts became a public issue, the countries that had supported the treaty began to unify in their opposition to it. By the end of the week, the United States recognized that it had no international support for its effort and was totally isolated.

When the negotiators for all the participating countries finally gathered in Geneva on May 21, 2003, for the vote to adopt the treaty, there were no dissents. Health and Human Services Secretary Tommy Thompson, head of the U.S. delegation, announced its capitulation and that it would support the treaty. A strong and comprehensive treaty, containing a road map for countries to follow to enact effective tobacco control measures, was adopted by consensus.

A little over a year later, on June 29, 2004, when the treaty closed for signature, 168 member states, nearly 90 percent of the countries involved, had signed and more than half the ratifications required for entry into force had been garnered. The FCTC has become one of the most rapidly embraced UN conventions. Expectations were that the treaty would achieve the required forty ratifications before the close of 2004, and it did.

Although this case study has dealt with the interaction between NGOs and nation-states in a discrete negotiation, its lessons have broader relevance to mounting challenges to U.S. government policy preferences.

There is no doubt, as this case study shows, that U.S. and foreign NGOs in alliance with other state and nonstate actors can have a substantial impact on short-term outcomes. Whether that also holds for long-term outcomes is yet to be seen. It is clear that the treaty, even without U.S. approval, is highly popular internationally. By the time the treaty closed for signatures, 168 countries had signed, and the fortieth ratification was secured on November 30, 2004. The treaty went into effect on February 27, 2005.

One could argue that the U.S. failure to impose its will in this case was because the Bush administration considered the treaty to be of secondary importance. That argument would emphasize that the administration did not oppose public health per se but instead merely gave primary concern to the trading privileges of one of the nation's largest exporters. Washington gave way because the loss did not undermine the most important administration objectives.

One could also posit that timing played a major role in the force with which the opposing countries held firm. When resolve and frustration finally coalesced and produced a strong treaty at INB 6, it was in the weeks leading up to the Iraq war. It is fair to suggest that many countries voted against the

U.S. position during this negotiation in order to vent their anger and feelings of impotence at being unable to avert U.S. plans to invade Iraq.

Finally, although U.S. desires were thwarted in much of the final language of the treaty, in those areas that were most central to U.S. needs, for example the language on trade, the United States either prevailed or was able to practice significant damage control. The final negotiated outcome on trade—silence with regard to pro-health language in the preamble—did not achieve U.S. goals of trade-primacy language, but it did thwart the desired language of the vast majority of delegates for health-primacy language.

Nonetheless, the final treaty represents a significant step forward for global public health, in both the provisions contained in the document and the catalyst it provided to energize and unite a new civil society force for change. Whether it represents a significant defeat for U.S. policy is yet to be determined, but for the countries involved in this negotiation, and the civil society that supported them, the defeat was real and justly deserved.

12

INTERNATIONAL PUBLIC OPINION
Incentives and Options to Comply and Challenge

DAVIS B. BOBROW

International public opinion often provides a context in which foreign actors can attempt to modify, evade, delay, or even resist what Washington would like to do and have others do. This chapter explores how international public opinion relates to challenges to U.S. government policy preferences. It presents a secondary analysis of poll responses given by a representative sample of the general public both inside and outside the United States. This analysis thus addresses both the domestic public opinion that political elites face within their own countries (that is, in those countries where polls were conducted) and the international public opinion that U.S. policy makers face.

Public opinion abroad has shifted in ways that reduce incentives for quick acquiescence to U.S. official preferences. The consequences of cooperation are weighing more heavily on compliant actors abroad as well as on the U.S. government. That does not generally mean that the international public is demanding direct confrontation with the United States, withdrawal from engagement with it, or commitment to alternative alignments and hard counterbalancing. Most foreign publics are more receptive to attempts to stand aside from, delay, divert, or modify U.S. government preferences than to direct, dramatically visible resistance.

I argue that international public opinion is important for the United States to consider because of the need to understand and anticipate challenges to American policies. I also introduce conservative rules of interpretation to employ when drawing inferences from poll responses. Furthermore, I analyze patterns of public opinion from readily available polls of high technical quality conducted mostly from September 11, 2001, through 2006 (see the appendix to this chapter). These polls covered particular national publics, and thus those publics are the unit of analysis here. All reported patterns and interpretations are of those aggregates.[1]

How International Public Opinion Matters

How might reported public opinion affect the policy choices of governments? In an extreme view, public opinion actually controls policy choices. Foreign political elites act as if they expect a referendum on what they have done vis-à-vis U.S. preferences, altering their positions to fit with what they think to be majority views. In my own view, international public opinion has a number of different functions that affect foreign elites. It is an indicator of the domestic political risks and rewards likely to result from a particular stance toward a U.S. policy preference. It also offers a clue as to how other non-U.S. elites are likely to behave toward a U.S. policy preference and whether there will be opportunities for challenge coalitions with other foreign actors. Global opinions may also be an instrument for bargaining with Washington to extract side-payments for support or offer foreign actors a credible excuse to use when trying to gain Washington's acceptance, even if grudging, of their inability to support a U.S. policy preference. Finally, foreigners may use their knowledge of U.S. public opinion to gauge domestic pressures on Washington to modify a particular policy and opportunities for challenge coalitions with American organizations and groups.

International public opinion may also serve a number of functions for U.S. government elites. It can indicate the domestic situation that foreign leaders will be facing. It may indicate the possibility of a Pyrrhic victory, in which foreign leaders who have complied with U.S. preferences are subsequently replaced by less compliant leaders. Global public opinion can also suggest whether policies requiring foreign contributions will actually generate those contributions promptly, in adequate volume, and for sufficient duration. It can clarify how large U.S. side-payments on other issues might need to be in order to secure compliance on a particular issue. Finally, international opinion, both pro and con, may help U.S. proponents of a policy develop strategies to gain domestic public support (i.e., positive public opinion in valued foreign countries, hostile opinion in negatively valued countries). Conversely, it may help U.S. opponents discredit a policy (i.e., negative public opinion in valued foreign countries, positive opinion in negatively valued countries).

International public opinion can constrain U.S. and foreign policy actors or serve as a resource as the major players engage in direct confrontations or joint attempts to modify policy. How others treat U.S. policy preferences and how the United States responds usually result from bargaining at both the domestic and international levels (Putnam 1988). Elites have less difficulty harmonizing the two bargaining levels when dealing with issues that are relatively low profile for pertinent national publics, receive scant media attention, and exhibit little apparent change from past policies. Policy elites with a strong grip on power at home have more latitude when it comes to bargaining; it is relatively safe for them to step outside the "zone of permissiveness" that public opinion offers. One kind of situation in which policy actors have considerable leeway is the absence of a competitive opposition with a clearly different stance on dealings with the United States. Another is when the next scheduled "mandate renewal" (e.g., a national election) is some distance in the future. A third situation of relative freedom for policy actors is when there is a high degree of public approval of incumbent policy performance on matters less related to U.S. foreign policy.

One or more of those facilitating conditions often is missing abroad or in the United States. With regard to foreign elites, since U.S. acts of commission and omission can substantially impact their society, they would be wise to pay close attention to U.S. public opinion that calls for Washington to maintain or alter its policies. For U.S. elites, wise policy choice involves recognizing how foreign populations view American actions and motives, making appropriate responses with regard to those views, and having some foresight about the American public supporting or at least not opposing a particular policy choice. If U.S. policy elites indulge in unwarranted optimism, they risk underestimating the costs and overestimating the benefits of Washington's policy emphases.

Treatment of Poll Responses

The summaries and interpretations of public opinion offered in this chapter are shaped by several decisions about how to treat poll responses. Those decisions accept some loss of information in favor of highlighting patterns of prima facie political relevance.

Distributions of responses are presented as crude scores on a seven-point scale rather than actual percentages (see table 12.1). The crude score categories may have significantly different implications for political elites' anticipations of public reactions and the associated risks and opportunities. The crudeness also takes into account well-known problems of margins of error as well as sensitivity to question and response wording, interview situations, and question order within surveys.[2] Due consideration of those problems cautions against

Table 12.1. Scoring conventions

Public opinion	Score	Net percentages	Thermometer (mean of x degrees)	Positive percentages	10-point scales
Massively supportive	+3	50 or more	75 or higher	75 or more	8 or higher
Predominantly supportive	+2	25 to 49	65 to 74	65 to 74	6.5 to 7.9
Supportive	+1	10 to 24	55 to 64	55 to 64	5.5 to 6.4
Split	0	9 to −9	45 to 54	45 to 54	4.5 to 5.4
Rejecting	−1	−10 to −24	35 to 44	35 to 44	3.5 to 4.4
Predominantly rejecting	−2	−25 to −49	25 to 34	25 to 34	2 to 3.4
Massively rejecting	−3	−50 or more	24 or less	24 or less	2 or lower

making too much of even statistically significant small percentage differences. The scoring rules also make comparable poll responses available only in different forms: both positive and negative responses that yield net percentages; thermometer judgments; only positive percentages; or points chosen on multi-point scales.

Poll responses are grouped (bundled) together based on substantive judgments about their linked relevance to public support for cooperation with or challenge to U.S. preferences. Policy elites often believe that public opinion bundles combine many facets or "faces of an issue," and so those elites try to manipulate the public profile of those issues. Multiple query information is reported (in parentheses) because responses to numerous ostensibly related queries warrant more interpretive confidence than answers to a single question. Rankings of a particular policy emphasis relative to others also are reported [in brackets] when available because relative priorities are politically important.

Opinion Patterns

Discussion of the content of international public opinion begins with issues emphasized in U.S. foreign policy in recent years: terrorism, the proliferation of weapons of mass destruction (WMD), and the Iraq venture. International support for challenges to U.S. policy may reflect broader appraisals of the United States and its role in international affairs. If foreign opinion is positive and thus favoring U.S. policy, the burden of persuading elites not to cooperate with the United States falls on those who would oppose, or at least not comply with, U.S. preferences. If foreign opinion is negative and thus disagrees with U.S. policy, the burden of persuasion falls on those who would comply.

The likelihood of challenges to U.S. policy is particularly strong when poll responses on such current issues as terrorism, WMD, and Iraq and responses about the United States in general and its international role share a prevailingly or negative pattern.

How much even prevailingly negative opinions suggest international public support for challenges may depend on the level of consensus about alternatives to U.S. leadership and centrality. Absent attractive alternatives, challenges to the United States seem more likely to range only from rhetorical flourishes to passive withholding of cooperation. That argues for exploring opinions about alternatives to U.S. unipolar dominance: bipolarity, stronger global international governmental organizations (IGOs) such as the UN, stronger regional organizations such as an enhanced European Union (EU), and having particular foreign nations lead others in challenging U.S. policies.

Finally, U.S. public opinion can affect foreign estimates of the domestic political incentives American elites must resist or accommodate in facing non-American policy preferences. Do challengers have encouraging prospects for potent coalitions with U.S. partners? Do they run significant risks of a punitive U.S. response and lingering American resentment? Moderate challenges of abstention, delay, and diversion seem less risky and more promising if the U.S. public shares foreign reservations about Washington's foreign policy preferences and favors accommodation to others.

Specific Issues

Opinions about the United States with respect to international terrorism, WMD proliferation, and the invasion and occupation of Iraq appear in table 12.2. Positive scores indicate agreement with or approval of the U.S. position and suggest receptiveness to compliance; negative scores indicate receptiveness to challenging U.S. policy.

The policy of the George W. Bush administration has emphasized the threat of terrorism and made it a priority. The first column of table 12.2 reports the extent to which publics view terrorism as a threat or policy priority by averaging responses to several questions. Those questions asked if terrorism posed an important threat in the world and in the public's own country; if it is one of the two most important issues for their country; what fears and worries citizens had about it; whether it should be a priority for the EU (asked of Europeans) and for the United States (asked of Americans); and if U.S. concerns about terrorism were warranted.

In terms of the scoring categories (rows) in table 12.1, few publics massively or predominantly rejected the notion that international terrorism posed a threat, but most rejected the notion or were split when opinions were pooled

Table 12.2. Terrorism, WMD, and Iraq

Country	Terrorism as threat and problem (2002–2006)	U.S. and terrorism (2002–2006)	WMD spread as threat and problem (2001–2006)	U.S. Iran, North Korea policy (2006)	Assessments of Iraq war (2002–2006)	Support for military participation (2002–2005)
WESTERN EUROPE						
Austria	−1.5 (13)	−1 (6)	1 [4] (2)		−2.5 (7)	−2
Belgium	−1.2 (13)	−0.9 (6)	1.5 [3] (2)		−3 (1)	−1
Denmark	−1.1 (13)	0.7 (6)	1.5 [3.5] (2)		−0.5 (7)	−1
Finland	−1.5 (13)	0.1 (6)	.5 [3.5] (2)		−2 (7)	0
France	0.2 (20)	−1 (1620)	1.3 [4.3] (12)	−3 (2)	−1.5 (32)	−2.5 (4)
Germany	0.2 (20)	1.1 (15)	1.4 [3.5] (12)	−2 (2)	−1.5 (30)	−2.5 (4)
Greece	−1.1 (13)	−3 (6)	3 [5] (2)		−2.4 (7)	−2
Iceland					−1.3 (6)	
Ireland	−1.3 (13)	0.1 (6)	2.5 [4] (2)		−1	2
Italy	0.1 (17)	0.5 (12)	1.8 [3.3] (5)	−2 (2)	−0.2 (9)	−1.3 (3)
Luxembourg	−1.4 (13)	−0.5 (6)	2 [4] (2)		−3	−1
Netherlands	−0.6 (15)	1.2 (8)	1.5 [3.8] (4)		−0.8 (10)	1.5 (2)
Portugal	−0.6 (15)	−1.5 (7)	3 [2.8] (4)	−1 (2)	−1.1 (9)	−1
Spain	1.2 (15)	−1.4 (9)	1.7 [4] (8)		−1.9 (21)	−2 (3)
Sweden	−1.5 (13)	0.7 (6)	2 [3] (2)		−1	1
Switzerland					−2.4	
United Kingdom	0.5 (20)	0.7 (16)	1.6 [2.3] (12)	−1.5 (2)	−0.1 (31)	−0.3 (4)
NORTH AMERICA						
Canada	−3	1.3 (3)	−2 [4]		−0.7 (15)	−3 (2)
United States	1.2 (45)	1.7 (53)	1.9 [2] (26)	0 (2)	−0.3 (347)	1.4 (101)
LATIN AMERICA						
Argentina	2	−2.5 (2)	−1 [2]	−3 (2)	−2.8 (7)	−3
Bolivia	1	2	−1 [2]			
Brazil	1	−1 (3)	1 [1]	−3 (2)	−0.8 (5)	−3
Chile		−2		−2 (2)	−2	−3
Colombia					−1.9 (6)	
Ecuador					−1.8 (6)	
Guatemala	1	3	−1 [3]			
Honduras	1	3	−1 [3]			
Mexico	2.5 (5)	−1 (2)	1.5 [2] (2)	−1 (2)	−3 (3)	−3
Peru	2	3	0 [2]			
Venezuela	1	3	1 [1]			
Uruguay					−2.9 (6)	
EASTERN EUROPE						
Albania					1 (6)	
Croatia	−3 (4)	−2 (2)				
Georgia					−0.9 (6)	

continued

Table 12.2. *continued*

Country	Terrorism as threat and problem (2002–2006)	U.S. and terrorism (2002–2006)	WMD spread as threat and problem (2001–2006)	U.S. Iran, North Korea policy (2006)	Assessments of Iraq war (2002–2006)	Support for military participation (2002–2005)
Kosovo					0.9 (6)	
Macedonia					−1.6 (6)	
Russia	2.3 (4)	0.4 (7)	0.1 [4] (8)	−2.5 (2)	−1.8 (28)	−3
Serbia					−2 (5)	
Ukraine	−2	3	−1 [3]			
EU ACCESSION COUNTRIES						
Bulgaria	−0.6 (13)	1.6 (7)	0.3 [3.5] (3)		−0.8 (6)	
Cyprus	−0.5 (12)	−2.5(6)	1.5 [6] (2)			
Czech Republic	−0.6 (12)	2.5 (7)	−0.5 [4] (3)			
Estonia	−0.5 (12)	1.3 (6)	2 [5] (2)		−1.5 (6)	
Hungary	−0.2 (12)	0.9 (7)	1 [4.5] (2)	−2 (2)	−3	
Latvia	−0.2 (12)	1 (6)	2 [3.5] (2)		−2.3 (6)	
Lithuania	−0.4 (12)	2 (6)	3 [4] (2)		−0.6 (6)	
Malta	−0.2 (12)	1.7 (6)	3 [4.5] (2)			
Poland	0 (15)	1.2 (12)	1.3 [3.2] (5)	0.5 (2)	−0.2 (12)	−2.3
Romania	−0.2 (12)	2.5 (6)	2 [5.5] (2)			
Slovakia	−0.7 (13)	1.6 (7)	0.8 [2.8] (3)			
Slovenia	−0.5 (12)	−1.2 (6)	2 [5] (2)			
CONFLICT AREA						
Egypt	1	−3 (3)	−0.7 (7)	−2.5 (2)	−2.8 (4)	
Israel		3			1.6 (6)	
Jordan	−2.5 (3)	−2.6 (6)	−1 [5] (8)		−2.1 (17)	−3
Kuwait		1			1 (4)	
Lebanon		−2 (4)	0 [2]	−2 (2)	−1.4 (8)	−3
Morocco	−3	−2.3 (3)			−2 (12)	−3
Pakistan	1 (3)	−2.4 (6)	−1.6 [1] (8)		−1.9 (25)	−2.7
Palestinian Authority		−3				
Turkey	−0.5 (15)	−2.4 (11)	0.5 [3] (8)	−3 (2)	−1.9 (28)	−3
United Arab Emirates		−3		−2.5 (2)	−3	
Uzbekistan	1 (2)		−1 [3]			
ASIA & PACIFIC						
Australia		−0.5 (2)		−1 (2)	−0.1 (9)	−1
Bangladesh	3	−1	−1 [1]			
China	−2 (3)	−0.7 (3)	−0.1 [4] (8)	−2 (2)	−2 (5)	−2
India	2.8 (4)	1.5 (4)	0 [3] (8)	−0.5 (2)	−0.9 (12)	−2.5
Indonesia	0 (3)	−1.6 (5)	−0.6 [5] (8)		−2.1 (8)	−3

continued

Table 12.2. *continued*

Country	Terrorism as threat and problem (2002–2006)	U.S. and terrorism (2002–2006)	WMD spread as threat and problem (2001–2006)	U.S. Iran, North Korea policy (2006)	Assessments of Iraq war (2002–2006)	Support for military participation (2002–2005)
Japan	1 (4)	0 (2)	1.4 [1] (8)		−2.1 (11)	−1
Malaysia	1 (2)				−1.9 (6)	
Myanmar	−1 (2)					
New Zealand		1			−0.8 (6)	
Philippines	2 (2)	1.5 (2)	0 [1]	1 (2)	0.2 (7)	−1
South Korea	−2 (4)	−2 (3)	−0.5 [2.5]	−1 (2)	−2.5 (12)	−1
Thailand	−1.5 (2)					
Vietnam	−1 (3)	2	−2 [3]		−2.6 (6)	
AFRICA						
Angola	0	2	−1 [2]			
Cameroon					−1.6 (6)	
Ghana	−2	2	−1 [2]			
Ivory Coast	1	3	−1 [3]			
Kenya	−1	1.5 (2)	−3 [3]	2 (2)	−1.7 (7)	
Mali		1	−1 [3]			
Nigeria	0	1.3 (3)	−0.1 [4] (8)	1 (2)	0.4 (13)	
Senegal	−2	−2	0 [2]			
South Africa	−1	1	−1 [2]		−1.4 (6)	−2
Tanzania	2	1	−2 [2]			
Uganda	2	2	0 [2]		−1.4 (6)	

Note: Ranks are in brackets. Numbers of queries are in parentheses with no entry if only one question was asked.

for the 2002–2006 period. A comparison of scores during George W. Bush's first term with those during the second shows that initially positive views substantially eroded among most EU 15 and accession country (EUAC) publics. There was little change in Asian publics, however.[3] The few publics with massive, predominant, or even supportive majorities in either period in which coping with terrorism was a high priority usually had experienced dramatic terrorist incidents (e.g., Spain, the United States, Russia, India, and the Philippines).[4] In short, widespread initial post-9/11 agreement with the U.S. emphasis on terrorism was replaced by generally diverging opinions. Much of the world no longer placed terrorism at the top of the priority list, where the Bush administration seemingly wanted it to be.

Has public opinion that supported, or at least did not massively or predominantly oppose, prioritizing terrorism favored the U.S.-preferred approach? Second column scores average opinions about the United States not being a cause of terrorism, American sincerity in opposing terrorism, a U.S.-

led counter-terrorism policy, and the correctness of U.S. counter-terrorism practices. Other than in the Central and Eastern European EUACs and Latin America, supportive majorities were few and geographically scattered. Massively or predominantly rejecting majorities were frequent in largely Islamic publics. Many EU 15 publics and those of several American allies in Asia and the Pacific (e.g., Australia and Japan) were split. When comparing scores from the first to the second Bush term, support declined and rejection increased. In sum, politicians in many countries have had growing domestic public opinion incentives to avoid clearly endorsing the U.S. approach to the war on terror. In only a few countries have there been incentives to generally endorse Bush policy. In largely Islamic countries politicians had very large incentives to publicly reject the Bush "war on terror" policies.

U.S. policy has emphasized coercive military action to counter international terrorism. Even at the peak of international sympathy shortly after 9/11, EU 15 publics were far more likely to be massively or predominantly supportive of civil contributions to the war on terror or, to a somewhat lesser extent, security assistance (base use and intelligence sharing) rather than military participation.[5] Public support for EU military participation in a U.S.-led war on terror predominated only in Denmark, the UK, France, Luxembourg, and the Netherlands. Those poll results were supportive of some European states joining a coalition of the willing but not of more encompassing EU or NATO military activity under U.S. leadership. As of 2003, public views supportive of even coalition of the willing military participation had diminished. European publics (the UK, France, Germany, Italy, the Netherlands, Portugal, and Poland) strongly supported economic sanctions but opposed the use of force against "another country harboring dangerous international terrorists" regardless of sponsorship by the United States, European Union, or both.

The third column of table 12.2 contains averaged scores and priority rankings [in brackets] for WMD proliferation as a general threat and a specific one (from Iran and North Korea), a focus for citizens' fears, a foreign policy priority, and one of the two most pressing world dangers.[6] Signs of strong public support for proliferation management efforts are large positive majorities (1.3 or more) considering WMD to be a threat, along with a high priority ranking (3 or higher). Signs of opposition or little support for intense action against WMD are large negative majorities and low priority rankings. National publics resembling the former included some EU members, Mexico, and Japan. Only a few publics resembled the latter category, but these were states that are crucial for U.S. proliferation management policies: Russia and China. Publics with only a supportive majority or a high priority rank may well accept that the spread of WMD presents a problem but not one that is severe enough to override attention to other issues. That pattern is widespread among EU 15, EUAC, Latin American, and African publics, and some in the Asia/Pacific region and the Middle East.

Even publics with a prevailing view of proliferation as a problem and threat may not support complying with Washington if they doubt the merits or motives of specific U.S. coping measures. The fourth column reports scores in 2006 for U.S. policy toward Iran and North Korea as proliferators. Only three publics were positive; only the publics of Poland, India, Australia, and the United States were split. The political incentives for many foreign elites to differentiate their country's stance from official U.S. counter-proliferation policies or to pay a high price for cooperating with them follow more from their publics' negativism about Washington than from widespread indifference to threats from WMD.

Averaged assessments of America's Iraq war are in the next column, and support for military participation in it is shown in the last column. The former column pools general evaluations of the war's justification and worth with judgments about its impacts on terrorism and world safety, the international system (perceived U.S. power and trustworthiness, American alliances, and the UN), Middle East stability, and the Iraqi people. Positive majorities were few (Albania, Israel, and Kuwait). Negative majorities, often predominant or massive, were the most frequent, suggesting that many governments would have domestic political incentives to challenge rather than comply with U.S. policies. There were, however, numerous split publics, including those of a number of troop contributors to the U.S.-centered coalition: Denmark, the UK, Italy, the Netherlands, Poland, and Australia. Their political circles and those of contributors with prevailing negative majorities (e.g., Japan and South Korea) may have had to justify sending troops by linkage: extracting compromises from the United States on other issues. When asked directly about military participation, publics were almost always strongly negative, further pointing to political risks for national elites complying with the United States.[7]

The domestic political incentives not to comply with U.S. requests for military cooperation in Iraq have also applied to reconstruction involvement (polling of the EU 15 in 2003–2004). Most publics massively placed the financial burden on the United States and only a few, usually among the militarily participating countries, had supportive majorities for a major EU or UN financial role. The United States and usually the EU were massively or predominantly rejected by most publics, which did not want them to have leading roles in managing reconstruction, the transition to sovereignty, and security provision. The UN seems to have been the default choice, with narrowly supportive or split publics.[8]

In sum, international public opinion has been for the most part prevailingly negative on cooperation with U.S. policy preferences on Iraq and the two other members of President Bush's "axis of evil."

Views of the United States

General opinions about the United States may influence publics' receptivity or resistance to prominent recent U.S. policies (such as those on Iraq and the war on terror). Those policies may also influence publics' general appraisals of the United States. Table 12.3 summarizes opinions on how the United States affects the rest of the world in general and specifically with respect to world peace and stability, environmental quality, and the international economy, as well as the likelihood that U.S. policies will continue to have a substantial impact on the world. Positive scores indicate favorable assessments of U.S. policies.

The first column averages evaluations of the overall impact of what the United States does (effects on the respondents' country, U.S. consideration for its interests, and American influence on the world and on the respondents' country).[9] There were very few predominantly or massively positive majorities, and those were usually in publics of security dependencies of the United States (Albania, Georgia, Kosovo, Israel, the Philippines). Advocates of compliance with the United States seem advantaged there. More publics predominantly or massively viewed the impact of U.S. policies as adverse and inattentive to their interests and those of the larger world (these were in France, Greece, the Netherlands, Spain, Canada, Argentina, Egypt, Jordan, Turkey, and Malaysia). Advocates of challenge seem advantaged there.

A still larger number of publics had small positive or negative majorities or were split. Their political elites lack strong domestic political incentives to pursue policies that are purely cooperative or oppositional toward the United States. Those elites instead must find a careful balance; the details of a particular circumstance may tip the scales one way or the other. The even division also suggests that either cooperation or challenge may seem viable to political elites in a strong position, while those weak on other grounds may find themselves with no unequivocally viable option.

The second column scores average responses to questions about U.S. contributions to world peace and to a statement suggesting that the United States does not have an excessive propensity to use force. The results are more prevailingly negative than those for America's overall international role. Predominantly or massively negative publics are not unusual in the EU 15 (Austria, Finland, France, Germany, Greece, and Spain), where there were no support-

Table 12.3. Appraisals of U.S. world impact

Country	In general (2001–2006)	On world peace (2002–2006)	On environmental quality (2001–2006)	On the international economy (2001–2005)	As the greatest power (2004, 2006)
WESTERN EUROPE					
Austria	−1.3 (5)	−2.4 (9)	−2.9 (7)	−1.3 (16)	
Belgium		−1.8 (8)	−2.6 (7)	−1.5 (16)	
Denmark	−0.6 (7)	−0.4 (9)	−3 (7)	−0.5 (16)	
Finland	−0.1 (4)	−2.8 (9)	−2.7 (6)	−1.1 (16)	
France	−2 (17)	−2.7 (11)	−3 (10)	−2.4 (19)	3
Germany	−1.7 (18)	−2 (11)	−2.9 (10)	−1.5 (19)	
Greece	−2 (3)	−2.6 (7)	−3 (7)	−2.3 (16)	
Iceland	−1.3 (3)	−3			
Ireland	0	−0.8 (10)	−1.3 (7)	0 (16)	
Italy	−0.6 (11)	−0.8 (10)	−1.6 (10)	−0.7 (19)	
Luxembourg	0 (5)	−1 (9)	−3 (7)	−1.3 (16)	
Netherlands	−2.3 (8)	−1.4 (9)	−2.9 (8)	−1.3 (16)	
Norway	−2				
Portugal	−0.4 (8)	−1.9 (10)	−2.1 (8)	−0.7 (17)	
Spain	−2.4 (10)	−2.3 (9)	−2.3 (7)	−2.1 (17)	3
Sweden		−1.5 (8)	−2.9 (7)	−0.9 (16)	
Switzerland	−1.8 (5)	−3			
United Kingdom	−0.5 (18)	−1 (11)	−2.3 (10)	−0.9 (19)	2
NORTH AMERICA					
Canada	−2 (5)	−1.5 (2)		−2.5 (2)	3 (4)
United States	2 (5)	0.1 (5)	−1		
LATIN AMERICA					
Argentina	−2.6 (10)	−2.7 (3)	−3	−3	
Bolivia	−1 (4)			−3	
Brazil	−1 (5)	−3 (2)	−3	−2	
Chile	−1 (2)	−2.5 (2)	−2		
Colombia	0.8 (4)	−2			
Ecuador	−1.8 (6)	−2			
Guatemala	1			−2	
Honduras	2 (2)			−1	
Mexico	−0.8 (5)	−2.7 (3)	−3	−1.5 (2)	1 (3)
Peru	−0.5 (3)			−2	
Uruguay	−2 (4)	−3			
Venezuela	1 (2)			−1	
EASTERN EUROPE					
Albania	3 (3)	−1			
Croatia	1	−3 (2)	−2 (3)	−1.2 (6)	

continued

Table 12.3. *continued*

Country	In general (2001–2006)	On world peace (2002–2006)	On environmental quality (2001–2006)	On the international economy (2001–2005)	As the greatest power (2004, 2006)
Georgia	1.6 (5)	1			
Kosovo	3 (3)	0			
Macedonia	−1.6 (5)	−3			
Russia	−1.8 (15)	−2.2 (5)	0	−1 (2)	2.7 (3)
Serbia	−1.7 (3)	−3			
Ukraine	−1.8 (4)			−2	
EU ACCESSION COUNTRIES					
Bulgaria	−1.2 (8)	−1.4 (7)	0.5 (6)	0.6 (13)	
Cyprus		−2.9 (6)	−3 (6)	−2.6 (12)	
Czech Republic	−0.5 (2)	0.9 (6)	0 (6)	1.2 (13)	
Estonia	0.8 (4)	−1.2 (7)	0.1 (6)	1.5 (12)	
Hungary	0	−1.1 (7)	−0.1 (7)	0.8 (12)	
Latvia	0 (2)	−1.4 (7)	0 (6)	1 (12)	
Lithuania	0.7 (3)	0.6 (7)	2 (6)	2 (12)	
Malta		0.5 (6)	1 (6)	1.5 (12)	
Poland	0.3 (6)	−1 (9)	0.8 (8)	0.9 (14)	
Romania	0.5 (2)	1.8 (6)	2.2 (6)	2.1 (12)	
Slovakia		−0.5 (6)	−0.3 (6)	0.4 (13)	
Slovenia		−2.5 (6)	−2.5 (6)	−1.1 (12)	
CONFLICT AREA					
Egypt	−2 (2)	−3	−3	−2	
Israel	2.2 (5)	2			2 (2)
Jordan	−2.6 (7)	−1.5 (2)		−2	
Lebanon	−1.4 (6)	−2 (5)	−2	−3	
Morocco	−1.7 (3)	0			
Pakistan	−1.4 (13)	−2.3 (3)		−2	
Turkey	−2.7 (11)	−2.7 (9)	−2.2 (6)	−2.6 (10)	
United Arab Emirates	−2	−2	−2		
Uzbekistan	1.8 (3)			−1	
ASIA & PACIFIC					
Australia	−1.6 (8)	−2.3 (3)	−2		
Bangladesh	−2			−2	
China	−0.8 (6)	−2.5 (2)	0		3
India	0.2 (2)	−1.5 (2)	2	−2	2
Indonesia	−0.8 (6)	−2.4 (4)	−1	−2	
Japan	0 (9)	−1.3 (3)		−3	3 (3)
Malaysia	−2.2 (7)	0			
New Zealand	−1.8 (4)	−2			

continued

Table **12.3.** *continued*

Country	In general (2001–2006)	On world peace (2002–2006)	On environmental quality (2001–2006)	On the international economy (2001–2005)	As the greatest power (2004, 2006)
Philippines	2.8 (7)	0.7 (3)	2	0	
South Korea	−1.3 (10)	−1.7 (4)	0	−2.5 (2)	2.5 (3)
Thailand	1.5 (2)				
Vietnam	−1 (6)	−2		−2	
AFRICA					
Angola	1			−2	
Cameroon	−0.6 (5)	−1			
Ghana	1			0	
Ivory Coast	0			−1	
Kenya	0.8 (6)	−1 (2)	2	1	
Mali	1 (2)			−1	
Nigeria	1.8 (7)	0.5 (2)	2	2	
Senegal	−2			−1	
South Africa	0.8 (6)	−1.5 (2)		−1	
Tanzania	1			−2	
Uganda	1 (6)	−1		0	

ive majorities. All Latin American publics polled were predominantly or massively negative. While EUAC publics were less negative than those of the EU 15, only Romania had a supportive majority. Primarily Islamic publics in the Middle East and Asia were strongly negative, and most Asian and African publics were negatively inclined. Many national elites have had to deal with publics largely believing that, or at best split on, the idea of U.S. preference for excessively militaristic and violent policies harmful to world and regional peace and stability.

On environmental quality, fourteen of the EU 15 publics were predominantly or massively negative on the U.S. contribution. Among the EUAC publics, many were split. All four Latin American publics polled had strongly negative judgments, while some Asian publics had strongly supportive majorities (India and the Philippines) as did the two African publics polled.

The fourth column combines assessments of U.S. contributions to the world economy (economic growth, reduction of poverty and inequality, globalization, and the absence of an economic threat from America). For most publics, scores were strongly negative about reducing poverty, far more so than for advancing growth. Indeed, evaluations of U.S. contributions to the latter were more positive for more publics than for any of the previous parts of table 12.3. For example, in most EU 15 publics the degree of negativism was less.

Nevertheless, only in the EUACs were national publics with positive majorities other than exceptional.

In sum, the first four columns suggest substantial negativism in most of the world about the international impact of the United States, albeit to a lesser extent in the EUACs and Africa. Those views suggest at least prevailing skepticism about the self-interest and collective interest gains from supporting U.S. government policy preferences. Before we assume that publics are receptive to challenging Washington directly, the results in the last column should be considered.

The few polled national publics all had majorities, usually very large ones, expecting the United States to be the world's greatest power for at least the next ten years, with the implied expectation that U.S. policies will continue to affect others significantly. The perceived likelihood of continuing American power may well lead many foreign publics to shun the prospect of pervasive, sustained bad relations with the United States. A nation that mounts extreme challenges might trigger U.S. retaliation and run great risks for very uncertain benefits. The perceived importance of good relations with a continuing American superpower can mute challenges, especially if foreign elites and publics have hopes that the United States will eventually behave more considerately. Having convictions that the United States is unswervingly or recurrently committed to damaging policies may encourage publics to support a quiet government campaign to build capacity for future direct challenges and to delay mounting any challenge until that greater capacity exists.

The implications of negative public assessments of how the United States affects the rest of the world may depend on several things. One is the extent to which those same publics view the United States positively in even more general terms. Another is whether those publics attribute U.S. foreign policy shortcomings to a specific (and temporary) presidency rather than to inherent, deeply rooted U.S. characteristics. A final factor is whether the international publics prefer U.S. involvement and even leadership to passivity and isolationism. Relevant opinions appear in table 12.4.

Generally favorable views of the United States suggest to what extent America has the "benefit of the doubt" or a halo when it comes to a wide range of specific policies for which Washington may seek acceptance or cooperation. The first column has most publics prevailingly positive in 1999–2000 at the end of the Bill Clinton presidency. That often eroded or vanished after 9/11 (except for many African publics). For the most part, scores fell with the invasion and occupation of Iraq and have not improved or have even worsened since then. Most major power allies in Europe and Asia seem split; Islamic publics are usually markedly negative. Split public opinion can dispose elites toward

Table **12.4.** Broad appraisals of the United States and the Bush administration

Country	Favorable (1999–2000)	Favorable (post-9/11–2006)	As a role model (2002–2005)	Bush foreign policies (2001–2006)	Problems are Bush, not U.S. values/nature (2002–2005)	Activism OK (2002, U.S. only 2006)	Desire strong leader (2002–2005)
WESTERN EUROPE							
Austria			−1 (24)				
Belgium			−1.1 (24)				
Denmark			−1.3 (24)				
Finland			−1.7 (24)				
France	1	−0.8 (9)	−0.8 (32)	−2.8 (13)	2.5 (4)	−1	−0.7 (3)
Germany	3	−0.2 (8)	−0.6 (32)	−2.3 (12)	2 (4)	0	1 (2)
Greece			0 (24)				
Ireland			0.3 (24)				
Italy	3	0.8 (5)	0.7 (32)	−1.4 (9)	1 (3)	−2	1 (2)
Luxembourg			−0.9 (24)				
Netherlands		0.8 (3)	−1.1 (25)	−2.2 (5)	2		2 (2)
Portugal		0	1.2 (25)	−2 (2)			
Spain		−1.8 (5)	−0.5 (28)	−2.7 (6)	1.7 (3)		0
Sweden			−0.8 (24)	−3			
United Kingdom	3	1 (9)	−0.3 (33)	−1.6 (13)	1.5 (4)	−2	1.5 (2)
NORTH AMERICA							
Canada		0.5 (4)	−0.6 (9)	−2.3 (4)	1.3 (3)	−2	2
United States		3 (4)		0.6 (67)		−1.5 (4)	1.8 (4)
LATIN AMERICA							
Argentina	0	−2	−2 (3)	−3	2	−3	
Bolivia	2	1	−2 (3)	−1	0	−3	
Brazil	1	−1 (2)	−1.7 (5)	−2.7 (3)	1 (2)	−2	
Guatemala	3	3	0.7 (4)		1	−2	
Honduras	3	3	1.3 (4)		2	−2	
Mexico	2	0.3 (3)	−0.5 (6)	−2.5 (2)	1	−3	3
Peru	2	2	0.3 (3)	0	2	−2	
Uruguay				−2			
Venezuela	2	3	1.3 (5)	0	0	−3	
EASTERN EUROPE							
Croatia			−0.4 (24)				
Russia		−0.2 (6)	0 (7)	−1.9 (7)	0 (4)	−2	0
Ukraine	2	3	0.7 (3)		2	0	
EU ACCESSION COUNTRIES							
Bulgaria	3	2	0.2 (29)		1	−2	
Cyprus			−1 (24)				

continued

Table 12.4. *continued*

Country	Favorable (1999–2000)	Favorable (post-9/11–2006)	As a role model (2002–2005)	Bush foreign policies (2001–2006)	Problems are Bush, not U.S. values/nature (2002–2005)	Activism OK (2002, U.S. only 2006)	Desire strong leader (2002–2005)
Czech Republic	3	2	0.3 (29)	−2	−2	1	
Estonia			−0.4 (24)				
Hungary			0.8 (24)				
Latvia			0.4 (24)				
Lithuania			0.6 (24)				
Malta			−0.1 (24)				
Poland	3	1.5 (6)	0.8 (29)	−0.3 (6)	0.5 (2)	−2	1.5 (2)
Romania	−1		0.4 (24)				
Slovakia	2	1	0.7 (28)		0	1	
Slovenia			−0.6 (24)				
CONFLICT AREA							
Egypt		−2.5 (2)	−2 (2)	−3	0	−3	
Israel		2 (2)	1.3 (4)	2.5 (2)	0		2
Jordan		−3 (5)	−1.2 (7)	−1.8 (5)		−2	
Kuwait		1	0.3 (3)	2	0		
Lebanon		−1.7 (3)	0 (6)	−2.5 (2)	1 (2)		
Morocco		−2 (2)	−0.3 (3)	−3 (2)	3		
Pakistan	−3	−2.1 (5)	−2.3 (6)	−1.6 (5)	1.3 (2)	−3	
Palestinian Authority		−3	−2.7 (3)				
Turkey	0	−2.5 (6)	−1.4 (30)	−2.3 (6)	0.7 (2)	−3	
Uzbekistan	1	3	1.3 (4)			−1	
ASIA & PACIFIC							
Australia		−0.5 (2)	−1 (3)	−1.5 (2)	1		3
Bangladesh		0			1	−3	
China		−1 (3)		−1.5 (2)	−1		
India		1.8 (4)	0 (3)	0.3 (3)	0.7 (2)	−3	
Indonesia	3	−1.2 (4)	0.2 (6)	−3 (2)	−1	−3	
Japan	3	0.4 (3)	0.8 (5)	−2 (3)	0 (2)	−2	2
Philippines		3	2 (3)	2	2	0	
South Korea	1	0.3 (3)	0.6 (8)	−1.3 (3)	−2 (2)	−2	2
Vietnam		1.5 (2)	0 (3)		2	−3	
AFRICA							
Angola		0	0 (3)		2	−3	
Ghana		3	2 (3)	−1	0	−3	
Ivory Coast		3	2.7 (3)		−1	0	
Kenya	3	3	1.7 (3)	−2	2	−2	

continued

Table **12.4**. *continued*

Country	Favorable (1999– 2000)	Favorable (post- 9/11– 2006)	As a role model (2002– 2005)	Bush foreign policies (2001– 2006)	Problems are Bush, not U.S. values/ nature (2002– 2005)	Activism OK (2002, U.S. only 2006)	Desire strong leader (2002– 2005)
Mali		3	−0.3 (3)		−2	−2	
Nigeria	0	2 (3)	2.7 (6)	0 (3)	1	−3	
Senegal		1	0 (3)		−1	0	
South Africa		2	1 (3)		1	−3	
Tanzania		0	0 (3)		0 (2)	−3	
Uganda		2	2 (3)		2	−3	

situation-specific choices about compliance with the United States; negative public opinion can lead them to avoid visible cooperation.

The third column reports assessments of the United States as a superior role model warranting emulation with regard to politics, business, science and technology, social policy, and quality of life. Judgments comparing the American "way" with that of one's own nation or the EU have most publics split or with slightly positive or negative majorities. African publics are especially likely to have large positive majorities and primarily Islamic publics in the Middle East, large negative ones. Underlying the average scores are repeated differences between positive assessments of the relative merits of competitive U.S. economic practices (private business and technology innovation) and negative assessments of U.S. social infrastructure (education and health care systems), social justice, and overall quality of life. In countries with split publics or slight majorities, acceptance of and support for importing U.S. practices selectively seems more palatable domestically than blanket adoption or rejection of them. Few publics predominantly or massively favored comprehensively embracing the American "way" in terms of the socioeconomic and governance practices that Washington has chosen to export.

Most of the summarized opinions on views of the United States were gathered during the presidency of George W. Bush, whose foreign policies mostly received negative majorities abroad, and those negative views were often predominant or massive (see the fourth column of table 12.4). Only the publics of Israel, Kuwait, and the Philippines were strongly positive; only the publics of Peru, Venezuela, Poland, India, and Nigeria were split. Of course, appraisals of Bush's foreign policy in particular and of U.S. foreign policy in general may influence each other. Given that appraisals of the U.S. international role were cool or negative, the extent to which publics attribute their negative views to the Bush presidency or more enduring American inclinations matters. The fifth column, with some exceptions, shows majorities giving more weight to the Bush presidency. That suggests assessments of the United States and its international role could improve during a new presidential administration with policy inclinations that are perceived differently. Foreign publics who see the United States as just going through a "bad patch" may encourage their political elites to pursue challenge strategies of delay and evasion to buy time for policy shifts by a successor U.S. administration and to avoid challenges likely to leave lasting resentment among Americans.

What overall approach to international affairs do foreign publics want from the United States, other than being different from that of George W. Bush? The penultimate column of table 12.4 has most publics viewing recent levels of U.S. international activism negatively, often by very substantial majorities. Only a few were even split. Yet national publics disagreed with each other on whether the United States errs on the side of excessive or insufficient international activism. In the last column, the preferences of the few publics polled for the United States to be a strong leader in international affairs do not seem to favor reduced activism. Scores reported elsewhere (Bobrow 2005) have the Western and Eastern European publics in favor of America playing a strong, activist leadership role but somewhat fearful of U.S. unilateralism. Yet the Japanese and Korean publics who shared a preference for the United States as a strong leader also thought U.S. activism was already excessive. Challenges supported by international public opinion seem about as likely to call for more U.S. international involvement as they are to demand less.

The opinion sets discussed to this point imply that many foreign publics (and thus elites) have views that incline them to consider alternatives to compliant cooperation with U.S. policy initiatives. Among most publics, the United States does not have the sort of policy "credit rating" (which would be manifest in large supportive majorities) that would encourage their elites simply to bandwagon with Washington. Yet more fragmentary responses suggest a continuing demand for and receptivity to American leadership in directions different from those of the Bush administration. Those isolated responses also reflect a recognition of the realistic need to get along with an American superpower. What alternatives to the status quo might then seem attractive to international publics?

Alternatives to Current American Predominance

The negative views of the United States discussed here do not necessarily amount to support for anything more than rhetorical challenges, grumbling, delay, and evasion. Prospective support for challenges with more assertive, sustained, and encompassing policy content seems stronger if international public opinion positively views one or more alternatives that would reduce America's unilateral capacity to shape and lead the world. Table 12.5 deals with several possibilities. These include bipolarity, especially with China or the EU rising to peer status with the United States; stronger IGOs, especially the United Nations; and collective foreign and defense policy action by the EU without it having superpower status. In the remaining tables, positive scores indicate that a public positively views an alternative, and negative scores indicate the opposite.

In the first column, international publics differ about whether the world would be safer with a second (unnamed) military superpower. Most Latin American and African publics were strongly negative when polled early in the period covered. In the EU 15, none of the publics were strongly negative then, and as of 2005 they were strongly positive. Asians were divided, with Chinese and Indians strongly positive and U.S.-ally publics in Japan, the Philippines, and South Korea opposed. Vietnamese public opinion was also negative on that issue. Similar divisions appear among conflict area and EUAC publics (with narrower margins). More specifically, in the second column, the desirability of China as a military peer of the United States met with rejection in "old" and "new" Europe, as well as in India and Japan. Support prevailed in China and most of the Islamic publics polled. A superpower or strong leadership role for the EU (third column) received strong support in Western Europe, Russia, and Turkey. Yet the type of power member publics strongly favored for the EU was civil rather than military in nature (fourth column). As for challenges, even member publics supporting the EU as a superpower strongly rejected having it balance and compete with rather than cooperate with the United States (fifth column). In sum, the publics supported neither China nor the EU as a future pole of comprehensive power approximately matching that of the United States.

Another alternative to constrain U.S. power might be a collective international governance regime of IGOs. By processing issues through IGOs in which the United States participates, governments with policy preferences different from Washington's may have a number of opportunities. They may have a better chance of delaying and diluting unwanted U.S. actions, diverting American resources to other issues, extracting side-payments for cooperating with the United States, and building coalitions with American political elements opposed to particular U.S. government preferences. Public opinion supportive of IGOs provides political elites with an incentive to use them for issue processing, whatever their ultimate effectiveness in resisting or modify-

Table 12.5. Alternatives to U.S. predominance

Country	World safer with another military power (2002–2005)	China as peer military power (2005–2006)	EU as superpower, strong leader (2002–2004, 2005 only for U.S.)	EU as civil power (2002–2006)	EU as balancing power, competing with U.S. (2002–2003)	Evaluation of UN and international governmental institutions (2002–2006)	Stronger UN (2002–2005)	Favorability of UN IGOs over U.S. (post-9/11–2006)
WESTERN EUROPE								
Austria				2 (4)		1.4 (6)		
Belgium				2 (4)		0.7 (6)		
Denmark				1.5 (4)		3 (6)		
Finland				1.7 (4)		2 (6)		
France	0.7 (3)	−2	3 (4)	1.5 (6)	−2.8 (5)	1 (11)	1.6 (7)	0.2
Germany	0.7 (3)	−3	2.5 (4)	2 (6)	−2.8 (5)	0.8 (11)	2.6 (7)	1
Greece				2.3 (4)		−1.3 (6)		
Ireland				1.3 (4)		2 (6)		
Italy			3 (3)	2.2 (6)	−3 (5)	1.7 (6)	2.1 (6)	2.5
Luxembourg				2.5 (4)		1.7 (6)		
Netherlands	2	−2	2 (4)	1.6 (6)	−2.8 (5)	1.5 (6)	2.3 (3)	0.7
Portugal			3	2.7 (5)	−2.5 (4)	1.9 (6)	3	1.9
Spain	3	−3		2.3 (4)		1.1 (8)	2.5 (4)	2.9
Sweden				1.5 (4)		2.7 (6)		
United Kingdom	0 (3)	−3	2 (4)	1.8 (6)	−2.6 (5)	1.6 (11)	1.6 (7)	0.6
NORTH AMERICA								
Canada	−0.5 (2)	−3				2.3 (3)	3 (2)	1.8
United States	−1.1 (14)	−3	0 (4)	3	−3 (4)	0.2 (15)	0.4 (36)	−2.8
LATIN AMERICA								
Argentina	−2					−2.5 (2)	2 (2)	−0.5
Bolivia	−2					2 (2)		1
Brazil	−1					−0.3 (3)	2.3 (3)	0.7
Chile							2 (2)	
Guatemala	−3					3 (2)		0
Honduras	−2					3 (2)		0
Mexico	−3					2.3 (4)	2.5 (2)	2
Peru	−2					2.5 (2)		0.5
Venezuela	0					2.5 (2)		−0.5
EASTERN EUROPE								
Russia	0.2 (3)	−3 (2)	3			1.2 (5)	1.3 (3)	1
Ukraine	−1					2.5 (2)		
EU ACCESSION COUNTRIES								
Bulgaria	1					2 (8)		0

continued

Table 12.5. *continued*

Country	World safer with another military power (2002–2005)	China as peer military power (2005–2006)	EU as super-power, strong leader (2002–2004, 2005 only for U.S.)	EU as civil power (2002–2006)	EU as balancing power, competing with U.S. (2002–2003)	Evaluation of UN and international governmental institutions (2002–2006)	Stronger UN (2002–2005)	Favorability of UN IGOs over U.S. (post-9/11–2006)
Cyprus				2.3 (4)		−0.7 (6)		
Czech Republic	−2			2.3 (4)		1.9 (8)		−0.1
Estonia				2.3 (4)		1.7 (6)		
Hungary				1.7 (4)		2.2 (6)		
Latvia				2 (4)		1.7 (6)		
Lithuania				3 (4)		1.5 (6)		
Malta				2.7 (4)		2.2 (6)		
Poland	0.5 (2)	−3	−1 (3)	2.6 (6)	−2.6 (4)	2 (8)	2.6 (5)	0.5
Romania		−3				2.3 (6)		
Slovakia	−1			2.3 (4)		1.9 (9)		0.9
Slovenia				2.3 (4)		0.9 (6)		−0.5
CONFLICT AREA								
Egypt	−2					0		2.5
Israel						−2	−2	−4
Jordan	0 (3)	3				1 (4)	1.5 (2)	4
Kuwait						3	0	2
Lebanon	1 (2)	0				−0.5 (2)	2.5 (2)	1.2
Morocco	−2					−1 (2)	1 (2)	1
Pakistan	3	3				0.1 (3)	−1 (2)	2.2
Palestinian Authority	−2 (2)					−3	3	0
Turkey	1 (3)	2	2			−0.4 (10)	0.8 (4)	2.1
Uzbekistan	−1					2.6 (5)		
ASIA & PACIFIC								
Australia						1	3 (2)	1.5
Bangladesh	0					2 (2)		
China	3	3 (2)				2.6 (7)	2 (2)	3.6
India	2 (2)	−1.3 (3)				2.1 (7)	2.5 (2)	0.3
Indonesia	0.5 (2)	2				1.2 (8)	2.3 (3)	2.4
Japan	−3	−3 (2)				−0.4 (11)	3 (2)	−0.9
Malaysia						1.6 (8)		4.6
Philippines	−2					3 (7)	2.5 (2)	0
South Korea	−1					0.4 (13)	1 (3)	0.1
Thailand						2.1 (8)		
Vietnam	−1					2.5 (10)		1

continued

Table 12.5. *continued*

Country	World safer with another military power (2002–2005)	China as peer military power (2005–2006)	EU as super-power, strong leader (2002–2004, 2005 only for U.S.)	EU as civil power (2002–2006)	EU as balanc-ing power, compet-ing with U.S. (2002–2003)	Evalu-ation of UN and interna-tional govern-mental institu-tions (2002–2006)	Stron-ger UN (2002–2005)	Favor-ability of UN IGOs over U.S. (post-9/11–2006)
AFRICA								
Angola	−2					3		3
Ghana	−2					3 (2)		0
Ivory Coast	−2					3 (2)		0
Kenya	−2					2.5 (2)		−0.5
Mali	−1					3 (2)		0
Nigeria	0					2.5 (4)	0	0.5
Senegal	0					3 (2)		2
South Africa	−1					3 (2)	2.5 (2)	1
Tanzania	−2					2 (2)		2
Uganda	−1					3 (2)		1

Note: Entries in the last column are calculated by subtracting the post-9/11 U.S. favorability score in table 12.4 from that for the UN and international institutions in the sixth column of this table.

ing U.S. policies. Foreign governments wanting to use IGO venues may even gain official U.S. acceptance of that strategy on grounds that it might dampen their own domestic public's opposition to U.S. preferences.

The last three columns of table 12.5 summarize evaluations of IGOs (including the UN and some special purpose institutions), support for strengthening the UN (in general, by making its mandate necessary for the preemptive use of force and by enlarging the Security Council), and the extent to which IGO favorability scores exceed those for the United States after 9/11. Most world publics had massively or predominantly favorable general IGO evaluations except those in the Middle East, patterns that recurred on the issue of strengthening the UN (only the Israeli and Pakistani publics had negative majorities). Making the UN the only legitimate source of a mandate for preemptive military attacks, a move that might seriously constrain the United States (and some of its allies), was rejected by the American, Israeli, and Pakistani publics; opinions in the UK were divided on that issue. Polling in mid-2002, not included in table 12.5, suggests that a UN mandate increases support among EU member publics for participation in a broad preemptive military intervention coalition with the United States. Publics in the UK, France, Germany, Italy, the Netherlands, and Poland were asked about supporting their nation's military participation in a U.S. attack on an Iraq having WMD or aiding Osama bin Laden—an attack that would have many or few Western casualties. Positing a UN mandate substantially increased support regardless of the other conditions. That result may indicate that those publics have more favorable opinions of IGOs than of the United States, as did many other publics.[10]

As discussed, European publics' views in table 12.5 called for the EU to become a superpower and strong leader in international affairs but not the large-scale military power required to play a full "balancer" role vis-à-vis the United States. That somewhat countervailing set of opinions calls for further exploration of European public opinion on the EU as a source of challenges to U.S. policies. Relevant scores appear in table 12.6.[11]

With few exceptions, EU 15 publics had far more positive views of EU than of U.S. contributions to world peace, environmental quality, and poverty reduction. With smaller differences, EU contributions were more favorably viewed for world economic growth, counter-terrorism, and globalization. EUAC publics, with very few exceptions, also favored the EU but often by a smaller margin. The margin in favor of the EU tended to increase in "new" and "old" Europe from the first to the second terms of George W. Bush. That increase even occurred for the issue of counter-terrorism, the topic on which appraisals of U.S. performance during the first Bush term most rivaled those of EU performance in the same period. The relative scores suggest that, across a range of international policy issues, there were substantial domestic incentives for EU politicians to advocate a European position and avoid quick and visible compliance with U.S. preferences.

Support for bold and sustained challenges seems doubtful, however, given the general favorability scores in the final column of table 12.6. The EU edge among EU 15 publics often falls short of that for most of the issue areas; some EUAC publics favor the United States over the EU. Europeans may well be more negative about contemporary U.S. programs for the issue areas in table 12.6 than they are enthusiastic about the general merits of the EU. That could follow from public dissatisfaction with EU performance on other issues. If that is true, public support for the EU as an alternative to America-centered unipolarity may well depend on citizens attaching high priority to foreign and defense concerns.

Table 12.7 reports opinions on steps the EU might take to be a stronger and more autonomous player in world affairs, the priority that should be given to foreign and defense issues, and overall EU performance on those issues. Positive scores in the first four columns indicate support for less reliance on and

Table 12.6. Evaluations of the EU relative to the United States

Country	For world peace (2003–2005)	For environmental quality (2003–2005)	For economic growth (2003–2005)	For poverty reduction (2003–2005)	In globalization (2003–2005)	In counter-terrorism (2003–2005)	General favorability (for EU 2002–2004, for U.S. post-9/11)
EU 15							
Austria	4.5	4.5	1.9	3.7	1.3	2.8	
Belgium	4.8	5.2	2.8	4.3	4.5	2.5	
Denmark	3.5	4.3	0.8	4	2.5	2.3	
Finland	5.8	5.1	2	2.4	3.5	1.4	
France	5.5	4.9	2.3	3.9	5	2.8	3.2
Germany	5.1	5.7	1.4	4	4.5	2.5	1.3
Greece	5.5	5.2	4.9	4.5	3.5	4.7	
Ireland	4.2	4.4	1.3	3	4.5	2	
Italy	2.8	3.2	1.5	2.4	3	1.1	1.6
Luxembourg	4.9	5.7	2.6	4.5	4.5	1.5	
Netherlands	4.1	4.9	2.2	4	4	1.4	0
Portugal	4.4	4	2	3.4	2	1	1.8
Spain	5	4	3	4.2	4.5	3.7	4.2
Sweden	4.5	4.9	0.7	3.3	2.5	1.1	
United Kingdom	3.1	4.3	1.3	2.5	2	0.1	−1
EUACs							
Bulgaria	3.8	2.5	1.3	2.2		1	−0.4
Croatia	5.5	4	2.3	4		4	
Cyprus	5.9	6	5.2	5.9		4.3	
Czech Republic	2.1	3	0.7	1.8		−0.1	−1.4
Estonia	3.7	2.8	1	1.7		0.9	
Hungary	4	2.8	1.1	2.4		0.8	
Latvia	4	2.7	1.5	1.3		1.3	
Lithuania	2.3	1	0.8	0.8		0.1	
Malta	2.6	2	1.1	2		1.1	
Poland	2.7	2.2	1	1.7		0.5	−0.4
Romania	1.2	0.8	0.8	1		−0.2	
Slovakia	3.5	2.7	1.7	2.9		0.8	0.4
Slovenia	5.5	5.4	3.1	4.2		0.7	
Turkey	4.5	4	4.1	4.8		2.3	4.8

Note: Scores for the United States are drawn from previous tables and from Bobrow 2005, and those scores are subtracted from scores for the EU. Most of the polled European publics were asked six questions about world peace, environmental quality, economic growth, and poverty reduction and seven questions about terrorism. Turkey was polled on each question not less than four times, and Croatia, not less than two. General favorability scores for the EU are based on eight or more questions, except in the case of Croatia, where five questions were asked.

compliance with the United States. In the next three columns, positive scores suggest making greater independence a priority. The final column's scores are for satisfaction with what the EU has been doing.

The first column scores average support for a common foreign policy (CFP) in general; a common position on international crises; an EU foreign minister; an EU seat on the UN Security Council (UNSC); and joint EU–national member government foreign policy decision making. Publics are massively or predominantly supportive except for Scandinavia, the UK, and Turkey, where there are only supportive majorities. In the next column, scores for a common defense and security policy (CDSP) pool support for it in general, a rapid reaction force, and joint EU–national member government defense and security policy decision making. Support for the CDSP is markedly less than for a CFP, especially in some of the EU 15 countries, but no public is negatively inclined and few are split. Third column scores indicate support for the EU and member national governments as the key loci of European defense decisions rather than NATO. Majorities, often massive or predominant, support that principle in most of the EU 15; support is less strong in most of the EUACs. In the fourth column, mostly massive or predominant majorities in every EU 15 and EUAC public would favor the EU being more independent of the United States. In sum, all four sets of indicators point to substantial public demand for moving away from followership of the United States and for Europe to face Washington with a unified foreign and defense policy.

The next three columns deal with CFP and CDSP content priorities in their own right and relative to other possible priorities for the EU. They also indicate the extent to which publics of member countries consider foreign and security issues to be important priorities.[12] Publics, with one exception, were split or had narrow negative majorities on whether the EU's importance in the world was one of the top three EU priorities; publics consistently gave the issue a very low ranking among competing priorities. The more recent polls showed a marked drop in support for placing that issue in the top three. Most publics split on placing the achieving of peace and security in Europe among the top three EU priorities, a massive decline from the strong majorities that favored doing so in the earlier polling years. Relative priority, however, remained consistently high. As for the top two priorities for member countries, foreign and security matters were consistently and massively denied that standing in all EU and EUAC publics; both issues had very low relative priority.

Publics thus offer their political elites little incentive to pursue world influence for the EU, which might interfere with other less political-military goals. Successes in that area are thus unlikely to compensate for perceived shortcomings on higher priority issues. Achieving peace and security in Eu-

Table 12.7. EU foreign policy and security policy

Country	Support for common foreign policy (2000–2006)	Support for common defense and security policy (2002–2006)	EU & national leadership preferred over NATO (2002–2005)	More independent of U.S. (2002–2005)	Assert world importance (2002–2005)	Achieve peace, security in Europe (2003–2005)	Foreign policy, defense country's most important issues (2003–2006)	Evaluation of EU foreign affairs, peace, and security (2003–2006)
EU 15								
Austria	2.3	1.4	3	2.4 (5)	−0.5 [14]	0 [3]	−3 [13]	0.5
Belgium	3	2.5	2.5	2.3 (5)	−1 [13]	0 [3.3]	−3 [14]	1.4
Denmark	1.4	1.2	1	2 (5)	−0.5 [14]	0.6 [2.4]	−3 [10]	1.4
Finland	1.6	0.6	3	2 (5)	−1.5 [14]	0.6 [2.5]	−3 [12]	1.1
France	2.7	2.4	2.5	1.8 (10)	−0.5 [13]	0 [3]	−3 [13]	0.9
Germany	2.8	2	2.5	1.4 (10)	0 [13]	0.6 [2.6]	−3 [11.5]	1.5
Greece	3	1.9	3	2.4 (5)	0 [14]	0 [2.6]	−3 [10.5]	1.6
Ireland	2	1.2	3	2.2 (5)	−0.5 [14]	−0.2 [4.4]	−3 [14]	1.6
Italy	3	2.6	2.5	2 (8)	−0.8 [13]	−0.2 [2.9]	−3 [13]	1.4
Luxembourg	2.8	2.3	3	2 (5)	−0.3 [13]	0.6 [2.2]	−3 [14]	1.7
Netherlands	2.6	2.1	2.1	2 (7)	−0.5 [12]	0.2 [2.2]	−3 [10.5]	1.2
Portugal	2.5	2.2	3	1.8 (6)	0 [13]	0.2 [2.8]	−3 [13]	1.1
Spain	3	1.9	3	2 (7)	−0.5 [13]	0 [3.2]	−3 [10]	1.6
Sweden	1.4	.9	3	2.2 (5)	−1.4 [14]	0.6 [2.9]	−3 [10.5]	0.8
United Kingdom	1.5	1.1	−0.3	1.5 (10)	−1.5 [13]	0.2 [3.9]	−3 [11]	−0.1
EUACs								
Bulgaria	2.7	2.5	1.3	3 (4)	1.5 [14]	0 [3]	−3 [11]	1.7
Croatia	2.7	3	1.5	3 (2)	−3 [10.5]	−2 [4]	−3 [9]	0.8
Cyprus	3	2.9	1.7	3 (4)	−0.5 [13]	0.4 [2.9]	−3 [6.5]	2.4
Czech Republic	2.3	2.4	2.3	3 (4)	−1.3 [14]	0.2 [3.2]	−3 [14]	1.7

Table 12.7. *continued*

Country	Support for common foreign policy (2000–2006)	Support for common defense and security policy (2002–2006)	EU & national leadership preferred over NATO (2002–2005)	More independent of U.S. (2002–2005)	Assert world importance (2002–2005)	Achieve peace, security in Europe (2003–2005)	Foreign policy, defense country's most important issues (2003–2006)	Evaluation of EU foreign affairs, peace, and security (2003–2006)
Estonia	2.6	2.5	1.7	3 (4)	−1.5 [13]	0.4 [3.4]	−3 [10.5]	2
Hungary	2.7	2.2	0.7	3 (4)	−0.8 [14]	0.6 [2.2]	−3 [14]	1.2
Latvia	2.8	2.7	0.3	3 (4)	−1.5 [12]	0.2 [2.6]	−3 [11.5]	1.9
Lithuania	2.8	2.3	0	3 (4)	−0.8 [13]	−0.2 [3.6]	−3 [12]	2.3
Malta	2.4	1.3	1.7	3 (4)	−0.8 [13]	−0.2 [3.3]	−3 [13]	1.7
Poland	2.8	2.5	0	1.5 (4)	−1.8 [14]	−0.1 [3]	−3 [12]	1.4
Romania	2.9	2.5	1	2.5 (4)	−1 [14]	0.2 [2.3]	−3 [13]	2.4
Slovakia	2.9	2.5	2	3 (4)	−0.5 [14]	0.2 [2.2]	−3 [13]	1.5
Slovenia	3	2.1	1.3	3 (4)	−1 [14]	0.2 [3.2]	−3 [11]	1.7
Turkey	1.9	1.2	1.3	2.2 (6)	−1.5 [14]	−0.6 [7.5]	−3 [10]	1.1

Note: Ranks are in brackets. For "CFP support," each of the EU 15 was queried twenty-one times and each of the EUACs, twenty times, with nineteen for Bulgaria, Romania, and Turkey and nine for Croatia; for "CDSP support," eighteen and seventeen respectively, and nine for Croatia; for "EU and national," the UK, France, Germany, Italy, and Poland had four queries, the Netherlands and the other EUACs had three, except for Croatia and the other EU 15, which had two; for "assert world" the EU 15 had six queries and the others five, except for Croatia with three; for "achieve peace" and "most important issues," the EU 15 had five queries and the others each had six; and for "evaluation," the EU 15 had eleven queries, and the EUACs had eight, except for Bulgaria, Romania, and Turkey with seven and Croatia with six. Queries on "more independent" are in parentheses.

rope can mobilize public demand, but probably only at times when publics see imminent threats. At those times and for those threats, public support for challenging what are thought to be selfish U.S. policies probably will be politically important.

In the final column, most publics had positive majorities on the EU's performance in the realm of foreign policy and security policy. These results would call into question any suggestion that there is significant public demand for major changes in the EU's international role. The EU foreign and defense policy status quo does not seem to face discontented majorities, and (according to table 12.6) it seems to provide a sense of superiority relative to the United States. Member publics hardly seem to want the changes in priorities needed for the EU to become the major locomotive for a new era of bipolarity or multipolarity. In sum, EU publics may support "soft" challenges to U.S. policies. These would be challenges that emphasize buying time through delay, evasion, and diversion so that Washington might change its position in response to other pressures. That sort of support discourages anything more than rhetorical or procedural disputes with the United States; it certainly would hinder steps that could raise the EU to superpower status. Most polled European publics (see table 12.4) would find those limits compatible with their hopes for post-Bush U.S. policy improvement.

Rallying Countries

Poll results also suggest how receptive public opinion might be to particular foreign governments rallying others to challenge U.S. policies. I reason that receptivity to the leader of a continuing coalition, regardless of issue or region, increases when the publics of the rallier and the rallied share positive views of the coalition and negative views of the United States. For shorter term issue- and incident-specific coalitions, publics may have split but not negative views of each other, as well as massive or predominant majorities opposed to the same particular U.S. policy preference. Such coalitions might focus on the United States as the provider of vital support to a state or movement their member publics view negatively as a common enemy or pariah. Alternatively, a coalition might focus on the United States as threatening or punishing a state or movement that member publics view positively. Pertinent scores appear in tables 12.8 and 12.9.

In table 12.8, the favorability score of the "column" country's public about the "row" country appears in each cell before the slash (/); that of the row country's public about the column country appears after the slash. Reciprocally positive entries combined with substantial majorities that are negative about the United States are rare indeed. That situation argues against the prospects

Table 12.8. How national publics view other countries (2002–2005)

	UK	France	Germany	Italy	Poland	Russia	China	Japan	India	South Korea	USA
UK											2.7/1
France	1.5/0										0.7/−0.8
Germany	2.3/1	2.8/3									1.9/−0.2
Italy	1/1	1/1	2/1								0.2/0.8
Spain		/2	/3				/0	/2			/−1.8
Poland	0/1	0/1.5	1/1.5	1/1							1/1.5
Russia	0/	0/2.5	0/3	0/	−1/						1/−0.2
Turkey	0/	−1/−1.5	0/0	−1/	−1/		/−0.8	2/1			0/−2.5
Egypt		/1	/2				/2	/2			/−2.5
Jordan		/0	/1				/0	/0			/−3
Pakistan		/0	/1				/3	/2			/−2.1
China	1.5/−2	0.7/2	0.4/2	0.4/	−0.4/	1.2/−3					0/−1
Japan	3/−2.5	3/2	2.5/3		3/	2.5/−3	−2.5/−1.7				2.8/−0.4
India	/1	/1.5	/1.5			/2	−2.5/−0.8	−2/2.3			2/1.8
Indonesia	/−3	/1	/2			/−3	/0	/2	/−1	/−2	/−1.2
Malaysia	/−2					/−3	/2	/3	/−1	/−1	/−3
Philippines	/1					/−1	/2	/2	/−1	/0	/3
Thailand	/0					/−3	/1	/1	/−3	/−2	
South Korea	/−2					/−3	1/−0.5	−1/−1.4	0/−2.8		0/0.3
Vietnam	/−3						/−2	/0	/−3	/−1	/1.5
Nigeria		/2	/2			/0	/2	/2			/2

Table 12.9. Various countries' views of possible pariah states (2003–2006)

	Iran	Syria	Palestinian Authority	Israel	Pakistan	Saudi Arabia	North Korea
EU							
Austria	0	1		−2	−1		−2
Belgium	−1	1		−2	0		0
Denmark	−1	1		−2	0		−2
Finland	0	2		−1	0		−1
France	−1.3 (11)	0 (3)	0	−0.6 (5)	−1	−1	−0.3 (4)
Germany	−1.6 (11)	0.7 (3)	−1	−0.4 (5)	0	−1	−2.2 (4)
Greece	2	3		−2	2		2
Ireland	−1	1		−2	0		−2
Italy	−1.3 (3)	0 (3)	0	−0.5 (2)	0	−1	0 (2)
Luxembourg	−2	0		−2	−1		−2
Netherlands	−2 (2)	−0.5 (2)	−1	−1 (2)	−1	−1	−2
Poland	−2	−1	−2	−2		−1	
Portugal	−2 (2)	−0.5 (2)	−1	−1 (2)	−1	−1	−2
Spain	−1.2 (9)	1 (2)		−1 (2)	1		−0.5 (2)
Sweden	0	2		−1	1		0
United Kingdom	−1.2 (11)	−0.7 (3)	0	−0.7 (6)	0	0	−2.2 (4)
NORTH AMERICA							
Canada	−2						−3
United States	−2.5 (9)	−2	−2 (2)	1.3 (11)		−1.2 (5)	−2.4 (5)
LATIN AMERICA							
Mexico				−1	−3		−3
EASTERN EUROPE							
Russia	0 (9)	2		0 (2)			0.7 (3)
CONFLICT AREA							
Egypt	1.1 (7)			−3			1
Israel	−3	−2					−2
Jordan	1.1 (8)	3		−3			0 (2)
Kuwait	0	1					−1
Lebanon	2	3					1
Morocco	2	1					1
Pakistan	2 (8)	2		−3			1 (2)
Palestinian Authority	2	2					1
Turkey	0.4 (9)	1		−3			1 (3)
ASIA & PACIFIC							
Australia	−2	−1					−3
China	0 (7)			−1	−2 (3)		−2.5 (4)
India	0.1 (7)			0	−2.5 (2)		0 (2)
Indonesia	−1 (8)	1		−3	−2 (2)		−0.4 (5)

continued

Table 12.9. *continued*

	Iran	Syria	Palestinian Authority	Israel	Pakistan	Saudi Arabia	North Korea
Japan	−1 (7)			0	−1.3 (3)		−3 (5)
Malaysia					−2 (2)		−2 (4)
Philippines							−1.5 (2)
South Korea	0	−1		0	−3 (2)		−2.9 (6)
Thailand							−3 (2)
Vietnam					−3 (2)		−3 (3)
AFRICA							
Nigeria	0	0		0			0.5 (2)

for sustained, multiple-issue challenge coalitions. Public opinion conditions that are relatively conducive to narrower and more temporary coalitions, however, may well be present in France, Germany, Italy, and Japan, and more arguably in Russia, China, and some polled Middle Eastern countries. Regionally, none of the publics of the possible Western European coalition members or leaders in table 12.8 have negative majorities about each other, but most lack strong negative favorability majorities about the United States. In Asia, publics of the major powers are for the most part negative toward each other (China and Japan, China and India, South Korea and Japan). Southeast Asian publics seem disinclined to take sides between China and Japan. The Japanese, Indian, and South Korean publics resemble many European ones in not being disposed to broadly and severely strained relations with the United States. Asian publics seem unlikely to agree with each other on support of a regional coalition or bloc rallied by any particular nation, let alone one broadly challenging the United States.

Table 12.9 reports views of possible pariah states. For which of those states do foreign publics have strongly negative views and might reasonably see the United States as their crucial supporter? Israel is the clearest case. With albeit more fragmentary data, results show that Pakistan could be a pariah state for Asian publics and Saudi Arabia for European publics. Negative majorities toward Israel are not limited to primarily Islamic publics, and pertinent European publics are not positive about the Palestinian Authority. The scores in table 12.9 suggest that targets of U.S. enmity that might provide a central theme for challenging the United States would be Iran (for some Middle Eastern and Asian publics) and Syria (for some Middle Eastern and European ones). In line with the UN voting patterns reported in chapter 6 of this volume, there have been significant public opinion incentives for challenging U.S. policies toward the Middle East. This is especially true for U.S.-backed regional military actions that could pose costs to third parties.

Receptivity of the U.S. Public

We have yet to consider to what extent American public opinion encourages challenges from abroad. In such cases, domestic pressure on the U.S. government to modify policies might conveniently be in line with foreign preferences. One set of indications compares views held by the U.S. public with those of other publics as reported in preceding tables. A foreign challenge seems more likely to be associated with a desired shift in U.S. policy if the modifications sought are popular with Americans. When these domestic and foreign preferences are aligned, there is a greater chance for transnational coalitions with American activists. Washington then faces not just foreign criticism but also domestic political pressure. Another set of indications, drawing on data introduced below, focuses on American views about the consequences of foreign judgments for the United States and whether those foreign judgments warrant adjustments to U.S. policy. A foreign challenge looks more promising if American public opinion acknowledges that there is something to be gained by accommodating foreign views. Some U.S. politicians and bureaucrats will then have domestic political incentives to align with the challenge.

In table 12.2, positive U.S. majorities viewing terrorism as a threat and the U.S. stance toward it differ from the split or negatively inclined public opinions common elsewhere, although domestic public views of the American stance have become less positive. For the whole time period of the polling, there seldom are contrasting massive or predominant majorities between the United States and other publics on international terrorism. There is little difference between the American public's view of WMD proliferation as a threat and the views of most other publics of the Global North, but publics of the Global South accord it less importance. The American public stands in greater contrast to many others on three issues. One is specific U.S. counter-proliferation policies (most other publics are very negative while the U.S. public is only split). The second issue is the Iraq war, with most others strongly negative and the Americans initially positive and then splitting or becoming narrowly negative. Third is the use of military force, with positive (albeit declining) U.S. majorities in contrast to often massively or predominantly negative majorities elsewhere.

Tables 12.3 and 12.4 show that Americans had more positive judgments about the United States and its general international impact than did most others (except for many of the EUAC publics). While U.S. public opinion was split on the issue of America's contribution to world peace and security, most other publics were negative, often by large majorities. On environmental quality contributions, the American public was prevailingly negative, but less so than most others. Unlike the strong negativism that many others held for Bush administration foreign policy, the U.S. public was again split. The trend in U.S. public opinion has been from positive to negative, but not enough to catch up with the growth of negativism among others. Like most others, the U.S. public had negative majorities on contemporary U.S. international activism, but, unlike most others, it was split on whether the United States engaged in too much or too little of that activity.

In table 12.5, U.S. majorities reject alternatives to America's sole superpower status that involve the rise of a military "balancer" (unnamed, or China or the EU). When the balancer is unnamed in the poll, the U.S. public's prevailing position is more negative than that of some major powers in Europe and Asia, but it is in line with that of the publics of many other countries. Most publics resemble America's public on the undesirability of China becoming a peer military power. The U.S. public generally agrees with most European publics in favoring a civil rather than military role for the EU, as well as transatlantic cooperation and collective action. As for IGOs, and especially the UN, being modifiers or alternatives to U.S. unipolarity, the split or negative American public opinion contrasts with the positive, often predominant majorities in most other publics that evaluate IGOs favorably and support strengthening the UN. Most other publics were either split or positive in favoring the UN as a center of international influence over the United States, but Americans massively preferred the United States to have the central role. Table 12.8 shows that the U.S. public often had more positive views of the other countries considered than those countries' publics had of the United States. Table 12.9 shows that the United States clearly differs from most others in its positive view of Israel, negative view of Syria, and the intensity of negativism about Iran and the Palestinian Authority.

In short, strong American majorities do not agree that the U.S. track record warrants broad foreign challenges. In addition, American public opinion does not show a strong rejection of many specific Washington policies or eschew a strong role as global leader. Yet the substantial positive majorities of a few years ago for the United States in general and for various specific issues have in many instances eroded to near even splits or narrow negative majorities. If that is a continuing trend, it may encourage foreign challengers and agents promoting a change in U.S. policies. It does not, however, confirm that current public demand is sufficient to sustain winning coalitions to effect major changes in America's world role or in many specific foreign policies.

The U.S. public has continued to favor others having more capacity to be effective supporters but not their having the military power to rival or check-mate Washington. It has favored more burden bearing by others, such as the EU, IGOs, and regional allies, but not more independent and authoritative decision making that could allow those other actors to constrain the United States. American public opinion differs from much of the world's less on specific policies (except for the Middle East) than it does on potential structural changes in the international system, how the United States affects others, and the use of force. There is an obvious tension between the U.S. public's preference for shared responsibility in managing world problems (rather than being the sole rule enforcer) and its coolness toward sharing power with other countries and IGOs.[13] The American public can see that accommodating the views of foreign governments and publics is useful and even necessary in order to get their help in advancing American interests. They can also see that accommodating foreign parties may lead to an undesirable and unnecessary sacrifice of American interests.

There is abundant evidence that the American public is aware of the negative views held by much of the international public. In polling for 2003–2006, predominant net majorities on average saw the U.S. world image worsening. That decline was seen as a major problem by net majorities (2004–2006), and in previous polling (2003–2004) substantial majorities professed it important that the United States have a positive rather than a negative image internationally. Predominant majorities have supported U.S. foreign policy taking into account the interests and approval of others and major allies in particular (an average score of +2.1 on eleven questions in 2001–2005).[14]

Responses to questions (in 2002 and 2004) about who has and should have influence on U.S. foreign policy gave foreign governments and publics scores above the midpoint on a degree of influence scale. Scores for foreign publics were greater than the current degree of influence attributed to them. For preferred future level of influence, scores for foreign governments and publics were greater than for U.S. interest groups (but not the president or Congress).

Foreigners do have some reasons to believe they will get support in the United States for policy accommodation, especially when challenges are perceived to follow from pro-American intent or at least not America-weakening motives. Foreign attempts to modify U.S. policies couched in terms of "loyal opposition" are more likely to secure partners in the United States than are ones featuring harsh general condemnation and especially violence against Americans. The "loyal opposition" perception is more likely when the U.S. public is already split or prevailingly negative on current U.S. lines of policy, as it increasingly has been in recent years.

The chances of U.S. public receptivity are greater if the foreign publics and governments seeking modifications are viewed positively by Americans and are thought to be important.[15] That implies more receptivity to, and less in the way of reprisals for, challenges from Europe than from Asia or other regions. As for individual nations, according to table 12.8 and other data, the UK and Japan seem especially well positioned to have their challenges well received by the U.S. public. Others viewed positively include Canada, Australia, Italy, the Netherlands, Poland, Mexico, Egypt, Israel, the Philippines, Taiwan, South Africa and, in recent years, India. After having challenged the Iraq invasion, Germany and France lost ground with the U.S. public but returned to the favored list of nations not later than 2005.[16]

Other evidence casts doubt on U.S. public support for accommodating foreign challenges. The public has been split on whether the Bush administration was sufficiently accommodating to foreign interests and preferences and on whether improving relations with allies should be a U.S. foreign policy priority.[17] While recognizing that international opinion was predominantly negative on the U.S. invasion of Iraq (an average score of +2.2 on six questions in 2003–2004), the U.S. public did in that period support the Iraq policy and was only split on the need for allied support (an average score of +.3 on six questions in 2002–2004). Further, a predominant majority separated their vote in the 2004 presidential election from their expectations about foreign reactions to the outcome.

In sum, American public opinion provides little encouragement to foreign elites about the likely success of direct and harsh challenges demanding quick policy shifts by Washington. It does, however, provide grounds for them to think that some kinds of challenges are not doomed to fail or incur high retaliatory costs. When spurred on by public opinion in their own nations, foreign political elites may be attracted to the softer challenge strategies of debate, delay, and diversion while refraining from active cooperation. Those sorts of challenges can have political value at home, pose little chance of burning bridges that would hinder future good relations with Washington, and help buy time for developments at home and abroad to induce desired policy shifts in Washington.

Appendix

Public Opinion Sources

All data come from national samples unless specifically indicated. Data are drawn from Bobrow and Boyer 2005 and the survey sources listed below.

Americans & the World. 2002. Conflict with Iraq. www.americans-world
    .org/digest/regional_issues/Conflict_Iraq.

AsiaBarometer Survey. 2003, 2004. See Inoguchi et al. 2005 and Inoguchi et al. 2006. Polling June–September 2003 and October 2004–November 2005. Urban samples.

BBC World Service. 2005. World Service Poll. Twenty-three-country poll finds strong support for dramatic changes at UN and for increased UN power. http://www.pipa. org/onlinereport/BBCworld. Polling November 2004–January 2005. Urban/major metropolitan samples in Brazil, Chile, China, India, Indonesia, Philippines, South Africa, and Turkey.

Chicago Council on Foreign Relations. 2004. Global views 2004: U.S. public topline report; comparing South Korean and American public opinion and foreign policy; Mexican public opinion and foreign policy; comparing Mexican and American public opinion and foreign policy. http://www.ccfr.org. Polling July 2004.

Chicago Council on Foreign Relations and German Marshall Fund. 2002. Worldview 2002: Comparing American and European public opinion. http://www.worldviews. org. Polling June 2002.

European Commission. 2001, 2003. Flash Eurobarometer. Nos. 114, 151, 151b. http:// www.europa.eu.int/comm/public opinion. Polling November 2001 and October 2003.

———. 2003–2004. Eurobarometer: Public opinion in the accessing and candidate countries, No. 2004.1; Public opinion in the candidate countries, Nos. 2003.3 and 2003.4; Polling in the candidate countries, No. 2003.2. http://www.europa.eu.int/ comm/public opinion. Polling May 2003–March 2004.

———. 2003–2006. Eurobarometer: Public opinion in the European Union. Nos. 58–66. http://www.europa.eu.int/comm/public opinion. Polling October 2002–October 2006.

———. 2005–2006. Special Eurobarometer. Nos. 214, 220, 222, 251, 255, 259. http:// www.europa.eu.int/comm/public opinion. Polling November 2004–June 2006.

Gallup International. 2001. Gallup International Poll on terrorism in the U.S. http:// www.gallupinternational.com. Polling October 2001.

———. 2002. Voice of the people: Global survey results give a thumbs down to U.S. foreign policy; poverty and not terrorism is the most important problem facing the world. http://www.voice-of-people. Polling July–August 2002. Urban samples in Bolivia, Bosnia, Brazil, China, Colombia, India, Pakistan, and Poland. Sample of seven regions in Indonesia, capital city in Peru, and peninsular Malaysia.

———. 2003. New Gallup International post war Iraq poll—global opinion from 45 countries. http://www.gallupinternational.com. Polling April–May 2003.

———. 2004. U.S. foreign policy effect: An overall negative opinion across the world. http://www.voice-of-people. Polling December 2003.

German Marshall Fund and the Compagnia di San Paolo. 2003. Transatlantic Trends 2003. http://www.transatlantictrends.org. Polling June 2003.

Globescan/Program on International Policy Attitudes (PIPA). 2004. Global public opinion on the U.S. presidential election and U.S. foreign policy. http://www.pipa. org. Polling May–September 2004. Urban samples in Brazil, China, Colombia, Dominican Republic, India, Indonesia, Kazakhstan, Peru, Thailand, Turkey, and Venezuela. Six main provinces in Tanzania.

Guardian Unlimited. 2004. What the world thinks of America. http://www. Guardian. co.uk/uselections2004/viewsofamerica/table. Polling September–October 2004.

New York Times. 2006. NYT–CBS News Poll. http://www.nyt.com. Polling October 2006 and historical.

Pew Research Center for the People and the Press. 2001. Bush unpopular in Europe, seen as unilateralist. http://people-press.org. Polling August 2001.

———. 2002–2006. Pew Global Attitudes Project: Spring 2006 survey, 15-nation survey final topline; spring 2006 survey, 6-nation survey final topline; May 2005 16-nation survey; 2004. A year after Iraq war, mistrust in Europe ever higher, Moslem anger persists; 2003 views of a changing world: Wave-2 update survey; 2003 America's image further erodes, Europeans want weaker ties: A nine-country survey; 2003 six-nation survey; 2003 forty-four-nation major survey; What the world thinks in 2002: How global publics view their lives, their countries, the world, America. http://people-press.org. Polling March–May 2006; April–May 2005; February–March 2004; April–May 2003; March 2003; November 2002–January 2003; July–October 2002. Urban samples in 2006 and 2005 polling in China, India, and Pakistan; in 2004 in Morocco and Pakistan; in 2003 in Brazil, Indonesia, Morocco, Nigeria, Pakistan, Poland, and Russia; in 2002 in Angola, Brazil, China, Egypt, Guatemala, Honduras, India, Indonesia, Ivory Coast, Mali, Pakistan, Senegal, Venezuela, and Vietnam.

———. 2003. Trouble behind, trouble ahead: A year of contention at home and abroad. 2003 year end report. http://people-press.org.

———. 2003. Two years later, the fear lingers. http://people-press.org. Polling July–August 2003.

———. 2003, 2005, 2006. News interest index: August 2006 final topline; February 2006 final topline; May 2005 final topline; March 2003 final topline. http://people -press.org. Polling August 2006, February 2006, May 2005, March 2003.

———. 2004. Foreign policy attitudes now driven by 9/11 and Iraq. http://people -press.org. Polling July 2004.

———. 2005. America's place in the world 2005. http://people-press.org. Polling October 2005.

———. 2005. Bush approval rating lower than for other two-termers. http://people -press.org. Polling January 2005.

———. 2005. NII/Social Security survey. http://people-press.org. Polling February 2005.

———. 2005. Public unmoved by Washington's rhetoric on Iraq. http://people-press .org. Polling December 2005.

———. 2006. Turnout survey final topline. http://people-press.org. Polling September–October 2006.

Program on International Policy Attitudes (PIPA). 2002. PIPA bulletin: October polling on Iraq. http://www.pipa.org. Polling September–October 2002.

———. 2007. Global views of the U.S. http://www.worldpublicopinion.org/pipa/pdf/ jan07/bbc. Polling November 2006–January 2007. Urban samples in Brazil, Chile, China, Egypt, Indonesia, Lebanon, Philippines, Portugal, Turkey, and United Arab Emirates.

PIPA Globescan. 2005. Global views on China; poll on global economy. http://www .pipa.org/OnlineReports/bbcworldpoll. Polling November–December 2004. Urban/metropolitan samples in Brazil, Chile, India, Indonesia, Philippines, South Africa, and Turkey.

PIPA-Knowledge Networks. 2002–2004. Opportunities for bipartisan consensus: What both Republicans and Democrats want in U.S. foreign policy; global public opinion on the U.S. presidential election and U.S. foreign policy; U.S. public beliefs and attitudes about Iraq; Americans on the war with Iraq; Americans on North Korea II; Americans on Iraq & the UN inspections; Americans on Iraq after the UN resolution. http://www.pipa.org. Polling December 2002–December 2004.

TNS Sofres. 2003. Transatlantic trends 2003: topline data. http://www.transatlantic trends.org. Polling June 2003.

United States Information Agency. 1995. America as a global actor: The U.S. image around the world. Washington: USIA Office of Research and Media Reaction. Polling in 1994. Urban or elite samples in Guatemala, Ghana, Honduras, India, Jordan, Kenya, Lebanon, Nigeria, Tanzania, and Senegal.

Washington Post. 2006. Washington Post–ABC News Poll. October 24 and December 12. Polling October and December 2006 and historical.

13

THE IMPLICATIONS OF
CONSTRAINED HEGEMONY

DAVIS B. BOBROW

As the preceding chapters have illustrated, challenges to official U.S. policies are abundant and varied. Many political leaders in the world do consider and make noncompliant choices other than violent resistance or hard counter-balancing. The reasons behind those choices as well as the details of their implementation have been explored for a variety of actors in international affairs (substate, state, nonstate, and multi-state) with a wide range of hard and soft power assets. The explorations ranged across various classes of substantive issues: political, military, economic, environmental, and public health. While much attention has been given to occurrences during the presidency of George W. Bush, many of the authors place those events in a context of tendencies, actions, interpretations, and experiences that pre-date his administration. Those contextual elements strongly suggest that the international affairs behaviors that are central to the subject of this book may wax and wane with different U.S. administrations but will not disappear with a different American president.

Each of the preceding chapters relates to the elements of the action/arena combinations introduced in chapter 1. These discussions lead me to analyze the actual use of those combinations and to suggest certain broad conclusions and implications that support or modify the assertions in chapter 1. There are, based on those implications and conclusions, possible prescriptions for U.S. policy that might forestall or deal effectively with the challenges of evasion, modification, and resistance. Policy that could manage such challenges would be better than policy that inspired further and more severe challenges.

Actions and Arenas

Table 13.1 is a modification of table 1.1 from chapter 1. Boldface entries in the cells refer to the chapter that discusses use of that particular action/arena combination to challenge the United States. Italicized entries signify modifications of the matrix suggested or stimulated by my reading of a particular chapter and my own thinking about its topic.[1] The numbers in the cells refer to chapter numbers, that is, 2 refers to Jeremy Pressman's chapter on Iraq; 3, to Siegmar Schmidt's on Germany; 4, to Steve Chan's on China; 5, to Ilter Turan's on Turkey; 6, to Thomas J. Volgy et al.'s on the G-7; 7, to Dennis M. Gormley's on the Missile Technology Control Regime (MTCR); 8, to Alexander Ochs and Detlef F. Sprinz's on global climate change (GCC); 9, to Diana Tussie's on international trade; 10, to Robert Kudrle's on tax competition; and 11, to Judith P. Wilkenfeld's on tobacco regulation.

The boldface entries indicate that there are examples of each type of arena and action, although not of each possible combination. A particularly large number of instances were reported for three arenas (unilateral, clubs and caucuses in U.S.-member IGOs and INGOs, and collective action networks with American participants). There were also many instances of three types of actions (bloc creation, rule expansion, and schedule delays).[2] The central foreign actor(s) in each chapter (except chapter 6 on the G-7) used more than one arena and more than one action. The G-7, while by definition limited to a particular arena, used more than one type of action. The italicized entries call for more comment since they go beyond summarization of what has previously been argued. They tag interpretive additions and modifications that suggest more general improvements to the actions/arenas matrix.

With regard to arenas, it may be useful to divide the category of "broad agenda institutions with the United States excluded." Its component categories could be institutions from which the United States deliberately excluded itself but could in principle still join and institutions whose essential character precludes U.S. membership. Illustrations of the former are the post-Kyoto GCC regime (discussed by Ochs and Sprinz) and the International Criminal Court; of the latter, the Mercosur agreement discussed by Tussie. Consideration of "collective action networks with American participants" may usefully distinguish three types of networks. In the first, the American participants are a major part of the executive branch. This arrangement amounts to a coalition with some foreign participants authorized by the president in order to modify congressional and/or NGO preferences. An example of this arrange-

Table **13.1** The initial framework revisited

Actions		Arenas			
	Unilateral	Broad agenda institutions with U.S. excluded	Coalitions of the unwilling	Clubs and caucuses in U.S. member IGOs, INGOs	Collective action networks with American participants
"Craziness," martyrdom	2,4				
Melting	2				
Counter-balancing	5			5	
Fait accompli	2,5,3,4	8	7		
Bloc creation	5	4,9,3	3,4,9	4,5,9,11	4,10,11
Rule-based retaliation	2,4			3,9,11	4,11
Rule expansion	2	3,4,9,8	9	3,4,6,8,9,11, 5,10	2,3,4,8,9,11, 10
Consent and exploit	2,4,5			4,7	
Consent and deceive	2			7,8	
Promise, protest, retraction	5				
Conditional support commitments	2,3,5,11		10	6	5
Schedule delays	2,4,5	9	9	3,4,9,6	4
Linkage to large side-payments	4,5,3	9,8	9	9,6	4
Standing aside	3,4	9	9	9,4,6	
Credible helplessness	3,4,5	8		7,6,11	

ment would be the State and Defense Departments' opposition to the arms embargo on Turkey (noted in chapter 5 by Turan). A second type of collective action network with American participants would be when NGOs and congressional factions push for a change in previous U.S. policy that the executive branch finds politically appealing (as in Kudrle's discussion of harmful tax competition). A third type of network would be when the American participants are NGOs, dissident bureaucrats, and congressional factions opposed to the current administration's preferences (as seen in Wilkenfeld's analysis of the Framework Convention on Tobacco Control during the administration of George W. Bush).

Turning to action possibilities, that of "'craziness' and martyrdom" may be sharpened by distinguishing between tangible, demonstrative acts (as noted in chapter 2 by Pressman, regarding Iraq) and rhetorical signals of a willingness to do so in the future (as noted in chapter 4 by Chan, regarding China).

Whether or not the German cabinet gave the United States warning or "due notice" of its position on Iraq (see Schmidt's chapter 3) suggests whether or not it simply presented Washington with a "fait accompli." A deliberate lack of surprise, that is, providing a warning, may or may not reduce the abrasiveness or effectiveness of a fait accompli, clarify U.S. blocking or retaliatory intentions, or induce concessions by the United States or third parties. If the fait accompli makes U.S. policy makers look bad at home or abroad, they are unlikely to admit readily to having been clearly forewarned. The extent of foreknowledge on the part of the United States is then often murky or contested, as with the Chinese demonstration in January 2007 of its ability to kill a satellite with a land-based missile and the forced downing of a U.S. intelligence collection airplane early in the Bush administration, not to mention the Chinese surge across the Yalu River in the Korean War.

Faits accomplis need not be physical acts. They can be hard-to-reverse communicative ones (e.g., Gerhard Schroeder's campaign position on Iraq [chapter 3] or the disclosure to the media of Bush's positions on the FCTC [chapter 11]) or even adoption and ratification of international treaties and agreements (e.g., the Marrakech Accords and Russian ratification of the Kyoto Protocol [chapter 8]).

As for "bloc creation," blocs can be revived in broad agenda institutions without U.S. membership, not just created from scratch (as Schmidt notes in chapter 3 about Germany and France in the EU). The revival/creation distinction for blocs may also apply to each of the other nonunilateral arenas, for example China and Russia in the U.S.-member MTCR (see Gormley's chapter 7).

The German case also raises the possibility that others may try to use "rule-based retaliation" to limit U.S. retaliation against them for noncompliance, not just to retaliate against the United States. The trade bargaining discussed in chapter 9 by Tussie suggests that others can use WTO rules and processes both to pressure the United States through complaint procedures and to constrain U.S. retaliatory moves against them for its trade grievances. In such a damage-limiting mode, the arenas of U.S.-member IGOs may be especially useful, as with the German use of NATO. Other maneuvers to limit U.S. retaliation may involve publicizing, both in the United States and globally, Washington's retaliatory threats and actions as violations of core American values or the lack of U.S. commitment to options that exemplify those values (as happened with the FCTC and on numerous occasions with Iraq). Chinese efforts to prevent the formation of a coalition of those willing to supply arms to Taiwan (noted in chapter 4) suggest that challengers may invoke a rule (e.g., no arms supply to secessionist parts of a state) to raise the prospect of future retaliation against third parties who might behave in a way that at least some Americans favor.

As with rule-based retaliation, "rule expansion" invokes informal norms and consensual values, not just formalized codes of behavior. Further thoughts on rule expansion are suggested by Gormley's analysis of the MTCR (chapter 7), Kudrle's of the *Harmful Tax Competition* project (chapter 10), and those on GCC and the FCTC (chapters 8 and 11, respectively). There may be a worthwhile, if hard to apply, distinction to be made between rule expansion in the form of stronger compliance and sanction measures for existing rules versus adding rules with expanded coverage. If the United States advocates some expansion of the former type while opposing expansion of the other, foreigners may be able and willing to mount a challenge by linking the issues for bargaining purposes or even charging normative hypocrisy. Also, there are more likely to be American associates for networks with foreigners that push conflicting positions on rule expansion. Especially in a context of rapid technological change and diffuse technology access, rules of both sorts, as in the MTCR, are likely to fall behind changes in the world while the United States and others jostle for advantage (as Gormley emphasizes in chapter 7). Financial globalization presents another aspect of rapid change and diverse interests in enforcement versus moves toward greater harmonization. The *HTC* project experience suggests the likely emergence of multiple collective action networks with foreign and American participants and little achieved rule expansion, unless the logjam is jolted loose by a dramatic common threat.

It seems worth noting that in the two chapters (8 and 11) discussing some foreign-driven actual rule expansion (regarding GCC and tobacco) the official U.S. position had changed from support to opposition. Perhaps that form of apparent U.S. defection motivates especially intense efforts by both foreign supporters of rule expansion and their American associates. Finally, as Kudrle observes in chapter 10, expanded rules for international behavior have sovereignty-limiting potential. If the United States is hypersensitive to even the appearance of sovereignty erosion, foreign advocates of rule expansion can expect to face intermittent U.S. "sovereignty eruptions."[3] An upwelling of sovereignty sensitivity will not hinder challengers if their interest is not so much to secure U.S. agreement as to cast doubt on Washington's normative sincerity or if the challengers are able and willing to sustain their challenge until an eruption subsides.

Turning to "consent and deceive" actions, the paucity of entries may be an artifact of the cases selected. Yet it seems at least as likely that the lack follows from the addiction to ambiguity ("wiggle room," "fuzziness") that political actors show in their agreements with each other and from their fondness for making exaggerated public claims about agreements reached. What may well be a consent and exploit move to a foreign actor might readily be interpreted by American officials as a consent and deceive action and vice versa.[4] Similar interpretive possibilities apply to "promise, protest, retraction" moves. Nevertheless, the perception that a particular U.S. president, let alone the United States in general, often makes consent and deceive moves may raise the odds of challenges (as may be illustrated by the EU reaction to President Bush not honoring the GCC treaty and environmental protection promises made early in his first term). From another angle, Americans and foreigners in a collective action network who want to blunt the ability of a particular challenger (e.g., North Korea) to modify U.S. behavior can benefit from depicting it as a chronic user of consent and deceive actions.

"Schedule delays" are fairly obvious. There is, however, a related possibility: schedule acceleration. The challenge takes the form of pushing for a faster timetable than the United States wishes. Examples may be found in the G-7 providing debt relief for the poorest countries, in Israeli accommodation to the Palestinians, or in an Israeli ceasefire and pullback from the recent invasion of Lebanon. Schedule delays are often packaged with or morph into "conditional support commitments." That may well have happened in the G-7 with regard to some aspects of the U.S. war on terrorism and Middle East matters. Going beyond the discussion in the introductory chapter, I would argue that challengers may in effect demand that third parties stay out of coalitions of the willing that the United States might favor. The conditions then are not limited to stipulating what the United States does or does not do, as illustrated in Chan's discussion of China's efforts to prevent the formation of a coalition of those willing to supply arms to Taiwan (chapter 4).

The action type involving "large side-payments" may be improved by a distinction between the potential or current challenger as a seeker after such inducements from the United States or as a provider of the side-payments. The latter might offer the United States a policy modification carrot and retaliation preventive or might offer third parties an inducement to join in a challenge. An example of providing large side-payments would be Germany's significant military commitments in Afghanistan and off the Horn of Africa (which were welcome to Washington and balanced against its dispute with the United States over Iraq [chapter 3]). Other examples of providing large side-payments include the EU's inducements to Russia to ratify the Kyoto Protocol and to large developing countries to undertake measures to limit GCC (chapter 8) and support by leaders of the G-20+ for special agricultural protections for particular commodities important to small and poor less developed countries (chapter 9). Based on what has occurred in other multilateral forums, one might expect that differences between the old members of the G-7 and new members of the G-8 (i.e., Russia) and eventual G-9 (with China), as suggested by Volgy et al. in chapter 6, may have the newcomers pressing the G-7 for large side-payments.

"Standing aside" often involves parties who simultaneously or sequentially combine this action with schedule delays, conditional support commitments, and linkage to large side-payments. Equivalent to abstaining from a vote, standing aside challenges particular new U.S.-preferred actions that require or at least would be much more effective and efficient with the challenger's participation (e.g., toughening sanctions on Iran). Perhaps standing aside moves should be ordered on a continuum. At the more challenging or even confrontational end would be moves that curtail previously established forms of cooperation with the United States on a matter of high priority for Washington with no ready substitute for the abstainer. The ability to make influential standing aside moves increases as a foreign actor meets both conditions (e.g., China's role in the Six-Party Talks on North Korea). A Germany that continues to allow U.S. use of military facilities and over-flights to support the Iraq war while standing aside from direct troop participation in it surely is doing "challenge limitation."

To conclude the discussion of the action/arena elements in table 13.1, one can say that "credible helplessness" involves pleading difficult political circumstances or insufficient tangible assets. That is, pleas can emphasize what seems unlikely to be acceptable to selectorates, including violations of established and legitimate institutional checks and balances. A challenger may of course make such a plea as a way of avoiding compliance with American preferences. There are, however, some other possibilities related to this type of action. If U.S. officials plead credible helplessness when challenged to do more, foreign challengers may discredit the claim by using the expertise of Americans in a collection action network (as discussed in chapter 11 on U.S. assertions about legal restraints on tobacco control) or using their influence in U.S. policy formation (as discussed in chapter 8 on GCC). If third parties decline to join a challenge on credible helplessness grounds, it is conceivable that leading challengers can undermine the claim by providing what are for the recipient large side-payments.

Broader Themes

The previous discussion and chapter-by-chapter analyses support the introductory assertion that others in the world possess and use a far more diverse portfolio of options than merely hard counter-balancing (against the United States) or bandwagoning (with the United States). There are substantial grounds for believing that violent challenges are far less prevalent than the less dramatic and less visually striking forms. In part, as illustrated, that is

because challenges can come from friends as well as neutrals and less antagonistic foes. In part, as illustrated in many of the case studies and in chapter
12, that fact suggests hope for "better" future American policies as well as the
need to avoid excessively straining relations with the United States, expected
to remain powerful for the foreseeable future.

No claim is made that all foreigners who differ from U.S. foreign policy
preferences use all the possibilities in the initial arenas/actions matrix, let
alone in the amended and expanded one just discussed. We should, however,
seriously consider that selective use follows more from constrained availability
(as Turan suggests in chapter 5) than from a lack of awareness of the matrix's
contents. In particular, awareness often includes using ostensibly shared-in-
terest "engagement" moves as well actions that suggest separation or opposition. In an era of cross-border flows of tangibles and intangibles, it may well be
the case, as Tussie illustrates in chapter 9, that others are increasingly willing
and able to mount a continuous stream of challenges by pooling expertise to
take advantage of new and cheap forms of information sharing and mobilization (as Wilkenfeld describes in chapter 11).

There are several implications. First, as availability changes, challenge actions will change as well. Second, potential challengers are attentive to what
others have done and are trying to do and to what the apparent consequences
are. Precedents and learning analogies are not limited to a challenger's own experience with the United States or other would-be hegemonic powers. Third,
given the variety of challengers and of policies that might be challenged, it
would be unwise to assume that the next round of challengers will simply em-
ulate the last. The chances are that future challenges will depend on both the
challengers' perception of likely opportunities and a positive evaluation of the
payoffs previously achieved. Engagement moves should be viewed for possible
asymmetric influence effects (as in Gormley's tale of activity inside the MTCR
in chapter 7). One common aspect of these implications, of which more will be
said later, is that American governmental and nongovernmental actors often,
although not always, can partially shape the choices a given challenger will
make on a given issue at a given time.

The domestic political environment of challengers and their assessments
and manipulations of U.S. domestic politics clearly matter a lot, as argued in
all of the preceding chapters. Challengers' domestic political factors surely do
include immediate opportunities to retain or gain power. Yet, as Schmidt observes in chapter 3, what is electorally expedient functions in a more long-term
context of broad convictions about legitimate and effective conduct and claims
of national and group autonomy. Those contextual features evolve over time
in readily observable ways, while short-term political expedients are harder

to foresee and require much more specific information and insight. It is hard to deny that the trinity of immediate expediency, broad convictions, and parochial claims operates for the United States as well. Thoughtful challengers monitor and project America's trinity, as in Chan's view of the Chinese analysis of the United States in chapter 4.

These observations about the importance of a domestic politics perspective are hardly fresh insights, although U.S. policy making often pays at most token lip service to them. What arguably gives them special importance are self-inflicted American handicaps in respecting and acting on those insights. In particular, high-level U.S. office holders in the executive and legislative branches often seem to deny the significance of the domestic politics of foreign countries as it shapes what foreigners do and do not do at home, in the United States, and elsewhere in the world. The significance of domestic politics in foreign countries instead seems to be acknowledged after challenges become critical (especially as they play out in U.S. domestic political contests). The significance attributed seems to wane if and when a challenge fades.

Many current and potential foreign challengers have cadres of America watchers who have access to their political elites and to national media and who have substantial understanding of how the United States works, competence in the English language, and networks of relationships with American persons and groups. Those corollaries of globalization and superpower standing are hard to ignore. Except for a few foreign countries or groups, one or more of those attributes do not characterize the American foreign policy process. Over a large number of issues and actors, others' understanding of the practical details of U.S. politics and policy making probably exceeds Americans' grasp of theirs. Furthermore, because of the regional and functional breadth of U.S. policy concerns and the impact the United States has on others, current and potential foreign challengers are likely to devote a major portion of their policy resources to dealing with the United States about a small number of issues and to maintain that focus for a long period of time. Again with few exceptions, America will not devote a major portion of its policy resources to a particular current or potential challenger or sustain a particular policy issue focus in relations with them for more than a few years. In sum, others are more likely to assign their "A team," adopt an extended time perspective about future U.S. behavior, and thus see value from continuing investments in collective action networks with Americans than are high-level U.S. officials in equivalent positions.

In addition, an increasing number of private and public American entities, for reasons of professional gain or policy conviction, are able and willing to provide guidance and resources for policy influence on and in Washington. When American entities find fault with current or emerging U.S. policy preferences, they are often likely to reach out to foreign associates working on whatever cause may be of concern. Indeed, as Kudrle implies in chapter 10, an NGO may even come to life for that purpose. That, too, is an unavoidable corollary of globalization. Foreigners who wish to mount challenges and are quite rich either in terms of wealth or rectitude may well find partnering up with available American entities attractive and feasible.

Even if one agrees with many of the conclusions and implications introduced up to this point, there are three sets of assumptions that some Americans might say make such conclusions unimportant for America's world standing and successful policy formation. For each assumption set, there is a counterpoint raised by the analyses in this book.

Assumption set I. At worst, after some grumbling others will do what the United States wants because they are convinced that America has one or more of four things. Those are (1) the punitive capacity to make them back down and the will and competence to use that punitive capacity; (2) the reward capacity to make foreigners secure and prosperous and the will and competence to use that capacity; (3) support among the vast majority of any given foreign population and the will and competence to use that support; and (4) the leadership capacity to muster broad international coalitions in joint action endeavors and the will and competence to use it.

Assumption set II. Whatever the content and style of U.S. policies, some foreign parties will object and try to manipulate U.S. policy because they have one or more of the following attributes: (1) an evil nature with vicious values; (2) a leadership reflexively committed to parochial short-term political expediency and thus anti-Americanism; (3) an ignorant or misinformed and exaggeratedly negative view of U.S. intentions and practices as well as chronic underestimation of U.S. attributes in the first set of assumptions; and (4) little policy latitude because of domination by a state or group that is an enemy of the United States.

Assumption set III. The third set of assumptions does not totally reject either of the first two sets. Instead, it suggests that the correct procedural and rhetorical style can significantly influence foreigners' convictions and actions. If the United States gets its style right, others will believe and act in ways that aid and abet the achievements the first set expects rather than in ways that hinder them. There is disagreement on what that style should be.

Some prescribe a style that procedurally shows respect and consideration through patient "consultation" in bilateral and multilateral forums as well as compliance with previously agreed to support commitments, codes of conduct, and dispute resolution mechanisms. Those behavior styles should be accompanied by a rhetoric of cooperation rather than command—rhetoric that values rather than hectors the other, recognizes the legitimacy of its felt concerns, and acknowledges its cultural norms and sensitivities. Allegedly, the recommended procedural and rhetorical style will bring others to view the United States as benign, thoughtful, and prudent and as a provider of club and public goods. Abrupt unilateralism procedurally and arrogance rhetorically will lead to opposite images, resulting in a loss of "hearts and minds." The choice of styles amounts to a choice between internationally palatable or domineering hegemony.

For others, the allegedly correct style differs fundamentally. In this alternative, procedure and rhetoric emphasize clarity, unswerving convictions, blunt talk, claims to special degrees of foresight and righteousness, and determination to proceed promptly with America's chosen policy, no matter what others might think. There is no good reason to back off from confrontation. Advocates of this style believe that it will instill sufficient awe (and perhaps shock) in enemies for them to at least postpone challenges or even give up in the belief that the United States starts what it promises and completes what it starts. Since advocates seldom doubt that the United States has superior capabilities and competencies, the point is to avoid signals of weak will, including indecisiveness. The choice of styles amounts to a choice between confident and credible or doubting and unreliable hegemony.

Each of these three assumption sets amounts to a view of international affairs that is out of touch with much, though not all, of the real world (as shown by the public opinion results in chapter 12 and in one or another respect by the other preceding chapters). With regard to the first assumption set, the rest of the world is hardly convinced that the United States has the capacity, will, and competence to punish its enemies and reward its friends by providing security and prosperity (chapters 2, 3, 4, 5, 6, 7, 9, 11, and 12). Indeed, there are substantial concerns that America's international impacts are more negative than positive and that few international actors are attracted to the U.S. system of politics, economics, and social support (chapters 8, 9, 11, and 12). U.S.-led policy cohesion and coalition formation are not easy or always very effective even among major allies in the G-7 or NATO. The same can be said when the issue is hindering missile proliferation in the MTCR, finding consensus on international political economy matters in an enlarged WTO, or unifying the Global North on the environment or OECD on regulatory matters (chapters 3, 5, 6, 7, 8, 9, 10, and 11). The declining face validity of the compliance-inclined assumptions can be seen in both opinions and actions, even in relatively well-disposed (or very dependent) parts of the world such as the EU accession states. Finally, the shifts, reversals, and splits in U.S. politics since the end of the Cold War may lead foreigners (chapter 4) or even Americans (chapter 12) to doubt the desirability and feasibility of the U.S. hegemony envisioned in assumption set I. The coffers of internationally recognized capability, will, and competence are not as full as assumed and are being drawn down more than replenished (chapter 6).

Assumption set II falls short in that challengers often do not fit its profile. While some challengers do, that profile surely does not apply to many of the not fully compliant actors discussed in this volume. Unwarranted reliance on this set of assumptions can lead to treating others possibly open to accommodation as "hopeless cases." The assumptions then legitimize harsh policies that discourage cooperation with the United States and encourage enmity. The second set of assumptions reeks of arrogance about moral stature, long-term vision, information superiority, and American capability, will, and competence. Beyond irritating others, the assumptions are conducive to U.S. underestimation of what others can and will do and to overestimation of the effectiveness of American countermeasures and preventives. The results can be challengers faring better than the U.S. administration expects and an erosion of beliefs that U.S. dominance is worth the cost, even if it were possible. Unsuccessful, or even unnecessary, applications of the second set of assumptions can, ironically, undermine confidence in the first set of assumptions.

Assumption set III, in either the palatable or domineering variant, assumes that reactions to American style primarily account for foreign choices about whether and how to challenge American policy preferences. For some Americans, this assumption set also underpins decisions on undertaking joint efforts with a foreign challenger. Style recommendations and criticisms, however, seem little more than a device useful for factional policy contests in U.S. and foreign political systems. Consider the political appeal of giving credit or blame to procedural or rhetorical style rather than more substantive matters of ends and means. The implication is that matters are as they appear on the surface, and that surface is a fundamental source of international friction or trust. I suggest instead that American style is at most the "final straw" triggering challenges, particularly public challenges. It matters primarily when there are no issues of policy substance on the table, or issues at stake so serious that the "final straw" that style might provoke actually kicks in, or issues so technically complex and esoteric that politicians have only style to talk about.

Discussions of style do of course allow us to avoid talking about substance. Political styles also resemble clothing styles in being relatively easy to change compared to, for example, ethnic grievances, diffused technologies, territorial losses, economic underdevelopment, or the incidence of major diseases. That avoidance of tougher issues can make pledges to change style or demands for a change in style politically attractive. It also means that savvy politicians and bureaucrats in many parts of the world know that styles can quickly change back to what they once were, and so they will hardly rely on the changes in themselves.

Each set of assumptions seems inadequate as a guide for the United States to anticipate, forestall, and cope with challenges that foreigners may mount. An appropriate way to conclude this book is to suggest that there be less debate about the relative merits of those sets of assumptions and more commitment to follow a short set of prescriptive rules.

First, start from the premise that the ends sought by a foreign entity and the United States are more often than not partially compatible and partially incompatible, that is, mixed motive games are the rule and not the exception. Second, for any current or potential challenge thought to matter for America's well-being, invest in determining what the mix of motives is for others and who can determine their relative weights in the other's policy process. In doing that, avoid projecting onto others what is particularly important for the United States. Third, take into account that for most issues, some collective action network that links policy actors abroad and in the United States already exists or it will appear and affect policy choice and sustainability. Fourth, concentrate on identifying and executing actions (of omission or commission, direct or indirect) that hold promise for strengthening within the foreign entity any elements who attach priority to ends compatible with U.S. goals. Fifth, concentrate on identifying and then avoiding any U.S. actions likely to do the opposite. Sixth, use a time perspective for policy planning and implementation that is no shorter than that of relevant foreigners.

Finally, never forget that the United States is not exactly the first hegemonic power to come down the street in many parts of the world. Those who live there have lots of practice and lore about strategies to evade, modify, and even resist a hegemon's policy preferences—and they often have cardinal interests they think will suffer unless they use those strategies.

NOTES

Chapter 1: Strategies beyond Followership

1. As Pentagon advisor Thomas Barnett wrote before the invasion of Iraq, "Our next war in the Gulf will mark a historic tipping point—the moment when Washington takes real ownership of strategic security in the age of globalization. . . . The Middle East is the perfect place to start. . . . The only thing that will change that nasty environment and open the floodgates for change is if some external power steps in and plays Leviathan full time" (Barnett 2003, 174, 228).

2. The terms in parentheses are from Ikenberry 2003, 4.

3. The last two circumstances are illustrated in Ikenberry 2003, the report of expert opinion posted on the U.S. National Intelligence Council Web site. The posting has disclaimers stating that the report reflects only the views of its author, but the Bush administration is not noted for posting documents on official Web sites that run counter to its policy inclinations.

4. On how such internal factors can affect international bargaining, see Putnam 1988; Evans, Jacobson, and Putnam 1993; Knopf 1993; Mo 1994; Mo 1995; Bueno de Mesquita 2002; Bueno de Mesquita et al. 2000.

5. On the former, South Koreans and Kurds might not fully agree with Thomas Barnett's claim that with regard to "exporting security . . . [the United States has] a very good track record" (2003, 228). On the latter, consider American assertions that some state and nonstate leaders are so evil that they cannot be allowed to survive.

6. The U.S. National Intelligence Council posted report provides an interesting set of generic nonfollowership options (Ikenberry 2003, 14–22). Strong points include detecting elements of engagement and entanglement, not just signs of distancing or explicit opposition, in possible strategies of resistance and modification; attempts to influence domestic politics in the United States; and specific actions by others as well as the use (and indeed even creation) of a variety of arenas in which to pursue resistance and modification. Less satisfactorily, the set is state-centric, even though some of the strategies can be used by nonstate actors. It does not call attention to evasion strategies. The generality of the categories (most obviously that of bargaining) may not clearly identify the sorts of issue-specific instrumental actions strategies involve. Finally, in

only some instances does it recognize combinations of strategic moves or actions and the arenas bundled with them.

The category scheme I suggest has only an informal, inductive character, which is based on my observations of a variety of state and nonstate actors dealing with global and regional great powers and on the written and oral ideas of many international affairs analysts and practitioners.

7. Quotations in this paragraph are from the unfortunately prophetic analysis in Dror 1971.

8. Publicly standing aside while covertly cooperating with Washington surely happens but does not pose the challenge described here.

9. Noncompliance specifics may be moderated when relevant foreign parties want to maintain U.S. membership in the organization and gain U.S. adherence to at least some of the organization's conventions.

10. Even if networks agree with current U.S. policy preferences, they may anticipate a need to counter pressures for unwanted policy changes.

Chapter 2: Modes of Iraqi Response to American Occupation

1. These three factors did not always have equal priority or were even relevant at all times from 1945 to 1991.

2. In 1983, USCENTCOM took over for Carter's Rapid Deployment Joint Task Force.

3. The United States conducted training exercises, sold arms to Gulf allies, prepositioned U.S. military equipment, and signed basing agreements.

4. The Bush administration was certain Iraq had nonconventional weapons. For an extensive list of statements, see http://lunaville.org/WMD/billmon.aspx.

5. Regime change, though often through less intrusive means such as a coup, has long been a favored way of installing or maintaining a U.S. ally (e.g., Iran in 1953, Guatemala in 1954, South Vietnam in 1963, Chile in 1973, Grenada in 1983, and Panama in 1989).

6. There also has been talk of new U.S. bases in Iraq that would not only help in the post-Saddam era for Iraq but would also give the United States instruments to defend its wider regional objectives. See Shanker and Schmitt 2003a; 2003b; Marten and Cooley 2005; Arato 2004, 24; and Linzer 2005.

7. On the absence of a pre-invasion al-Qaeda–Iraq link, see *The 9/11 Commission report* 2004, which states, "[T]o date we have seen no evidence that these or the earlier contacts ever developed into a collaborative operational relationship. Nor have we seen evidence indicating that Iraq cooperated with al Qaeda in developing or carrying out any attacks against the United States" (66).

8. On Iraqi Shiites more generally, see Cole 2003b; Nakash 1994; and Shanahan 2004.

9. For the full text of the fatwa, see Feldman 2004, 140.

10. See Chandrasekaran 2003; and Prof. Juan Cole's blog, Informed Comment, for November 26, 2003, www.juancole.com/2003/11/sistanis-fatwa-trumped-bremer-rajiv.html.

11. Chandrasekaran 2003, A01ff. I draw on this article by Chandrasekaran for much of this story.

12. "Iraq Coalition Casualty Count," http://www.icasualties.org, accessed February 8, 2005.

13. Bremer argues that Sistani made a new demand after the agreement of November 2003: direct elections for the interim government (Bremer 2006, 242). Sistani's initial position prior to the November agreement was that the constitution drafters should be elected. The assumption, as Bremer had outlined in an op-ed in the *Washington Post* on September 8, 2003, was that the Iraqis would gain sovereignty after the constitution was written. In other words, sovereignty would be restored to an elected Iraqi government. The agreement of November 2003 reversed the order of writing a constitution and restoring sovereignty, thus creating a new situation for Sistani to consider: the CPA handing sovereignty to an unelected government selected by caucuses. It could be called a new demand, but it was made in the context of a new U.S. proposal.

14. Williams and Constable 2004; and a not-for-attribution interview with a U.S. official of the CPA, February 2005.

15. Interview with a U.S. official of the CPA, February 2005.

16. "The political transition in Iraq: the report of the fact-funding mission," http://www.un.org/News/dh/iraq/rpt-fact-finding-mission.pdf, 12, accessed February 15, 2005. See also Chandrasekaran 2006, 205–207.

17. They were Ahmed Chalabi (Iraqi National Congress), Abdul Aziz Hakim of the Supreme Council for Islamic Revolution in Iraq, Ibrahim Jafari of the Dawa party, Mowaffak Rubaie, and Muhammed Bahr Uloum (a Shiite cleric).

18. This pronouncement was enshrined in article 4 of the TAL: "The system of government in Iraq shall be republican, federal, democratic, and pluralistic."

19. Interview with an American observer of Iraqi politics, February 2005. The Kurdish Web site is http://www. krg.org.

20. Interview with an American observer of Iraqi politics, February 2005. See also Galbraith 2004.

21. For more on article 61(c), see Diamond 2006, 173–75.

22. "The Kurdistan Regional Government is recognized as the official government of the territories that were administered by the that [sic] government on 19 March 2003 in the governorates of Dohuk, Arbil, Sulaimaniya, Kirkuk, Diyala and Neneveh" (Law of Administration for the State of Iraq for the Transitional Period, March 8, 2004, http://www.cpa-iraq.org/government/TAL.html, accessed February 4, 2005).

23. See Diamond 2006, 166, for a more mixed assessment.

24. Jabr was named finance minister in the government formed by Nouri al-Maliki after the elections in December 2005; his move out of Interior was supported by some Sunni Arab and U.S. officials.

25. An excellent article from which I draw material is Silverstein 2006.

26. See "Iraq" in *World Report 2006* (Human Rights Watch, January 2006), http://hrw.org/english/docs/2006/01/18/iraq12215.htm, accessed September 28, 2006.

27. http://www.whitehouse.gov/news/releases/2005/01/20050130-2.html, January 30, 2005.

28. The official Web site of the Independent Elections Commission of Iraq used slightly different English names: Unified Iraqi Coalition, Kurdistani Gathering, Twafoq Iraqi Front, National Iraqi List (Allawi's list), and Hewar National Iraqi Front. See "Certification of the Council of Representatives Elections Final Results," February 10, 2006, http://www.ieciraq.org/final%20cand/IECI_Decision_Certified_Results_of_ CoR_Elections_En.pdf, accessed September 28, 2006.

29. http://www.globalsecurity.org/military/world/iraq/igc.htm.

30. http://www.c-span.org/campaign2000/transcript/debate_101100.asp.

31. Excerpts from the U.S. National Intelligence Estimate, "Trends in Global Terrorism: Implications for the United States," April 2006, http://www.dni.gov/press_ releases/Declassified_NIE_Key_Judgments.pdf; Foreign Affairs Select Committee, British House of Commons, "Foreign Policy Aspects of the War against Terrorism," July 2, 2006, HC-573, http://www.publications.parliament.uk/pa/cm200506/cmselect/ cmfaff/573/573.pdf; Benjamin and Simon 2006; and Pressman 2006.

Chapter 3: The Reluctant Ally

I am greatly indebted to my Ph.D. candidates Cornelia Beyer and Marcus Menzel and my colleague Bernhard Stahl for their comments and assistance.

1. François Duchêne originated the term as a metaphor to describe the European Community in the 1970s.

2. The Constitutional Court defined two conditions for out-of-area operations: approval by an absolute majority of the Bundestag and only then with legitimation by a system of collective security such as that provided by the UN, the Organization for Security and Cooperation in Europe (OSCE), or even NATO.

3. How deep and emotional the impact of the experience of Srebrenica still is could be witnessed in July 2005, exactly ten years after the massacre: official commemorations, attended by heads of states and leading politicians, took place in Germany and in many other European countries.

4. In December 2001 the Bundestag decided that Germany would deploy nearly eighteen hundred soldiers to support the then-interim government of Hamid Karzai (Wagener 2004, 96–97). The troops made up nearly a third of the fifty-five hundred soldiers of the International Security Assistance Force (ISAF). By June 2003 Germany increased the number of troops to twenty-five hundred, and in July 2005 Defense Minister Peter Struck announced that an additional eight hundred soldiers would be sent to Afghanistan. Germany was providing the largest national contingent of the seven thousand European soldiers deployed in Afghanistan. The German Development Service (DED), in cooperation with NGOs, started a range of local peace initiatives carried out by a special branch called the Civil Peace Service (see http://www .ziviler-friedensdienst.org/english/main.html).

5. See, for example, *Frankfurter Allgemeine Zeitung,* August 8, 2002, 1.

6. Before the invasion started in March 2003 the U.S. government never officially asked for German troops in case of a war.

7. Other contributions to the debate stress changes in domestic U.S. society and politics as causes of the shift in American foreign policy and the rift in transatlantic relations. Harald Müller (2004), one of the most respected specialists on transatlantic

relations, views the rise of the religious right and its political alignment with neocon-servatives as the impetus for the radical changes in U.S. foreign policy.

8. Kagan's provocative and pessimistic arguments have initiated a controversial discussion among German intellectuals and between Germans and Americans. See "Gulliver vs. Lilliput: Robert Kagans 'Macht und Schwäche' in der Debatte," in *Blätter für deutsche und internationale Politik* 11 (2002): 1345–58. The title, taking up the meta-phor of Gulliver in Lilliput land reveals the extent to which Kagan's arguments were accepted in general; nonetheless many authors accuse Kagan of oversimplification. The exchange of letters between German and American intellectuals took place in that somewhat left-wing-oriented German journal from May to October 2002. Sur-prisingly, the dense network of various organizations such as the Fulbright program and the Atlantic Bridge could neither influence the course of events nor the debate during the crisis.

9. In a more historical context, this metaphor reactivates different alarming memo-ries of the German *Sonderweg*, of a Germany anchored neither in the East nor in the West (hence the "Third Way") and trying to become the hegemonic power in Europe in World Wars I and II.

10. Quoted in *Frankfurter Allgemeine Zeitung*, August 5, 2002, 1.

11. Further, some of the younger generation are less concerned with the importance of transatlantic relations and worry about expanded restrictions on civil liberties in the United States.

12. For example, Gordon and Shapiro claim that "Schroeder chose to campaign shamelessly and relentlessly against the United States and a possible war in Iraq" (2004, 10). Politicians, journalists, and academics with decades-long advocacy of close German-American relations regard the moralistic and emotional tone of such com-mentary as signs of a broken norm and advocate more moderate discourse to help to renew the transatlantic alliance.

13. At a party conference in June 1999 Foreign Minister Fischer was even personally attacked with a paint bomb during a debate about Kosovo.

14. Speaking at the University of Landau, Dieter Roth, former director of one of the most respected polling institutes (Forschungsgruppe Wahlen, headquartered in Mann-heim), stated that the Iraq war issue increased Schroeder's popularity to an extent that could not be overcome by the opposition.

15. Also, the upper house of the German parliament, the Bundesrat, in which the CDU had a clear majority, cannot interfere in foreign policy.

16. Cooperation by German intelligence services in providing target intelligence to the United States at the beginning of the Iraq war has been denied by the German gov-ernment. It has also denied the domestically sensitive allegations of cooperation with the CIA rendition program in Bush's war on terror.

17. Memorandum von Deutschland, Frankreich und der Russischen Föderation zur Lage im Irak, http://www.bundeskanzler.de/Neues-vom-Kanzler-.7698.469107/a.htm, accessed August 28, 2004.

18. It is probably misleading to label the behavior of the German government as strategic. A strategy involves a plan designed to achieve a long-term goal consisting of interim goals and a sequence of actions using specific instruments.

19. The poll is in the Transatlantic Trends series of the German Marshall Fund of the United States, www.transatlantictrends.org/index.cfm.

20. The "grand coalition" was politically necessary since the elections did not result in a clear majority and coalitions with smaller parties were not possible.

Chapter 4: Soft Deterrence, Passive Resistance

An earlier version of this essay was presented at the annual meeting of the International Studies Association, Honolulu, March 1–5, 2005.

1. Exemplary works expounding on these themes include Fukuyama 1992; Huntington 1988 and 1999; Kennedy 1987; Keohane 1984; Keohane and Nye 1977; Krauthammer 1991; Nye 1990; and Rosecrance 1976.

2. Power-transition theory has evolved from its original formulation (Organski 1968; Organski and Kugler 1980). For more recent appraisals of the research program based on this theory, see DiCicco and Levy 1999; and Kugler and Lemke 1996 and 2000. The salience of issues raised by this theory is attested to by a recent workshop held by the Sino-American Security Dialogue Group in China, entitled "'China's Rise' and U.S.-China Relations in the 21st Century: Power Transitions and the Question of 'Revisionism.'" Tammen et al. (2000) provide a general application of power-transition theory to the international situation at the beginning of the twenty-first century, with attention to China as the leading challenger to U.S. hegemony. A. I. Johnston (2003) addresses specifically the question of whether China is a status quo power. That the power-transition theory has received so much attention at a supposed "unipolar moment" points to the mixture of confidence and anxiety and the cross-currents in both U.S. policy and academic circles referred to previously.

3. Actual historical reality is considerably more complicated than these assertions. The relationship between the United States and the United Kingdom was acrimonious before 1895. They were bitter, even hostile, rivals in the Western hemisphere as well as Asia and the Pacific (Vasquez 1996). Moreover, the United States and Germany had both long overtaken the UK before the outbreak of both world wars, which were precipitated more by German concerns about a rising Russia/Soviet Union than a declining UK (Copeland 2000). In addition, there have been peaceful power transitions when a democracy overtook a nondemocracy and vice versa. Recent examples include a reunited Germany gaining ascendance over Russia in economic size and, measured in purchasing-power parity, China surpassing Japan. For a more extended treatment of power-transition theory applied to Sino-American relations, see Chan 2004.

4. Levy 1987 provides an insightful discussion on the motivation behind preventive wars. Copeland 2000 studies this motivation in several historical episodes, including the concerns and calculations of German leaders prior to World Wars I and II. Schweller 1992 argues that democracies are unlikely to launch a preventive war due to the nature of their political institutions and ethos. The U.S. invasion of Iraq in 2003, justified explicitly by the Bush administration as an attempt to prevent Saddam Hussein from acquiring weapons of mass destruction, clashes with this argument.

5. Scholars tend to agree that China has behaved constructively in multilateral institutions and adhered to their rules and procedures. See Pearson 1999 and Lardy 1999

for China's conduct in international economic regimes. Samuel Kim's study on Chinese participation in the United Nations (1979) is dated but still relevant.

6. These injunctions and their application during the Warring States period of Chinese history received extensive treatment in classic Chinese military texts (the Seven Military Classics, including Sun Tzu's *The Art of War*). Ralph Sawyer offers two exemplary references to the pertinent strategic ideas at work: "By acting submissively, feigning loyalty, and playing upon King Fu-ch'ai's desires for victory and power over the northern Chou states through Po P'i's persuasions, [the kingdom of] Yueh insidiously deflected attention away from itself and ensured that [the kingdom of] Wu would dissipate its military strength and energy"; and "[w]henever possible [King Kou-chien] increased [King] Fu-ch'ai's arrogance, played upon his desires, and encouraged him in his deluded campaigns against Ch'i in the north" (Sawyer 1994, 108, 121). For all their supposed comparative advantage in appreciating and capturing the nuances of traditional cultural perspectives, there is among Sinologists writing about contemporary military and diplomatic affairs a general dearth of sensitive and sophisticated scholarship on Chinese strategic thought and conduct. Much of their research fails to go beyond ritualistic references to the so-called Middle Kingdom syndrome and the supposed importance of "face" to the Chinese. Indeed, the prevalent mode of analysis by U.S. academics writing on Chinese foreign policy tends to follow the Western, Clausewitzean tradition emphasizing armament procurement and alliance behavior. For two exceptional attempts to relate to Chinese cultural legacies in strategic matters, see Johnston 1995 and Nathan and Ross 1997.

7. This injunction incorporates the idea of turning the tables on the opposition and administering to the other its own medicine, but its subtlety extends beyond these meanings. The story from which this injunction is supposed to have originated also refers to the exposure of contradictions in another person's arguments or rationale. Indeed, the Chinese concept for contradiction derives from the combination of characters for spear and shield. My shorthand reference to role reversal does not quite capture all these ideas plus the notion of exploiting the inherent contradictions in the other's position.

8. Shambaugh 1996 analyzes how this U.S. debate is likely to be interpreted and received in China.

9. This literature ostensibly owes its intellectual pedigree to Immanuel Kant's treatise on perpetual peace (1795), in which he argued that a republican form of government, a cosmopolitan outlook, and a pacific union of like-minded states would provide the foundation for durable international peace. Contemporary scholars deduce or infer from Kant's seminal presentation that competitive and pluralistic politics, economic interdependence, and normative socialization in the rules of foreign conduct can dampen the danger of militarized disputes and even wars among states. Many have reported evidence lending support to this proposition.

10. A representative and particularly cogent example of the huge and growing literature on the concept of democratic peace is Russett and Oneal 2001.

11. Peter Gries quotes a Chinese analyst at a Foreign Ministry think tank: "[I]ncreasing regionalism is an important way to restrain American hegemonism" (2004, 7).

12. Hirschman 1945 is the classic study on the use of economic statecraft. For a more recent treatment of economic coercion and bargaining power, see Wagner 1988.

13. America's China watchers seem disposed to assume that international treaties, norms, and organizations should be applied to constrain and transform China. They seldom appear to consider the possibility that others, including China, may use the same international treaties, norms, and organizations to restrain the United States. This omission is surprising because, after all, Washington's disenchantment with some international organizations (e.g., the International Labor Organization and the United Nations Educational, Scientific, and Cultural Organization) is well known, as are a long list of its refusals to support international agreements.

14. On conflict involving asymmetric dyads, see Mack 1975 and Paul 1994. These studies are also pertinent to why Davids sometimes prevail over Goliaths.

15. See, for example, Schroeder 1994a and 1994b on the rarity of balancing behavior when states face a hegemonic threat. On passing the buck and bandwagoning, see Christensen and Snyder 1990 and Schweller 1994.

16. Again, there seems to be nothing culturally unique about "martyrdom" approaches to national defense; recall, for example, references to the Alamo, Masada, and kamikaze.

Chapter 5: The United States and Turkey

1. The categories are drawn from Gilpin 1981, 29.

2. For accounts of this relationship in English and in Turkish see Sander 1979; Harris 1972; and Rustow 1987.

3. An excellent summary of Cypriot history and the Cyprus problem until the 1974 crisis can be found in Bölükbaşı 1988. Kissinger 2000 (chap. 7) devotes considerable space to the history of the Cyprus conflict. See also Rustow 1987, chap. 5; Firat 1997, chap. 3.

4. Sönmezoğlu 1995, 7–28; Sander 1979, 225–41.

5. Sönmezoğlu 1995, 14. There is a very good summary of the period in Lenczowski 1990, 92–104.

6. The most detailed study of the Johnson letter has been conducted by Haluk Şahin (2002). The full English-language text of the letter and İnönü's response are in *Middle East Journal* (1966): 386–93.

7. This thesis is advanced in a highly convincing manner by Bölükbaşı 1993 and Şahin 2002, 102–103. The same interpretation is offered in Harris 1972, 114.

8. Nasuh Uslu makes this argument (1999, 125).

9. The following account has relied mainly on Erhan 1996; Harris 1972, 191–98; and Sönmezoğlu 1995, 57–67.

10. Erhan suggests that anti-Turkish ethnic lobbying was behind this (1996, 114).

11. Turkey had again threatened to intervene on the island unless Greece withdrew the troops that it had there in excess of the numbers allowed by treaties. See Uslu 2000, 206–18; Bölükbaşı 1988, 138–43.

12. The summary of events relies mainly on Bölükbaşı 1988, 188–92.

13. Bölükbaşı 1988, 193. Kissinger 2000, 192–239, gives an account of the events and the secretary of state's own analysis.

14. For example, Turkey said yes to a proposal by Kissinger to adopt a system of cantonal administration (Bölükbaşı 1993, 205).

15. The developments during the administration of President Ford are summarized in Lenczowski 1990, 142–47.

16. Some have speculated that the U.S. government was not opposed to enhanced Turkish presence on the island because it would help restrain Makarios, who was thought to be close to the Soviet Union. There is no evidence to support this speculation.

17. The Gulf War and the problems deriving from it have been treated in detail in Gözen 2000.

18. The rest of this account largely draws from Yetkin 2004.

19. The discussion is focused on Turkey's attempt to change U.S. policy. If that were not the case, other observations about actions could be added. For example, the Turkish plan to stage an intervention on the island in order to retaliate against atrocities committed by Greek Cypriots was rule based in that it was in conformity with the provisions of the agreements that gave Cyprus its independence. One might also suggest, with tongue in cheek, that Turkey had promised to intervene on the island, protested the U.S. pressure to stop the operation, but retracted its decision.

20. The repeated communication to U.S. officials of the need for parliamentary approval surely brought with it schedule delays and involved pleas of at least temporary credible helplessness. The importance of the last as a deliberate Turkish move to avoid eventual compliance with U.S. policies seems doubtful if the AKP government thought that it would secure parliamentary passage of the site utilization resolution.

Chapter 6: Resistance to Hegemony within the Core

1. We assume that the United States continues to be committed to the status quo, even after the end of the Cold War. Reasons for this assumption include our belief that it derives enormous benefit from the institutions it built and the policies it pursued with respect to security and economic issues during the Cold War. Since 1989, U.S. strength has increased vis-à-vis other "major powers" and yet the United States has not sought to comprehensively change global institutions created during the Cold War (see, e.g., Volgy and Bailin 2003), even though substantial lip service has been paid to a "new world order." Attempts to develop major new global regimes involving environmental and human rights issues have been strongly resisted by U.S. policy makers.

2. We refer to this condition as critical but not "necessary" since realists and neorealists argue that, even without policy disagreements, others may resist hegemony for balancing purposes. Yet we are not aware of many situations in the recent history of international politics where such "balancing" was not accompanied by policy disagreements.

3. One could argue further that policy dissension is a weak form of resistance. Larger powers can, through dissenting, rationally view their actions as making it more difficult for the hegemon to pursue its preferences as well as signaling unwillingness to cooperate. In either case, the hegemon may have to modify its preferences.

4. The term G-7 refers to the original seven members: Canada, France, Germany, Italy, Japan, the UK, and the United States. When referring to the G-8, we include Rus-

sia as a new member, at least in a symbolic sense. Reference to the G-6 indicates the other six original members, without the United States.

5. We consciously avoid the term "power" in favor of the more restrictive term "strength," meaning material capabilities.

6. Our concepts of strength are operationalized using material capabilities. We are mindful, however, that material strength is often accompanied by other types of capabilities (see, e.g., Ikenberry and Kupchan 1990).

7. See Hasenclever, Mayer, and Rittberger 1996; and Keohane 1984. Relational strength and structural strength differ, in part due to the assumption that maintaining the status quo requires different kinds of strength than changing the nature of an existing world order. An intermediate step between the two is to engage in incremental changes to existing structural arrangements (e.g., NATO expansion, the shift from the General Agreement on Tariffs and Trade [GATT] to the WTO), requiring less structural strength than creating a "new world order" (Volgy and Bailin 2003).

8. For operationalizations of these concepts, and the validation techniques used to verify that our measures correspond to these concepts, see Volgy and Bailin 2003 and Volgy and Imwalle 2000.

9. Relational strength is operationalized as the economic and military share of all great power resources, yielding three measures: an economic, a military, and an aggregated (average) share for each great power. For the operationalizations of the measures, their validation, and the sources used, see Spiezio 1990 and Volgy and Imwalle 2000.

10. The dimension of structural strength reported here takes the form of an external strength index, composed of all resources made available for foreign policy activity, modified by increases in international system complexity and the autonomy of the state. The external strength index includes military spending as part of all foreign policy resources, but its treatment differs from the way in which it is used for the relational measure since the two indexes are not correlated. Also different from the relational strength measure, structural strength is measured not in comparison to other states, or to the system as a whole, but by identifying a single point in time for a given state and then measuring changes from that point in time, while taking into account both the growth in complexity of the system and changes to a state's autonomy in the system. This is done because there are measures available for autonomy and system complexity but not for structural strength for myriad states that would be part of the "denominator" required for comparison with the entire international system. Thus, while we can compare changes in the "relative" strength of great powers over time, the structural measure only shows whether or not the "structural" strength of a state has increased or decreased compared to its demonstrated strength at an earlier point in time.

11. For a recent sampling of noneconomic issues being addressed by the G-7, see www.g7.utoronto.ca.

12. See Volgy and Bailin 2003, 93. Collective strength far exceeds the highest level of power concentration of Britain in the nineteenth century, or that of the United States after 1945 (Spiezio 1990; Volgy and Imwalle 1995).

13. For examples, see Erlanger 1997, A6; Cohen 1999. For an example of when such conflicts were minimized, see Sciolino 2002.

14. For example, on December 23, 1983, President Sandro Pertini announced a com-

plete withdrawal of Italian troops from Beirut, arguing that U.S. forces "are there in defense of Israel, and not of peace, and they are bombarding Lebanon with tons of bombs" (*Facts on File*, December 31, 1983).

15. For examples, see Bueno de Mesquita 1975; Bueno de Mesquita and Lalman 1992; Huth et al. 1993; Signorino and Ritter 1999.

16. Space considerations prohibit discussing in-depth results using the alliance portfolio data. They reflected only one major break among G-7 states. It occurred at the very end of the Cold War, and it lasted only two years.

17. For example, while caucuses may function to increase group cohesiveness in the UNGA, there is no G-7 caucus.

18. There is one reason why they might: to attain a position of leadership of the Group 77 states. This would apply to major states such as Russia and China. The G-7 states, however, do not seek to lead those Group 77 states that are fundamentally opposed to the international economic status quo. For a rigorous, empirical, and successful test of the validity of these assertions, see Volgy, Frazier, and Stewart Ingersoll 2003. There is one way in which policy cohesion cannot be measured well by UNGA voting commonality. The measure is based on the cohesiveness of the group *in response to* contested resolutions. While there is a broad array of such resolutions, they fail to capture the full array of activities occurring in the international environment, and clearly the agenda of the UNGA is not controlled by the G-7.

19. We use principal factors factor analysis, replicating the methodology used in recent successful efforts (e.g., Russett and Kim 1996) to identify dimensions of voting issues, except that we raise the threshold for minimum variance by 50 percent to address concerns that this method uncovers too many dimensions (Voeten 2000). For the methodology and its results, see Volgy, Frazier, and Stewart-Ingersoll 2003.

20. See Iida 1998. The equation for calculating the defection ratio is:

Defect = [defections/(7 * # of resolutions)] * 100
Where: Defect = defection ratio
Defections = number of defections in UN roll call votes
7 = number of G-7 members

21. The lack of correspondence between changes in General Assembly defection and G-7 defection ($r = -.0372$; ns) indicates that G-7 defection scores are not in response to the same dynamics driving other members of the UNGA.

22. The average defection scores range from a high of 36.1 percent for Japan to a low of 22.91 percent for the UK.

23. The average G-6 defection from U.S. baseline voting during the Cold War was 24.7 percent, and it increased after the Cold War to 34.4 percent (an increase in defection of 39 percent).

24. Might G-6 states continue to vote cohesively while searching for alternatives to the coalition with the United States? We believe that this measure carries sufficient validity to reflect such attempts. For example, in the late 1990s Japan sought to develop a new coalition with China in order to find an alternative to the dominance of the IMF in Asia. We find increasing Japanese defection scores in UNGA voting during this period. Such behavior is also compatible with the international public opinion patterns discussed in chapter 12 of this volume.

25. We see the conflict over Iraq not as a failure of the G-7 to cooperate in response to an emerging interstate war threatening the status quo but as a response to the United States using high levels of coercion as an instrument of "regime change." As an example of global economic threat, in the midst of substantial conflict over Iraq, the G-7 unanimously demanded that OPEC states reduce oil prices to a "level consistent with lasting economic prosperity" (*International Herald Tribune,* May 24, 2004, 1).

26. The U.S. State Department and the RAND Corporation have been collecting data on international terrorism starting with 1968, the year marking the start of "modern international terrorism" (Hoffman 2003, 46).

27. See http://www.state.gov/s/ct/rls/pgtrpt. Sharp reductions in international terrorist acts in the immediate aftermath of 9/11, following the attacks on al-Qaeda and the Taliban regime, appear to be temporary and understate terrorist activity occurring in both Iraq and Afghanistan. For deterrence of terrorism, see Brophy-Baermann and Conybeare 1994.

28. See Davenport, Moore, and Poe 2003; Ben-Yehuda and Mishali-Ram 2003.

29. See, for example, Bueno de Mesquita et al. 2000; Bueno de Mesquita 2002; Keohane and Milner 1996; Risse-Kappen 1991.

30. We assume that key policy makers are motivated both by their desire to stay in office and, by pursuing a series of policy preferences (both foreign and domestic), to do a "good job" in office (Bueno de Mesquita 2003). We assume that the desire to stay in office is paramount since without it policy preferences cannot be pursued. The dynamics of staying in office vary across political systems but involve democratic mechanisms in all of the G-7 states.

31. Even in states where policy makers have experienced extensive domestic terrorism, the risk of now introducing international terrorism may have considerable impact on the survival of the government. Witness the electoral costs of Spanish participation in the Iraq war and the fall of the government after the Madrid transit attacks occurred on the eve of national elections.

32. We suspect a substantial interaction between selectorate turmoil and perceived security risks. France, the strongest G-7 opponent of American initiatives, has both a large Arab population in the selectorate and a history of difficulties in battling terrorism on French soil.

33. For a formal model of these relationships and how to aggregate them from the state to the G-7 level, see Volgy et al. 2004.

34. Ikenberry 2001. Also see Haggard and Simmons 1987; Hasenclever, Mayer, and Rittberger 1996; Keohane 1984; Martin and Simmons 1999.

35. This variable also allows us to assess the influence of possible autocorrelation in the equation.

36. For military expenditures, we use the Stockholm International Peace Research Institute (SIPRI) yearbooks; for GDP data, annual estimates are from the International Monetary Fund. See Spiezio 1990; Volgy and Imwalle 2000.

37. Data used are available at http://www.prio.no/cwp/ArmedConflict/. We are grateful to Nils Petter Gleditsch for access to them. An alternative data set on intrastate conflicts is that of the updated COW project (Sarkees, Wayman, and Singer

2003). That set concludes in 1997 and does not as yet provide publicly the broader range of intrastate conflicts of Gleditsch et al. 2002.

38. See http://www.state.gov/documents/organization/10297.pdf, and http://www.state.gov/www/global/terrorism/annual reports.html.

39. Data on crises are from the International Crisis Behavior Project (http://www.icbnet.org/). We are grateful to Jonathan Wilkenfeld for sharing the latest updates. The interstate war data are from the Uppsala project at http://www.prio.no/cwp/ArmedConflict/.

40. These results, of course, do not negate the possible importance of relative state strength for other matters, including the likelihood that a strong state may be able to override policy dissension within the group.

41. The age of the G-7 limits our analysis to a maximum N of 26. Prudence then leads us to confine our analysis to no more than four independent variables in each model.

42. This assertion has two very important caveats. First, the G-7 maintains its current membership, an assumption that may be severely challenged in the near future. Second, the U.S. administration continues to commit itself to this multilateral forum. Despite the Bush administration's unilateralism over Iraq, the Kyoto Protocol, and so on, it has continued with the G-7 process.

43. G-6 reactions to U.S. support for an aggressive Israeli response to Hezbollah in Lebanon in 2006 further underscored these difficulties within the group.

44. See, for example, Bueno de Mesquita 2003 on the differences between democratic and nondemocratic leadership.

45. For an excellent empirical analysis of differences in orientation to security issues between the United States, Russia, and China, see Lake 2004.

Chapter 7: Thwarting U.S. Missile Defense from within the Missile Technology Control Regime

1. Among the thirty-four nations currently holding equal status within the MTCR is Russia, and two states, Israel and China, are "adherents" to the regime's guidelines, though not formal participants. There is a push by certain regime states to add China to the list of formal members. See http://www.mtcr.info/english/index.html for background on MTCR activities.

2. The NPR remains classified, but major portions were leaked on its publication and are found at http://globalsecurity.org/wmd/library/policy/dod/npr.htm.

3. It did that by deploying a few ground-based interceptors (GBIs) at Fort Greely, Alaska, in early autumn 2004.

4. Without adequate testing of Pyongyang's nascent missiles and any accompanying countermeasures, the issue of equivocal effectiveness cuts two ways—neither the offense nor defense will have been tested sufficiently to foster any confidence in real-world performance (Rubin 2003).

5. Their mere presence in Israel furnished enough reassurance to the Israeli public to keep their decision makers from intervening in the war and splitting the coalition apart at a critical point.

6. Patriot missile defense batteries are theoretically capable of shooting down low-flying cruise missiles and UAVs, but the horizon limits of their own ground-based radar mean they must depend on a sensor deployed on an airplane or balloon to alert the fire battery in enough time to engage the incoming missile.

7. A combination of human error, onboard technical malfunction, and computer incompatibility between the Federal Aviation Administration (FAA) and the Transportation Security Administration caused U.S. security personnel to mistake the Kentucky governor's airplane for a terrorist threat (Spencer S. Hsu, *Washington Post*, July 8, 2004). An intelligent and committed terrorist is unlikely to fly a small airplane, manned or unmanned, above an altitude of 3,000 feet, where the FAA's radars would be able to detect and query the aircraft's transponder to establish its intentions.

8. With the Soviet Union no longer dispensing Scuds to its client states, North Korea is left as the chief supplier of MTCR-restricted ballistic missiles.

9. To demonstrate just that, New Zealand engineer Bruce Simpson created a Web site titled "Do-It-Yourself Cruise Missile," where he documented his effort to build one in his garage for under five thousand dollars (http://www.interestingprojects.com/cruisemissile/; "DIY cruise missile thwarted," BBC News Online, December 9, 2003, http://news.bbc.co.uk/go/pr/fr/-/1/hi/world/asia-pacific/3302763.stm).

10. In a leaked memorandum, the chief of staff of Defense Minister Alain Richard of France argued not only that the missile exceeded the MTCR range threshold by two hundred kilometers but also that there were several nonproliferation reasons for vetoing the sale. Over the Defense Ministry's objections, President Jacques Chirac approved the sale (Gormley 2001).

11. In late 2004, Russian press reports had an entire group of unemployed missile specialists from the State Missile Center, Makeyev Design Bureau, departing Chelyabinsk, at the start of the Yeltsin era, for work on North Korea's ballistic missile program. See "Russia: Press Report Alleges 'Large Group' of Missile Developers Went to Work for North Korea during Yeltsin's Tenure," Chelyabinsk *Ural-Press-Inform* in Russian, November 26, 2004 (Foreign Broadcast Information Service [FBIS] translated text).

12. "Russia Establishes Victory Prize for Arms Makers; *Iskander* System Profiled," *Moscow Channel One TV*, in Russian, February 2005 [FBIS translated text]. Terminal maneuverability certainly would make the Iskander more difficult but not impossible to intercept.

13. Bush administration officials have claimed that Chinese state-owned corporations transferred missile technology to Pakistan, Iran, North Korea, and Libya, justifying the imposition of economic sanctions sixty-two times in George W. Bush's first term—compared with only eight times during Bill Clinton's two terms ("Bolton Warns China's Alleged Proliferators of Weapons Technology," *Tokyo Kyodo World Service*, in English, February 7, 2005).

14. Because they do not threaten Russian and Chinese strategic missiles, boost-phase interceptors could remain uncontrolled.

15. The Bush administration's overly aggressive articulation of the preemption doctrine has yielded unintended and unwarranted consequences, including a potentially

dangerous global scramble among copycat states to adopt their own preemption doctrines. The United States should recast preemption as a last resort, not a license to legitimate aggression, and exercise great care in implementing not only the defensive components of its new denial strategy but also the offensive ones. This pertains especially to arming heretofore nuclear strategic missiles with conventional warheads (Gormley 2006b).

16. Early in 2002, the Bush administration established a confidential interim policy governing the export of UAVs otherwise meriting Category I treatment (a strong presumption to deny transfer). Increasingly in demand to enhance the prospect of precision delivery of conventional weapons, large reconnaissance UAVs were seen as a weapon support mechanism for discriminating forms of warfare, not as delivery systems for WMD. But the stark reality is that large UAVs can also deliver five-hundred-kilogram payloads to ranges over three hundred kilometers (Gormley and Speier 2003).

17. The MTCR does not cover penetration aids for cruise missiles such as towed decoys or terrain bounce jammers, which, when specifically designed to match their delivery vehicles, make it much more difficult for missile defenses to succeed. The same holds true for a variety of technical countermeasures designed to improve ballistic missile performance against missile defenses.

18. China's transfers of M-11 missile components to Pakistan and C-802 anti-ship cruise missiles to Iran (several of which subsequently ended up under Hezbollah's control) are illustrative.

Chapter 8: Europa Riding the Hegemon?

An earlier version of this chapter was presented at the annual meeting of the International Studies Association, Honolulu, March 2–5, 2005. We are grateful for comments by Davis Bobrow and Guri Bang.

1. This ranking includes CO_2 emissions from fossil fuels and cement as well as the most powerful five non-CO_2 gases. Currently, percentages of total emission can be computed only for the year 2000.

2. This holds true even if European states did not directly participate in most of these crises, e.g., in Vietnam or the Cuban missile crisis.

3. This and the following section draw on Bodansky 2001 and, in part verbatim, on Sprinz et al. 2004.

4. The precise interpretation of this obligation is a major topic of current research (see, e.g., O'Neill and Oppenheimer 2002). No consensus has yet been found as to what "dangerous anthropogenic interference" means and how such dangers should be addressed.

5. The ten countries that joined the EU in 2004 do not figure into the compliance obligation of the EU because they each have separate treaty obligations.

6. This section draws, in part verbatim, on Busby and Ochs 2005.

7. BBC News, July 19, 2001, http://news.bbc.co.uk/1/hi/sci/tech/1446313.stm (accessed January 31, 2005).

8. http://org.eea.eu.int/documents/newreleases/tec2-2004-en (accessed August 12, 2004).

9. http://www.bmu.de/erneuerbare_energien/kurzinfo/doc/3988.php (accessed February 18, 2005).

10. http://europa.eu.int/comm./environment/climat/pdf/background_[a[er.pdg (accessed January 20, 2005).

11. *US News & World Report,* March 11, 1997, http://www.usnews.com/usnews/news/ap1103/index/htm (accessed December 14, 1999).

12. A good overview is given in Yacobucci and Powers 2005.

13. The U.S. states are Connecticut, Delaware, Maine, Massachusetts, New Hampshire, New Jersey, New York, Rhode Island, and Vermont. Maryland, the District of Columbia, Pennsylvania, and some eastern Canadian provinces are "observers."

14. http://www.wupperinst.org/Sites/Projects/rg2/1085.html (accessed August 29, 2004).

15. The original EU position was to keep sinks (the CO_2 absorption capacity of terrestrial ecosystems) out of the negotiations because of acknowledged accounting difficulties.

16. Since the United States does not participate in the Kyoto Protocol, Europeans will be able to sell U.S. industries their allocations, but the U.S. allocations are unlikely to be recognized as a Kyoto currency and so would not be bought by Europeans or others participating in the Kyoto system.

17. In June 2005 a Gallup Poll asked, "Should your government abide by Kyoto?" The results were that 42 percent answered yes, 23 percent said no, and 35 had no opinion (Lydia Saad, "Are Americans Cool to Kyoto? " Gallup Poll, June 21, 2005, cited in Brewer 2006).

18. For example, on Iraq, Europe is too divided to even advance a credible strategy of its own.

19. Material for the first two points is, in part verbatim, from the cited contributions to Ochs and Venturelli 2004.

20. Ideally, this would include all GHG emissions since the onset of industrialization.

Chapter 9: Developmental Opposition in International Trade Regimes

This chapter has benefited from Cintia Quiliconi's parallel research at FLACSO and her generous comments and insights.

1. The G-20 agenda proposed more radical cuts to domestic support measures provided by developed countries, including a capping or reduction of domestic support measures used by them. On market access, the coalition proposed a blended formula under which "each member will contribute to a substantial improvement in market access for all products, in an effective and measurable way." On export subsidies, the G-20 proposed the elimination "over an x period of export subsidies for the products of particular interest to developing countries," and further that "members shall commit to eliminate over a y period export subsidies for the remaining products."

2. NAFTA and other subregional agreements with the United States have opted for the negative list scheme.

3. Latinobarómetro 2004. The poll interviewed 18,600 persons in a total of seven-

teen Latin American countries. Additional public opinion information is discussed in chapter 12.

Chapter 10: U.S. Defection from the OECD "Harmful Tax Competition" Project

1. For a recent discussion of the OECD that notes its relative neglect in the academic literature, see Porter and Webb 2004.

2. One recent estimate of U.S. losses from individual evasion puts the number of culprits at about 750,000 and annual tax losses at $20 billion to $40 billion (Baucus and Grassley 2004). Annual U.S. corporate tax losses may range from $10 billion to $20 billion (Sullivan 2004, 15).

3. Territorial systems must be especially careful to guard against the siphoning of profits from home operations to lower-tax areas.

4. States became ever smaller relative to the total supply of lendable funds; hence the supply curve to any one of them moved closer to the horizontal. Just how close to horizontal it is for some very large countries, such as the United States, remains in dispute.

5. In 2001 the average effective EU marginal rate was four percentage points below the United States' 24 percent, while the average effective rate of only two European states was higher than that of the United States (Engen and Hassett 2002, 23, 24). The standard statutory U.S. rate was 35 percent.

6. Pass-throughs to other governments leave the federal government accounting for only a bit more than half of direct expenditures (Rosen 2002, 14, 473).

7. Such evasion became particularly straightforward after the introduction of the euro in 1999 across all the EU states except Britain, Sweden, and Denmark.

8. This includes placing intellectual property in the "harmful" jurisdiction and also a process known as "stripping," in which profits from home country activity are moved offshore by the payment of contrived debt charges.

9. Owners may obviously reside in many countries; they seldom live in low income tax havens.

10. The haven characteristics in this paragraph are those of production, sham, headquarters, and secrecy tax haven, respectively (Kudrle and Eden 2003).

11. Unless noted, factual material in this section is drawn from Easson 2004 and Webb 2004.

12. For lists of tax havens, see Kudrle and Eden 2003, 48–49.

13. They also differ from each other in many dimensions, including specialization in various financial activities and the extent of involvement in scandals of various kinds (Suss et al. 2002; Sharman 2004).

14. Luxembourg and Switzerland continued to abstain, seeing no reason that the particular questionable activities in which they specialized should be singled out. OECD rules formally allowed more than abstention; they could have vetoed the entire project.

15. *HTC* excluded "treatment of interest on savings instruments, particularly bank deposits" on grounds that such matters would be considered later and that a special Working Party was considering them (OECD 1998, 10).

16. Parts of *HTC* virtually duplicate the language of the European Code of Conduct of 1996 (Mutti 2003, 87–88). The EU also decided in 1998 to enforce the state aid rules of the Treaty of Rome more strictly (Easson 2004, 1048). All of this vividly illustrates pervasive European concern about "harmful tax competition."

17. Some committing early to cooperation with the OECD and avoiding the black-list, such as Cyprus, would have faced a real challenge with either insubstantiality or ring fencing (Hope 2000, 6) had those criteria not been dropped from the project in 2001.

18. The difficulty of such a definition was foreseen in paragraph 55 of *HTC* (OECD 1998, 24).

19. O'Neill suggested that the administration consider the abolition of a separate corporate income tax in May 2001, claiming that others in the administration also favored such a move (Shales 2001).

20. This interpretation is bolstered by the contemporary testimony of Donald C. Alexander, director of the Internal Revenue Service in the Clinton administration (Alexander 2001). The OECD had pointed out that the "foreign sales corporations" fell under the scope of the project only to the extent that they deal with financial services, and this narrow focus would have applied to subnational regimes as well. But *HTC* was originally intended to be only the opening shot in an attack on suspect tax practices.

21. After O'Neill took his first shots at the OECD project, seven previous IRS directors, including three Republicans, expressed the collective view that O'Neill misunderstood the project and that its success was vital for the integrity of the U.S. tax system (Johnston 2001, 1). Automatic, as opposed to upon-request, information sharing would have created a major political divide centering on the adequacy of foreign information control regimes, but any such dispute remains for the future.

22. The final budget request of the outgoing Clinton administration seemed to regard those two elements as the sole requirements for tax haven compliance (Sheppard 2001, 2021).

23. Pressure from many of the same groups that opposed the *HTC* project all along got the Bush administration to make such reporting necessary for citizens of only sixteen countries, including the major EU members (U.S. Mission to the European Union 2002).

24. This call to withdraw from the OECD prompted a vigorous rebuttal coauthored by Senator Charles Grassley, a Republican from Iowa (Baucus and Grassley 2004).

25. Some business groups, such as the United States Council for International Business (2004), openly embraced the refocused project.

26. The previously discussed surrogate, de facto "ring fencing," was also dropped, but it had not been officially adopted as an indicator for the havens. In the OECD countries, however, the criterion was retained.

27. The original deadline was July 31; it was subsequently changed to February 28, 2002.

28. See the *Progress Report* (OECD 2001). Luxembourg and Switzerland again abstained as they had for both previous reports, and they were joined by Belgium and Portugal, which objected to dropping "no substantial activities" while "ring fencing" was retained (for them).

29. The noncooperating list in July 2004 had six countries, none of which was among the tax project holdouts: the Cook Islands, Myanmar, Indonesia, Nauru, Nigeria, and the Philippines (Financial Action Task Force 2004).

30. The OECD produced a model for an exchange of information agreement in April 2002. It was developed jointly by a working group of the Forum that included both OECD and haven countries.

31. In 2002 the IMF, OECD, and World Bank proposed an international tax dialogue (ITD) to coordinate activity and share lessons among international organizations and country governments on a broad range of tax matters. The UN participates as an observer (http://www.itdweb.org/).

32. Because all such acts could be justified as a state's attempt to enforce its own tax laws, nothing done or threatened appears to have violated international law (Gross 2003, 394, 400).

33. Some of these financial centers were identified years later as jurisdictions from which cooperation was to be sought largely to increase the effectiveness of the European Union Savings Directive (McCloskey 2004, 1236). The newly cited havens were Barbados, Brunei, Costa Rica, Dubai, Guatemala, Hong Kong, Macao, Malaysia (Labuan), the Philippines, Singapore, and Uruguay.

34. Progress is likely to come in small increments rather than a sudden *volte-face*. Complete abandonment of bank secrecy, for example, would take revision of the Swiss constitution. For a discussion of recent progress with the United States, see Cantley 2004.

35. Even Switzerland, Andorra, Liechtenstein, Monaco, and San Marino are obligated to cooperate by providing information in cases of criminal tax fraud (Gnaedinger 2004). Some of the sharpest responses to OECD action on this and many other issues have come from the International Trade and Investment Organization (ITIO), composed mainly of Commonwealth countries (http://www.itio.org, accessed June 28, 2005). Antigua and Barbuda withdrew from their earlier information sharing commitment to the OECD in October 2003, citing the EU Savings Directive exception as the reason.

36. Confidential author telephone interviews, summer 2005.

37. The unfolding of the *HTC* project has even been portrayed as an example of the power of argument and the usefulness of a constructivist approach to understanding international relations (Webb 2004; Sharman 2004). That approach may well illuminate parts of the story for some actors, but the case for its centrality remains to be made. The interests of states and/or the interests of dominant groups within them appear quite consistent with what took place.

38. If the welfare of the Caribbean and the South Pacific was really important to the OECD governments, they could have provided economic support far more efficiently than by caving in to specious arguments about jurisdictional legitimacy.

39. By 2004 nearly all of the original tax havens had subscribed to a report that stated, "All countries, regardless of their tax systems, should meet [high standards of transparency and information exchange for both criminal and civil taxation matters] so that competition takes place on the basis of legitimate commercial considerations. ... In particular, it is important to prevent the migration of business to economies that

do not engage in transparency and effective exchange of information for tax purposes" (OECD 2004b, 2).

40. The success of the CFP with members of the Congressional Black Caucus, dozens of whom signed a letter opposing the HTC project, was an impressive but limited inroad to Democratic ranks (Sheppard 2001, 2019).

41. For a thoughtful discussion of some of the inner workings of the OECD, see Porter and Webb 2004.

42. In the MAI disaster the OECD was blindsided by both elements of domestic civil society and nonmember states (Graham 2000).

43. As Diana Tussie makes clear in chapter 9 of this volume, the Bush administration's overall posture had a similar, or perhaps greater, impact on Latin American attitudes.

Chapter 11: Saving the World from Big Tobacco

1. See generally, Office of the Surgeon General 2004; Campaign for Tobacco Free Kids, "Health harms from smoking and other tobacco use."

2. "Scarce family resources are spent on tobacco products instead of on food, or essential needs. If poor people did not smoke . . . potentially 10.5 million fewer people would be malnourished in Bangladesh" (Debra Efroymson et al., *Hungry for tobacco: An analysis of the economic impact of tobacco consumption on the poor in Bangladesh,* quoted in de Beyer et al. 2001, 210–11; and de Beyer and Bridgen 2003, 10).

3. Quotations from the report (UN Economic and Social Council 2004) appear in Deen 2004.

4. Personal communication to the author, 2003.

5. See also Manheim 2003.

6. This and subsequent quotes from Patricia Lambert are from an interview she gave to Boston-based Infact (now Corporate Accountability International) during the filming of its documentary, *Overcoming the Odds: A Story of the First Global Health and Corporate Accountability Treaty* (2004).

7. These groups included the Campaign for Tobacco-Free Kids and the American Cancer Society in the United States, ASH Thailand, the International Non-Governmental Coalition against Tobacco (INGCAT), and the Consumers Association of Penang (Malaysia).

8. My account of the history of the Framework Convention Alliance (FCA) is based on personal recollections of members of FCA, notes taken at meetings, FCA Alliance Bulletins, e-mail traffic, and direct participant observation.

9. The discussion on structured network is based in large part on a draft of a discussion paper (Brecher et al. 2004).

10. Margaret Keck and Kathryn Sikkink define advocacy networks as "forms of organization characterized by voluntary, reciprocal and horizontal patterns of communication and exchange." These organizations exchange information and provide a means of communication among participants so that they can develop a common language and frame issues for groups and the public. Framing, they argue, is particularly important as it is a "conscious strategic effort by groups of people to fashion and share

understandings of the world and of themselves that legitimize and motivate collective actions" (Keck and Sikkink 1998, 8).

11. A growing concern for civil society is its ability to achieve a balance in participation between NGOs from industrialized nations and those from developing countries. See UN Non-governmental Liaison Service 2004.

12. The technical seminars and the distribution of information over the years evolved into what Dr. Derek Yach, former WHO executive director for noncommunicable disease and mental health, called "the best university of global tobacco control" (B. Simpson, "Smoke Out!" *Johns Hopkins Pubic Health,* spring 2003, quoted in Yach et al. 2007).

13. The United States consistently and persistently argued that First Amendment protection of freedom of speech applied to the commercial speech of tobacco companies.

14. See the following documents on the Campaign for Tobacco-Free Kids Web site: *Global initiatives; How do you sell death?; Trust us, we are the tobacco industry; Golden leaf, barren harvest; Public health, international trade, and the Framework Convention on Tobacco Control,* http://tobaccofreekids.org/.

15. The World Health Organization conducts much of its business through its regional offices: AFRO, the African region; PAHO, the Pan American Health Organization, for North and South America and the Caribbean; SEARO, Southeast Asia; WPRO, the western Pacific; EURO, Europe; and EMRO, the eastern Mediterranean.

16. "According to the Center for Responsive Politics (CRP), in the previous election cycle, the tobacco companies gave more than $6 million in soft money, mainly to the Republican party. Between 1995 and the end of 2002, Philip Morris alone donated more than $10.7 million (about $9 million to Republicans), making it number four on the all-time soft-money donor list" (Berdik 2004). For undoubtedly much the same reason, the European Union was constrained by German tobacco interests and Japan followed the interests of Japan International, which opposed all regulatory rules in the body of the treaty, relegating them to a protocol.

17. "The draft of the international anti-tobacco treaty . . . was packed with options for alternative wording setting out differing and often competing policy options on taxation, marketing, labeling and anti-smuggling measures," according to Derek Yach, head of WHO anti-smoking campaign (quoted in Fowler 2001). "The language we have creates options for a strong treaty. There's also language that could make it a weak treaty—but all the language is clear." As I was quoted at the time, "It is heartening that nations from Africa, Asia, the Middle East . . . that are the latest targets of the tobacco industry's marketing barrage have taken strong positions and have succeeded in keeping them under consideration as the negotiating process moves forward" (Fowler 2001).

18. This language is similar to that in the General Agreement on Tariffs and Trade, article XXb: "Subject to the requirement that such measures are not applied in a manner which would constitute a means of arbitrary or unjustifiable discrimination between countries where the same conditions prevail, or a disguised restriction on international trade, nothing in this Agreement shall be construed to prevent the adop-

tion or enforcement by any contracting party of measures: . . . (b) necessary to protect human, animal or plant life or health."

19. As with the quotes from Patricia Lambert, those from Dr. Otto are from an interview he gave to Infact in preparation for its documentary film on the treaty.

20. Quoted in Campaign for Tobacco-Free Kids, "Leading U.S. Public Health Groups Tell U.S. Delegation to Tobacco Treaty Negotiations: Go Home" (press release), February 25, 2003.

Chapter 12: International Public Opinion

An earlier version of this paper was presented at the annual meeting of the International Studies Association, Honolulu, March 2–5, 2005.

1. I have formally avoided the ecological fallacy by drawing no inferences to subnational opinion or subnational combinations of opinions (Langbein and Lichtman 1978). Informally, when very high percentages of a national public share opinions on several items in the same survey those opinions are likely to be held by a substantial portion of poll respondents.

2. Those problems are compounded in some especially useful surveys that were administered in many different cultures and languages.

3. Scores for Latin American and African publics are only for Bush's first term of office. See Bobrow 2005 for a fuller set of first term scores.

4. Poll respondents expressed their opinions about top policy priorities in relation to diverse sets of possible threats and problems, of which terrorism was one. Europeans were asked about the possible threat or problem of U.S. economic competition, Islamic fundamentalism, U.S. unilateralism, immigrants, Israel-Arab military conflict, and WMD in Iran and North Korea. South Koreans were asked about AIDS/the Ebola virus/other potential epidemics, global warming, the development of China as a major power, economic competition from low-wage countries, U.S. unilateralism, world population growth, North Korea becoming a nuclear power, the rise of Japanese military power, Sino-Japanese rivalry, a large number of illegal foreign workers, and tensions between China and Taiwan. For the Mexican public, the questions posed were about world environmental problems, the development of China as a world power, chemical and biological weapons, economic competition from the United States, drug trafficking, and world economic crises. Europeans were also asked about their fears of other scenarios: a world war, a nuclear conflict in Europe, a conventional war in Europe, an accidental launch of a nuclear missile, an accident in a nuclear power station, the spread of NBC (nuclear, biological, chemical) weapons of mass destruction, ethnic conflicts in Europe, organized crime, and epidemics. Other possible worries suggested to publics in Asia and Uzbekistan were poverty, economic inequality in society, fair world trade, environmental problems, wars and conflicts, natural disasters, globalization, health issues, domestic economic problems, global recession, crime, human rights, corruption, lack of democracy, illegal drugs and drug addiction, refugee and political asylum problems, unemployment and difficulties getting employment, education, the domestic social welfare system, ethics in science, the aging of society, the fast pace of social and technological improvement, the threat from powerful industries, religious fundamentalism, overpopulation, and moral decline/spiritual decadence.

Europeans were asked about EU priorities with regard to enlargement, getting closer to European citizens by informing them more about the EU, implementing the euro currency, fighting poverty and social exclusion, protecting the environment, guaranteeing food quality, protecting consumers and guaranteeing the quality of products, fighting unemployment, reforming EU institutions, fighting organized crime and drug trafficking, asserting the political and diplomatic importance of the EU around the world, maintaining peace and security in Europe, guaranteeing the rights of the individual and respect for democracy in Europe, and fighting illegal immigration. As for priorities for their own individual countries, EU and EUAC publics were also asked about crime, public transport, the economic situation, rising prices/inflation, taxation, unemployment, defense/foreign affairs, housing, immigration, the health care system, the educational system, pensions, and protecting the environment. Publics in forty-four countries were asked if various problems significantly affected their country, including crime, group conflict, corrupt political leaders, moral decline, poor quality drinking water, poor quality public schools, immigration, and emigration. U.S. publics were periodically posed two relevant batteries of questions. Other possible critical threats to U.S. vital interests have recently included: chemical and biological weapons, unfriendly countries becoming nuclear powers, AIDS/the Ebola virus/other potential epidemics, immigrants and refugees, the Israel-Arab military conflict, Islamic fundamentalism, global warming, economic competition from low-wage countries, the development of China as a world power, world population growth, India-Pakistan tensions, and economic competition from Europe. Other possible foreign policy goals included protecting American jobs, preventing the spread of WMD, securing energy supplies, stopping the influx of illegal drugs, controlling and reducing illegal immigration, maintaining worldwide military superiority, improving the global environment, combating world hunger, strengthening the UN, protecting American business interests abroad, protecting weaker nations against foreign aggression, helping to improve the standard of living of less developed countries, and helping to bring a democratic form of government to other nations.

5. For poll results used for this paragraph, see Bobrow 2005.

6. Priority rankings are based on responses to the sets in note 4 (above) that have a WMD component and a forty-four-nation survey battery on major world problems whose other possibilities were religious and ethnic hatred, infectious disease/AIDS, pollution and the environment, and the rich/poor gap.

7. The splits in Finland, Ireland, and Sweden were only for participation in postwar international peacekeeping operations (PKO).

8. For results bearing on this paragraph, see Bobrow 2005.

9. The questions asked of Americans were about the U.S. effect on others, consideration of others' interests, and general influence on the world.

10. Entries in the last column of table 12.5 subtract the U.S. favorability score from that for the UN and other IGOs, with possible results ranging from +6 to −6.

11. Most columns' entries subtract the U.S. score in tables 12.2, 12.3, or 12.4 from that for the EU, with possible scores from +6 to −6. Those in the economic growth, poverty reduction, and globalization columns use subsets of questions used for the international economy column in table 12.3 (Bobrow 2005).

12. Rankings are based on poll responses regarding the battery of issues listed in note 4 above, with world importance and peace and security in Europe as choices, and on priorities for their own country (the set that begins with "crime, public transport").

13. The average shared responsibility score was +2.1 on eight queries (2001–2004).

14. This interpretation was illustrated by responses to questions on the possible U.S. use of force to destroy North Korean nuclear weapons. Support was massively predominant—if military force were employed with the approval of the UN, U.S. allies, and South Korea. With opposition from one of them, support declined. With opposition from two, opinion was split or negative.

15. Challenges from those viewed as abhorrent and unimportant validate the challenged U.S. policies. Hostile U.S. public reactions seem especially likely in response to negative public opinion and challenging actions from Iran, Middle Eastern Islamic states and movements, Cuba, and North Korea.

16. Even in 2003, a predominant U.S. majority was against punishing Germany and France for challenges on Iraq in the UN.

17. The average score was +.3 on twelve questions regarding foreign interests and preferences (2001–2005).

Chapter 13: The Implications of Constrained Hegemony

1. No attempt has been made to provide a representative sample of foreign challenges to U.S. policy preferences, and the entries should not be interpreted as being based on that type of sample.

2. Pressman's treatment does not explicitly call attention to the collective action network arena. However, his allusion to the actions of some exiles in Washington before and during the Iraq invasion fit in that arena. So too do the activities of the Kurds, particularly in the period a few years after the U.S. occupation began.

3. The United States is of course not alone in its recurrent sensitivity to prospective sovereignty erosion.

4. For example, Gormley's report in chapter 7 that China formally stated its own interpretation of MTCR conventions after gaining adherent status is more suggestive of consent and exploit activity than of consent and deceive.

REFERENCES

Alexander, D. C. 2001. Alexander testimony at Senate Government Affairs Investigations panel hearing on tax havens. *Tax Notes Today* 19 (July).

Arato, Andrew. 2004. Constitution-making in Iraq. *Dissent* 51(2):21–28.

Barnett, Michael, and Raymond Duvall. 2005. Power in international politics. *International Organization* 59(1):39–75.

Barnett, Thomas P. M. 2003. The Pentagon's new map. *Esquire,* March, 174ff.

Barringer, Felicity. 2006. Officials reach California deal to cut emissions. *New York Times,* August 31.

Barzani, Nechirvan. 2005. Kurdistan and Iraq. *Washington Times,* January 28.

Baucus, M., and C. E. Grassley. 2004. Finance leaders urge appropriators to drop OECD funding provision. *Tax Notes Today* 17 (November).

Baumert, Kevin, and Jonathan Pershing. 2004. *Climate data: Insights and observations.* Report prepared for the Pew Center on Global Climate Change.

Benjamin, Daniel, and Steven Simon. 2006. Of course Iraq made it worse. *Washington Post,* September 29.

Bennett, D. Scott, and Allan Stam. 2000. *EUGene:* A conceptual manual. *International Interactions* 26:179–204. http://eugenesoftware.org.

Bennett, D. Scott, Allan Stam, and Matthew Rupert. 2003. Comparing measures of political similarity: An empirical comparison of S versus T_b in the study of international conflict. *Journal of Conflict Resolution* 47(3):367–93.

Ben-Yehuda, Hemda, and Meirav Mishali-Ram. 2003. The ethnic-state perspective in international crises: A theoretical framework applied to the Arab-Israeli conflict, 1947–2000. *International Interactions* 29:1–26.

Berdik, Chris. 2004. Tobacco industry saves on soft money, spends on advertising and lobbyists. *CorpWatch,* July 28.

Bergsten, C. F., T. Horst, and T. H. Moran. 1978. *American multinationals and American Interests.* Washington, DC: Brookings Institution.

Bergsten, Fred. 2000. Toward a tripartite world. *Economist,* July 13, 23–26.

Bernstein, Richard, and Ross H. Munro. 1997. The coming conflict with America. *Foreign Affairs* 76 (March–April): 18–32.

Bobrow, Davis B. 2001. Visions of (in)security and American strategic style. *International Studies Perspectives* 2:1–12.

———. 2002. A changing American world role? *Zeitschrift fur Poliltikwissenchaft* 12(1):83–96.

———. 2005. Anti-Americanism and international security: Indications in international public opinion. Anti-Americanism Working Papers, Center for Policy Studies, Central European University, Budapest.

Bobrow, Davis B., and Mark A. Boyer. 2005. *Defensive internationalism: Providing public goods in an uncertain world.* Ann Arbor: University of Michigan Press.

Bodansky, Daniel. 2001. The history of the Global Climate Change Regime. In *International relations and global climate change,* ed. Urs Luterbacher and Detlef F. Sprinz. Cambridge, MA: MIT Press.

Bölükbaşı, Süha. 1988. *Turkish-American relations and Cyprus.* Lanham, MD: University Press of America.

———. 1993. The Johnson Letter revisited. *Middle Eastern Studies* 29 (July).

Borón, A. 2004. La izquierda latinoamericana a comienzos del siglo XXI: nuevas realidades y urgentes desafíos. *Observatorio Social de América Latina* 5, no. 13 (January–April): 41–56.

Brecher, Jeremy, Tim Costello, Suren Moodliar, and Kim Folz. 2004. Making social networks work. The North American Alliance for Fair Employment, April 23. http://www.fairjobs.org.

Bremer, L. Paul, III, with Malcolm McConnell. 2006. *My Year in Iraq.* New York: Simon & Schuster.

Brewer, Thomas L. 2006. U.S. public opinion on climate change issues: Update for 2005. http://faculty.msb.edu/brewert/documents/USPublicOpinionupdate-for2005.doc. Posted January 12, 2006.

Brophy-Baermann, Bryan, and John A. C. Conybeare. 1994. Retaliating against terrorism: Rational expectations and the optimality of rules versus discretion. *American Journal of Political Science* 38:196–210.

Brown, Eryn. 2001. The World Health Organization takes on big tobacco (but don't hold your breath). *Fortune,* September 17.

Brown, Michael E., et al. 2000. *America's strategic choices.* Rev. ed. Cambridge, MA: MIT Press.

Bueno de Mesquita, Bruce. 1975. Measuring systemic polarity. *Journal of Conflict Resolution* 19:187–216.

———. 2002. *Predicting politics.* Columbus: Ohio State University Press.

———. 2003. *Principles of international politics: People's power, preferences, and perceptions.* Washington, DC: Congressional Quarterly Press.

Bueno de Mesquita, Bruce, and David Lalman. 1992. *War and reason: Domestic and international imperatives.* New Haven: Yale University Press.

Bueno de Mesquita, Bruce, James D. Morrow, Randolph M. Siverson, and James Smith. 2000. Political institutions, political survival, and policy success. In *Gov-*

erning for prosperity, ed. Bruce Bueno de Mesquita and Hilton Root, 59–84. New Haven: Yale University Press.

Busby, Josh, and Alexander Ochs. 2005. From Mars and Venus down to Earth: Understanding the transatlantic climate divide. In *Beyond Kyoto: Meeting the long-term challenges of global climate change,* ed. David Michel, 35–76. Washington, DC: Brookings Institution.

Bush, George H. W., and Brent Scowcroft. 1998. *A world transformed.* New York: Random House.

Bush, George W. 2002. *The National Security Strategy of the United States of America.* http://www.whitehouse.gov/nsc/nss.

———. 2003. President Bush discusses freedom in Iraq and Middle East. Remarks by the President at the 20th Anniversary of the National Endowment for Democracy, United States Chamber of Commerce, Washington, D.C., November 6. http://www.whitehouse.gov/news/releases/2003/11/20031106–2.html

Business and Industry Advisory Committee to the OECD (BIAC). 1999. *A business view of tax competition.* Paris: OECD (June).

Campaign for Tobacco-Free Kids. 2001. *Golden leaf, barren harvest.* http://www.tobacco freekids.org/campaign/global/FCTCreport1.

———. 2001. *How do you sell death?* http://www.tobaccofreekids.org/campaign/global/FCTCreport2.

———. 2001. *Public health, international trade, and the Framework Convention on Tobacco Control.* http://www.tobaccofreekids.org/campaign.global/framework/docs/Policy.

———. 2001. *Trust us, we are the tobacco industry.* http://www.tobaccofreekids.org/campaign/global/framework/docs/TrustUs.

Cantley, Beckett G. 2004. The new tax information exchange agreement: A potent weapon against U.S. tax fraud? *Houston Business and Tax Law Journal* 4:231–58.

Cassidy, J. 2004. Tax code. *The New Yorker,* September 6.

Castañeda, J. G. 1993. Can NAFTA change Mexico? *Foreign Affairs,* September–October.

Center for Freedom and Prosperity. 2004. House leadership urges permanent withdrawal of "misguided, Clinton-era regulation." April 26. http://www.freedomandandprosperity.org/press/p04–26–04/p04–26–04.shtml

Chan, Steve. 2003. Power, satisfaction, and popularity: A poisson analysis of U.N. Security Council vetoes. *Cooperation and Conflict* 38:339–59.

———. 2004. Exploring some puzzles in power-transition theory: Some implications for Sino-American relations. *Security Studies* 13:1–39.

Chan, Steve, and Alex Mintz, eds. 1992. *Defense, welfare, and growth: Perspectives and evidence.* London: Routledge.

Chandrasekaran, Rajiv. 2003. How cleric trumped U.S. plan for Iraq. *Washington Post,* November 26.

———. 2004a. Iraqi Council Shiites walk out of session on constitution. *Washington Post,* February 28.

———. 2004b. Iraqi panel pivots on U.S. plan. *Washington Post,* February 17.

———. 2006. *Imperial life in the emerald city.* New York: Knopf.

Chao, Elaine L. 2003. Speech presented at National Lawyers Convention, Twenty-first Anniversary, the Federalist Society, November 14. http://www.ngowatch.org/ChaoAddress.

Chelala, Cesar. 2001. U.S. should not ease its stand against tobacco. *Boston Globe,* August 20.

Cheney, Dick. 2002. Vice president speaks at VFW 103rd national convention. August 26. http://www.whitehouse.gov/news/releases/2002/08/20020826.html.

Christensen, Thomas J., and Jack Snyder. 1990. Chain gangs and passed bucks: Predicting alliance patterns in multipolarity. *International Organization* 44:137–68.

Cohen, Roger. 1999. Uncomfortable with dependence on U.S., Europe aims for new parity. *New York Times,* June 15.

Cole, Juan. 2003a. The United States and Shi'ite religious factions in post-Ba'thist Iraq. *Middle East Journal* 57(4):543–66.

———. 2003b. The Iraqi Shiites. *Boston Review,* November–December.

———. 2004. Transition to What in Iraq? Stanford Institute for International Studies, May 11.

Commission to Assess the Ballistic Missile Threat to the United States. 1998. Executive summary of the commission's report. Washington, DC: GPO.

Copeland, Dale C. 2000. *The origins of major war.* Ithaca, NY: Cornell University Press.

Dalgaard-Nielsen, Anja, 2003. Gulf war: The German resistance. *Survival* 45(1): 99–116.

Davenport, Christian A., Will H. Moore, and Steven C. Poe. 2003. Sometimes you just have to leave: Domestic threats and forced migration, 1964–1989. *International Interactions* 29:27–56.

de Beyer, Joy, and Linda Waverley Bridgen, eds. 2003. *Tobacco control policy: Strategies, successes, and setbacks.* Washington, DC: World Bank, Research for International Tobacco Control.

de Beyer, Joy, Chris Lovelace, and Ayda Yurekli. 2001. Poverty and tobacco. *Tobacco Control* 10:210–11.

Deen, Thalif. 2004. Smoking chokes progress on U.N. millennium goals. *United Nations,* June 8.

Defense Science Board. 1998. *Report of the Defense Science Board Task Force on Nuclear Deterrence.* Washington, DC: Office of the Under Secretary of Defense for Acquisition and Technology.

Dembinski, Matthias. 2003. *Ein Sturm im Wasserglas? Deutsche Außenpolitik im Zeichen transatlantischer und europäischer Verwerfungen.* Frankfurt: HSFK-Report 12.

Demertzis, M. 2000. A note on fiscal federalism: A case for Europe? Unpublished manuscript.

DeSoysa, Indra, John R. Oneal, and Yong-Hee Park. 1997. Testing power transition theory using alternative measures of national capabilities. *Journal of Conflict Resolution* 41:509–28.

Der Spiegel. 2002. Freund oder Feind? (special issue on U.S.-German relations) 40:112–23.

Diamond, Larry. 2006. *Squandered victory: The American occupation and the bungled effort to bring democracy to Iraq.* New York: Henry Holt.

DiCicco, Jonathan M., and Jack Levy. 1999. Power shifts and problem shifts: The evolution of the power transition research program. *Journal of Conflict Resolution* 43:675–704.

Donfried, Karen. 2005. Germany after the elections: Implications for U.S.-German relations. Testimony before the U.S. House of Representatives, Committee on International Relations, Subcommittee on Europe and Emerging Threats. Washington, November 9.

Doran, Charles F. 1989. Systemic disequilibrium, foreign policy role, and the power cycle: Challenges for research design. *Journal of Conflict Resolution* 33:371–401.

Drahos, P. 2003. When the weak bargain with the strong: Negotiations in the World Trade Organization. *International Negotiation* 8:79–109.

Dreazen, Yochi J. 2005. Basra violence challenges U.S. strategy. *Wall Street Journal,* September 21, A12.

Dror, Yehezkel. 1971. *Crazy states: A counterconventional strategic problem.* Lexington, MA: Heath Lexington Books.

Easson, A. 2004. Harmful tax competition: An evaluation of the OECD initiative. *Tax Notes International Magazine* 34 (June 7): 1037–78.

Elmore, Richard F. 1985. Forward and backward mapping: Reversible logic. In *Policy implementation in federal and unitary systems: Questions of analysis and design,* ed. Kenneth Hanf and Theo A. J. Toonen, 33–70. Boston: Martinus Nijhoff.

ENDS Environment Daily. 2004. New EU renewables target "will be set in 2007." *ENDS Environment Daily* 1674, May 26. http://www.environmentdaily.com/articles/index.cfm?action=article&ref=16741&searchtext=energy&searchtype=all.

Engen, E., and K. A. Hassett. 2002. Does the U.S. corporate tax have a future? *Tax Notes 30th Anniversary Issue,* 15–27.

Erhan, Çağrı. 1996. *Beyaz Savaş: Türk-Amerikan İlişkilerinde Afyon Sorunu.* Ankara: Bılgı.

Erlanger, Steven. 1997. Clinton basks at summit; some Europeans are cool to U.S. *New York Times,* June 21.

———. 2002. Germany joins Europe's cry that the U.S. won't consult. *New York Times,* February 13. http://www.nyt.com.

Esson, Katharine. 2004. The millennium development goals and the WHO FCTC: An opportunity for global partnership. Presentation at FCTC IGWG, June 21. http://www.who.int/tobacco/areas/communications/events/en/mdgs_tobaccocontrol.

European Commission. 2004. *MEMO/04/44: Questions & answers on emissions trading and national allocation plans.* Brussels, March, updated January 6, 2005. http://europa.eu.int/rapid/pressReleasesAction.do?reference=MEMO/04/44&format=HTML&aged=1&language=EN&guiLanguage=en#fn1.

European Environment Agency. 2006. *Greenhouse gas emission trends and projections in Europe.* Copenhagen: European Environment Agency.

Evans, Peter B., Harold K. Jacobson, and Robert D. Putnam, eds. 1993. *Double edge diplomacy: International bargaining and domestic politics.* Berkeley: University of California Press.

Fay, Kevin. 2002. *Bush administration climate proposal: A significant contribution.* http://www.abanet.org/environ/committees/climatechange/newsletter/mar02/fay.htm, accessed June 15.

Fearon, James D. 1995. Rationalist explanations for war. *International Organization* 49:379–414.

———. 2006. Iraq: Democracy or civil war? Testimony to the U.S. House of Representatives, Committee on Government Reform, Subcommittee on National Security, Emerging Threats, and International Relations, September 15.

Feinberg, R. 2003. The political economy of United States' free trade agreements. *World Economy* 26(7):1019–40.

Feldman, Noah. 2004. *What we owe Iraq.* Princeton: Princeton University Press.

Fidler, David P. 2003. World Health Organization's framework convention for tobacco control. *ASIL Insights,* March 28. http://www.asil.org/insights/insigh100.htm

Financial Action Task Force. 2004. Non cooperating countries and territories (NCCTs). http://www1.oecd.org/fatf/NCCT_en.htm

Financial Stability Forum. 2000. Financial Stability Forum releases grouping of Offshore Financial Centers (OFCs) to assist in setting priorities for assessment. http://www.fsforum.org/publications/PR_OFC00.pdf.

Fırat, Melek M. 1997. *1960–1971 Arası Türk Dış Politikası ve Kıbrıs Sorunu.* Ankara: Siyasal Kitabevi.

Fowler, Jonathan. 2001. Tobacco control talks make progress. Associated Press, November 29.

Frankel, Glen. 1996. U.S. aided cigarette firms in conquests across Asia. *Washington Post,* November 17.

Fukuyama, Francis. 1992. *The end of history and the last man.* New York: Free Press.

Gaddis, John Lewis. 2002. A grand strategy of transformation. *Foreign Policy* 133 (November–December): 50–57.

Galbraith, Peter. 2004. Iraq: The bungled transition. *New York Review of Books* 51(14), September 23.

George, Alexander L. 1980. Domestic constraints on regime change in U.S. foreign policy: The need for legitimacy. In *Change in the international system,* ed. Ole R. Holsti, Randolph M. Siverson, and Alexander L. George, 233–62. Boulder, CO: Westview Press.

German Marshall Fund (GMF). 2005. *After the U.S. election: A survey of public opinion in France, Germany, and the United States.* February 7. http://www.gmfus.org.

Gilpin, Robert. 1981. *War and change in world politics.* New York: Cambridge University Press.

Ginsberg, Roy H. 2001. *The European Union in international politics: Baptism by fire.* Lanham, MD: Rowman & Littlefield.

Giridharadas, A. 2001. Saved havens: The treasury coddles tax cheats. *New Republic,* August 27–September 3, 23–24.

Gleditsch, Nils Petter, Peter Wallensteen, Mikael Eriksson, Margareta Sollenberg, and Havard Strand. 2002. Armed conflict 1946–2001: A new dataset. *Journal of Peace Research* 39:614–37.

Gnaedinger, C. 2004. EU signs savings tax agreements, Swiss plan ok'ed. *Tax Notes International* 36 (December 13): 899.

Goodman, Ellen. 2003. Torching the tobacco treaty. *Boston Globe,* May 3.

Gordon, Philip, and Jeremy Shapiro. *Allies at War: America, Europe, and the Split over Iraq.* New York: McGraw-Hill, 2004.

Gordon Report. 1981. *Tax havens and their use by United States taxpayers—An overview.* Washington, DC: U.S. Treasury, duplicated.

Gormley, Dennis M. 1999. Track it, then attack it. *Defense News,* January 18.

———. 2000. Defusing China's threat to Taiwan. *Defense News,* March 24.

———. 2001. *Dealing with the threat of cruise missiles.* Oxford: Oxford University Press.

———. 2003. Missile defence myopia: Lessons from the Iraq war. *Survival* 45(4): 61–86.

———. 2006a. Cruise control. *Bulletin of the Atomic Scientists* 62(2):26–33.

———. 2006b. Securing nuclear obsolescence. *Survival* 48(3):127–48.

Gormley, Dennis M., and Lawrence Scheinman. 2005. Implications of proposed India-U.S. civil nuclear cooperation. http://www.nti.org/e_research/e3_67a.html.

Gormley, Dennis M., and Richard Speier. 2003. Controlling unmanned air vehicles: New challenges. *Nonproliferation Review* 10(2):66–79.

Goulder, R. 2004. TNI interview: Jeffrey Owens. *Tax Notes International Magazine* 33 (March 29): 1189.

Government Accountability Office. 2003. *Missile defense: Knowledge-based practices are being adopted, but risks remain.* Washington, DC: GAO.

Gözen, Ramazan. 2000. *Amerikan Kıskacında Dış Politika: Körfez Savaşı, Turgut Özal ve Sonrası.* Ankara: Liberte.

Graham, M. 2000. *Fighting the wrong enemy: Antiglobal activists and multinational enterprises.* Washington, DC: Institute for International Economics.

Gries, Peter H. 2004. China eyes the hegemon. Unpublished manuscript.

Gross, J. B. 2003. OECD defensive measures against harmful tax competition: Legality under WTO. *INTERTAX* 31(11):390–400.

Grubb, Michael. 2001. The UK and European Union: Britannia waives the rules? In *Climate change after Marrakech: The role of Europe in the global arena (German Foreign Policy in Dialogue—A German E-Newsletter on German Foreign Policy),* ed. D. Sprinz. http://www.deutsche-aussenpolitik.de.

Grubb, Michael, and Richard Stewart. 2004. Promoting climate-friendly technologies: International perspectives and issues. In *Towards a transatlantic consensus on climate change,* ed. Alexander Ochs and Aldo Venturelli. Loveno, Italy: Villa Vigoni.

Gupta, Joyeeta, and Lasse Ringius. 2001. The EU's climate leadership: Reconciling ambition and reality. *International Environmental Agreements* 1:281–99.

Haass, Richard. 1997. *The reluctant sheriff: The United States after the Cold War.* New York: Council on Foreign Relations Press.

———. 2002. Defining U.S. foreign policy in a post–post–cold war world. www.state.gov/s/p/rem/9632.

Haggard, Steph, and Beth Simmons. 1987. Theories of international regimes. *International Organization* 41:491–517.

Hamilton, A. 2003. U.S. Treasury official defends nonresident alien interest reporting regulations. *Tax Notes International Magazine* 30 (May 12): 541.

Harnisch, Sebastian. 2004. Deutsche Sicherheitspolitik auf dem Prüfstand: Die Nonproliferationspolitik gegenüber dem Irak. In *Deutsche Sicherheitspolitik. Eine Bilanz der Regierung Schröder*, ed. Sebastian Katsioulis Harnisch and Christos Overhaus Marco, 173–200. Baden-Baden: Nomos.

Harris, George S. 1972. *Troubled alliance: Turkish-American problems in historical perspective, 1945–1971.* Washington, DC: American Enterprise Institute.

Hasenclever, Andreas, Peter Mayer, and Volker Rittberger. 1996. Interests, power, knowledge: The study of international regimes. *Mershon International Studies Review* 40 (supplement 2):177–228.

Heady, C. 2002. The truth about tax burdens. *OECD Observer.* March. http://www.oecd observer.org/news/fullstory.php/aid/651/The_truth_about_tax_burdens.htm.

Hellmann, Gunther. 2002. Der "deutsche Weg": Eine außenpolitische Gratwanderung. *Internationale Politik* 57(9):1–8.

———. 2004. Von Gipfelstürmern und Gratwanderern: Deutsche Wege in der Außenpolitik. *Aus Politik und Zeitgeschichte* 11:32–39.

Henze, Paul B. 1987. Out of kilter: Greeks, Turks, and U.S. foreign policy. *National Interest* 8 (summer): 71–82.

Herron, Kerry G., et al. 2000. *Mass and elite views on nuclear security: U.S. national security surveys, 1993–1999.* Albuquerque: UNM Institute for Public Policy, University of New Mexico.

Herron, Kerry G. and Hank C. Jenkins Smith. 2006. *Critical masses and critical choices: Evolving public opinion on nuclear weapons, terrorism, and security.* Pittsburgh: University of Pittsburgh Press.

Higgot, R. 2004. Multilateralism and the limits of global governance. Paper prepared for the conference Learning from the Crisis: Where Do We Go for Global Governance? Buenos Aires, May.

Hines, James R. 1999. The case against deferral: A deferential reconsideration. *National Tax Journal* 52(3):385–404.

Hippler, Jochen. 2003. Unilateralismus der USA als Problem der Internationalen Politik-Konsequenzen für globale Problemlösungen, die Vereinten Nationen und die Entwicklung des Völkerrechts. *Aus Politik und Zeitgeschichte* 12:3–10.

Hirschman, Albert O. [1945] 1980. *National power and the structure of foreign trade.* Expanded ed. Berkeley: University of California Press.

Hodge, Carl Cavanagh. 2004. *Atlanticism for a new century.* Upper Saddle River, NJ: Prentice Hall.

Hoffman, Bruce. 2003. The logic of suicide terrorism. *Atlantic Monthly,* June, 40–47.

Hope, K. 2000. Cyprus starts to heed calls to mend its offshore ways: OECD pressure has brought pledges of full compliance with the international campaign against tax evasion. *Financial Times,* August 16, 6.

Horner, F. 2001. Where is the organisation going? International Tax Planning Association, summary of the June 17–19, 2001, meetings. http://www.itpa.org/open/summaries/berlin2001s.html.

Houghton, John Theodore, and Intergovernmental Panel on Climate Change. 1996. *Climate change 1995: The scientific basis: contribution of working group I to the second assessment report of the Intergovernmental Panel on Climate Change.* Cambridge: Cambridge University Press.

———. 2001. *Climate change 2001: The scientific basis: contribution of working group I to the third assessment report of the Intergovernmental Panel on Climate Change.* Cambridge: Cambridge University Press.

Hufbauer, G. C., and J. M. Van Rooij. 1992. *U.S. taxation of international income: Blueprint for reform.* Washington, DC: Institute for International Economics.

Huntington, Samuel P. 1988. The U.S.—decline or renewal? *Foreign Affairs* 67:76–96.

———. 1999. The lonely superpower. *Foreign Affairs* 78:35–49.

Hurrell, A. 2004. Hegemony and regional governance in the Americas. Global Law Working Paper 05/04, New York University.

Huth, Paul, Christopher Gelpi, and Scott Bennett. 1993. The escalation of great power militarized disputes. *American Political Science Review* 87(3):609–23.

Iida, Keisuke. 1988. Third World solidarity: The Group of 77 in the UN General Assembly. *International Organization* 42(2):375–95.

Ikenberry, G. John. 1989. Rethinking the origins of American hegemony. *Political Science Quarterly* 104(3):375–400.

———. 1998–1999. Institutions, strategic restraint, and the persistence of American postwar order. *International Security* 23(3):43–78.

———. 2001. *After victory: Institutions, strategic restraint, and the rebuilding of order after major wars.* Princeton: Princeton University Press.

———. 2003. Strategic reactions to American preeminence: Great power politics in the age of unipolarity. http://www.cia.gov/nic/confreports_stratreact.html.

Ikenberry, G. John, and Charles A. Kupchan. 1990. Socialization and hegemonic power. *International Organization* 44(3):283–315.

Ikle, Fred C., and Albert Wohlstetter. 1988. *Discriminate deterrence: Report of the Commission on Integrated Long-Term Strategy.* Washington, DC: GPO.

Inoguchi, Takashi, Miguel Basanez, Akihiko Tanaka, and Timur Dadabaev. 2005. *Values and life styles in urban Asia: A cross-cultural analysis and sourcebook based on the AsiaBarometer survey of 2003.* Tokyo: Institute of Oriental Culture, University of Tokyo, Special Series 19; Mexico City: Siglo XXI Editores.

Inoguchi, Takashi, Akihiko Tanaka, Shigeto Sonoda, and Timur Dadabaev, eds. 2006. *Human beliefs and values in striding Asia.* Tokyo: Akashi Shoten.

International Chamber of Commerce. 2000. Harmful tax competition. http://www.iccwbo.org/home/statements_rules/statements/2000/harmful_tax.asp

Janning, Josef. 2002. Lange Wege, kurzer Sinn? Eine außenpolitische Bilanz von Rot-Grün. *Internationale Politik* 57(9):9–18.

Joffe, Josef. 2003. Continental divides. *National Interest,* spring, 157–60.

Johnston, Alastair Iain. 1995. *Cultural realism: Strategic culture and grand strategy in Chinese history.* Princeton: Princeton University Press.

———. 2003. Is China a status quo power? *International Security* 7:57–85.

Johnston, D. C. 2001. Former I.R.S. chiefs back tax havens crackdown. *New York Times,* June 9.

Kagan, Robert. 2002a. Macht und Schwäche: Was die Vereinigten Staaten und Europa auseinander treibt. *Blätter für deutsche und internationale Politik* 10:1194–206.

———. 2002b. Power and weakness. *Policy Review* 113, May–June.

Kahn, Herman. 1960. *On thermonuclear war.* Princeton: Princeton University Press.

Kant, Immanuel. [1795] 1957. *Perpetual peace.* Trans. Lewis White Beck. New York: Bobbs-Merrill.

Karp, Regina. 2005–2006. The new German foreign policy consensus. *Washington Quarterly* 29(1):61–92.

Kaufman, Marc. 2003. U.S. seeks to alter anti-tobacco treaty: "Reservations" clause sought as way out of some provisions. *Washington Post,* April 30.

Kay, David. 2003. Interim Report of the Iraqi Survey Group. https://www.cia .gov/cia/public_affairs/speeches/2003/.

Keaney, Thomas A., and Eliot A. Cohen. 1993. *Gulf War air power survey: Summary report.* Washington, DC: GPO.

Keck, Margaret E., and Kathryn Sikkink. 1998. *Activists beyond borders.* Ithaca, NY: Cornell University Press.

Keen, M., and J. E. Ligthart. 2004. Cross-border savings taxation in the European Union: An economic perspective. *Tax Notes International Magazine* 33 (February 9): 539–46.

Kelly, Mick. 2006. Asia-Pacific partnership meets: The inaugural meeting of the Asia-Pacific Partnership on Clean Development and Climate (AP-6) took place in Sydney, Australia, January 11–12th 2006. *Tiempo Climate Newswatch.*

Kennedy, Paul. 1987. *The rise and fall of the great powers: Economic change and military conflict from 1500 to 2000.* New York: Random House.

Keohane, Robert O. 1984. *After hegemony: Cooperation and discord in the world political economy.* Princeton: Princeton University Press.

Keohane, Robert O., and Helen Milner. 1996. *Internationalization and domestic politics.* Cambridge: Cambridge University Press.

Keohane, Robert O., and Joseph S. Nye. 1977. *Power and interdependence: World politics in transition.* Boston: Little, Brown.

Khagram, Sanjeev, James V. Riker, and Kathryn Sikkink, eds. 2002. *Restructuring world politics: Transnational social movements, networks, and norms.* Minneapolis: University of Minnesota Press.

Kiernan, V. G. 1991. *Tobacco: A history.* London: Hutchinson Radius.

Kim, Samuel S. 1979. *China, the United Nations, and world order.* Princeton: Princeton University Press.

Kissinger, Henry. 2000. *Years of renewal.* New York: Touchstone Books.

Knopf, Jeffrey W. 1993. Beyond two-level games: Domestic-international interaction in the intermediate range nuclear forces negotiations. *International Organization* 47(4):599–628.

Knox, MacGregor, and Williamson Murray, eds. 2001. *The dynamics of military revolution, 1300–2050.* Cambridge: Cambridge University Press.

Krauthammer, Charles. 1991. The unipolar moment. *Foreign Affairs* 70:23–33.

Kudrle, R. T., and L. Eden. 2003. The new attack on tax havens: Will it work, will it last? *Stanford Journal of Law, Business, and Finance* 9 (autumn): 37–68.

Kugler, Jacek, and Douglas Lemke, eds. 1996. *Parity and war: Evaluations and extensions of the war ledger.* Ann Arbor: University of Michigan Press.

―――. 2000. The power transition research program.. In *Handbook of War Studies II,* ed. Manus I. Midlarsky, 129–63. Ann Arbor: University of Michigan Press.

Lake, David A. 2004. Hierarchy in international relations: Authority, sovereignty, and the new structure of world politics. Paper prepared for the annual meeting of the American Political Science Association, Chicago.

Langbein, Laura I., and Allan J. Lichtman. 1978. *Ecological inference.* Beverly Hills, CA: Sage.

Lardy, Nicholas R. 1999. China and the international financial system. In *China joins the world: Progress and prospects,* ed. Elizabeth Economy and Michael Oksenberg, 206–30. New York: Council of Foreign Relations.

Latinobarómetro. 2004. Encuesta Latinobarómetro 2004 una década de mediciones, una década de evolución. http://www.latinobarometro.org.

Layne, Christopher. 1993. The unipolar illusion: Why new great powers will rise. *International Security* 17:5–51.

Lemke, Douglas, and Suzanne Werner. 1996. Power parity, commitment to change, and war. *International Studies Quarterly* 40:235–60.

Lenczowski, George. 1990. *American presidents and the Middle East.* Durham, NC: Duke University Press.

Levy, Jack S. 1987. Declining power and the preventive motivation for war. *World Politics* 39:82–107.

―――. 1997. Loss aversion, framing, and bargaining: The implications of prospect theory for international conflict. *International Political Science Review* 17:179–95.

Lindstrom, Gustav. 2003. *Shift or rift: Assessing U.S.-EU relations after Iraq.* Paris: European Union Institute for Security Studies.

Linzer, Dasfna. 2005. U.S. uses drones to probe Iran for arms. *Washington Post,* February 13.

Mack, Andrew. 1975. Why big nations lose small wars: The politics of asymmetric conflict. *World Politics* 27:175–200.

MacKenzie, Donald, and Graham Spinardi. 1995. Tacit knowledge, weapons design, and the uninvention of nuclear weapons. *American Journal of Sociology* 101(1):44–99.

Manheim, Jarol. 2003. Biz-War: Origins, structure and strategy of foundation-NGO network warfare on corporations in the United States. Paper presented at the American Enterprise Institute, Washington, DC, June 11.

Mansfield, Edward. 1993. Measuring the international distribution of power. *International Review of Sociology* 101(1–2):263–82.

Marten, Kimberly, and Alexander Cooley. 2005. Permanent military bases won't work. *International Herald Tribune,* February 3.

Martin, Lisa L., and Beth Simmons. 1999. Theories and empirical studies of international institutions. In *Exploration and contestation in the study of world politics,* ed. Peter J. Katzenstein, Robert O. Keohane, and Stephen D. Krasner. Special issue of *International Organization.* Cambridge, MA: MIT Press.

Mastanduno, Michael. 1997. Preserving the unipolar moment: Realist theories and U.S. grand strategy after the cold war. *International Security* 21:49–88.

Mathews, Jessica Tuchman. 2002. U.S.-Europe: Estranged partners. Remarks to the Open Forum, U.S. Department of State, Washington, DC, January 11.

Maull, Hanns W. 1990–1991. Germany and Japan: The new civilian powers. *Foreign Affairs* 69(5):91–106.

———. 2004a. Deutsche Außenpolitik: Von der Stagnation in die Krise. In *Jahrbuch Internationale Politik 2001/02,* ed. von W. Wagner, K. Kaiser, H. W. Maull et al., 177–88. Bonn: Deutsche Gesellschaft für Auswärtige Politik; Munich: Oldenbourg-Verlag.

———. 2004b. Germany, Iraq, and the crisis of the transatlantic alliance system. Opinion editorial no. 2, August 28. http://www.deutsche-aussenpolitik.de/digest/op-ed_inhalt_02.php.

———. 2007. Zivilmacht. In *Handbuch der deutschen Außenpolitik,* ed. Siegmar Schmidt, Reinhard Wolf, and Gunther Hellmann. Wiesbaden: VS-Verlag.

McCloskey, W. 2004. OECD's McCloskey shares Berlin meeting highlights. *Tax Notes International Magazine* 34 (June 21): 1235.

McDonnell, Patrick H. 2006. Into the abyss of Baghdad. *Los Angeles Times,* October 23.

McMahon, K. Scott, and Dennis M. Gormley. 1994. *Controlling the spread of land-attack cruise missiles.* Marina del Rey, CA: American Institute for Strategic Cooperation.

Mearsheimer, John, J. 2001. *The tragedy of great power politics.* New York: Norton.

Mendelsohn, Jack. 2000. The impact of NMD on the ABM Treaty. In *White Paper on National Missile Defense,* ed. Joseph Cirincione et al. Washington, DC: Lawyers Alliance for World Security.

Mertler, Craig A., and Racel A. Vanatta. 2002. *Advanced and multivariate statistical methods: Practical application and interpretation.* Los Angeles: Pyrczak.

Millot, Mark Dean. 1993. Facing the emerging reality of regional nuclear adversaries. *Washington Quarterly* 17(3):50–51.

Mo, Jongryn. 1994. The logic of two-level games with endogenous domestic coalitions. *Journal of Conflict Resolution* 38(3):402–22.

———. 1995. Domestic institutions and international bargaining: The role of agent veto in two-level games. *American Political Science Review* 89(4):914–24.

Modelski, George. 1987. *Long cycles in world politics.* Seattle: University of Washington Press.

Morgenthau, Hans. 1952. Another great debate: The national interest of the United States. *American Political Science Review* 46(4):961–88.

Müller, Friedemann, and Michael Oppenheimer. 2004. Climate change: The case for long-term targets. In *Towards a transatlantic consensus on climate change,* ed. Alexander Ochs and Aldo Venturelli. Loveno, Italy: Villa Vigoni.

Müller, Harald. 2003. Terrorism, proliferation: A European threat assessment. Institute for Security Studies, Chaillot Papers (58).

———. 2004. Das transatlantische Risiko: Deutungen des amerikanisch-europäischen Weltordnungskonflikts. *Aus Politik und Zeitgeschichte* 3–4:7–17.

Mutti, J. H. 2003. *Foreign direct investment and tax competition.* Washington, DC: Institute for International Economics.

Nakash, Yitzhak. 1994. *The Shi'is of Iraq.* Princeton: Princeton University Press.

Narlikar, A., and D. Tussie. 2004. The G20 at the Cancun Ministerial: Developing countries and their evolving coalitions in the WTO. *World Economy* 27(7):947–66.

Nathan, Andrew J., and Robert S. Ross. 1997. *The Great Wall and the empty fortress: China's search for security.* New York: Norton.

Neuss, Beate. 2003. Wozu brauchen wir die Amerikaner noch? Das transatlantische Verhältnis (What are the Americans useful for? Transatlantic relations). *Die politische Meinung* 4(401):5–13.

———. 2004. Elitenwandel und außenpolitische Orientierung: Ein Grund für das transatlantische Zerwürfnis? (Change in elite attitudes and foreign policy orientation: A cause of the transatlantic divide?) *Die politische Meinung* 3(412):51–60.

Niedermayer, Oskar. 2003. "Wandel durch Flut und Irak-Krieg?" In *Bilanz der Bundestagswahl 2002,* ed. Eckhard Jesse, 37–70. Wiesbaden: Westdeutscher Verlag.

The 9/11 Commission report. 2004. New York: Norton.

Nye, Joseph S. 1990. *Bound to lead: The changing nature of American power.* New York: Basic Books.

———. 2001. The "Nye Report": Six years later. *International Relations of the Asia-Pacific* 1(1):95–103.

Ochs, Alexander. 2005. *Gleneagles.* German Institute for International and Security Affairs, July. http://www.swp-berlin.org/de/common/get_document.php?id=1330, accessed November 1, 2006.

Ochs, Alexander, and Aldo Venturelli, ed. 2004. *Towards a transatlantic consensus on climate change.* Loveno, Italy: Villa Vigoni.

Office of the Surgeon General. 2004. *The health consequences of smoking: A report of the Surgeon General.* Washington, DC: Public Health Service, U.S. Department of Health and Human Services.

O'Neill, Brian C., and Michael Oppenheimer. 2002. Dangerous climate impacts and the Kyoto Protocol. *Science* 296:1971–72.

O'Neill, P. 2001. Statement of Paul H. O'Neill before the Senate Committee on Governmental Affairs Permanent Subcommittee on Investigations. OECD Harmful Tax Practices Initiative. July 18. U.S Department of the Treasury, Office of Public Affairs. http://www.ustreas.gov/press/releases/op486.htm.

Organization for Economic Co-operation and Development (OECD). 1998. *Harmful tax competition: An emerging global issue.* Paris: OECD.

———. 2000a. *Framework for a collective memorandum of understanding on eliminating harmful tax practices.* Paris: OECD.

———. 2000b. *Towards global tax cooperation: Progress in identifying and eliminating harmful tax practices. Report to the 2000 Ministerial Council Meeting and Recommendations by the Committee on Fiscal Affairs.* Paris: OECD.

———. 2001. *Project on harmful tax practices: The 2001 progress report.* Centre for Tax Policy and Administration, November 14.

———. 2004a. A process for achieving a global playing field. OECD Global Forum on Taxation, Berlin, June 3–4. http://www.oecd.org/dataoecd/13/0/31967501.pdf.

———. 2004b. *Project on harmful tax practices: The 2004 progress report.* Centre for Tax Policy and Administration, February.

Organski, A. F. K. 1968. *World politics.* New York: Knopf.

Organski, A. F. K., and Jacek Kugler. 1980. *The war ledger.* Chicago: University of Chicago Press.

Ott, Herman E., and Sebastian Oberthür. 2001. Breaking the impasse: Forging an EU leadership initiative on climate change. Heinrich Böll Foundation. http://www.boell.de/downloads/oeko/PapersNr3en.pdf, accessed August 29, 2004.

Overhaus, Marco. 2006. Civilian power under stress: Germany, NATO, and the European security and defence policy. In *Germany's uncertain power: Foreign policy of the Berlin Republic,* ed. Hanns Maull, 66–78. Basingstoke, England: Palgrave.

Pape, Robert A. 2005. Soft balancing against the United States. *International Security* 30(1):7–45.

Paul, T. V. 1994. *Asymmetric conflicts: War initiations by weaker powers.* New York: Cambridge University Press.

Pearson, Margaret M. 1999. China's integration into the international trade and investment regime. In *China joins the world: Progress and prospects,* ed. Elizabeth Economy and Michael Oksenberg, 161–205. New York: Council of Foreign Relations.

Peto, Richard, Alan D. Lopez, Jillian Boreham, et al. 1996. Mortality from smoking worldwide. *British Medical Bulletin* 52:12–21.

Pew Center on Global Climate Change. 2002. *Analysis of President Bush's climate change plan.* http://www.pewclimate.org/policy_center/analyses/response_bushpolicy.cfm, accessed February 1, 2005.

Pfaff, William. 1992. America as outsider: Washington plays with fire. *International Herald Tribune,* June 15.

Phillips, N. 2001. Regionalist governance in the new political economy of development: Relaunching the Mercosur. *Third World Quarterly* 22(4):565–81.

———. 2003. Hemispheric integration and subregionalism in the Americas. *International Affairs* 79(2):257–79.

Picciotto, Sol. 1992. *International business taxation: A study in the internationalization of business regulation.* New York: Quorum Books.

Pikayev, Alexander A., et al. 1997. *Russia, the U.S., and the missile technology control regime.* Oxford: Oxford University Press.

Porter, T., and M. Webb. 2004. The role of the OECD in the orchestration of global knowledge networks. Paper prepared for the International Studies Association Annual Meeting, Montreal.

Pressman, Jeremy. 2006. Is balancing the wrong question? Power and influence in international politics. Paper presented at the American Political Science Association annual meeting, Philadelphia, September 3.

Putnam, Robert D. 1988. Diplomacy and domestic politics: The logic of two-level games. *International Organization* 42(3):427–60.

Rabe, Barry G. 2002. Statehouse and greenhouse: The states are taking the lead on climate change. *Brookings Review* 20(2):11–13.

Rasler, Karen, and William R. Thompson. 1994. *The great powers and global struggle, 1490–1990.* Lexington: University Press of Kentucky.

Report of the Canberra Commission on the Elimination of Nuclear Weapons. 1996. http://www.wagingpeace.org/articles/1996/10/03_butler_chaining.htm.

Reuter, P., and E. M. Truman. 2004. *Chasing dirty money: The fight against money laundering.* Washington, DC: Institute for International Economics.

Riggs, John A., ed. 2004. *A climate policy framework: Balancing policy and politics. A report of an Aspen Institute Climate Change Policy dialogue, November 14–17, 2003.* Aspen, CO: The Aspen Institute.

Risse-Kappen, Thomas. 1991. Public opinion, domestic structure, and foreign policy in liberal democracies. *World Politics* 43:143–75.

Rosecrance, Richard, ed. 1976. *America as an ordinary country.* Ithaca, NY: Cornell University Press.

Rosen, H. S. 2002. *Public finance.* 8th ed. New York: McGraw-Hill Irwin.

Rosi, Eugene J., ed. 1973. *American defense and détente: Readings in national security policy.* New York: Dodd, Mead.

Ross, Andrew L., Michele A. Flournoy, and David Mosher. 2002. What do we mean by "transformation"? *Naval War College Review* 55(1):27–42.

Roy, Denny. 1994. Hegemon on the horizon? China's threat to East Asian security. *International Security* 19:149–68.

Rubin, Alissa J. 2004. Iraqi silence indicts U.S. occupiers. *Los Angeles Times,* May 16.

Rubin, Uzi. 2003. A comparative review of the technologies of missile defense and their countermeasures. Report from Rubincon Defense Consulting Ltd.

Rudolf, Peter. 2006. The transatlantic relationship: A view from Germany. In *Germany's uncertain power: Foreign policy of the Berlin Republic,* ed. Hanns Maull, 137–51. Basingstoke, England: Palgrave.

Ruggie, J. R. 1998. *Constructing the world polity.* London: Routledge.

Rumsfeld, Donald H. 2002. Joint press conference with British Secretary of State for Defense Geoffrey Hoon, June 5, 2002. http://defenselink.mil/transcripts/transcript.aspx?transcriptID=3488.

———. 2004. Prepared testimony of U.S. Secretary of Defense Donald H. Rumsfeld before the Senate Appropriations Committee, Defense Subcommittee, May 12, 2004.

Russett, Bruce M. 1970. *What price vigilance: The burdens of national defense.* New Haven: Yale University Press.

Russett, Bruce, and Soo Yeon Kim. 1996. The new politics of voting alignments in the UN general assembly. *International Organization* 50:629–52.

Russett, Bruce M., and John R. Oneal. 2001. *Triangulating peace: Democracy, interdependence, and international organizations.* New York: Norton.

Rustow, Dankwart A. 1987. *Turkey: America's forgotten ally.* New York: Council on Foreign Relations.

Şahin, Haluk. 2002. *Johnson Mektubu.* Istanbul: Gendaş.

Sander, Oral. 1979. *Türk-Amerikan İlişkileri: 1947–1964.* Ankara: Siyasal Bilgiler.

Sarkees, Meredith Reid, Frank Whelon Wayman, and J. David Singer. 2003. Interstate, intra-state, and extra-state wars: A comprehensive look at their distribution over time, 1816–1997. *International Studies Quarterly* 47:49–70.

Sauer, Tom. 2003. Limiting national missile defence. *International Network of Engineers and Scientists against Proliferation.* http://www.inesap.org/bulletin22/bul22.htm.

Sawyer, Ralph D. 1994. *Sun Tzu: The art of war.* Boulder, CO: Westview Press.

Schelling, Thomas C. 1960. *The strategy of conflict.* Cambridge, MA: Harvard University Press.

Schmidt, Siegmar, Reinhard Wolf, and Gunther Hellmann, eds. 2007. *Handbuch der deutschen Außenpolitik.* Wiesbaden: VS-Verlag.

Schröder, M., et al., eds. 2002. *Klimavorhersage und Klimavorsorge* (Climate Prediction and Precautionary Measures). Berlin: Springer.

Schroeder, Paul W. 1994a. *The transformation of European politics, 1763–1848.* New York: Oxford University Press.

———. 1994b. Historical reality vs. neo-realist theory. *International Security* 19: 108–48.

Schwarz, Hans-Peter. 2004. Die deutsche Außenpolitik nach dem Irakkrieg. *Politische Studien* 55(393):78–91.

Schweller, Randall L. 1992. Domestic structure and preventive war: Are democracies more pacific? *World Politics* 44:235–69.

———. 1994. Bandwagoning for profit: Bringing the revisionist state back in. *International Security* 19:72–107.

Schweller, Randall L., and David Priess. 1997. A tale of two realisms: Expanding the institutions debate. *Mershon International Studies Review* 41:1–32.

Sciolino, Elaine. 2002. European Union acts to admit ten nations. *New York Times,* December 14.

Scott, C. 2004. OECD targets additional financial centers in tax haven crackdown. *Tax Notes International Magazine* 34 (June 14): 1101.

Semple, Robert B., Jr. 2005. Christie Whitman rides to the defense of her Grand Old Party. *New York Times Online,* February 1, 2005.

Sessler, Andrew M., et al. 2000. *Countermeasures: A technical evaluation of the operational effectiveness of the planned U.S. National Missile Defense System.* Cambridge, MA: Union of Concerned Scientists.

Shadid, Anthony. 2004a. Iraqi cleric yields on elections. *Washington Post,* February 27.

———. 2004b. Shiites march for elections in Iraq. *Washington Post,* January 20.

Shadid, Anthony, and Rajiv Chandrasekaran. 2003. Leading cleric calls for elections in Iraq. *Washington Post,* November 30.

Shah, Saeed. 2004. U.S. states defy Bush with carbon trading plan. *Independent,* November 12.

Shales, Amity. 2001. O'Neill lays out radical vision for tax. *Financial Times,* May 21, 1.

Shambaugh, David. 1991. *Beautiful imperialist: China perceives America, 1972–1990.* Princeton: Princeton University Press.

———. 1996. Containment or engagement of China? Calculating Beijing's responses. *International Security* 21:180–209.

Shanahan, Roger. 2004. The Islamic Da'wa party: Past development and future prospects. *Middle East Review of International Affairs* (MERIA) 8(2).

Shanker, Thom, and Eric Schmitt. 2003a. Rumsfeld denies the U.S. has plans for permanent Iraq bases. *New York Times,* April 22.

———. 2003b. Pentagon expects long-term access to key bases. *New York Times,* April 20.

Shapiro, Ira. 2002. Treating cigarettes as an exception to the trade rules. *SAIS Review: A Journal of International Affairs* 22 (January): 87–96.

Sharman, J. 2004. The bark *is* the bite: International organizations and blacklisting. Unpublished manuscript.

Sheppard, L. A. 2001. News analysis—It's the bank secrecy, stupid. *Tax Notes International Magazine* 22 (April 23): 2018.

Signorino, Curtis S., and Jeffrey Ritter. 1999. Tau-b or not tau-b: Measuring the similarity of foreign policy positions. *International Studies Quarterly* 43:115–44.

Silverstein, Ken. 2006. The minister of civil war. *Harper's Magazine,* 313:1875.

Smith, W., and P. Korzeniewicz, 2005. Transnational social movements, elite projects, and collective action from below in the Americas. http://falcon.arts.cornell.edu/sgt2/contention/documents/BSmithpaper2.doc.

Smyth, Gareth, and Krishna Guha. 2005. Kurdish pledge of "no compromise" on Kirkuk raises fears of conflict. *Financial Times,* January 28.

Sönmezoğlu, Faruk. 1995. *ABD'nin Türkiye Politikası: 1964–1980.* Istanbul: Der Yayinlari.

Speier, Richard. 2000. Can the missile technology control regime be repaired? In *Repairing the regime,* ed. Joseph Cirincione, 205–16. Washington, DC: Routledge.

Spiezio, K. Edward. 1990. British hegemony and major power war, 1815–1939: An empirical test of Gilpin's model of hegemonic governance. *International Studies Quarterly* 34:165–81.

Sprinz, Detlef F., Anja Bauer, Jette Krause, Kathrin Birkel, and Ruben Zondervan. 2004. *International Environmental Policy.* PolitikON. http://www.politikon.org, e-learning course, accessed April 1, 2004.

Stam, Alan C. III. 1996. *Win, lose, or draw: Domestic politics and the crucible of war.* Ann Arbor: University of Michigan Press.

Starkey, Brigid, Mark Boyer, and Jonathan Wilkenfeld. 1999. *Negotiating a complex world: An introduction to international negotiation.* New York: Rowman & Littlefield.

Strange, Susan. 1989. Toward a theory of transnational empire. In *Global changes and theoretical challenges: Approaches to world politics for the 1990's,* ed. Ernst-Otto Czempiel and James N. Rosenau. Lexington, MA: Lexington Books.

———. 1996. *The retreat of the state.* Cambridge: Cambridge University Press.

Sullivan, M.A. 2004. News analysis: Shifting of profits offshore costs U.S. Treasury $10 billion or more. *Tax Notes International Magazine* 36 (October 4): 12.

Suss, E. C., O. H. Williams, and C. Mendis. 2002. Caribbean offshore financial centers: Past, present, and possibilities for the future. IMF Working Paper.

Szabo, Steven. 2004a. Germany and the United States after Iraq: From alliance to alignment. *International Politics and Society* 1:41–52.

———. 2004b. *Parting ways: The crisis in German-American relations.* Washington, DC: Brookings Institution Press.

———. 2006. Parting ways. The German-American relationship after Iraq. In *Germany's uncertain power: Foreign policy of the Berlin Republic,* ed. Hanns Maull, 122–36. Basingstoke, England: Palgrave.

Talbot, Brent J. 2004. American-led coalition or unilateral action? The question of American hegemony in the 21st century. Paper presented at the annual meeting of the International Studies Association, Montreal, March 17–20.

Tammen, Ronald L., Jacek Kugler, Douglas Lemke, Allan C. Stam III, Mark Abdol-lahian, Carole Alsharabati, Brian Efird, and A. F. K. Organski. 2000. *Power transitions: Strategies for the 21st century.* New York: Chatham House.

Tanzi, V. 1995. *Taxation in an integrating world.* Washington, DC: Brookings Institution.

Taylor, A. J. P. 1961. *The origins of the second world war.* New York: Atheneum.

Taylor, Allyn. 2002. Global governance, international health law and WHO: Looking towards the future. *Bulletin of the WHO* 80(12):975–80.

Taylor, Allyn, Frank Chaloupka, Emmanel Guindon, and Michaelyn Corbett. 2000. The impact of trade liberalization on tobacco consumption. In *Tobacco control in developing countries,* ed. Prabhat Jha and Frank Chaloupka, 356–58. Oxford: Oxford University Press.

Tenscher, Jens. 2005. Bundestagswahlkampf 2002: Zwischen strategischem Kalkül und der Inszenierung des Zufalls. In *Wahlen und Wähler: Analysen aus Anlass der Bundestagswahl 2002,* ed. Jürgen Falter, Oscar Gabriel, and Bernhard Weßels, 102–33. Wiesbaden: Verlag Sozialwissenschaften.

Tobacco-free initiative. 2004. *World Health Organization.* http://www.who.int/tobacco/about/en/.

Tussie, D. 2003. *Trade negotiations in Latin America: Problems and prospects.* London: Macmillan Press.

United Kingdom. Department of Trade and Industry. 2003. *Energy white paper: Our energy future—creating a low carbon economy.* London: UK Stationery Office.

United Nations. 1992. *United Nations Framework Convention on Climate Change.* http://unfccc.int/resource/docs/convkp/conveng.pdf, accessed March 26, 2003.

———. Economic and Social Council. 2004. Item . . . of the provisional agenda, Tobacco or Health, Ad hoc Inter-Agency Task Force on Tobacco Control, Report of the Secretary General, June 8. Substantive session for 2004, New York, 28 June–23 July. http://www.un.org/esa/coordination/ecosoc/.

———. Non-governmental Liaison Service (NGLS). 2004. We the people: Civil society, the UN and global governance: Report of the Panel of Eminent Persons on UN-Civil Society Relationship. *NGLS Roundup* 113 (June).

United Nations Framework Convention on Climate Change (UNFCCC). 2004a. Kyoto Protocol to enter into force 16 February 2005 (press release). Bonn, November 18.

———. 2004b. *United Nations Framework Convention on Climate Change: Status of ratification,* May 24. http://unfccc.int/resource/conv/ratlist.pdf, accessed January 21, 2005.

United States. Central Intelligence Agency. 2000. *Unclassified report to Congress on the acquisition of technology related to weapons of mass destruction and advanced conventional munitions.* https://www.cia.gov/library/reports/archived-reports-1/jan_jun2000.htm.

———. 2002. *Foreign missile developments and the ballistic missile threat to the United States through 2015.* http://www.fas.org/irp/news/2002/01/bmthreat-2015.html.

———. Congress. Senate. 1997. Resolution expressing the sense of the Senate regarding the conditions for the United States becoming a signatory to any international agreement on greenhouse gas emissions under the United Nations Framework Convention on Climate Change.

———. 2005. To express the sense of the Senate on climate change legislation (S.AMDT.866).

United States. Department of Defense. 2004. *FY04 report to Congress on PRC military power.* http://www.defenselink.mil/pubs/d20040528PRC.pdf.

United States. Department of State. 2005. Vision statement of Australia, China, India, Japan, the Republic of Korea, and the U.S. for a new Asia-Pacific partnership on clean development and climate, July 28. Washington, DC.

United States. Department of the Treasury. Office of Public Affairs. 2003. United States and Aruba sign agreement to exchange tax information. Statement by Treasury Secretary John Snow. JS-1018. November 21.

United States. White House. 2001. Executive order: Federal leadership on global tobacco control and prevention. January 18. http://clinton5.nara.gov/library/hot_releases/January_18_2001_2.html.

———. 2002. *Global climate change policy book.* http://www.whitehouse.gov/news/releases/2002/02/climatechange.html.

———. Office of the Press Secretary. 2001. President Bush discusses global climate change. June 11. http://www.whitehouse.gov/news/releases/2001/06/20010611-2.html.

———. 2005. President and Danish Prime Minister Rasmussen discuss G8, Africa. July 6. http://www.whitehouse.gov/news/releases/2005/07/20050706-3.html.

United States Council for International Business. 2004. Letter to Senator Ted Stevens. October 26. http://www.uscib.org/docs/Appropriations_bill_letter.pdf.

United States Mission to the European Union. 2002. Treasury proposes sharing some tax information with EU, other countries. http://www.useu.be, accessed June 1, 2005.

Uslu, Nasuh. 1999. Türk Tarafı Açısıdan Kıbrıs Sorununun Boyutları. *Liberal Düşünce* 4 (winter): 13.

———. 2000. *Türk-Amerikan İlişkilerinde Kıbrıs.* Ankara: 21. Yüzyıl Yayınları.

Vasquez, John A. 1996. When are power transitions dangerous? An appraisal and reformulation of power transition theory. In *Parity and war: Evaluations and extensions of The War Ledger,* ed. Jacek Kugler and Douglas Lemke, 35–56. Ann Arbor: University of Michigan Press.

Victor, David G. 2004. *Climate change: Debating America's policy options.* New York: Council on Foreign Relations.

Voeten, Erik. 2000. Clashes in the assembly. *International Organization* 54:185–215.

Volgy, Thomas J., and Alison Bailin. 2003. *International politics and state strength.* Boulder, CO: Lynne Rienner.

Volgy, Thomas J., Derrick V. Frazier, and Robert Stewart Ingersoll. 2003. Preference similarities and group hegemony: G7 voting cohesion in the UN General Assembly. *Journal of International Relations and Development* 6:51–70.

Volgy, Thomas J., and Lawrence E. Imwalle. 1995. Hegemonic perspectives on the new world order. *American Journal of Political Science* 89:819–32.

————. 2000. Two faces of hegemonic strength: structural versus relational capabilities. *International Interactions* 26:229–51.

Volgy, Thomas J., Lawrence E. Imwalle, and John E. Schwarz. 1999. Where is the new world order? Hegemony, state strength, and architectural construction in international politics. *Journal of International Relations and Development* 5:51–70.

Volgy, Thomas J., Kristin Kanthak, Derrick V. Frazier, and Robert Stewart Ingersoll. 2004. The G7, international terrorism and domestic politics: Modeling policy cohesion in response to systemic disturbances. *International Interactions* 30:191–209.

Wagener, Martin. 2004. Auf dem Weg zu einer "normalen" Macht? Die Entsendung deutscher Streitkräfte in der Ära Schröder. In *Deutsche Sicherheitspolitik: Eine Bilanz der Regierung Schröder,* ed. Sebastian Harnisch, Christos Katsioulis, and Marco Overhaus, 89–118. Baden-Baden: Nomos.

Wagner, R. Harrison. 1988. Economic interdependence, bargaining power, and political influence. *International Organization* 42:461–83.

Walt, Stephen M. 2005. Taming American power. *Foreign Affairs* 84(5):105–20.

Walton, John, Jeremiah A. Barondess, and Stephen Lock, eds. 1994. *The Oxford Medical Companion.* New York: Oxford University Press.

Waltz, Kenneth N. 1979. *Theory of international politics.* New York: Random House.

————. 1993. The new world order. *Millennium* 22:187–95.

Webb, M. C. 2004. Defining the boundaries of legitimate state practice: Norms, transnational actors and the OECD's project on harmful tax competition. Unpublished manuscript.

Williams, Daniel. 2004. Iraqi Kurdish leader demands guarantees. *Washington Post,* January 18.

Williams, Daniel, and Pamela Constable. 2004. U.S. rebuffs cleric on Iraqi vote plan. *Washington Post,* January 13.

Winkler, Rainer. 2004. Die Irak-Krise im Bundestagswahlkampf 2002. *Dias Analyse,* no. 1, September 2003. http://www.dias-online.org.

Wohlforth, William. 1999. The stability of a unipolar world. *International Security* 24:1, 5–42.

————, ed. 2003. *Cold war endgame: Oral history, analysis, debates.* University Park: Pennsylvania State University Press.

Wohlstetter, Albert. 1964. Analysis and design of complex systems. In *Analysis for military decisions,* ed. E. S. Quade, 103–48. Santa Monica, CA: RAND, R-387-PR.

————. 1968. Theory and opposed systems design. In *New approaches to international relations,* ed. Morton A. Kaplan, 19–53. New York: St. Martin's Press.

Wolfers, Arnold. 1952. National security as an ambiguous symbol. *Political Science Quarterly* 67(4):481–502.

World Bank. 1999. Curbing the epidemic: Governments and the economics of tobacco control. Development in Practice, World Bank, Washington, DC.

World Health Organization. 2004. Tobacco-free initiative. http://www.who.int/tobacco/about/en/.

Wright, Robin, and Alan Sipress. 2004. Kurds' wariness frustrates U.S. efforts. *Washington Post,* January 9.

Wright, Tom. 2005. Tax evaders keep step ahead of EU. *International Herald Tribune,* May 25, 1.

Yach, Derek, Heather Wipfli, Ross Hammond, and Stan Glantz. 2007. Globalization and tobacco. In *Globalization and health,* ed. Ichiro Kawachi and Sarah Wamala, 39–67. Oxford: Oxford University Press.

Yacobucci, Brent D., and Kyna Powers. 2005. *Climate change legislation in the 108th Congress.* CRS Report for Congress. Washington, DC: Congressional Research Service.

Yetkin, Murat. 2004. *Tezkere: Irak Krizinin Gerçek Öyküsü.* Istanbul: Remzi Kitabevi.

Zaborsky, Victor. 2004. Does China belong in the missile technology control regime? *Arms Control Today,* October. http://www.armscontrol.org/act/2004_10/Zaborsky .asp.

CONTRIBUTORS

Davis B. Bobrow is professor (emeritus) of public and international affairs and political science at the University of Pittsburgh. His books include *Policy Analysis by Design* (1987, with John Dryzek) and *Defensive Internationalism* (2005, with Mark Boyer), and he has authored or coauthored more than one hundred book chapters and articles on various aspects of international affairs and public policy. He has held senior staff positions and consultancies with major U.S. government agencies; visiting appointments in policy-related programs in East Asia, Europe, and Israel; and the presidencies of the International Studies Association, the National Association of Schools of Public Affairs and Administration, and the Association of Professional Schools of International Affairs.

Steve Chan is professor of political science at the University of Colorado, Boulder. He has held Fulbright visiting appointments in Singapore and Taiwan. His research addresses issues pertaining to the nexus between globalization processes and domestic policy performance, rationalist explanations of outcomes of extended deterrence and war termination, the relationship between changing national capabilities and international conflict, and the evolving pursuit of security and prosperity in East Asia. His work has been published in a dozen books and about two hundred articles and book chapters.

Derrick Frazier is assistant professor of political science at the University of Illinois, Urbana-Champaign, with additional faculty appointments in the arms control, disarmament, and international security (ACDIS) and international studies programs. His areas of expertise include international conflict, conflict management, international security and U.S. foreign policy. In addition to research on the G-7 and international terrorism, Dr. Frazier is currently engaged in research on third-party management of interstate conflict and regional security.

Dennis M. Gormley is senior lecturer in security and intelligence studies at the University of Pittsburgh and senior fellow at the Monterey Institute's Center for Nonproliferation Studies. He previously held senior positions with the Blue Ridge Consulting Group, the Pacific-Sierra Research Corporation, and the U.S. Harry Diamond Laboratories. He has written and advised widely on intelligence, military strategy and transformation, missile proliferation, missile defense, and nonproliferation policy and has been a research associate at the International Institute for Strategic Studies.

Kristin Kanthak is assistant professor of political science at the University of Pittsburgh. Her research focuses on legislative behavior, particularly that of the U.S. Congress. Her work has appeared in the *American Political Science Review, Public Choice,* the *Journal of Theoretical Politics,* and *International Interactions.*

Robert T. Kudrle is Orville and Jane Freeman Professor of International Trade and Investment Policy, Hubert Humphrey Institute of Public Affairs and the Law School at the University of Minnesota. Much of his recent research has examined economic relations among industrial countries. A Rhodes Scholar, he has served as a consultant and expert witness for the Antitrust Division of the U.S. Department of Justice and as a consultant to the Internal Revenue Service, Canadian Department of Consumer and Corporate Affairs, UN Center on Transnational Corporations, Overseas Private Investment Corporation, Agency for International Development, and Urban Institute. He has been a vice president of the International Studies Association and coeditor and editorial board member of the *International Studies Quarterly.* He currently serves on the editorial boards of the *International Political Economy Yearbook* and the *Minnesota Journal of Global Trade.*

Alexander Ochs is senior research associate in the Global Issues Research Unit of the German Institute for International and Security Affairs (SWP, http://www.swp-berlin.org), Europe's largest foreign policy think tank. He also serves as project manager of the International Network to Advance Climate Talks (INTACT, http://www.intact-climate.org), an initiative committed to promoting the climate change issue on the transatlantic and global political agenda. He has organized a series of high-level policy meetings on climate change and coedited *Sustainable Climate Protection Policies* (2000). His chapter "From Mars and Venus Down to Earth: Understanding the Transatlantic Climate Divide," appeared in the SAIS Center for Transatlantic Relations book *Climate Policy for the 21st Century* (2004). He has held teaching positions in International Relations at the Freie Universität and the Humboldt University in Berlin.

Jeremy Pressman is assistant professor of political science at the University of Connecticut. He previously taught at Harvard University and was associated with the Middle East Project of the Carnegie Endowment for International Peace. He coauthored *Point of No Return: The Deadly Struggle for Middle East Peace* (1997, with Geoffrey Kemp) and has published contributions to *Current History, International Studies Perspectives, Journal of Conflict Studies,* the *New York Times, Security Studies,* the *Washington Post,* and *International Security.*

Siegmar Schmidt is professor of political science and chair of the international relations and comparative government departments at the University of Landau. Other appointments have been as the Willy-Brandt (DAAD) Chair at the University of the Western Cape, and at the universities of Trier, Mainz, Munich, and that of the Federal Armed Forces of Germany. He has written numerous books and articles on democracy promotion, German foreign policy, the evolution of the European Union, and political development in South Africa and Eastern Europe.

Detlef F. Sprinz is a senior fellow with the Potsdam Institute for Climate Impact Research (PIK) and teaches international relations and social science methodology at the Faculty of Economics and Social Science, University of Potsdam, Germany. His research and publications encompass international regimes and their effectiveness, international environmental policy, and modeling political decisions. He is coeditor of *International Relations and Global Climate Change* (2001, with Urs Luterbacher) and of *Models, Numbers, and Cases: Methods for Studying International Relations* (2004, with Yael Wolinsky-Nahmias), in addition to numerous journal articles. See http://www.sprinz.org for further details.

Robert Stewart-Ingersoll is assistant professor at Grand Valley State University. In addition to his work on G-7 foreign policy cohesion, his research focuses on the relationship between globalization and human rights and the roles of regional powers within regional security complexes.

Ilter Turan is professor of political science at Istanbul Bilgi University where he has been rector. Previous appointments were at Koc University and Istanbul University, and he has held visiting appointments at the universities of

Kentucky, Arizona, Iowa, Wisconsin, and California (Berkeley). He has published widely in English and Turkish on Turkish political development, political behavior, political culture, Turkish political institutions, and Turkish foreign policy. He is a frequent commentator in Turkish media and currently is a political columnist for the economics daily *Dünya*.

Diana Tussie is senior research fellow in international relations at FLACSO Argentina (Latin American School of Social Sciences) and CONICET (the National Council for Technical and Scientific Research). She is director of the FLACSO Buenos Aires Research Program on International Economic Institutions and of the Latin America Trade Network. She is the editor of *The Promise and Problems of Trade Negotiations in Latin America* (2003) and the author of *The Environment and International Trade Negotiations: Developing Country Stakes* (2000). She has served as Argentina's undersecretary for international trade policy and as an alternate member of the Mercosur Trade Commission.

Thomas J. Volgy is professor of political science at the University of Arizona and executive director of the International Studies Association. His most recent book is *International Politics and State Strength* (2003, with Alison Bailin), and he has authored or coauthored articles in numerous publications, including the *American Journal of Political Science, International Studies Quarterly, World Politics, Journal of Politics,* the *Nation,* and the *New Republic.* He has been a U.S. delegate to the CSCE and an Atlantic Council Fellow and has undertaken numerous international assignments for USAID and the National Democratic Institute.

Judith P. Wilkenfeld was director for international programs at the Campaign for Tobacco-Free Kids, where she was responsible for building U.S. and international support for the Framework Convention on Tobacco Control. She was a member of board of directors of the Framework Convention Alliance on Tobacco Control and served for two years as vice-chair of the Scientific Advisory Committee on Tobacco Product Regulation for the World Health Organization. Previously, she served as special advisor for tobacco policy in the U.S. Food and Drug Administration's Office of the Commissioner and as assistant director of the Division of Advertising Practices in the U.S. Federal Trade Commission. She also was the lead attorney in several successful litigations against tobacco companies' deceptive advertising and marketing practices. She served on the editorial board of the *Journal of Public Policy and Marketing, Tobacco Control,* and the *Food and Drug Law Journal.*

INDEX

Action on Smoking and Health (ASH), 208, 210, 294n8

actions. *See* policy actions

Afghanistan: al-Qaeda in, 22; Germany's role in, 41, 45, 48, 51, 54, 60, 278n4; reconstruction efforts in, 45, 61

Albania, 231, 232

Allawi, Iyad, 28, 35, 278n28

al-Qaeda, 22, 76, 139; and Iraq, 24, 39, 40, 46, 59, 276n7

al-Sadr, Muqtada. *See* Sadr, Muqtada al-

al-Sistani, Ayatollah Ali. *See* Sistani, Ayatollah Ali al-

Andorra, 196, 197, 293n35

Argentina, 129, 172, 173, 176, 179, 180, 232

Association of Southeast Asian Nations, 14, 69, 71

Australia: climate policy, 149, 152, 160; and the Framework Convention on Tobacco Control (FCTC), 211, 214; public opinion, 230, 231, 257

Austria, 154, 188, 197, 232

ballistic missiles: export policy, 129, 132; and the Hague Code of Conduct, 141, 142; Scud missile, 127, 129, 130, 288n8; Shihab missile, 132, 137; U.S. defense, 123–27. *See also* cruise missiles;

Missile Technology Control Regime (MTCR)

Barzani, Massoud, 30, 31–32

Belgium, 57, 154, 188, 197, 230, 292n28

Blair, Tony, 6, 105, 118, 160, 161

bloc creation, 14–15, 55, 80, 98, 264

Brahimi, Lakhdar, 27–28, 40

Brazil, 172, 173, 176–77, 178, 180

Bremer, L. Paul: and development of Iraqi governance, 25–28, 40, 277n13; and the Kurds, 30, 32. *See also* Coalition Provisional Authority (CPA)

Britain: and Cyprus, 82–83, 87–88; Iraq policy, 29, 56, 105, 118; missile program, 131, 132, 133. *See also* Blair, Tony; United Kingdom

broad agenda institutions, 17, 55, 59, 166, 262, 264

Brundtland, Gro Harlem, 210, 212

Bush, George W.: climate policy, 144, 155, 156–57, 159, 266; and the Framework Convention on Tobacco Control (FCTC), 205, 212, 214, 219, 220; and Germany, 47, 57, 58, 59, 60, 61; Iraq policy, 26, 34, 35, 38, 90, 91; missile defense program, 123, 127, 128, 140–41, 289n16; national strategy statement, 4; Nuclear Posture